THE POLITICAL ECONOMY OF CIVIL SOCIETY AND HUMAN RIGHTS

As a result of the revolutions in Eastern Europe and the collapse of Communism, the idea of civil society has been revived and is now at the center of political discussion. It is generally agreed that building genuine civil societies is the only true means of furthering the cause of democracy and human rights. It is also widely agreed that only the institutions of civil society are capable of reconciling the sometimes conflicting demands of individual liberties and the common good.

The Political Economy of Civil Society and Human Rights is one of the first studies of its kind, and provides a far-ranging, systematic analysis of the multifaceted notion of civil society. It shows in detail how the three main orders of civil society – the moral-cultural, the political, and the economic – while autonomous, are closely interrelated and interact in a synergetic manner. This study also shows how the logics that are constitutive of the various realms of civil society are all instances of communicative rationality – a rationality of dialogue and discourse. The work concludes by arguing that the only sure way of achieving international justice is by the construction of civil societies world-wide.

G. B. Madison is Emeritus Professor of Philosophy at McMaster University, Canada, and has held positions at the universities of Paris and Toronto. He has edited three collections of philosophical essays and is the author of several books on political theory and contemporary European philosophy. He has written extensively on issues relating to economic methodology, globalization, and civil society.

ROUTLEDGE STUDIES IN SOCIAL AND POLITICAL THOUGHT

THE POLITICAL ECONOMY OF CIVIL SOCIETY AND HUMAN RIGHTS

G. B. Madison

Routledge
Taylor & Francis Group

LONDON AND NEW YORK

First published in 1998
by Routledge

2 Park Square, Milton Park, Abingdon, Oxon OX14 4RN
711 Third Avenue, New York, NY 10017, USA

Routledge is an imprint of the Taylor & Francis Group, an informa business

Transferred to Digital Printing 2007

First issued in paperback 2016

Typeset in Garamond by
RefineCatch Limited, Bungay, Suffolk

Brtitish Library Cataloguing in Publication Data
A catalogue record for this book is available from the British Library

Library of Congress Cataloguing in Publication Data
Madison, Gary Brent.
The political economy of civil society and human rights/G. B. Madison.
p.   cm.
Includes bibliographical references and index.
1. Civil society.   I. Title.
JC336.M33   1997
301–dc21   97–8645

ISBN 978-0-415-16677-5 (hbk)

ISBN 978-1-138-97873-7 (pbk)

Publisher's Note
The publisher has gone to great lengths to ensure the quality of
this reprint but points out that some imperfections in the
original may be apparent

A ma mère
Lela G.

CONTENTS

CONTENTS

INTRODUCTION

[I]gnorance, forgetfulness or contempt of the rights of man are the sole causes of public misfortune and governmental depravity. . . . The final end of every political institution is the preservation of the natural and imprescriptible rights of man. These rights are those of liberty, property, security, and resistance to oppression.

(Déclaration des droits de l'homme et du citoyen, 1789)

The following reflections on civil society and human rights have been provoked by the most significant series of world events to have occurred in the living memory of those who, like the author of this book, came of age in the post-World War II period. I am referring naturally to the events leading up to the collapse of the Berlin Wall in 1989. The revolutionary events in Eastern Europe that year – and the subsequent ones that resulted in the demise of the Soviet Union itself on Christmas Day 1991, when the Red Flag was lowered over the Kremlin for the last time – signaled not only the end of a long drawn-out Cold War but the end as well of an entire era. This was the era of "actually existing Socialism," an era that began with the Bolshevik revolution in Russia in 1917 which set for the remainder of the century the parameters within which humanity was destined to articulate its greatest hopes as well as its worst fears. As that astute observer of East European affairs, Timothy Garton Ash, stated at the time, 1989 "was the year communism in Eastern Europe died. 1949–1989 R.I.P." (Ash 1990, p. 131). Václav Havel, who passed from being a political prisoner under the communists to being the president of a newly liberated Czechoslovakia, has not hesitated to assert that "[t]he fall of the Communist empire is an event on the same scale of historical importance as the fall of the Roman empire" (Havel 1993, p. 10). Yet another social observer, the leading French sociologist Alain Touraine, has referred to "the memorable events of 1989" as "the most exhilarating to have occurred since mid-1789" (Touraine 1995, p. 348).

Touraine is referring of course to the French Revolution two hundred years earlier, and his remark points to one of the most significant features of the revolutions of 1989: like the American Revolution and the French

Revolution in its early stages, the East European revolutions were attempts to institute liberal democracy; as such they amounted to a rejection of the way of viewing revolution that had prevailed from the Jacobins to the Bolsheviks. The significance of the revolutions of 1989 is that they marked (it is to be hoped) the end of what in Chapter 4 I refer to as "revolutionism," i.e., the long-prevalent and highly tenacious belief that the "good society" can be brought into being by violent means – in other words, the core tenet of revolutionary Socialism which held that the end justifies the means. Czechoslovakia's "velvet" revolution served as a paradigm of this "new thinking" (to borrow an expression from Mikhail Gorbachev). Although world historical events often require a long process of interpretation and reinterpretation in order for their meaning or significance to become clear – when late in his life Chou En Lai was asked what he thought was the significance of the French Revolution, he is purported to have replied, "It's still too early to say" – interpreting the significance of the revolutions of 1989 poses no great difficulties. (In fact, thanks to recent work by historians such as François Furet, the "meaning" of the French Revolution is clearer now than at any other time in the past.) What above all helps in interpreting the events of 1989 is that the leading actors in the various social movements leading up to the demise of totalitarian rule were unanimous in declaring that their express goal was that of bringing into being what they referred to as *civil society*.

The idea of civil society is, to be sure, an old idea in liberal political philosophy dating back to the eighteenth century. For a very long time, however, it was an idea that political theorists (social scientists in particular) had tended to ignore. As Francis Fukuyama quite rightly observes: "Until recently, civil society was a relatively neglected subject of analysis: in the West, it was often taken for granted as an inevitable concomitant of modernization, while in the East it was denounced by Marxists as fraudulent" (Fukuyama 1995, p. 8). Thus, one of the most significant features of the revolutions of 1989 was the way in which the principal actors (members of Poland's Solidarity, Czechoslovakia's Civic Forum, etc.) put to new, effective use an old idea in Western political philosophy – thereby reminding Westerners of the perennial significance of an idea that they themselves had long lost sight of.

What in particular the Easterners demonstrated – the significant lesson they offered the world – was the extreme relevance of the old idea of civil society to the new freedom and democracy and human rights movements spreading over the surface of the globe at the present time. "The idea of civil society," one writer observes, "has enjoyed a spectacular renaissance in recent years, as citizens from Warsaw to Lusaka, Santiago to Beijing, have struck with a vengeance at entrenched autocratic regimes" (Lewis 1995, p. 173). After 1989, writers dealing with the issue of democratization have come to use the terms "democracy" and "civil society" interchangeably. And for good reason: the fact of the matter is that any meaningful attempt to institute democracy and respect for human rights requires the creation of civil society. In other words, "democracy" and "human rights" are words devoid of any real meaning outside the context of "really existing" civil society. Without the institutional guarantees provided by the structures of civil society, human rights are without substance, and at the limit human life itself tends to have "no more importance than cigarette ash flicked in the wind," in the words of the Chinese-American human rights activist and long-time prisoner of the Chinese gulag, Harry Wu (see Wu 1995 and Tyler 1995b). "Civil society," it could be said, designates a specific kind of *régime*, namely, that ensemble of socio-political arrangements which are expressly based on the principles of democracy and human rights. The notion of civil society, I maintain, is an altogether basic and all-inclusive notion in the theory of democracy.

The revival, in actual practice, of the idea of civil society calls for a renewed theoretical analysis of the concept itself. This is the task this book assigns itself. To explore the many ramifications of the concept of civil society, as this book seeks to do, is to engage in an exercise in *political economy* in the classical sense of the term. A systematic analysis of the idea of civil society must necessarily be "interdisciplinary" and must cover a great deal of ground, dealing not only with the economic and political structures germaine to civil society, but with the social-cultural arrangements appropriate to it as well. Since a multifaceted study of such a sort amounts in the final analysis to a reflection on the human condition itself – "man" being by nature, as Aristotle said, a social-political animal (*zoon politikon*) – the political economy of civil society is inevitably, as Adam Smith might say, a branch of moral philosophy.

Despite the complexity of the subject matter a study such as this necessarily has to deal with, the basic structure of this book is fairly simple. Chapters 1 and 2 are meant to serve as an overall introduction to the detailed analyses that follow, pointing up, as it were, the need for analyses such as these. In these chapters I document how, thanks to the revolutions of 1989, the idea of civil society has once again emerged as the central concept of democratic political theory – but I also attempt to show how other on-going developments in both the East (ethnic nationalism) and the West (adversarial multiculturalism) render the triumph of the idea anything but certain. I must confess that I cannot quite bring myself to share Francis Fukuyama's optimistic belief that subsequent to "1989" and the end of Communism, liberalism has finally and definitvely triumphed over its antiliberal adversaries (see Fukuyama 1989 and 1992). The fact of the matter is that, as Julio Maria Sanguinetti stated in his 1995 inaugural speech as President of Uraguay: "We might see a time of servitude or a time of liberty."[1]

Not only is the liberal idea of civil society a concept that needs to be analyzed scientifically (i.e., analytically), it is also, given the forces at work in the present-day world that continue to militate against what it stands for, an idea whose *moral superiority* needs to be argued for philosophically. This constitutes the dual task assigned to Chapters 3, 4, and 5, which make up the main body of this work. In these chapters I seek both to explicate and to defend the various societal arrangements constitutive of civil society. For purposes of analysis I break civil society down into three "orders" – the moral-cultural, the political, and the economic – each of which is centered on a particular goal or object, these being, respectively, truth, justice, and prosperity. In addition I seek to show how each order is animated by a "logic" peculiar to it, as well as how these different logics are related to each other (how, in other words, they are "synergetic"). This necessitates detailed considerations of a host of diverse issues, and from a number of different disciplinary points of view: political, economic, and philosophical. Key topics to be considered range all the way from the nature of representative democracy and the market economy to the nature of truth itself. What nevertheless guarantees to these varied reflections an underlying unity is the methodological approach that prevails throughout this study: the work as a whole is an exercise in *hermeneutics*, that is to say, it is an attempt to work out an overall *interpretive account* of the social world.

There is, moreover, a thematic thread that runs throughout the entire book. What I wish to demonstrate above all is how the logics that are constitutive of the various realms of civil society are all instances of what that discipline known as philosophical hermeneutics terms "communicative rationality." What makes humans properly human is that, as the ancient Greeks insisted, they are rational beings. What makes a society both civil and democratic – what makes civil society a "rational society" – is the way in which it is animated throughout by that form of rationality that hermeneutics labels "dialogical" or "communicative" and whose chief features I shall attempt to describe in the course of this study. It is my belief that an approach to civil society and human rights from the point of view of communicative rationality is such as to make it possible to overcome the modern fact/value dichotomy which has for so long bedeviled the social sciences and which has resulted in what I believe to be an altogether spurious distinction between so-called "value-free" science and partisan, culture-bound ideology. It is my belief that approaching issues pertaining to democracy and civil society from the point of view of communicative rationality can provide not only the best intellectual or scientific account of these issues, it can also serve to show how civil society as portrayed in this book is, as the ancient Greeks would again say, the *best* form of human being-in-the-world. My approach, in other words, is at one and the same time analytic and normative, conjoining both fact and value.

In analyzing the essential features of civil society I have perforce limited my perspective to that of the nation-state, since there is not, and cannot be, any such such thing as a "world society," widespread talk of a "new global village" notwithstanding. The most important framework in which the peoples of the world can work for their own betterment is that of the particular state-entities to which they happen to belong. And yet the world in which we now live is one of ever-increasing internationalization or globalization. Thus, any analysis of democracy from the point of view of the concept of civil society would be incomplete without a consideration of the issue of *democratization*, i.e., the creation of civil society in the world as a whole. Accordingly, I attempt in an appendix to this book to bring to bear on international issues – chiefly those of democratization and development – lessons learned from the analysis of the idea of civil society within the context of the nation-state. It is in fact my contention that this approach – from the local to the global, so to speak – is, from a methodological point of view, the most fruitful approach to international issues that can be taken. Indeed, considerations of issues such as "international justice" or the supposed "right to development" which are *not* based on a prior understanding of issues such as social justice and economic rights as they pertain to civil society within the context of the nation-state tend not only to be hopelessly abstract but, more often than not, conceptually confused as well. One can, for instance, deal meaningfully with the question as to the obligation, if any, that richer nations have towards poorer nations only if one has previously resolved the question as to the obligation, if any, that richer citizens have towards their poorer co-citizens in any particular civil society. In addition, if one already has a proper understanding of human rights in relation to the idea of civil society, one will not make the error – one which is not only widespread but also extremely detrimental to the cause of human rights – of confusing the supposed rights of states within the international arena with the human rights of the individuals who are citizens of these states. In short, once one has achieved an understanding of the core features of the idea of civil society, one has gained a means for analyzing – from the point of view of democratic theory – any and every society in the world and for, as well, dealing in a fruitful way with the question of international relations; one has, as it were, gained possession of a conceptual skeleton key, a kind of universal *passe-partout*.

One feature of this book that the reader will readily notice is the extensive use I make of end notes. There is a reason for this. Being, as it is, the most basic and all-inclusive of concepts in the theory of democracy, the idea of civil society is, as I have mentioned, an extremely complex and multifaceted one. I have, in the main body of the text, attempted to deal with as many ramifications of the idea as seemed feasible. But there are numerous other facets of the idea that need at least to be noted, and this is one function the end notes are meant to serve. There are numerous others. The notes are meant not only to provide supporting evidence for assertions made in the text (one of the customary function of notes), they are meant also to provide additional background information on this or that issue (e.g., the economic notion of "general equilibrium") which might enable the general reader to better grasp the significance of a particular topic under discussion, but with which it would be inappropriate to overburden the main text; they are also meant to inform the reader of additional topics that could profitably be explored in order further to flesh out the idea of civil society, as well as to point the reader in directions that could be followed up in this regard. I said above that while the subject matter of this book is highly complex, its basic structure is fairly simple. An analogy is perhaps in order. From a structural point of view this book could be likened to a Gothic cathedral, such as Chartres or Notre-Dame de Paris. Gothic cathedrals, as anyone who has ever visited one knows, are extremely complex structures with numerous portals, towers, alcoves, chambers, triforia, aisles, ambulatories, crypts, aspses, chapels, even secret passageways (which in this text correspond to what is not said explicitly but which is nevertheless intended) – not to mention gargoyles and elaborate statuary, stations of the cross, etc. And yet, in their basic structure, Gothic cathedrals are the epitome of simplicity: their general form, that of intersecting nave and transept, is the simplest form there is in the world, that of the Roman cross. So likewise this book. Its nave is civil society, and its transept is human rights; just as nave and transept together make up the basic design of a Gothic cathedral, so civil society and human rights combined constitute a study in the political economy of democracy. To pursue the metaphor for yet a moment, the numerous end notes in this study can be viewed as so many side chapels, sites which the reader may choose momentarily to visit, or simply to by-pass, proceeding instead straight down the central aisle towards the high altar. The cathedral metaphor could be updated, should one so prefer. Today's cybernauts of the far-flung Internet may, if they should care to, view these notes as a non-electronic version of a hyper (or, perhaps more appropriately, hypo) text, which in its intricacies they are free to explore or not, as the mood suits them.

"All men are created equal. They are endowed by their creator with certain inalienable rights, among these are life, liberty, and the pursuit of happiness." These are words made famous by the author of the American Declaration of Independence, but it is not Thomas Jefferson whom I am quoting. The author here is Ho Chi Minh, and the words in question form the opening lines of the Declaration of the Democratic Republic of Vietnam, dated September 2, 1945. The words announced the beginning of a long struggle against French colonial rule and for national independence and territorial integrity. Vietnam is now not only a unified and independent country; like former socialist countries elsewhere in the world, it is also a country seeking to create a market economy and the rudiments of civil society.

If I quote the former leader of (formerly) communist Vietnam, it is in order to suggest that democracy and human rights are notions possessing universal significance and are "relevant" to all peoples of the world. They are notions that express universal aspirations on the part of humanity everywhere. As cultural inventions, they may be of Western origin, but in their meaning and significance they are notions that are applicable in all cultures where people are struggling to assert their basic dignity as free human beings. As one sociologist specializing in Afrian studies observes: "Cultures are not holistic entities. . . . If human rights analysts rid themselves both of spuriously dichotomous analytical categories and of spurious perceptions of homogeneity in both 'traditional' and 'modern' . . . societies, then it will be easier to see . . . the pertinence of rights for all state societies" (Howard 1990, pp. 172–73).

Democracy and human rights may be notions that are, as it were, universally "valid," but what are their chances of being universally recognized, in actual fact? What is likely to be the outcome of the post-1989 liberal revolution? Francis Fukuyama notwithstanding, the future cannot be predicted – but it can be made. The future – that which eventually "will have been" – is the realm of freedom *par excellence*, of freedom in the making. What the future will turn out to be is a function of the choices we make, or fail to make, of what we do, or fail to do. Responsibility for humanity's future is ours alone. This study attempts, by means of its theoretical analyses, to shed some light on the nature of the choices that must be made in the realm of everyday *praxis* if freedom and democracy are eventually to prevail worldwide.

1

THE IDEA OF CIVIL SOCIETY

THE YEAR OF TRUTH

The year 1989 will go down in history as the *annus mirabilis*, the Year of Wonders. This was the year when the unexpected unexpectedly happened, and with a suddenness that was truly breathtaking. In the space of a few weeks, or even a few days, the entire post-World War II order in Eastern Europe (as it was then called) broke down, bringing to an end the division of Europe and a Cold War that had seemed interminable. The most eloquent symbol of this spiritual break-down was the physical collapse of the Berlin Wall, a well-designed and heavily fortified structure that itself seemed to be destined to remain in place for the foreseeable future. So much so, in fact, that there was no lack of ready pundits to chide Ronald Reagan for being "out of touch with reality" when only a few years earlier, in 1987, standing before the Brandenburg Gate, he challenged Gorbachev to live up to his declared policy of "openness" (*glasnost*) by exclaiming: "General Secretary Gorbachev, if you seek peace, if you seek prosperity for the Soviet Union and Eastern Europe, if you seek liberalization: Come here to this gate! Mr. Gorbachev, open this gate! Mr. Gorbachev, tear down this wall!" (Canon 1991, p. 774).

When, as if in a delayed response to Reagan's incantation, the Iron Curtain did come crashing down a few years later (Gorbachev, as if in response to Reagan, having given the signal that it should so happen), this event without precedent in the post-war era sounded the death knell of Communism in Europe. Indeed, it announced (for all those who had the ears to hear) the demise of the socialist ideal itself. Only the most obdurate of ideologues could any longer continue to deny that this ideal had proven itself as bankrupt as the desolate economies it had spawned. As Ralf Dahrendorf stated in his reflections on the revolutions of 1989: "[T]he point has to be made unequivocally that socialism is dead, and that none of its variants can be revived" (Dahrendorf 1990, p. 42). Ronald Reagan had of course predicted this momentous development when in 1982 (three years before Gorbachev's rise to power) he declared before the British Parliament in Westminster,

1

THE IDEA OF CIVIL SOCIETY

paying tribute to Marx by employing Marx's own mode of discourse, that it was the Soviet Union that "runs against the tide of human history" and that "the march of freedom and democracy . . . will leave Marxism-Leninism on the ash-heap of history" (Canon 1991, pp. 314–15).

When in 1989 the Verdict of History did finally come down (and for the reasons that Reagan had predicted in his Westminster address), it was especially painful for those Marxists who had managed to hold on up until then to their comforting belief in the inevitability of the Great Proletarian Revolution. With unmitigated cruelty, the Dialectic of History itself conspired, by means of one of its customarily ironic Ruses of Reason, to "falsify" in the most undeniable of ways the Marxist reading of history. Any honest, i.e., intellectually consistent, Marxist had now to concede, painful though this be, that History itself had spoken and had relegated Socialism to the scrap heap of history. One such "post-Marxist" made the following confession in 1991, which is too revealing not to be quoted at length. Referring to Marx's core notion that the course of history is determined by the interplay between the "means of production" and the "relations of production," Michael Lebowitz stated:

> The dreams of many have been dashed by the failures of actually existing socialism. For those who consider themselves Marxists, however, there are special complications. Few others are so congenitally disposed to accept historical experience as the Verdict of History.
>
> The real as rational is the particular petard which has deprived Marxists of their footing. Prepared to accept every apparent crisis of capitalism as the reward for patient perseverance, as the revelation that the old is indeed dying, we look in shock at a machine gone mad. In the light of the economic and political crises of actually existing socialism (hereafter AES), the Marxian conception of history appears as the intellectual weapon not of the proletariat but, rather, of capital. . . . [T]he present era of social revolution in the countries of AES is proof that socialism fetters the development of productive forces. . . .
>
> When the relations of production fetter the development of productive forces, an era of social revolution begins and a new set of productive relations emerges. Thus, a classic Marxist textbook case: the fettering of productive forces by the common ownership of means of production [Socialism], social revolution [the revolutions of 1989] and . . . [ellipses in original] capitalism. Twist and turn as they may, those Marxists who accept the thesis of the primacy of productive forces cannot escape the unambiguous logic of their own lessons.
>
> (Lebowitz 1991, pp. 348–49, 358)

With the well-developed sense of black humor they had nourished as a result of having lived for some forty-odd years under a socialist regime (and under socialist indoctrination), the Hungarians summed up the message of

2

history in this way: "What is Socialism? It is the long and painful transition period between capitalism and . . . capitalism." On a more serious level, one of the more remarkable testimonies to the bankruptcy of Marxism in the Soviet Union itself was provided by Alexander Yakovlev, one of Gorbachev's closest collaborators who had been in charge of communist ideology and propaganda, in a book drafted during the twilight years of the regime. In 1988, at a time when Yakovlev held a leading position in the Central Committee of the Communist Party, he remarked: "It's time to say that Marxism was a utopia and a mistake from the very beginning. . . . Pure communism is pure death" (Yakovlev 1993, pp. xvii, 222).

Not even that cherished ideal of Western leftists, that of a "mixed economy" or a "third way," survived the collapse of "actually existing socialism" in Eastern Europe. (The "Swedish model" appealed to by those reborn communists who now called themselves "social democrats" was subsequently to reveal itself, in the Swedish elections of 1991, to be as economically unviable as the state socialism in regard to which it was touted as an alternative.[1]) The only question of real significance was no longer: is there an as-yet undiscovered alternative to both capitalism and socialism? but rather: how rapid should the move to a capitalist or market economy be? Gorbachev's failure to realize this and to assess properly the Verdict of History was undoubtedly the main reason for his ultimate downfall.[2] As one observer of the Russian scene has remarked: "[T]he Gorbachev period . . . was a transition to nowhere" (Sakwa 1994, p. 45). Gorbachev's fatal indecisiveness in pushing through the necessary economic reforms (such as those called for in the 1990 Shatalin "Five-Hundred-Day Plan" which he initially endorsed, only, as usual, to back off from it subsequently[3]) and his endless see-sawing back and forth were, of course, understandable. Remaining to the bitter end a defender of Communism (albeit a Communism with a would-be "human face"), he no doubt realized instinctively that to abandon central planning altogether would be to deliver a fatal blow to the Soviet Union itself which, given the pent-up resentment of the outlying "Republics" and the "nationalites problem," could continue to exist only if Moscow remained the "center" of the empire (whence the intrinsic absurdity of the Ryzkov plan that Gorbachev finally endorsed in November 1990 and which, in opposition to the Shatalin plan, called for a *centrally planned* move to a decentralized, market economy [!]). As a matter of fact, *perestroika* was doomed to failure from the outset, since it was based on the idea of a "socialist market economy," which is a contradiction in terms.[4] All attempts to find a "third way" in the form of "socialism with a human face" are doomed to failure. As one Polish Solidarity activist very aptly remarked, "socialism with a human face" is nothing more than "totalitarianism with the teeth knocked out" (see Ash 1989, p. 266).[5] Or, as Robert Conquest has said, "socialism with a human face" "sounds like the Phantom of the Opera" (Conquest 1993, p. 25).

In the case of the highly developed economies of late-modernity – and for reasons that we shall examine in greater detail in Chapter 5 – there simply is, in strictly economic terms, *no* alternative to a "capitalist" or market economy.[6] (Should one wish to talk about *capitalism* "with a human face" – in other words, a genuinely postmodern Capitalism, i.e., an economic system centered on the principles of communicative rationality[7] and human rights – that indeed would be a meaningful topic of discourse.) In any event, once a decision has been made to move to a market economy, that move must be global, not piecemeal, and should (for reasons having to do with the "logic" of social orders to be discussed more fully in Chapters 3, 4, and 5) be effected as rapidly as possible. Various liberalization measures – such as price deregulation; fiscal, monetary, and credit restraints; currency reform; trade liberalization; and, above all, privatization of state-owned firms and downsizing of government bureaucracies (many members of which will be adversely affected by reforms and who will accordingly pose a major threat to their successful implementation) – should be undertaken simultaneously.[8] A "gradualist" approach to reform is a sure recipe for failure, given the fact that serious market-oriented reforms are contrary to the vested interests of those who have benefited, and continue to benefit, from a command economy (or, as in the case of Latin America, a statist one) and who can therefore be expected to attempt at every turn to do their best to subvert these reforms.[9]

Ultimately, as the Swedish economist Anders Aslund has noted, "It is a question of all or nothing" (Aslund 1989)[10] – as, it must be said, it oftentimes is in human affairs; one cannot always escape the necessity of having to make hard choices. Reasons for both across-the-board and radical change are suggested by György Varga, editor of the Hungarian journal *Figgelö*, who observes:

> Systemic change and economic transformation should be considered simultaneously. The transformation of Hungary's political system and its economic system are mutually dependent and reinforce one another. Although the full transformation will take time, a market economy should be created with all deliberate speed because the values of political pluralism are most in harmony with autonomous decentralized economic decision-making. A market economy promotes such values as entrepreneurship, tolerance, and willingness to compromise.
>
> (Varga 1992, p. 20)

The comparative situations of Russia and Ukraine are instructive in this regard. As one specialist in Russian politics declared in 1994 (before Ukraine finally bit the bullet and began the marketization of its economy):

> The contrasting experience of post-communism in the two countries lends credence to the view that in such a transition there is only one speed, and that is full steam ahead. Anything else, and the country is

4

caught between two worlds, one struggling to be born, and the other refusing to die.

(Sakwa 1994, p. 69)

After the failure of Socialism to make good on its promises, one Polish economist is reported to have confessed, "I know how to turn an aquarium into a fish soup, but I don't know how how to turn a fish soup back into an aquarium." Indeed, there is no way to do so. While it is the case that "gradual" measures often lead free countries down the road to serfdom, once they have passed a "point-of-no-return" there are no "gradual" measures that can lead them back in the opposite direction on the same road. They have to find a different road altogether, a new path to a new liberty. For countries which have been plunged into the depths of serfdom, no such course has yet been charted, although there is no lack of theories on how it can be done – "transitology" is a science still in the making. The path to a new liberty can be found out only by trial and error, and with an immense amount of pain and suffering. As Yakovlev has rightly observed in regard to the situation in his country, the heartland of Socialism itself: "Russia is called upon to find its own way of returning to civilization, of reviving the structures and values of civil society" (Yakovlev 1993, p. 222).[11] Even in economically developed Western democracies, attempts to reverse the trend towards statism (attempts, so to speak, to reverse the course on the road to serfdom) by reducing chronic budgetary deficits on the part of government and excessive governmental, bureaucratic interventionism in all aspects of people's lives proves not to be an easy matter.

As the case of Eastern Europe demonstrated, the search for a "middle way" amounted to prolonging the life of a decrepit system that, by the logic of things human, cannot be "reformed" but must instead be killed off if a new, more rational – and more humane – system is to be born. As one specialist in Russian history has observed:

> It is in the logic of such a total system [a centrally planned economy] that it should end in total collapse. The structure is so tight, and everything is so interconnected, that any attempt at liberalization inevitably skids off into dissolution. And the intrinsic irreformability of communism is no longer a question of opinion; it is now a matter of historical fact. There is no middle way between the integral preservation of such a system and its collapse.

(Malia 1992, p. 60)

The famous Yugoslav ex-communist, Milovan Djilas, one of the first of a long line of courageous dissidents, has stated: "[S]ometime during the 1970s I realized that communism could not be reformed." During the Gorbachev era, Djilas argued that efforts to liberalize Communism could lead only to its collapse.[12] The dilemma confronting socialist regimes in an age of new

5

economic realities is that they cannot survive if they do not change, but they cannot change and still survive. A "reformed" communist can only be a dead communist.

In rejecting the idea of a "third way" for his own country, Václav Havel summed up well the general sentiment of the Easterners when he remarked: "The 'third way' is the fastest way to the Third World." And as Havel's homonym, Václav Klaus, subsequently prime minister of the Czech Republic, has stated:

> To pursue a so-called third way is foolish. We had our experience with this in the 1960s when we looked for socialism with a human face. It did not work, and we must be explicit when we say that we are not aiming for a more efficient version of a system that has failed.
>
> (as cited in Novak 1993, p. 47)

After "1989" it was difficult to determine what, if anything much at all, in either East or West, was left of the Left.[13] As Pierre Mauroy, prime minister of France's first socialist government in the early 1980s, confessed in 1990 shortly after the upheaval in Eastern Europe: "We thought we could find a third way, but it turned out there isn't one" (as cited in Lipset 1991, p. 183).

Timothy Garton Ash, an eyewitness to the revolutionary events in Eastern Europe, observed at the time: "This was the year communism in Eastern Europe died. 1949–1989 R.I.P." (Ash 1990, p. 131). 1989 and the death of Communism at last served to confirm the scientific predictions of Ludwig von Mises and F. A. Hayek, who in the 1930s had argued that Socialism is an economically irrational system and cannot be expected to "work."[14] 1989 finally proved them right, and thus served to validate the position long defended by adherents to the Austrian School of economics.[15] 1989 was therefore not only a year of death; as such, it was also the Year of Truth. No one, anywhere, even in the most far-flung of underdeveloped countries, could any longer deny the obvious: Socialism was indeed dead – R.I.P. The end of everything signified by the word "Socialism" was the message – the "truth" – that in 1989 the Easterners were trying to get through to the West. As Havel stated in an address to the Polish parliament (*Sejm*) in January 1990: "We have awakened and we must awaken those in the West who have slept through our awakening" (Havel 1990, p. 19). Or as Garton Ash remarked at the time: "They [the Easterners] are all saying, and for the left this is perhaps the most important statement: there is no 'socialist economics,' there is only economics" (Ash 1990, p. 105).[16] For his part, Ralf Dahrendorf summed up nicely the message the Easterners were trying to get through to the West when in 1988 he stated: "Accepting the 1980s means above all that there is no way back to the cozy days of social democracy [the supposed 'third way']. There is only a way forward to new liberty" (Dahrendorf 1988, p. 175).[17] It is precisely this "way forward to new liberty" – which the Easterners were telling us is in fact the "old" liberty of the eighteenth century liberal revolutions – that this book seeks to explore.[18]

THE REBIRTH OF AN IDEA

The "Year of Truth" was the term used by Garton Ash to characterize the Wonder Year, 1989 (see Ash 1990, Chapter 6). This was a most appropriate term, since as Havel, formerly a prisoner in the Czech socialist gulag and subsequently – after 1989 – the president of a free Czechoslovakia (subsequently divided into the Czech Republic and Slovakia), has never tired of reminding us, life under "actually existing Socialism" was nothing more than one constant, infinitely reiterated and, perhaps most importantly, *self-conscious lie*. Physical torture and repression were, of course, a mainstay of the socialist regimes of Eastern Europe (without which they could not have continued to exist),[19] but far more degrading was the *spiritual* degradation and affront to human dignity wrought by their forcing their citizens to live, day in and day out, in innumerable self-conscious and self-demeaning lies, in, that is, a continual denial of their own reason and intelligence. (The fact that, for structural reasons, i.e., by reason of the very nature of the regime itself, totalitarian regimes of a socialist sort require that their subjects "internalize" the lies and hypocrisies of the ruling ideology is what principally serves to differentiate these types of regimes from authoritarian regimes of a more traditional sort [e.g., Franco's Spain], which generally demand only external obeisance to the [limited] power interests of the ruling elite – mere physical compliance, as it were.)

Garton Ash was undeniably one of the most astute observers of the unfolding logic of events in Eastern (or, as it is now once again called, Central) Europe throughout the 1980s. As an unusually perceptive hermeneut of human events, he was also able to pinpoint that core notion which, in a complex and multifaceted way, served both to motivate and to legitimate the struggle for freedom and democracy on the part of the Easterners. The notion that was central to the Eastern Europe *refolutions* (to use Ash's appropriate neologism, combining "revolution" and "reform") was the idea of a *civil society* – an old idea, to be sure, long-familiar to the West (though still a highly "radical" notion in those parts of the world dominated by illiberal forces such as Islamic fundamentalism), but which in the West had long since dropped out of philosophical-political discourse – as, that is, a major thematic and organizing concept (i.e., a concept that can serve as a kind of "nucleus" around which all the other terms in a given political vocabulary, such as that of liberal democracy, can "crystallize," generating thereby a coherent structure, or what I shall be referring to as a "logic"). As Ash remarks:

7

A concept that played a central role in opposition thinking during the 1980s was that of "civil society." 1989 was the springtime of societies aspiring to be civil. Ordinary men and women's rudimentary notion of what it meant to build a civil society might not satisfy the political theorist. But some such notion was there, and it contained several basic demands. There should be forms of association, national, regional, local, professional, which would be voluntary, authentic, democratic and first and last, not controlled or manipulated by the Party or Party-state. People should be "civil": that is, polite, tolerant, and, above all, non-violent. Civil and civilian. The idea of citizenship had to be taken seriously.

(Ash 1990, p. 147)

Referring to the text just quoted, Ralf Dahrendorf has also highlighted the all-importance of the notion of civil society: "Civil society is the key" (Dahrendorf 1990, p. 163). It is the underlying thesis of this study that the concept of *civil society* can serve as a crystallizing notion in our current attempts to think a post-1989 or, more generally, a postmodern politics. The concept of civil society, I maintain, is that concept which both designates and defines a certain state of affairs, outside of which those other most prominent concepts in current political discourse, viz., democracy and human rights, are, and must forever remain, totally vacuous.

In other words, the underlying thesis of this study is that the institution of civil society, in any country whatsoever, is the necessary "condition of possibility" of democracy, i.e., of a regime dedicated to the respect, recognition, and enhancement of universal *human rights*. In the absence of an "actually existing" civil society any proclamation of human rights is empty and meaningless, just as any claim to democratic governance is hypocritical and vain. To actually exist, human rights must be *institutionalized* (such that they then accurately designate certain modes of concrete social *praxis*).

But what exactly is "civil society"? That is the question to which this study, in its overall orientation, will seek to provide an answer, even though it cannot hope to do full justice to the wide range of issues that would have to be explored in any systematic attempt to flesh out the notion of civil society. One can, however, begin to appreciate just how far-ranging and all-inclusive this core notion of political discourse is when one realizes that, in order fully to explicate it, one would have to explore in detail issues such as: the relation between the private and public realms; the place of the family in civil society; the relation between the public realm and the state; the role of the state in society; the role of volunteer and professional associations, social movements, and political parties; the role of the market economy in civil society; the role of the state in a civil market economy; multiculturalism and minority rights; individual versus group rights; communitarianism versus liberalism; social trust and solidarity; the concept of spontaneous orders and social synergy; the relation between private interests and the public good; the notion of economic rights; social justice; civil society versus the welfare state; civil society and the struggle for democracy in the third world; international justice and the role of non-governmental organizations in international democratization and development, as well as the link, if any, between democratization and development. This is by no means an exhaustive list.

The point needing to be stressed in the present context is that it was precisely this (so to speak) overdetermined notion of civil society that (so to speak, again) determined the course of events leading up to "1989." The struggle against socialist totalitarianism *was* the struggle for civil society, as the activists involved themselves clearly realized. The Polish Solidarity activists, for instance, referred to this as "social self-organization." In order to overthrow totalitarianism, the Easterners returned to the storage closet of old Western ideas, took out the idea of civil society, dusted it off, and put it to work, both conceptually and praxially. As one reformist member of the now-defunct Hungarian communist politburo remarked at the time: "We want to abolish the Party-state. We want to reintroduce the principles of Montesquieu in modern form" (see Ash 1989, p. 295). This is why Garton Ash was quite correct when, addressing the question as to what the West could learn from the liberal revolutions in Eastern Europe, he stated:

> If I am right in my basic analysis, they can offer no fundamentally new ideas on the big questions of politics, economics, law or international relations. The ideas whose time has come are old, familiar, well-tested ones. (It is the new ideas whose time has passed.)
>
> (Ash 1990, p. 154)[20]

This should by no means be taken as a criticism. To appreciate the true worth (and usefulness) of an "old" idea oftentimes demands creative insight. As Nietzsche remarked, "Not that one is the first to see something new, but that one sees as *new* what is old, long familiar, seen and overlooked by everybody, is what distinguishes truly original minds" (Nietzsche 1964, #200). The pursuit of novelty for novelty's sake is a strictly modernist obsession ('avant-guardism') which accordingly should have no place in a genuinely postmodern philosophy of politics.

Socialism, which until roughly the 1980s was thought to be the wave of the future and the newest of the new (and thus, according to modernist logic, the best) of social/political ideas,[21] was nothing if not social experimentation on a truly colossal scale, and the damage it inflicted on civilized (i.e., as Havel would say, "civil") forms of human relations (and on the physical environment as well) was equally without precedent in human history. Is it therefore any wonder that the people of Russia should express their most profound political/social aspirations when they declare their desire to return to or reinstitute a "normal society"? In this respect "1989" was truly remarkable and "original" in proclaiming the end of "revolutionism" or "utopianism" (as Boris Yeltsin called it).[22] Although Francis Fukuyama clearly was guilty of excess optimism in announcing the "end of history" and the definitive triumph of the old, eighteenth-century liberal ideas (all of which are summed up in the notion of civil society), he could nevertheless argue convincingly that, henceforth, there was simply no real alternative to them (see Fukuyama 1989 and 1992).

It was precisely this sort of thing that the Easterners were (as it were) trying to tell people in the West. According to Havel, the end of Communism – along with the unbridled communitarian ideal it embodied – signals the ultimate bankruptcy of the modernist utopian project in general. It confronts, as he has said, politics with the need to find "a new postmodern face."[23] Since postmodernism is not a "new" period in history, one which simply displaces modernity (see Madison 1994b), a genuinely postmodern politics can, without the slightest impropriety, adopt as its core idea the modern, Enlightenment notion of civil society (and classical liberal values in general). In fact, this is precisely what it must do. The central task of postmodern political theory must be that of rearticulating in a conscientiously postmodern, i.e., postmetaphysical (postfoundationalist and post-essentialist) way, the core ideas of modern Enlightenment liberalism – for instance, the idea of human rights (*les droits de l'homme et du citoyen*, as the *Déclaration* of 1789 put it). Anything else would amount to a regression to premodernity and to the fundamentally illiberal and inegalitarian forms of social life characteristic of what Tocqueville referred to as the *ancien régime* (see Tocqueville 1955).[24]

Thanks to the courage of the people of Eastern Europe in combating socialist totalitarian oppression and, in the process, their unabashed appeal to some of the "oldest" of liberal political notions of Western origin (which Westerners had themselves long since tended to discount), the notion of civil society is once again on the discursive agenda. Symptomatic of this is a book of Adam Seligman's, *The Idea of Civil Society*. As Seligman mentions: "Two centuries after its origins in the Enlightenment, the idea of civil society is being revived to provide an answer to the greater good of society and, similarly, how society can advance the interests of the individuals who comprise it" (Seligman 1992). This is a revealing remark (Seligman himself takes due note of the contributions of the Easterners to the revival of this "old" notion). As I shall argue in Chapter 4, the idea of civil society is the only conceptual means of resolving what is perhaps the most basic and persistent problem in political philosophy: how to reconcile private interests and the public good.[25] The idea of civil society also allows for a reconciliation of the demands of *culture*, i.e., particularity and community, with the requirements of *civilization*, i.e., individuality and universality. As I shall wish to argue, the idea of civil society is an extremely useful – indeed, indispensable – notion for political analysis.

To put the matter another way, the idea of civil society is not only an important analytical concept for political *science*, it is also the core concept of political *philosophy*, and it is, for that very reason, a supremely normative or *ethical* notion which, properly explicated, can serve to "ground" political *praxis* in sound ethical theory (albeit one which is thoroughly antifoundational, i.e., "hermeneutical").[26] For the only politics truly worthy of the name is not the politics of late modernity, based as it is on the modern notion of a "value-free" political science (which, in its implicit justification of ideology as such, can serve to justify the most unequal distribution of power) but a politics of postmodernity which takes seriously the demand of the early modern, eighteenth century American revolutionaries, i.e., in their time-honored phrase, that of the "equal liberty of all." Civil society, to the degree that it effectively exists, is nothing other than (as Hegel might say) the reciprocal, and therefore equal, recognition of all by all. It designates a state of affairs which, as the French hermeneuticist Paul Ricoeur has said, "allow[s] the freedom of each to be realized without harm to the freedom of others" (Ricoeur 1969, p. 53). In fact, the heart and soul of civil society is, in the words of Claude Lefort, "a mutual recognition of liberties, a mutual protection of the ability to exercise them" (Lefort 1986, p. 366). What Kant called "a universal civic society" (Kant 1963, p. 16)[27] is one which is founded on the idea of individual freedom ("the freedom of all") and universal human rights.

CIVIL SOCIETY AND HUMAN RIGHTS

It took the revolutions of 1989 to pointedly remind Westerners of the enduring validity of the idea of civil society, as well as the concomitant idea of human rights. For a number of years, Western intellectuals of a poststructuralist or deconstructionist sort (the "philosophers of 1968," as Luc Ferry and Alain Renaut aptly dubbed them [see Ferry and Renaut 1990]) as well as the American neopragmatist Richard Rorty had castigated the old, eighteenth century notion of "inalienable human rights" as a hopelessly "metaphysical" concept that should be relegated to the rubbish heap of history.[28] The notion of human rights was supposedly only one of the more blatant expressions of "humanism" (as Heidegger pejoratively referred to it), a Western, "bourgeois" (as the Marxists used to call it), "logocentric" idea designed exclusively for oppressing non-Western peoples and forcing them to submit to Western hegemony ("neo-" or "postcolonialism"). The poststructuralist abandonment of the idea of human rights notwithstanding, it was precisely this notion that the oppressed peoples of Eastern Europe and China resolutely appealed to in their struggle for freedom and democracy. 1989 amounted to a wake-up call to these intellectuals; it is as if 1989, first in China and then in Eastern Europe, caught the avant-garde poststructualists off guard and theoretically unprepared for understanding the meaning of the events (the real revolutions of 1989 – not merely the *ersatz* "revolution" of 1968) unfolding around them. They have, since then, been rushing to catch up with the locomotive of history (to borrow an expression from V. I. Lenin). Throughout the years in which a nostalgia for *mai '68* reigned supreme and stifled any attempts at genuine critical thinking (Michel Foucault, *enfant terrible* of the "establishment," as he liked to portray himself, being a case in point), a genuinely critical thinker such as Claude Lefort, former ultra-leftist and Trotskyist, never tired of reminding Westerners of the intrinsic, antitotalitarian value of the notion of universal human rights.

The fact of the matter, as Lefort clearly realized throughout all the years after 1968, is that there was no better conceptual tool than the notion of universal human rights with which to deconstruct totalitarianism – the goal long sought after not only by the peoples of Eastern Europe but also by those Westerners who had managed, though not without difficulty, to remain immune to all the widespread hoopla over "détente" and "peaceful coexistence." The reason why the idea of civil society is so useful in attacking totalitarianism is that it is the very antithesis of the totalitarian ideal. Thus, in order to appreciate the basic meaning of civil society, one should contrast it with the state of affairs to which it is most directly opposed, viz., totalitarianism.

This point bears emphasizing. Since 1989 the terms "democracy" and "civil society" have for all practical purposes become interchangeable. "Democracy" refers to an "ideal type" in political typology, one which is the polar opposite of totalitarianism (it is "an ideal type of the polar variety," as Sartori puts it [1987, I, pp. 200, 202]). Thus, as I have said, perhaps the best way to get a grip on the often elusive and unstable idea of civil society is to define it *a contrario*: civil society is everything that totalitarianism is not. This is in effect the "method" I shall be following throughout this study, and it accounts for the particular definition of civil society that I shall be defending.

What totalitarianism itself is, is altogether clear. The chief characteristic of a totalitarian regime – "the hideous system [in the words of Alexander Yakovlev] of statism, bureaucratic absolutism, economic ruin, and spiritual suppression of the individual" (Yakovlev 1993, p. 55) – is that it represents a systematic and ruthless attempt to subordinate all aspects of social life – political, economic, cultural, religious, etc. – to the dictates of an all-powerful State (itself under the total control of a self-coopting elite) – or, if it cannot quite manage that, to suppress them altogether. As John Paul II has observed: "the totalitarian State tends to absorb within itself the nation, society, the family, religious groups and individuals themselves" (John Paul II 1991, §45). Or, as Sartori says: "[T]otalitarianism denotes the imprisonment of the whole of society *within* the state, the all-pervasive political domination over the extra-political life of man. . . . [It is] the destruction of everything that is spontaneous, independent, diversified, and autonomous in the life of human collectivities" (Sartori 1987, I, p. 198).

The "totalitarian project" is that of the total "politicization" of society (see Berger 1986, p. 179). Actually, this is not an altogether apt description (although it may quite accurately serve to designate a major force at work in Western societies), for in claiming a monopoly over politics itself ("the leading role of the Party"), totalitarianism actually destroys the political realm altogether, i.e., that public realm in which citizens can freely and peacefully seek to mediate their social-political differences. As the Soviet historian Leonid Batkin accurately observed in 1988:

> Politics had disappeared from our society's life since the late twenties.
> ... Politics disappeared as a *specific* contemporary sphere of human activity where the differences in class and group interests are displayed and clash with each other, where there is direct public comparison of positions, and where methods are sought to bring them to some dynamic compromise. Politics disappeared – and thus *everything became "political."*[29]

The revolutions of 1989, conducted in the name of civil society, amounted to a revolt against this sort of politicization of society, against "a system where everything was political except politics" (Malia 1992, p. 70). They amounted to a revolt of society itself against an oppressor state. Ironically, perhaps, the totalitarian state was one that, while attempting to engulf all of society, at the same time set itself apart from the society ("the masses") of which it claimed nevertheless to be the voice. Actually, in totalitarian regimes even the state was made subordinate to the Party,[30] which led a *private* life of its own, one which in the USSR and China became indistinguishable from that of Western mafias.[31] Socialist regimes, their egalitarian ideology notwithstanding, invariably tend, by reason of the logic of the system, to become nothing more than institutionalized corruption. "The sole point of the system," Peter Boettke has pointed out with respect to the Soviet Union, "was to concentrate benefits on those in power and disperse the costs on the citizens" (Boettke 1993, p. 8).[32] The extra-societal (and extra-public) status of the socialist ruling elites (the "New Class" as Milovan Djilas dubbed it [Djilas 1957]) was well illustrated by the East German *nomenklatura* who lived in splendid isolation (and extraordinary comfort) behind the guarded walls of Wandlitz, their residential compound outside Berlin.

Unlike the revolution of 1917, the revolutions of 1989 were in no way "orchestrated" by a tightly-knit band of professional ideologues but were effected by loosely organized social groups or *Bürgerbewegungen* (citizens' movements) – Solidarity in Poland, the Civic Forum in Czechoslovakia, the Democratic Forum in Hungary, the New Forum in East Germany – whose motto was (in the words of the Polish Solidarity activists) "the self-organization of society." The idea (revolutionary not only with regard to the state-Socialism of the East but also, to a considerable degree, with regard to the state-welfarism of the West as well) was that it was not the state but individuals who, in free association, should, as much as possible, organize their own lives in common.[33]

In contrast to the oppressive homogeneity of the totalitarian state, a civil society is one which expressly seeks to safeguard the autonomy of the different spheres of human agency (social, political, economic, cultural, etc.). In contrast to the monolithic totalitarian state, a civil society is an intrinsically *pluralistic* (decentralized and polycentric) society. Indeed, a civil society is one whose *moral raison d'être* is, in the time-honored words of Wilhelm von Humboldt that John Stuart Mill reproduced in his celebrated *On Liberty*, the promotion of "the highest and most harmonious development of [man's] powers." From this arises "individual vigor and manifold diversity" (see Mill 1947, p. 57).

This supremely moral demand requires that individuals be accorded those constitutional guarantees that are necessary if they are to be able to pursue their own self-development, their own individual destiny, in freedom and "security" (as Montesquieu would say). Thus if, as Claude Lefort puts it, "Totalitarianism is based on the ruins of the rights of man" (Lefort 1986, p. 246),[34] a civil society is in contrast grounded firmly on the recognition of fundamental human rights. And as Lefort has also correctly observed, the appeal to human rights was the chief weapon of Eastern dissidents in their struggle to institute a "normal," i.e., civil, society.[35] It was precisely because the notion of human rights was so central to the revolutions of 1989 that these revolutions were of a nontraditional sort, i.e., nonviolent, "velvet" revolutions. The distinguishing feature of these revolutions was that they were decidedly "postmodern," i.e., their animating principle was not that of revolutionary violence but rather that of dialogue or communicative rationality; they were "self-limiting" revolutions (a topic to be discussed more fully in Chapter 4).[36]

Over the course of the last several years, the notion of human rights has come to occupy a central position in political discourse and has, as well, revealed itself to be one of the most effective weapons in the world-wide struggle for freedom and democracy. This notwithstanding, a great deal of confusion continues to surround the notion. Not all the rights enjoyed by people are, properly speaking, human rights. Human rights differ from those rights which belong to people by virtue of their belonging to a particular *group* of people. Rights of the latter sort would more properly be called "privileges," "prerogatives," or "perquisites." In premodern, aristocratic societies people enjoy different "rights" depending upon the class, caste, or estate of which they are members. There can be, and in fact are, such things as group rights, but they must be clearly distinguished from *human* rights. Indeed, since group rights are always particular and serve only particular interests and are thus neither universal nor universalizable, they almost invariably tend to conflict with human rights (as in the case of certain types of affirmative action which in point of fact amount to reverse discrimination). Human rights are by definition always *universal* and belong to individuals *as such*.

Another way of expressing the matter would be to say that human rights are those rights that belong to people simply by virtue of the fact that they are *human* beings, not because they are beings of this or that sort, belonging to this or that race, color, sex, religion, or what-have-you. As one leading analyst of the notion of human rights puts it: "To have a human right, one need be nothing other than a human being, nor do anything other than be born human" (Donnelly 1989, p. 144).[37] Human rights are, as it were, "birthrights." Or as Peter Anyang' Nyong'o of the African Academy of Sciences in Nairobi has said: "From our [African] point of view . . . human rights are universal. . . . All human beings are equal and are endowed by their Creator with basic rights that belong to them as human beings, and not as people of this or that color, continent, sex, nationality, or religion" (Nyong'o 1992, p. 92).[38] In other words, human rights, *les droits de la personne*, are *individual* rights, rights that belong to people for no other reason than the fact that they are, as Kierkegaard would say, "existing individuals."

This is a point that bears emphasizing, since it is often overlooked by communitarian critics of liberalism (the notion of human rights is a quintessentially liberal notion). As Donnelly has pointed out, human rights are "rights of individuals only. . . . [They] define persons as individuals and give prima facie priority to the claims of individuals over society and other social groups" (Donnelly 1989, p. 151).[39] One of the main contentions of Donnelly's analysis is "that the processes of state-building and economic 'modernization' have created individuals who are in need of human rights and that the individualism of human rights need not be possessive or atomistic – in fact, cannot be possessive or atomistic if human rights are to be realized" (Donnelly 1989, p. 143). The greatest threat to the rights and freedoms of citizens has always come, and always will come, from the state. Whence the need to enshrine ("entrench") these rights in constitutional Bills of Rights. In our times (and in the developed world), the state usually appeals to the interests of "society" when it sets out to repress the liberties of its citizens. As Donnelly also quite correctly observes:

> For all the talk of excessive individualism, the problem in the world today is not too many individual rights but that individual human rights are not sufficiently respected. . . . The balance [between the individual on the one hand and the State and Society on the other] is already (always?) tilted against the individual. The only likely result of advocating collective human rights, let alone the so-called human rights of states, is a further strengthening of the forces of repression. . . . Human rights are a rare and valuable intellectual and moral resource in the struggle to right the balance between society (and the state) and the individual. Unless we preserve their distinctive character, and stand

15

firm on their character as individual rights, their positive role in the struggle for human dignity may be compromised.

(Donnelly 1989, p. 149)

The communitarian attempt to place "collective rights" on an equal footing with individual (human) rights has been objected to by Jürgen Habermas, who has cogently argued that in a civil society or what he calls a "constitutional democracy" even such things as "cultural rights" must be viewed as rights pertaining to individuals, not groups. Modern Western societies are ever increasingly multicultural societies, and, as Habermas observes, the liberal notion of human rights "is by no means blind to cultural differences" (Habermas 1994, p. 112). Although, as Habermas points out, the notion of collective rights is "alien" to the principles of liberal democracy (Habermas 1994, p. 116), liberal political theory is nevertheless quite capable of finding a place among basic human rights for rights to "cultural self-determination." The reason is that, contrary to the one-sided view of liberalism put forward by liberalism's communitarian critics, liberal theory does not rest on an atomistic view of the human subject; it fully recognizes the "intersubjective" nature of human subjectivity (a point to which I shall return in Chapter 3) – and thus the need for individuals to situate themselves within specific cultural contexts. In this respect, "cultural rights" are simply variants on basic individual rights guaranteeing individuals the right to free association and freedom from discrimination. In a civil society or a constitutional democracy everyone must have the right to belong to a particular "culture" and the right to contribute to the flourishing of that culture.

This, however, does not mean that "cultures" (ethnic groups) themselves have rights. If it is a basic right of individuals in a free society to criticize any inherited belief, this means that in a constitutional democracy no group, purely as such, can be accorded special rights designed to guarantee its "survival." "For to guarantee survival," Habermas points out, "would necessarily rob the members of the very freedom to say yes or no that is necessary if they are to appropriate and preserve [as well as, Habermas adds elsewhere, transform] their cultural heritage" (Habermas 1994, p. 130). In a free society, the survival of any cultural or ethnic group must be dependent solely on the free adherence and loyalty to it on the part of its members; it cannot be constitutionally guaranteed. "The ecological perspective on species conservation," Habermas appropriately notes, "cannot be transferred to cultures" (Habermas 1994, p. 130; see also Madison 1982, pp. 7–8). The attempt to preserve cultures by legal means, to, in the words of Charles Taylor, "ensure [their] survival through indefinite future generations" (Taylor 1994, p. 41 n) reminds one of what in *The Rights of Man* Tom Paine called the folly (and injustice) of one generation attempting to legislate for all future generations. "There never did, there never will, and there never can," Paine wrote in opposition to Edmund Burke and his attack on the notion of the rights of man, "exist a parliament, or any description of men, or any generation of men, in any country, possessed of the right or the power of binding and controlling posterity to the *'end of time.'*" The logic of human rights dictates that "Every age and generation must be free to act for itself, *in all cases*, as the ages and generation which preceded it. The vanity and presumption of governing beyond the grave is the most ridiculous and insolent of all tyrannies" (Paine 1995, p. 438).

Human rights are thus always rights of individuals, not of groups. And the fundamental *raison d'être* of human rights is that of enabling ("empowering") individuals to, as Paine would say, act for themselves, to exercise human agency in the pursuit of what the ancient Greek philosophers called the "good life." One of the best definitions of "man" is that he is the acting animal, *animal agens*. As an economist and an acute observer of human affairs, Ludwig von Mises observed:

> nothing is more certain for the human mind than what the category of human action brings into relief. There is no human being to whom the intent is foreign to substitute by appropriate conduct one state of affairs for another state of affairs that would prevail if he did not interfere. Only where there is action are there men.
>
> (Mises 1978, p. 71)[40]

Only humans are capable of *acting* (animals "behave" but do not "act," since action is by definition teleological or intentional, requiring what philosophers used to refer to as "freedom of the will"). Moreover, the notion of human action is inseparable from that of the human *individual*, as Paul Ricoeur has said, "The only reality, in the end, are individuals who do things" (Ricoeur 1985, p. 216). Society or the State do not "do" anything, since they are not *agents*. To be sure, individuals sometimes act "in the name" of society or the State, but this sort of action on their part must, in a liberal society, always be open to public scrutiny (by other individuals) since, as public choice theory has amply demonstrated, this sort of action is not infrequently a cover for the pursuit of the strictly private interest of the individuals involved (see Buchanan and Tullock 1965).

The reason why *action* is such an important notion (and the reason why the freedom to act according to the dictates of one's own conscience is so vital) is that, as existential philosophers have duly noted, "man" is that being who, strictly speaking, has no "essence." Human beings "make" themselves, and they do so by means of their *action* (as Marx very rightly observed). As the French phenomenologist, Maurice Merleau-Ponty, pointedly remarked: "Man is a historical idea, and not a natural species" (Merleau-Ponty 1962, p. 170). Or as James Buchanan, Nobel Laureate in Economics, has observed, man should be considered to be not so much a "natural" animal as an "artefactual" one:

17

[he] is an artefactual animal bounded by natural constraints. We are, and will be, at least in part, that which we make ourselves to be. We construct our own being, again within limits. We are artefactual, as much like the pottery shards that the archaeologists dig up as like the animals whose fossils they also find.

(Buchanan 1979, pp. 94–5)

Herein lies the philosophical basis for the notion of *human dignity*, which it is precisely the function of human rights to ensure. As Donnelly observes: "Civil, political, economic, social, and cultural rights all clearly arise from the idea of innate personal dignity" (Donnelly 1989, p. 144). In his book Donnelly apparently does not feel the need to spell out the reasons for speaking of personal or human dignity (for him, it goes without saying that humans should be treated with dignity). A philosophical "grounding" for the notion of human dignity is nevertheless called for at some point or other. One such "grounding" is furnished by the author of a book entitled, appropriately enough, *The Acting Person* (Wojtiła 1979, p. 79). Pope John Paul II has long been an ardent spokesman for the notion of human dignity, and thus, accordingly, for the notion of human rights. An important statement of his in this regard was his 1991 papal encyclical, *Centesimus Annus*, in which he sought to discern the significance of the revolutions of 1989 and which we shall consider in greater detail when we examine the notion of a civil market economy in Chapter 5. In his various writings the Roman Pontiff has shown how what Donnelly refers to as "the idea of innate personal dignity" is itself dependent upon "the concept of the person as the autonomous subject of moral decision" (Donnelly 1989, p. 144). The reason why John Paul II maintains that "the fundamental error of socialism is anthropological [i.e., philosophical] in nature" (John Paul II 1991, §13) is because the notion of human dignity is inseparable from a philosophical anthropology ("theory of man") whose basic premise must be that human beings are first and foremost free agents who by means of their creative agency not only transform the world around them but who also in the very process transform themselves as well and who are thus (or who should be allowed to be) responsible to and for themselves – responsible for who they are, and responsible also for remaking themselves into subjects different from who, at any given time, they merely are.[41] The philosophical basis or justification for human rights is that they are what allow individuals to defend their dignity, which is to say, their freedom and capacity for creative initiative and enterprise, in all the various orders of civil society, the nature or logic of which we shall explore in greater detail in Chapters 3, 4, and 5.[42]

18

2

A NEW THREAT TO AN OLD IDEA

THE NEW TRIBALISM

No sooner had the idea of civil society emerged triumphant from the rubble of totalitarianism than it was put to a rude test. I am referring of course to the wave of ethnocentric nationalism that, after 1989 and in varying forms and degrees, swept over Eastern Europe – there being no longer a repressive totalitarian State to hold it in check. As one commentator has observed: "At the very moment democrats enjoyed their greatest modern victories since 1945, in Eastern Europe, the potential for a populist authoritarianism grew threatening again" (Maier 1993, p. 147). However distressing this development may have been for democratic reformers and human rights activists, it should have come as no surprise (at least when viewed in retrospect). It is in fact perfectly in line with the logic of things, and was thus in a sense "predictable." To appreciate how this is so, it may be useful to backtrack for a moment.

In an earlier work, invoking (with Tocqueville in mind) what I called the Law of Progressive Leftist Development, I maintained that given the logic or internal dynamism of Socialism (the demands, in particular, of the egalitarian ideal), there is an unavoidable tendency for socialist regimes to advance ever further down the road to serfdom. The reason for this is that equality as Socialism conceives of it (equality of conditions or outcomes) can be achieved and maintained only if all those natural tendencies that are apt to produce an inequality of conditions are continually and ruthlessly repressed. However, all such attempts (such as War Communism under Lenin[1] or Mao's Great Leap Forward) inevitably result in economic disaster. This is why it invariably happens that, in occasional moments of lucidity, socialist governments ease up on enforcing equality and allow, however reluctantly, for a liberalization of the economy (cf. Lenin's New Economic Policy or Deng Xiaoping's reforms ["It's glorious to get rich"]). However, as I argued, liberalization measures such as these can never be allowed to take their full course, for this would inevitably undermine the regime itself.[2] As a general rule, when people are granted economic freedom they usually end up

19

demanding political freedom as well, i.e., full-fledged liberal democracy - as the cases, to cite but two, of Taiwan and South Korea demonstrate (see in this regard Scalapino 1989). Inevitably, therefore, a counter-reaction on the part of the bureaucratic elite ensues, and the pendulum in socialist countries swings back the other way. The Khruschev thaw is followed by the Brezhnev freeze-over: Deng's liberalization measures call forth the Tiananmen crack-down. Socialist regimes are thus forever condemned to oscillate to and fro between ideological purism and economic realism in a monotonous eternal return of the same. The "end of history" trumpeted by the prophets of Socialism actually amounts to nothing more than (in Hegel's words) "the repetition of the same majestic ruin" (Hegel 1956, p. 106). A cycle without end, alternating between reform, regression, and stagnation – in an eternal recurrence (see Madison 1986, pp. 190–93).[3]

Earlier in this book, I argued that when socialist regimes do seek to implement the reforms that would make them economically viable, they run the risk of collapsing altogether. What Tocqueville said of "bad" governments is especially true of totalitarian ones: "The most dangerous moment for a bad government is when it seeks to mend its ways." Thus in an earlier work, composed in the early 1980s, I hazarded the prediction that the Soviet regime, to the degree that it sought to make itself economically viable, could not be expected to last for long (Madison 1986, p. 249). Is there a contradiction here, between saying, on the one hand, that socialist regimes are destined to stagnate forever and that, on the other hand, they are condemned to collapse altogether? Not really. It simply amounts to saying that when socialist totalitarian regimes do seek to overcome stagnation and "reform" themselves, these reforms, if successful, will inevitably result in the self-destruction of the regimes themselves.[4]

Socialist regimes are immensely resistant to change due to the fact that, as was mentioned in Chapter 1, they are forms of institutionalized corruption. This is what above all accounts for their tendency to endure indefinitely in a never-ending monotony. Strictly speaking, only factors extrinsic to the system (and its logic) can bring about fundamental change in the system, i.e., any thoroughgoing liberalization. These factors may themselves be either internal or external. By "internal" I do not mean internal to the *system* but, rather, to the *country* – factors such as natural disasters or financial or economic crises of the first order (such as, precisely, the one that befell the Soviet Union in the 1980s). External factors would be military or other forms of pressure brought to bear on the country (such as support for underground opposition movements like Solidarity, which was heavily supported throughout the 1980s by both the American and Vatican governments, and the massive American military build-up under Reagan).

Moreover, it is important to note that when socialist totalitarian regimes which have existed for any significant length of time *do* collapse, they leave behind nothing but a pile of rubble, the clean-up of which necessitates an arduous "transition period," not unlike that faced by countries devastated by war. Precisely because it is of the essence of a totalitarian regime to want to absorb into the Party-state all aspects of society, to destroy any form of social life independent of it, when it does finally disintegrate, the damage to society can in the meantime have been so extensive that there no longer exist any foundations on which a normal, civil society can be erected. As Alexander Yakovlev stated after the collapse of the Soviet Union: "We must admit the most important points of our building have rotted inside. In fact, there is nothing left inside to rebuild upon; the foundation has to be built from scratch" (Yakovlev 1993, p. 107).

And it is not only human society but nature itself that bears the scars of these attempts to realize a worker's paradise on earth. The living legacy of Socialism is that of, as Yakovlev calls it, "ecological vandalism" (Yakovlev 1993, p. 76; see also p. 70) on a truly mind-boggling scale. The classic case was pehaps East Germany. When, after the fall of the regime, outsiders were able to witness first-hand the ravages of Socialism, the European Community proclaimed the former DDR "the most polluted country in the world" (although, by all current accounts, Russia itself ranks as one of the most ecologically devastated countries in the world).

This brings us back to the issue of nationalism. In the light of what has been said, it should come as no surprise that after the destruction of whatever rudiments of civil society they may have possessed before totalitarianism sidetracked them from the main line of History,[5] the peoples of Eastern Europe found themselves with little else, in most instances, to fall back upon than the ethnic and nationalistic passions of an earlier time. As Seymour Martin Lipset observes:

> Totalitarian systems sought systematically to eliminate groups mediating between the individual and the state, and so have left their successors without effective civil societies. This reduced the possibility for *organized* opposition by reducing group effectiveness generally, leaving individuals ill-suited for innovative activities like entrepreneurship or anything else that Tocqueville included under the heading of "civil partnerships." The countries of the former Soviet empire are now trying to cope with the consequences of the suppression of civil society, which makes it hard to consolidate democracy or foster economic entrepreneurship.
>
> (Lipset 1993, p. 47)

The former socialist countries are, as it were (*par la force des choses*), obliged to return to the point in history where they left off before plunging into the dark night of totalitarian rule. As a political theorist in Tbilisi has observed:

Totalitarianism's decades-long assault on the structures of civil society has left behind a rubble of atomized individuals who are searching frantically for a common principle on which to base their new lives together. In this situation, nationalism comes to the fore as the major – if not the only – principle capable of holding society together. But since the nationalist *political* tradition has been interrupted, the *ethnic* element has become especially strong.

(Nodia 1992, p. 18)[6]

Because the newly emergent (or reemergent) nationalism in Eastern Europe is of an exclusionist sort and is based on the supposed uniqueness of one's own *Volkgeist*, it is readily transformed, Julia Kristeva observes, "into a repressive force aimed at *other* people and extolling *one's own*" (Kristeva 1993, p. 54). The distressing thing about the resurgence of ethnic nationalism is that, by making it excessively difficult to construct a genuine civic culture common to all the inhabitants of an existing country, it compounds immensely the difficulties involved in making the transition to a market economy, a necessary condition for a genuine civil society (as we shall see in more detail in Chapter 5). Ethnic nationalism, or what Daniel Chirot has termed "reactive nationalism," i.e., a nationalism "that is based on fear and resentment of the outside world, that demands communal solidarity of the entire nation, regardless of the cultural and individual differences which exist" (Chirot 1994, p. 416), tends invariably to degenerate into a new tribalism, and because of this it poses the greatest threat to the ideal of civil society appealed to by the revolutionaries of 1989. The reason for this is that, by privileging group rights (based on "nationality," ethnicity, race, religion, etc.) over individual rights, ethnic nationalism stands squarely opposed to the implementation of individual, i.e., human, rights, the condition for the creation of a genuine civil society and a market economy. There exists, to my knowledge, no instance where an ethnic obsession has facilitated democracy and human rights, and there is no lack of instances where it has actively frustrated democratization, to a greater or lesser degree; the list of the latter is practically endless: Romania, the former republics of the Soviet Union, Burma, Sri Lanka, Afghanistan, Indonesia, Ethiopia, the Sudan, sub-Saharan Africa, and, of course, the former Yugoslavia (to cite but a few instances [see in this regard Donald L. Horowitz 1993]). It is therefore with justification that Conor Cruise O'Brien asserts: "Nationalism and democracy are qualitatively different and incommensurable" (O'Brien 1991, p. 29).

To the degree that nationalism (ethnonationalism) gained ascendancy in Eastern Europe, what tended to occur was not the long-hoped for transition to a civil society based on individual human rights but rather the transition from one form of collectivism to another. As one Yugoslav has observed:

The nationalism that has recently emerged in this context is distinctly undemocratic. . . . Because of the structural similarities between

22

communism and this brand of nationalism, it has been relatively easy to move from one ideology to the other – that is, from one form of collectivism to the other. The former was based on class, represented by the Communist Party; the latter is founded upon ethnic homogeneity, presented by the national leader. Both systems neglect the individual and undermine the notion of rights to equal citizenship.

(Pesic 1993, pp. 100–1)[7]

As this writer goes on to say: "Citizenship rights are treated not as individual rights extended equally to all, but as the collective rights of ethnic or 'national' groups. The nation is understood as a kind of superfamily." When a nation is understood as "a kind of superfamily" or "community" and not as a genuine civil society, one can expect family squabbles to break out on a continual basis. Interethnic warfare becomes almost inevitable, as the case of Yugoslavia so vividly demonstrated. In such a case, the old nineteenth-century-type calls for the "national self-determination of peoples" can only mean the suppression of individual human rights (for those who are not members of the ethnic or "national" majority) and the total destruction of civil society; in sum, a renewed Hobbesian "war of all against all" and the very opposite of civility.

It may be noted that ethnic nationalism entails the suppression of human rights not only for ethnic minorites, but also for the members of the ethnic majority themselves, since, as the text of Vesna Pesic cited above indicates, the focus of ethnic nationalism is invariably on some charismatic leader who, for his own personal interests (power), fans the flames of ethnic hostility. Ethnonationalism is thoroughly self-serving on the part of the local leaders who encourage it, and it functions, after the demise of socialist ideology, as the primary fulcrum of political mobilization. It is, of course, absolutely inimical to democracy and to the free self-determination of the people themselves. "National self-determination (*Selbstbestimmung*)," the great rallying cry of the German people in the 1930s, generally means, in point of fact, the self-affirmation (*Selbstbehauptung*) of a nationalist leader, not the freedom of citizens (the word "self" in "self-determination" is altogether misleading, for the only "self" or "subject" here is, as Claude Lefort might say, the body of the King). For the helpless citizenry, the transition from totalitarianism to nationalism is a classic case of going from the frying pan into the fire.

Ethnic nationalism, while understandable as a response to the near-total destruction of civil society wrought by socialist totalitarianism, is nonetheless *absurd* – for a number of reasons. Ralf Dahrendorf signals some of them in the following remarks:

The idea of national self-determination has its attractions for people who feel lost in the modern world. It appears to offer a sense of belonging and of meaning, embodied in powerful symbols such as flags and anthems as well as passports and constitutions. People – some people at any rate – are prepared to die for the independence of their nation. It would be wrong to discount such a powerful force. Yet national self-determination remains one of the more unfortunate inventions of international law. It ascribes a right to peoples when rights should always be those of individuals. As a result, it invites usurpers to claim this right on behalf of peoples in whose name they speak while at the same time trampling on minorities, and sometimes on the civil rights of all. . . . If one allows the so-called right to self-determination to prevail over the basic rights of individual citizens, the result is likely to be a nation-state without liberty, and there is no shortage of examples.

(Dahrendorf 1990, p. 148)

Besides the fact that it often gives rise in a rather farcical manner to what Freud called the "narcissism of minor differences," ethnic nationalism is absurd in a fundamental, logical sense of the term. Abraham Lincoln expressed the matter well when, in the course of one the greatest trials history has ever placed upon a civil society, he said to the Southern secessionists in his First Inaugural Address (1861): "Plainly, the central idea of secession is the essence of anarchy" (Lincoln 1989, p. 220). By this he meant that the position of the secessionists was self-contradictory and thus self-destructive, i.e., logically absurd. It was absurd in that in attempting to secede from a democratic state (based on the principles of majority rule and respect for minority rights) they were setting a precedent that would be destructive of any government they themselves should establish in turn. When for reasons of ethnic nationalism a people rejects the ideas of democracy and civil society, "anarchy or despotism in some form is all that is left," as Lincoln so aptly said. Eastern Europe after the fall of Socialism is a case in point (the former Yugoslavia managed to conjoin both anarchy and despotism).[8]

Just as the Easterners woke up the West by reminding it of the enduring validity of the idea of civil society, so perhaps there is also a wake-up lesson that the phenomenon of ethnic nationalism can deliver to the West.

CIVIL SOCIETY VERSUS COMMUNITY

In the preceding chapter I raised the question as to what, after 1989, was left of the Left. Where have all the erstwhile Marxists disappeared to? The answer of course is that in the East the Party bosses and *apparatchiki* of the various socialist states effected an overnight conversion from the ideology of class warfare to the ideology of nationalism; ethnicity, *Kultura, Blut und Boden* replaced Marxist ideology as a convenient *causa belli*. But what about Western socialists? To what have they been able to transfer their allegiance and bellicosity ("class-warfarism") after the bankruptcy of Marxist ideology? Given

24

the fact that the socialist mind-set is deeply ingrained in human nature,[9] it is not to be expected that Western leftists would simply fold up their tents and walk away from their great mission in life, i.e., that of being radical critics of the "status quo."

The answer as to where the "radicals" have gone is not difficult to come by, at least in the case of a significant portion of them. Seymour Martin Lipset suggests the answer when, remarking on how "even if socialism is now a dirty word, the contest between [the so-called "left" and "right"] is by no means over," he observes how "leftist" has traditionally meant "favoring greater emphasis on community and equality, with the state as the primary instrument of reform" (Lipset 1993, p. 55). "Community" has indeed become the *mot d'ordre* of much of the post-Marxist left. This of course is not surprising, since what the Russian philosopher Alexander Zinoviev calls "communality" is indeed a persistent element in socialist thinking (see Hoskin 1990, pp. 29–31).[10]

"Communitarianism" is the Western counterpart to Eastern ethnocentric nationalism – a sort of "kinder, more gentle" version of the latter, as it were. The common element of both is, as Lipset points out, a reliance on political means, i.e., the state, to resolve social issues. The common element, in other words, is a pronounced obliviousness to one of the principal requirements of a genuine civil, which is to say, free society, i.e., the freedom of society from the state. Consider for instance that Western phenomenon referred to as "multiculturalism." Robert Hughes, art critic for *Time* magazine and uncompromising critic of the follies of both left and right, has written in this regard:

> The academic left professes to see in [multiculturalism] the seeds of radical promise: Marxism has passed through the fires of its own dissolution and is reborn as a "hero with a thousand faces" – multiculturalism. . . . [W]hat's left of the Left would like to endow ordinary internal differences within a society – of gender, race and sexual pattern – with the inflated character of nationhood, as though they not only embodied cultual differences but actually constituted whole "cultures" in their own right. "Queer Nation," indeed!
>
> (Hughes 1993, p. 75)

The term "multiculturalism" is, in itself, fairly neutral, and there is no reason why it should not be taken to mean something positive, viz., tolerance and respect for minorities having cultural and religious backgrounds different from those of the majority and a guaranteeing to them the right to maintain their customs and traditions through voluntary association. As Hughes remarks:

> Multiculturalism asserts that people with different roots can coexist, that they can learn to read the image-banks of others, that they can and

should look across the frontiers of race, language, gender and age without prejudice or illusion, and learn to think against the background of a hybridized society. It proposes – modestly enough – that some of the most interesting things in history and culture happen at the inter-face between cultures. It wants to study border situations, not only because they are fascinating in themselves, but because understanding them may bring with it a little hope for the world.

(Hughes 1991, pp. 83–4)

In point of fact, however, the multiculturalism that the new radicals would like to make mandatory and a matter of government-enforced policy is anything but the sort of thing Hughes describes. It amounts instead to a form of *separatism* that "denies the value, even the possibility, of such a dialogue. It rejects exchange. It is multiculturalism gone sour, fermented by despair and resentment" (Hughes 1993, p. 84). It is a formula not for cultural diversity but for cultural (or racial or ethnic) segregation. As practised by the "politics of difference," multiculturalism is something altogether different from what traditional liberal thought upheld under the heading "pluralism." "[H]onoring our distinctions, as peoples of a particular heritage and indi-viduals of particular gifts," Jean Bethke Elshtain notes, "is far different from the current construction of 'difference' as a form of group homogeneity that brooks no disagreement or distinction *within* and can maintain itself only as a redoubt *against* threatening 'enemies' from without" (Elshtain 1995, p. xiv). Even though Richard Rorty has expressed his sympathies for the "politics of difference" and even though he has said that "any left is better than none," he has nevertheless recognized that, as he says: "Multicultural-ism is turning into the attempt to keep these communities [within the nation, conceived of as a community of communities] at odds with one another" (Rorty 1994, p. E 15).

At the heart of multicultural separatism lies a philosophical view of the relation of the Self and the Other that is of a very peculiar sort. In spite of all the poststructuralist talk of "otherness" and "plurality," what we have to deal with here is a pseudo-plurality and a view of the Self that *opposes* it to the Other. The implicit assumption is that the relation between the Self or the Same and the Other is *dichotomous*; one cannot be and remain the "same" while opening oneself to, and learning from, the "other." Thus, those multiculturalists who emphasize "particularity" at the expense of universality view cross-cultural contacts as simply the means whereby a domineering, Western culture seeks to subjugate ("colonize") the cultures of various third world countries. This stance indeed amounts, as Hughes (1993) says, to a rejection of dialogue and exchange; it entails not respect for the Other (from whom one might learn something, even something about one-self) but rather an uncivil intolerance for everything "other." The "politics of difference" boils down to a "politics of identity" of an exclusionary sort.

26

The philosophical thesis implicitly at work here is that *only the Same can understand the Same*, only Like can know Like. As one North American Indian writer once declaimed, only Indians should be allowed to write novels about Indian life (this particular person, taking on the role of intellectual terrorist, was prepared to exert whatever pressure she could to prevent publishers from publishing books on Indian life by non-Indians). So much for the basic human right to freedom of expression! So much also for the imagination, which is nothing if it is not the ability to see things as others might. As Hughes points out, separatism of this sort is the opposite of "real multi-culturalism, generous and tolerant on both sides"; it is the opposite of diversity (Hughes 1993, p. 149). How, one is inclined to wonder, would people of this sort account for the fact that the single most insightful interpretation of the American way of life (from which Americans still continue to learn a great deal about themselves) was produced not by an American but by a foreign tourist who spent only nine months in the country, viz., Alexis de Tocqueville? The philosophical fact of the matter is, as Paul Ricoeur has said, "Our understanding of ourselves passes through others."

While there may be no such thing as a culturally and historically (and gender) invariant human nature ("essentialism"), is there nevertheless not something like a common human condition? Are not humans, always and everywhere, confronted, as humans, with the same "boundary situations" (as Karl Jaspers called them), e.g., adversity, suffering, guilt, the contingency or uncertainty of existence, mortality, sexuality . . . ? And in observing how different peoples, in different places and times, have interpretively responded to these common enigmas or dilemmas, can we not learn something about ourselves, about what it means to be human? This cannot of course be allowed by those multiculturalists who indulge in an uncritical rejection of the very notion of universality (and thus, in effect, the very notion of humanity) and who instead extol without qualification the virtues of "local-ism" or "particularity." "Like the racists before them," one French writer observes, "contemporary fanatics of cultural identity confine individuals to their group of origin. Like them, they carry differences to the absolute extremes, and in the name of the multiplicity of specific causalities destroy any possibility of a natural or cultural community among peoples" (Finkielkraut 1995, p. 79).

Multiculturalism of the isolationist sort is as absurd as is ethnocentric nationalism. Consistently implemented, it would entail the demise of the human sciences, which are nothing if not attempts to understand differing forms of life (social, cultural, psychological, historical, and so on). As Clifford Geertz has remarked: "The essential vocation of interpretive anthropology is . . . to make available to us answers that others, guarding other sheep in other valleys, have given [to the existential dilemmas of life], and thus to include them in the consultable record of what man has said" (Geertz 1973, p. 30). History itself (i.e., historiography), which is one of the prime means by which any people comes to an understanding of itself, would have to be scrapped, since it is by definition the attempt to understand other people and other ways of life (of past times). The logical outcome would be book burning on a scale unimaginable even by Hitler's Nazi legions.

Behind the simple-minded idea that only the Same can understand the Same lies a fundamental philosophical (or epistemological) error, that of equating understanding with *empathy*. This is the error of thinking that to understand the other, one must be able to "put oneself in their shoes," i.e., must be able to *relive* their experiences as they themselves lived them, to, in effect *be* them. As that discipline known as philosophical hermeneutics has demonstrated, however, understanding is improperly viewed when it is viewed as a merely *reproductive* activity. The reason why we can genuinely understand other forms of life is because understanding is *not* a simple mirroring process and a coinciding or becoming-one with that which is to be understood, as modernism took it to be, but is always a matter of creative *interpretation* or, as Paul Ricoeur would say, transfiguration. Interpretation is the means by which temporal or cultural distances are bridged, without for all that being abolished. Because understanding is always a matter of interpretation, it is always possible to achieve a genuine understanding of the other, without having to actually become the other.[11] The Russian culture critic Mikhail Bakhtin expressed this point in "intercultural hermeneutics" well when he said:

> In the realm of culture, outsidedness is a most powerful factor in understanding. It is only in the eyes of *another* culture that a foreign culture reveals itself fully and profoundly (but not maximally fully, because there will be cultures that see and understand even more). A meaning only reveals its depths once it has enountered and come into contact with another, foreign meaning: they engage in a kind of dialogue, which surmounts the closedness and one-sidedness of these particular meanings, these cultures. We raise new questions for a foreign culture, ones that it did not raise itself; we seek answers to our own questions in it.
>
> (Bakhtin 1986, p. 7)

A bad theory (such as, in this case, the notion that only the same can understand the same) generally translates into bad practice, and the socially divisive character of separatist multiculturalism is well reflected in the aggressive affirmative action programs it invariably tends to spawn. The old socialist ideal – the (re)distribution of social benefits by political means[12] – is fully at work here. One of the code words for this sort of governmental intrusion into society is "employment equity" – which has nothing to do with equity (justice as fairness) and everything to do with social engineering on a truly grand scale by an army of bureaucrats. Contrary to the rhetoric of the "equity" activists, the situation they are working at bringing into being is not one of "inclusiveness" but, in fact, one of exclusiveness that pits different groups in society against one another in their competition for political favors. The "politics of identity" is nothing more than a spoils system designed to favor some at the expense of others.

Politics is invariably corrupted when it becomes generally accepted that the prime function of government is not to insure the rights and liberties of its citizens but to guarantee directly their economic well-being by means of entitlements, transfer payments, quota systems for employment, and the like. As one social analyst has remarked, "rent-seeking [securing public support for one's private interests] is inevitable and can be expected to increase or decrease in response to the extent (and hence the value) of the state's control over resources" (Palmer 1984, p. 3). At the same time that politics is corrupted, society is politicized, a phenomenon that resulted in the destruction of civil society in the Eastern Europe. At the limit (or beyond a certain point of no-return) multiculturalism of the sort described above leads to the breakdown of civil society in much the same way as does ethnic nationalism in the former socialist countries. As Hughes also remarks:

> People once used a dead metaphor – "balkanization" – to evoke the splitting of a field into sects, groups, little nodes of power. Now, on the dismembered corpse of Yugoslavia, whose "cultural differences" (or, to put it plainly, archaic religious and racial lunacies) have been set free by the death of Communism, we see what that stale figure of speech once meant and now means again. A Hobbesian world: the war of all on all, locked in blood feud and theocratic hatred, the *reductio ad insanitatem* of America's mild and milky multiculturalism.
>
> (Hughes 1993, p.13)

The consequences of this (politicized) approach to social issues can only be disastrous for the maintenance of a civil society. When one's opportunities are not a function of one's individual abilities but of one's group affiliations, it is inevitable that groups will be led to compete with one another for their government allotments. This results in "rent-seeking" and a consequent corruption of politics. Politics ceases to be concerned, as it ought to be in a genuine civil society, with the *common good*, becoming instead the arena wherein special interest groups vie with one another in order to maximize, at the expense of others (opportunities are always scarce), their own private interests as a group. Politics, as the American Founding Father John Adams would say, becomes a sordid "scramble for the loaves and fishes."[13]

A prime manifestation of the *incivility* produced by a multiculturalism gone mad and obsessed with ferreting out "systemic" imbalances of power between groups is the barbarous intolerance engendered by attempts to enforce, by means of fascist-like intimidation ("thought vigilantism" [Rauch 1993]), "politically correct" modes of behavior. The underlying premise of this form of adversarial multiculturalism is that no member of a minority

29

group should ever feel offended by having their "self-esteem" called into question (this rule applies only to "oppressed" minorities, not to the white male "majority" who are by definition the oppressors and who can therefore legitimately be insulted to no end). Advocates of legal penalties against "symbolic harms" would equate merely offensive and insulting language with actual bodily harm, or the threat thereof. Naturally, the first victim of this sort of intellectual fraudulence and the unlimited censorship it entails is freedom itself, for as legal theorist Ronald Dworkin has observed, the essence of liberty "is freedom to offend" (Dworkin 1991, p. 13; see also Dworkin 1992).[14]

The antics of the politically correct "language police" would be risible, were it not for the fact that they have resulted in the ruin of many a person's career for remarks on their part deemed to be "racist" or "sexist."[15] Actually the charge of racism or sexism would be best directed at the politically correct themselves, since they tend to think only in stereotypes and to view everything in the light of a racial or sexual bias. To maintain, as many of them do, that no black or no woman can be racist or sexist is itself a stereotyping, racist or sexist position. The editors of a journal dedicated to an "inclusive vision of gender equality" remark in this regard:

> [I]t is tragic that in the last decade or so the willingness to engage in serious stereotyping has returned on a large scale. And the major player in this highly regressive development has been neo-feminism. A movement that began with so much promise, to help liberate society from group think regarding gender, has become a major purveyor of stereotypes – notably, of the evil-male/innocent-female victim iconography.
>
> ("Why *Balance* Is Needed," 1994 p. 12)

The irony of the situation is that attacks on free speech and the prohibition of "offensive" language in the name of combating "racism" or "sexism" actually tend to promote racism and sexism by promoting a racist and sexist mind-set; it is normal and fully to be expected that when social relations are regulated primarily on the basis of group attributes such as race or sex, and not on the basis of respect for the equal rights and dignity of individuals, tensions between different groups will be exacerbated ("The toxic winds of racism blow in more than one direction")[16] – in the same way that ethnocentrism calls forth ever more ethnocentric rivalry. As one writer pointedly observes: "A multicultural America may seem benign in a classroom syllabus, but we shouldn't be surprised if the result is conflict in the streets" (Hacker 1993, p. 22).

The phenomena of political correctness and adversarial multiculturalism are bound up with another pathological phenomenon particularly in evidence in our times: the cult of the "victim."[17] As Hughes remarks, "our new-found sensitivity decrees that only the victim shall be the hero" (Hughes

1993, p. 7).[18] Western culture has indeed become a culture of complaint, a culture of conspicuous offense-taking animated by, as Richard Rorty would say, "the need to stay as angry as possible" (Rorty 1994). Those aspiring to the ersatz respectability afforded by victimhood status can now avail themselves of the entrepreneurial services of a host of psychotherapists adept at "recovering" long-repressed, made-to-measure memories of childhood abuse.[19] The cult of the victim has its roots deep in the human psyche; it is the manifestion of a disease of the soul that Nietzsche, skilled philosopher-physician that he was, diagnosed as resentment or, better said, *ressentiment* – and which he perceived to be the motivating force in the socialist mindset and the reason for its eternal vindictiveness. The appeal to the "rights of the victimized" that we hear voiced today on every conceivable occasion is, to a very large extent, nothing more than a rancorous politics of *ressentiment*. As the Belgian-Canadian political theorist, and former Marxist, Marc Angenot has observed: "An immense market of *ressentiment* has opened up in the cultures of the end of the century" (Angenot 1992).[20] *Ressentiment* is the self-justifying "ideology" of the self-anointed "victim" who reasons, as Angenot says, in the following fashion: "I am oppressed, poor, impotent, ignorant, servile, vanquished – and that is my glory, it is what permits me to *make myself immediately superior*, in my ideological fancy, to the rich, the powerful, the talented, the successful." This "revenge of the vanquished" asserts that one's misfortunes are the exclusive fault of the "other," who must be made to pay on the spot for one's own perceived misfortunes.

Because it is "hostile to dialogue and compromise," as Angenot points out, the politics of *ressentiment* is the simulacrum of politics, of the democratic politics appropriate to a civil society. Appealing to past harms, real or imagined (it makes little difference), it demands special, compensatory treatment for an unspecified length of time in the future.[21] *Ressentiment* is the key factor at work in today's unholy alliance of aggressive, quota-based affirmative action programs and ethnocentric, narcissistic multiculturalism (what Angenot refers to as "gregarious egocentrism"). As Angenot observes:

> The growing *ressentiment* has contributed to the promotion of a new ideology of rights – thought of not in terms of the rights of citizenship and universality, but of a vociferous "right to be different." An exchange or market for exclusivist demands has been established, irreconcilable and irreducible ones on the part of ethnic, cultural, sexual, and other such groups. Western societies have become societies of *différends* (Jean-François Lyotard) where grudges and complaints do not point to a rule of justice ... where nothing, moreover, makes comprehensive sense or produces lasting effects.
>
> (Angenot, unpublished)

In the politics of *ressentiment*, justice is reduced to the juggling of special interests, universality to particularity, equal rights to preferential treatment.

The paternalistic Welfare State thrives on these litiginous *différends*, since they cannot be resolved by the rule of law but only by bureaucratic fiat. And thus it is not in the least surprising that this new market in exclusivist, group-based rights should be welcomed by modern governments, ever eager as they are to transform *citizens* into *clients*, as Alexis de Tocqueville pointed out over a hundred and fifty years ago when he expressed his fear that the new democratic egalitarianism he witnessed first-hand in America might give rise to nothing more than *"une nouvelle physionomie de la servitude"* (Tocqueville 1961, I, 1, 2).

The politics of *ressentiment* will always choose, in Tocqueville's words, "equality in servitude" over "equality in freedom," for the latter is dependent upon the universalist idea of equal human rights and the equal dignity of all individuals, but it is precisely this idea that, in its vindictiveness, the communitarian politics of *ressentiment* rejects. The politics of *ressentiment* is, as Angenot points out, a form of *tribalism*, and "tribalistic narcissism" is quite simply incompatible with a genuine recognition of otherness and plurality, with the equal liberty of all. The resentful reject the notion of equal human rights and the universal rules of fair treatment, demanding instead special, unequal ('pro-active") treatment of their own tribal groups. This spells the end of the notions of "equality before the law" (*isonomia*) and "the equal liberty of all" (*isegoria*), notions vital to any functioning democratic or civil society.

What we are dealing with here is, in one of its forms, what Rhoda E. Howard has called "reverse cultural imperialism." This is the argument, voiced by certain "third world" aficionados, that universal human rights, the rights of the individual as opposed to the tribal group, are a Western construct ("eurocentric") and thus something alien to non-Western cultures, and thus also, it is said, a form of oppression in their regard ("neocolonialism"). The argument goes as follows (I quote Howard): "[D]ebate, the idea that people holding initially opposing views can persuade each other through logic and reason of their position, is rejected as a form of thought typical of rationalist and competitive Western society. Western thought . . . silences the oppressed" (Howard 1992a, p. 6). This new form of "primitivism," "cultural absolutism," or "romantic communitarianism," as Howard variously refers to it, is yet another instance of the politics of *ressentiment*. The inverted system of values it rancorously appeals to amounts to a perverse denial of the fact that, as Howard says, "it is precisely the central human rights premises of freedom of speech, press and assembly that all over the world permit the silenced to gain a social voice" (ibid.).

Politically correct multiculturalism is indeed aggressively anti-Western in its insistence that all cultures and cultural practices are, in every respect, equally valid and deserving of respect – except, of course, for Western culture (or civilization) which is declared to be intrinsically "hegemonic" and the source of all evil and injustice in the world: "In an attempt to accommodate diversity, many educators and social critics now treat all ideas as equally deserving of respect, except those that sprang from Western civilization" (Park 1995, p. E 15). Western science in particular, radical feminists insist, was invented so as to maintain white male dominance.[22]

As Angenot points out, probably the only effective antidote to the politics of *ressentiment* is what he calls "the desire for justice – a justice with universal scope." He says: "All thought of citizenship, of the universal, of the universality of rules of justice, of dialogue, of the cosmopolitan and a non-partioned-off pluralism is an antidote to *ressentiment*." Whether or not this antidote will prove effective, it is certainly the only formula for a politics not of *ressentiment* but of *civility*, one that seeks to promote, in the words of Václav Havel, "an atmosphere of tolerant solidarity and unity in diversity based on mutual respect, genuine pluralism and parallelism" (Havel 1992a).

A WORD OF WARNING FROM THE EAST

As if in response to the post-Marxist mania for "communities" or, as the Germans might say, *Gemeinschaftlust*, Havel, that indefatigable spokesman for the idea of a genuinely civil society, issued, four years after the revolutions of 1989, a word of warning to the West. He urged the West not to lose sight of its traditional values and ideals, in particular that of "a civic society based on peaceful co-existence between different ethnic groups and cultures." Among these values and ideals, he said, "are respect for the uniqueness and the freedom of each human being, the principles of a democratic and pluralistic political system, a market economy, and a civic society with the rule of law" (Havel 1992d, p. 3). Only the idea of "a broad civic society," he said, can smother "the demons of nationalist collectivism." Today's Europe, he said (and one could say the same of North America), lacks an "ethos," government having become increasingly a matter of catering to "various lobbying groups" with bureaucrats wrapping "base and narrow-minded interests in noble, high-sounding words." Ethnocentrism and demands for national self-determination, he sought to remind the West, are the politics of the past. A politics of the future (what Havel also refers to as a postmodern politics) must be based firmly on "the certainty that only democracy, individual human rights and freedoms, and the civil principle can guarantee the genuinely full development of even that aspect of one's identity represented by membership in a nationality" (ibid.).

It is hard to find fault with Havel's assessment of the situation, since it bespeaks an authentic moral conscience, animated as it is by the ideals of "decency, reason, responsibility, sincerity, civility, and tolerance." These are indeed, as Garton Ash would say, the old ideas whose time has finally come, and they are the main elements in the idea of a civil society. It is this idea that must henceforth serve as the core notion of the politics of postmodernity, in both East and West.

In an era of globalization and ever-increasing world-wide interdependence

– in what Havel calls "today's planetary civilization" (Havel 1992c, p. 12) – there can be no return to the cozy comforts of an idealized, premodern *community* (*Gemeinschaft*). Present-day communitarianism, driven by a romantic nostalgia for premodern (face-to-face) communities, represents a counter-force to postmodern globalism, being, as it were, the more benign counter-part to the resurgent ethnic nationalism of the former socialist countries, as well as to the neopatrimonialism still rampant in many of the more backward countries of the third world. The word "civil," like the word "civilized," refers to an urbane, "city" mode of existence. A city is not a "community," as a village may be, but a place where all sorts of people from all sorts of disparate backgrounds are thrown together – and must accordingly learn the civic virtues that will permit them to live together in peace and in respect for their mutual rights. As one American offical remarked, objecting to the excesses of a divisive multiculturalism: "The issue is not multiculturalism. We agree with that. The question is, are you also going to talk about the political and moral values that are essential for us to live together?" (Reinhold 1991, p. 47).[23] By the nature of things, these values, human rights being among them, can only be *universal* values, not "local" (communalist) ones.

Central to any actually existing civil society is the principle of voluntary or civic association. "Social self-organization" was the watchword of the Polish Solidarity movement, and it was also that feature of the early American republic that so impressed Tocqueville. Americans, Tocqueville readily noted, were the most individualistic people on earth – and yet they were also the people who were most ready and willing to unite in voluntary association for community projects and the advancement of the common good.[24]

"Individualism" (and an emphasis on universal individual rights) need therefore in no way stand in opposition to the interests of "community." However, from a human rights point of view, only those "communities" are morally acceptable that fully respect the rights of their individual members. One such right is the right to "opt out" of a community and join another (in their talk of "community," communitarians often seem to ignore the fact that in "modern" society individuals usually belong to a number of different communities, both at any given time and over the course of their lives). In a free, civil society, there is no reason why people, if they are so inclined, should not be allowed to form communist-type communities (such as religious communes or Israeli *kibbutzim*) in which their individuality is sub-merged in the life of the collectivity – so long, that is, as they retain the option of opting out of them at any time. If individuals do not enjoy the freedom to opt out of a community – even if it is one into with they were born, such as a tightly knit religious community – "communitarianism" is simply a recipe for unfreedom.[25] Freedom can readily become a meaningless term if the rights of the group (to, for instance, the maintenance of its own existence) are accorded priority over those of the individual (see in this regard Donnelly 1989, p. 151).[26] Thus, to speak in classical terms, *Gemeinschaft* must always be subordinate to *Gesellschaft*, or, to borrow a terminological distinction from anthropologist Victor W. Turner, *communitas* must be subordinated to *societas*. Individuals can often give greater meaning to their lives by belonging to this or that community, but if this meaning is to be achieved in conformity to the principle of human dignity (the freedom to follow the dictates of one's own conscience in the pursuit of one's own destiny), communities must always be situated within, and be limited by, the overarching framework of civil society, with its guarantees of individual freedoms and rights of a cultural, political, and economic nature.

RETHINKING CIVIL SOCIETY

As our analysis of totalitarian society indicated by a kind of *via negativa*, "civil society" means the freedom of society from the state, and it also means the freedom of individuals, within society, to pursue their own destinies in voluntary association with others. Given the renewed threats to the idea of civil society on the part of both ethnocentric nationalism and radical communitarianism, it is obvious that the idea of civil society, however self-evident its virtues were to eighteenth century enlightenment thinkers as well as to the revolutionaries of 1989, stands in need of defense. This is precisely what Václav Havel was attempting to tell the General Assembly of the Council on Europe. Moreover, an adequate defense of the idea requires that it be transposed from the modern (eighteenth century) context of its origin and be *rethought* in, as Havel would say, a postmodern context. This is what the following chapters will attempt to do.

A common way of defining civil society is to say that it is that public realm which is intermediate between the state (political life), on the one hand, and the sphere of purely private life, on the other, i.e., the family. This way of approaching the issue often results in equating civil society primarily with those social relations (of a materialist sort) that are mediated by the market (these economic relations, moreover, usually being equated with pure selfishness and an egotism that pits one member of society against all the others). This is one of the more unfortunate legacies of Hegel's celebrated treatment of civil society in his *Philosophy of Right*. In German "civil society" translates as *bürgerliche Gesellschaft*, and the word Bürger is dangerously ambiguous; it can mean either "citizen" or "bourgeois." A market economy is an indispensable element in any genuine civil society, but civil society is much more than a *bürgerliche Gesellschaft*, if by *Bürger* one means *bourgeois*. This is of course the way Marx interpreted Hegel's use of the word *Bürger*, which allowed him to turn the whole idea of civil society to ridicule.[27] The individual human rights proclaimed by civil society, *les droits de l'homme et du citoyen*, Marx proclaimed, are in fact nothing more than legal privileges granted ostensibly to all citizens but in reality only to one class of citizens, i.e., the bourgeoisie, such rights being nothing more than a licence granted to it to exploit the working class. True, universal freedom will only come when bourgeois civil society (money and the right to private property)[28] is super-seded and replaced by a classless (communist or propertyless, and thus undifferentiated) community (*Gemeinwesen*). Ever since, those within the Marxist tradition have disparaged the notion of human rights, referring to them derisively as mere "bourgeois rights."[29] After Marx, and thanks to his deconstructive reading of Hegel, the idea of civil society fell into a kind of intellectual limbo – until, simultaneously with the demise of Marxism, it was resurrected in "1989."

Now that the old idea of civil society has finally been revived, it is important that it be reconceptualized and that the Hegelian understanding of it be superceded if the notion of universal human rights is to be made both meaningful and defensible (since, as I mentioned in Chapter 1, the notion of human rights is meaningless outside of the context of civil society). This point should be emphasized, since the "Hegelian" way of viewing civil society still prevails in much of the literature. Thus, for instance, Larry Diamond, one of the editors of the *Journal of Democracy*, defines civil society

> as an intermediary entity, standing between the private sphere and the state. Thus it excludes individual and family life, inward-looking group activity (e.g., for recreation, entertainment, or spirituality), the profit-making enterprise of individual business firms, and political efforts to take control of the state.
>
> (Diamond 1994, p. 5)[30]

This way of viewing the matter is, in my opinion, unfortunate (even though, for the sake of convenience, I have myself tended to speak in the customary fashion in the preceding pages), and one of the principal aims of this book is to overcome this unduly restricted way of conceiving of civil society. My aim, in short, is to revive, in a postmodern context, a pre-Hégelian, more extensive conception of civil society – such as, for instance, is to be found at the beginning of the liberal tradition in John Locke, who used the terms "civil society" and "political society" interchangeably and for whom civil society was coextensive with what Cicero would have called the *res publica*, i.e., a free society *in its entirety* (see Locke 1952, ch. 7). Following, as it were, Cicero, I choose to view civil society not as an entity *intermediate* between the "family" and the "state" (as does White [1994]) but as *society organized in a particular way*; the advent of civil society – a *res publica* – does not merely *add to* previously existing social and governmental arrangements but fundamentally *transforms* them.[31]

The important point in this regard is that the idea of civil society be seen to be the *core concept* of democratic political theory and, as such, as an *all-inclusive* concept. Just as "totalitarianism" designates a complete form of society, a social "whole," so likewise does "civil society" or "democracy." The crucial difference between these two forms of social organization is that while totalitarian society is uniform and undifferentiated ("total rule"), civil society is essentially and irreducibly *pluralist* or *polycentric*. A civil society is a society composed of distinct yet overlapping *orders*, these orders being nothing other than the sedimented results of human agency in different spheres of life. They are, as Michael Novak nicely puts it, so many "spheres of liberty" (Novak 1993, p. 112).

For the purposes of analysis, I shall single out three such orders: the moral-cultural order, the political order, and the economic order.[32] I shall argue that each order has its own relative autonomy and operates according to its own logic. Authentic democracy, as John Paul II would say, is possible only when these "spheres of autonomy" are respected (see John Paul II 1991, §45). In the following chapters I shall attempt to analyze in detail the logic proper to each of the three orders.[33] It will be one of the main contentions of this book that no civil society can be said fully to exist where individual agents are not endowed with the freedoms and rights appropriate to each of the three major spheres of human agency. As classical liberals would have said, freedom is indivisible: no one can be genuinely free who is not free culturally, politically, and economically.

I shall also argue – and this will constitute the guiding theme of my entire analysis – that while the logic of each order is distinct and irreducible to that of the others, they nonetheless all derive from a common "principle," as Montesquieu would say. Drawing my inspiration from that discipline known as philosophical hermeneutics, I shall call this principle *communicative rationality*, and I shall attempt to show how, in working itself out, this principle determines, in a fully coherent fashion, the configuration of each order. I hope to demonstrate thereby that what the term civil society designates is nothing less than a thoroughgoing institutionalization of communicative rationality in all spheres of human agency – cultural, political, and economic.[34]

3

THE MORAL-CULTURAL ORDER

THE IMPORTANCE OF IDEAS

In the realm of human affairs ideas are all-important, since, as was mentioned in Chapter 1, human beings are, *qua* human, historical or cultural beings – and are thus, as such, "products" (artifacts, as Buchanan put it) of the very ideas they form of themselves. As John Maynard Keynes remarked, it is ideas, not vested interests, that are decisive, for good or evil. Adversaries though they were in other respects, Keynes and Ludwig von Mises were in basic agreement on this score. "The history of mankind," Mises asserted around about the same time, "is the history of ideas. For it is ideas, theories and doctrines that guide human action, determine the ultimate ends men aim at and the choice of means employed for the attainment of these ends" (Mises 1981, p. 518). What indeed, one might well ask, can account for the decades-long, insane, and thoroughly counter-productive attempt to implant a socialist paradise on earth – Martin Malia has aptly described the "institutionalized phantasmagoria of 'developed socialism'" as "in fact a social theatre of the absurd" (Malia 1994, pp. 14–15) – if it be not the intrinsic and altogether beguiling power of a particular idea?[1] "It is what men think," Mill wrote in his treatise on government, "that determines how they act" (Mill 1958, p. 14).

Since they are decisive in shaping the course of human history, ideas ultimately can be neither verified nor refuted by having recourse to something outside the realm of ideas – outside the realm of human cultural practices in general. All appeals to so-called "objective" realities – biological determinants, material forces, the "nature of things," divine providence, and so on – are, in fact, appeals to yet other *ideas*, namely, the ideas that some people have entertained about what these "realities" supposedly are. This is why Mises also asserted:

> Facts *per se* can neither prove nor refute anything. Everything is decided by the interpretation and explanation of facts, by the ideas and the theories. . . . It is ideas that make history, not the "material

38

productive forces," those nebulous and mystical schemata of the materialist conception of history.

(Mises 1981, p. 46)

The moral-cultural order is the realm *par excellence* of ideas – scientific, philosophical, literary, etc. – and, since what people refer to as "nature" is determined, not by nature itself, but by the ideas they form of it (these ideas being constitutive of the *meaning* people attach to the word "nature"), the realm of ideas – culture – is the realm of *freedom*, the freedom of the "human spirit," of creative interpretation. It is in the nature of ideas that they demand to be taken on their own terms and to be assessed on the basis of their own merits. Thus, the core Marxist idea which postulates that the political and cultural realms are mere "superstructures" and that ideas are determined by material economic forces – the idea, in other words, that there is no freedom in the realm of ideas (even on the part of the Marxist?) – is an idea that is, in fact, *meaningless*, in that it undermines – in what it asserts – its own claim to validity as an idea. When theorists debunk ideas in the way Marxists are prone to do, they are denying – in actual practice (something that has come to be known as a "performative self-contradiction" [see Apel 1990]) – their own claim to intellectual respectability as theorists. As another economist and contemporary of Keynes and Mises, Frank H. Knight, said, the Marxist (or some such similar) idea that ideas are not to be taken seriously is "self-stultifying."[2]

In the last analysis, "bad" ideas can be refuted only by appealing to better ideas. No idea, as such, can be refuted (or justified) simply by appealing to "nature"; all such appeals are designed to terminate the free discussion of ideas and are rhetorical in the bad sense of the term. As Knight very aptly remarked: "The appeal to 'nature' has always been a slogan or *Kampfwort*; it has been used to beg the question [one of the main rhetorical fallacies known as *petitio principii*] in favor of any position which a particular writer or school happened to wish to defend or promote – or against any one singled out for condemnation" (Knight 1982, p. 340). Human nature (small "n") being what it is, people are more often than not inclined to condemn or anathematize those with whom they disagree than to discuss critically the merits of their ideas (as the contemporary phenomenon of political correctness so vividly demonstrates). As rhetorical theory insists, however, *ad hominem* attacks on one's opponents in no way amount to a refutation of their ideas. Although in common parlance people are said to be "arguing" when they hurl invectives at their opponents ("racist," "sexist," "fascist," "bourgeois liberal," etc.), adversarial confrontations of this sort have in fact nothing to do with *argumentation* in the proper sense of the term. Genuine argumentation is always concerned with giving *reasons* (or counter-reasons), and it always seeks to be rationally persuasive, even to the person with whom one is arguing. This amounts to saying that no genuine argument or discussion can

39

occur if one does not *respect* (at least in one's mode of comportment) the person of one's opponents or interlocutors (i.e., their "sense of judgment"). *Ad hominen* attacks on someone whose ideas one dislikes or disagrees with may oftentimes be an effective tactic for silencing that person, but they can never refute his or her ideas. Victories achieved in this way are hollow victories, and the ideas one thinks one has defended in this manner can lay no legitimate claim to being *true*.[3]

If, as a great many people claim, it is the case that rights entail obligations, then it is most certainly the case that the fundamental human or civil right to freedom of expression on the part of the individual entails the obligation on the part of every other individual to respect this right and to positively allow people, of whatever persuasion, to "speak their minds." Human rights are, after all *mutual* rights. The essence of civil society is, as Lefort has said, "a mutual recognition of liberties, a mutual protection of the ability to exercise them" (see p. 11). The supreme reason for instituting civil society (the "rule of law") is that of creating *an open space* in which the human spirit can flourish in freedom and in which individuals can exercise, without fear, their democratic, human rights to freedom of conscience and expression.

Another way of expressing the matter would be to say that the right to follow the dictates of one's own conscience, which is another way of saying the "right to privacy," is in a civil society a fundamental *social* right. For a postmodern liberalism, as one commentator remarks,

> The private sphere is no longer pre-social, no longer literally "inside" man set in opposition to the external world – as it had been in traditional liberalism. It is rather *in* the social world, a product of our [collective] choice, of a language for describing ourselves which we have learned from tradition and continue consciously to affirm.
>
> (Auerbach 1987, p. 27)

This is why, in her study of totalitarianism, Hannah Arendt declared: "To abolish the fences of law between men – as tyranny does – means to take away man's liberties and destroy freedom as a living political reality; for the space between men as it is hedged in by laws is the living space of freedom" (Arendt 1973, p. 466). Or, as Justice Louis Brandeis said, the right to privacy or, as he put it, the "right to be let alone" is "the most comprehensive of rights and the right most valued by civilized man." Thus, in order that individuals may be free to pursue the truth according to their own lights and in order that their ideas may receive the hearing they deserve and be assessed on their own intrinsic merits, the moral-cultural order of a civil society must be *autonomous*, free from coercive pressures of either a political or economic sort. (In a totalitarian society, in contrast, the function of the cultural sphere is reduced to that of serving the ideological purposes of the Party-state, to which it is totally subordinate.)[4]

This is not to say that between the various autonomous orders of civil society there are not numerous and complex overlappings. There are cultural, political, and economic aspects to every one of the three orders – without, however, it being the case that any one order occupies an absolutely central position. Thus, for instance, from one point of view the political order encompasses the other two (politics being, as Aristotle said, the "architectonic science"), in that a civil market economy cannot exist without the appropriate political-legal framework, and a cultural realm based on the free exchange of ideas cannot exist or be maintained without the appropriate constitutional guarantees that only the political-legal order can provide. From another point of view, the cultural order could be said to be central, in that it is precisely in this realm that the *ideas* of both a free market economy and a democratic polity receive their legitimation; it is only the cultural realm that can determine what is or is not essential to the make-up of a democratic polity or a market economy. From yet another point of view, however, the economic realm is all-important, in that political decisions must always be made with an eye to their economic ramifications and cultural institutions must take account of economic realities. Simply put, while having their own intrinsic logic, the three orders are nevertheless symbiotic and operate in a synergic fashion.

If the business of the political order is to produce justice and social stability, and if the business of the economic realm is to produce economic well-being (prosperity), the business of the moral-cultural order is the production of *truth* (or, to be more precise, truths in the plural, i.e., general agreements as to the worthiness of this or that idea). Democratic theory maintains that truth is to be determined neither by the highest economic bidder nor by the coercive powers of the state but always and only by means of free and open discussion seeking general, uncoerced agreement. Let us then consider in greater detail the logic peculiar to "the market place of ideas."

COMMUNICATIVE RATIONALITY

A civil society is a society in which people behave towards one another with civility. In the moral-cultural order, in everything having to do with beliefs or ideas, behaving with civility means behaving according to the dictates of *reasonableness*. The realm of ideas is the realm of discussion and debate, and the essence of reasonableness is, as Rhoda Howard says, "the idea that people holding initially opposing views can persuade each other through logic and reason of their position" (see p. 32). To behave reasonably also means behaving with good will, with, that is to say, the willingness to make the effort to understand the point of view of other people and the readiness to make concessions and to grant that one's opponent may, in any given dispute, turn out to be right (one must be prepared, as the French very aptly say, to *donner raison à son adversaire*).

The supreme *raison d'être* of the institutions of civil society, the most humane of all forms of social organization, is to encourage or foster in all three of its basic orders – economic, political, cultural – the development in human beings of that which is (potentially) most human about them. For as the ancient Greek sophist Protagoras, one of the first defenders of democracy, noted, it usually takes a deliberate effort against nature for people to realize what is best in their nature. Or as Michael Ignatieff has more recently observed in his survey of the "new nationalism," it may be that liberal civilization "runs deeply against the human grain and is only achieved and sustained by the most unremitting struggle against human nature" (see Ignatieff, as cited by Judt 1994, p. 48).

What, it might well be asked, is it to be (properly) human? The traditional philosophical definition of "man" is that he is the "rational animal" (*animal rationale*). What, however, is reason or rationality, that *differentia* which makes humans specifically human? In our modern, technocratic times, there is a strong tendency to equate reason or rationality with mere technological or instrumental rationality, what Max Weber referred to as *Zweckrationalität* and which he pessimistically predicted would become the dominant force in social organization, imprisoning humans in a bureaucratic "iron cage."

Instrumental rationality is means–end rationality; it is that exercise of reason whose purpose it is to determine the "best" – meaning, in this instance, the most *efficient* (not necessarily, by any means, the most ethical) – means for achieving given ends. When bureaucrats speak of "rationalizing" this or that aspect of social life (e.g., university administration), they mean nothing more than this; instrumental rationality is simply a form of cost-benefit analysis wherein that is deemed "best" which (supposedly) achieves the "same" result and which costs less in terms of time, money, or effort. In human affairs, technological-instrumental considerations are, it goes without saying, always extremely important; however, by their very nature, they can never determine the *ends* humans, *qua* humans, should aim at. As Frank Knight (whose views on rationality will be considered in more detail in what follows) insisted: "Economic rationality, as efficiency in the use of given means to achieve given individual or group ends, excludes a large part of the purposive [rational] life of men as social beings" (Knight 1982, p. 345). In other words, while technological-instrumental or economic-rational considerations are factors people will want to take account of in pursuing whatever ends they do pursue, they cannot, of themselves, dictate (by means of some kind of logical "decision procedure") what these ends themselves *should* be. They are, above all, totally useless in determining what the supreme end of life – what the ancient Greek philosophers referred to as the "good life" – should be (both for the individual and for society as a whole). All animals (to the degree that they have passed the Darwinian survival test) are "economizing" animals, but humans, to the degree that they lead properly human lives, are something more than that, as Aristotle long ago pointed out.

42

Only human beings are capable of voluntarily sacrificing their lives (the height of absurdity from a mere efficiency point of view) for the sake of ends that are only ideally possible – such as, for instance, the ever-elusive ideal of justice.[5] If humans are indeed "rational animals," then it necessarily follows that reason, in the properly human sense, cannot be reduced to mere technological-instrumental ("economizing") reason.

Reason in the most distinctly human sense is what a phenomenologist like Maurice Merleau-Ponty and hermeneuticists, who, like Calvin Schrag, situate themselves within the hermeneutical-rhetorical tradition, generally refer to as *communicative rationality* (reason as discourse, communicative praxis).[6] Merleau-Ponty, for instance, explicitly linked up "rationality" with "communication" and maintained that reason is essentially an *appeal to the other*, a dialogical attempt to arrive at mutual understanding (see Madison 1993, p. 34). While communicative rationality is the core notion in contemporary philosophical hermeneutics and in, as well, the Frankfurt school of Critical Theory as represented by Jürgen Habermas, many of the central features of the notion were spelled out much earlier in this century by Frank Knight, whose originality of thought in this matter merits being duly noted.[7] Knight, the foremost representative of the "Chicago School" of economics in the 1930s and the leading American economist of his times, was, throughout his writing, most insistent on debunking the economic (technological-instrumental) myth of "economizing man."

Reason, in the properly human sense, is not a property ("faculty") of human beings as isolated individuals; human beings can be said to be rational only to the degree that they are *social* beings.[8] This is what Aristotle meant when he defined "man" as both the rational animal and the *zoon politikon*, the political or social animal.[9] Just as no one can be free by themselves (as isolated, atomistic individuals – the celebrated Robinson Crusoes of laissez-faire economics, a notion that Marx quite rightly castigated), so also no one can be rational by themselves; like freedom, rationality is a matter of "mutuality." One of the main things that Knight objected to in thinking of a merely "economic" or crudely utilitarian (instrumentalist) sort (and in *laissez-faire* thinking in general) was its tendency to take the individual as something merely "given." "[T]he individual," he insisted, is not "given" but "is largely *made* [emphasis added] what he is by institutional processes" (Knight 1982, p. 264). "Man," he said, "is social as a feeling, knowing, thinking, desiring, and acting *individual*" (p. 276).[10] Since the individual (as a free and rational being) is a social being through and through, individuals can be said to be free and rational only to the degree that they exist in a free and rational *society* (i.e., a society in which "social reason" – communicative rationality - prevails): "The existence of man as a free individual is a function of free society" (Knight 1982, p. 363). Indeed, that entity sometimes referred to as *homo sapiens* can properly be said to be a *human* being only to the degree that it exists in a free society: "Men cannot live, as human beings, outside of *free* society, outside of association based on free agreement as to the nature of the society (meaning its constitution and laws) and its activities, and free agreement and disagreement within this framework" (Knight 1982, p. 227).

What Knight is in effect saying here is that individuals can properly be said to be human, i.e., free, only to the degree that they are members of a social "framework," this framework being, specifically, what Knight referred to as a *discussion community*.[11] To be human, i.e., rational, is to engage in communicative rationality; it is, in other words, to engage in free discussion (deliberation) as to what is to count as "true" and as to the ends that humans should pursue and the manner in which they should pursue them. It is this which confers meaning on a life, transforming thereby mere biological (and "economizing") existence into a properly human mode of being (unlike grasshoppers, even ants, Aesop and La Fontaine tell us, are fully capable of exercising "economic" rationality). As the Greeks also pointed out, man, the "rational animal," is also, and *as such*, the "speaking animal"; human reason is indeed *communicative* reason. Writing in the tradition of Aristotelian rhetoric as rearticulated in the 1960s by the Belgian scholar Chaim Perelman, the well-known American literary critic, Wayne Booth, expresses this position nicely when he states that from the point of view of classical rhetoric, the human person or "self"

> is *essentially* rhetorical, symbol exchanging, a social product in process of changing through interaction, sharing views with other selves. Even when thinking privately, "I" can never escape the other selves which I have taken in to make "myself," and my thought will thus always be a dialogue.
>
> (Booth 1974, p. 126)

The human being is that being which possesses the *logos* (*zoon logon ekon*). Reason (*ratio, logos*) is the "faculty" or (in less metaphysical language) the ability to speak, the ability, that is, by means of language (*logos*), to give "reasons" (*rationes, logoi*) – the ability, in other words, to persuade and to be persuaded (of the truth or rightness of this or that). In short, "reasonableness" is the ability to listen to the speech of others as well as the ability to respond to these others by means of civil discourse rather than brute force. As the Theory of Argumentation (the New Rhetoric) maintains (see Perelman 1979, as well as Madison 1989a), persuasion (in the proper rhetorical sense of the term) is the opposite of coercion; when, in the exercise of communicative rationality, one attempts to persuade another, one is appealing to their just judgment and to their free agreement or "assent" (as Booth would say). In other words, one is according them respect as conversational partners and is treating them humanely, in accordance with the principle of human dignity. Language (communicative rationality) is therefore that which enables humans to be human, to be truly political or social animals.[12]

*

THE MORAL-CULTURAL ORDER

If the reason for proclaiming human rights is the protection of human dignity (a point I take to be axiomatic), and if what makes humans properly human is that they are communicatively rational beings, i.e., beings possessing the *logos*, the "faculty of speech" as Knight puts it (Knight 1982, p. 345), it follows that what is absolutely vital to any *philosophical* justification of human rights is a well worked-out theory of communicative rationality. The old liberal notion of "natural rights" may in its time have amounted to a *coherent* philosophical position (see Shapiro 1986 and, more importantly, Strauss 1953), but arguments "from nature" (*physei*, as Aristotle would say) are no longer philosophically *sustainable* since all appeals to "nature" are thoroughly metaphysical, i.e., speculative. Moreover, the metaphysical worldview that subtends the notion of natural rights derives, and is inseparable, from a particular theological (Judeo-Christian) worldview. However appealing such a worldview may be for some people, in an age of global – and multicultural – civilization no adequate philosophical defense of *universal* human rights can rest on any such culturally relative worldview. If humans have, or should have, rights, it is not because of some imagined character they possess as isolated, atomistic individuals existing in a "state of nature" (or because they are creatures of a Judeo-Christian God). What we now refer to as human rights are, as Knight observed, not natural but *social*, "they are conceivable only in relation to other men and as generated by a combination of harmonious and conflicting interests" (Knight 1982, p. 327). Because they emerge out of, and are "grounded" in, free discussion aiming at mutual recognition, human rights are not "natural" rights but *rational rights*.[13] These rational rights are fundamental rights for the simple reason that without them human beings cannot live in the kind of political or social environment that allows them to realize their humanity. "Grounding" human rights in the phenomenon of communicative rationality is the only kind of philosophical defense of them that does not need to be buttressed up by fanciful metaphysical speculation but which, on the contrary, is self-justificatory or "self-grounding" (see Madison 1986, pp. 275–79).

The essential link between rationality and linguisticality (civil discourse) was clearly noted by Knight.[14] Let us take explicit note of some of the principal or "essential" characteristics of "discussion" or communicative rationality that Knight sought to highlight. The first thing to note (obvious though it may be) is that the purpose or goal of free, communicatively rational discussion is the attainment ("discovery") of what people call "the truth." Actually, to speak of "the truth" can be highly misleading. As philosophical hermeneutics insists, there is no such thing as *the* truth, meaning an answer to any inquiry (the "pursuit of truth") that could ever be said to be either absolute or final: "Nothing properly called absolute truth is possible for any principle or proposition, or even the simplest fact" (Knight 1982, p. 353). As Albert Camus said in his *Myth of Sisyphus*: "[T]here is no truth, but merely truths" (Camus 1955, p. 32). "Discussion," by its very nature (i.e., so

45

long as it remains "free," i.e., free from arbitrary closure), is on-going and never-ending. No "truth" can ever claim to be final; in a civil or democratic society no one may claim the right to have the "final say" or the "last word." As Gadamer has said: "The ongoing dialogue permits no final conclusion. It would be a poor hermeneuticist [read: rational inquirer] who thought he could have, or had to have, the last word" (Gadamer 1990a, p. 579). In a democratic society, "truth" refers not to some end-state to be arrived at at some time or other but is always of a *processual* or on-going nature; people can be "in the truth" only so long as the "conversation of mankind" (Oake-shott 1962) is allowed to continue and to develop, in all the realms of civil society, i.e., only so long as individuals are guaranteed their right to express freely their opinions, which is another way of saying their right at any time to call any prevailing consensus ("status quo") into question. Paradoxical though it might at first appear, truth can exist only so long as people have the right to change their minds as to what is or is not true, which amounts to saying: only so long as the "truth" itself is open to change. It can exist only so long as there continues to exist an on-going, open-ended conversation in the realm of the cultural, the political, and the economic. Truth can exist only so long as people *continue* to seek it out. Truth is indeed never something that simply *is*; it has to be *made*, and made ever anew, in the on-going process of communicative rationality.

Anticipating, as it were, the hermeneutical notion of truth, Knight was altogether correct in announcing the "revolutionary" nature of the notion of truth that he, as a liberal theorist (in fact, a *postmodern* liberal theorist, *avant la lettre*) was putting forth when he said: "The core of liberalism – what most distinguishes it from other views of life – is a manifold revolution in the conception of truth." "To say . . . belief is free," he went on to say, "is to say that truth is inherently 'dynamic,' subject to change and actually growing and changing" (Knight 1982, pp. 468–69). In short, truth is *process*, not *stasis*. "The *process* of inquiry through discourse thus becomes more important than any possible conclusions, and whatever stultifies such fulfillment becomes demonstrably wrong" (Booth 1974, p. 137). If truth is not, by means of free, open discussion, allowed to change and "grow," there can be no truth, at any time along the way. Like a living organism, truth either continues to grow and develop, or it withers away and dies. Thus, what is all-important is the open-ness (*glasnost*, as the Russians would say) of the discussion process itself. "Allowing a bad idea to be discussed," one scholar aptly observes, "kills it while discussion of good ideas leads to better ideas" (Parnas 1994, p. 7).

To say that there is no absolute or final truth amounts to saying, indirectly, what the essence of truth is. To say that there is no absolute or final truth is to say that truth is a matter of the temporary and provisional *agreements* that a free community of inquirers (e.g., scientists) happen to arrive at at any given time; "agreement is the only test of truth" (Knight 1982, p. 350). The notion of truth that Knight adumbrated in the 1930s was indeed philosophically revolutionary.[15] Truth, he was saying, is not, as traditional philosophy always maintained, a matter of perfect "correspondence," at any given moment, between ideas in the "mind" and things in the "external" world (*adequatio intellectus et res*).[16] A conception of truth of this sort (the paradigmatic Western conception of truth) is in fact meaningless – in that there is no possible way that "truths" so conceived could ever be "verified" (on this view of things, one would have to be a Baron Münchausen, capable of stepping outside of oneself and comparing from a God's-eye point of view one's "subjective" ideas with "objective" realities in order ever to know if one possessed the truth, or didn't). Although to say so will undoubtedly scandalize the absolutists, it is nevertheless the case, from a phenomenological (or "matter-of-fact") point of view, that "truth" is whatever any appropriate community of inquirers, operating in accordance with the argumentative or rhetorical protocols of their own discipline, happen, for whatever (relevantly persuasive) reasons, to decide it to be; it is a matter of "warrantable assertion," as Wayne Booth would say (Booth 1974, p. 11). If, for instance, the community of physicists, operating on the basis of what are currently held to be the "laws of nature," have decided in the great majority to adhere to the "big bang" theory rather than the "steady state" hypothesis, then that is what the truth of the matter is. Which obviously is not to say that this truth may not become *passé* at some time in the future (could Newton ever have anticipated Einstein?).

What this amounts to saying is that, in a civil society, truth is always of a "democratic" nature. This is not to say that truth is merely a matter of majority vote, in any particular intellectual or ideational area (e.g., science). Even in the political order (as we shall see in the following chapter), politically *just* decisions are never simply a matter of what the majority merely happens to agree upon. It could in fact be said that democracy, in either the political or cultural sense of the term, is characterized more by challenges to consensus than by actual achievements of consensus. Nevertheless, the fact remains that in a civil or democratic society, "the truth" can never be determined by an isolated group of "experts" but can only result from a general agreement (which must, in the course of things, be almost always something less than a total consensus) arrived at by bona fide discussants in the cultural, political, and economic orders. This is why, as we have seen, Knight maintained that "agreement is the only test of truth." More specifically: "[Another] feature of the liberal conception of truth is that it is a social category; its only test is unanimous acceptance in some community of discussion. Further, truth as social is ultimately democratic" (Knight 1982, p. 469).

From a postmodern point of view, "the truth" must be understood as that consensus or agreement at which a community of inquirers freely arrives. However, the notions of consensus or agreement must not be misconstrued.

It must be admitted that Knight commits a linguistic infelicity (and is unfaithful to the basic thrust of his own thought) when, as in the text just cited, he speaks of a "unanimous" acceptance or agreement. In a free society, unanimity is not necessarily a virtue; it is only totalitarian society that values unanimity (conformity) above all else.[17] A free society is precisely one which, within the bounds of reasonable and civil disagreement, not only tolerates but actually encourages a diversity of opinion as to what the truth is ("dissent"). This, it seems to me, is the point that John Stuart Mill was attempting to make in one of the great classics of liberty when he wrote in 1859:

> If all mankind minus one, were of one opinion, and only one person were of the contrary opinion, mankind would be no more justified in silencing that one person, than he, if he had the power, would be justified in silencing mankind.
>
> (Mill [1947], p 16; Chapter 2, lines 28–32)

The "liberal" theory of truth defended in the 1930s by Frank Knight was, therefore, of a different sort than the theory of truth defended in more recent times by Jürgen Habermas. According to Habermas, a true, right, or just decision or opinion must be one that *everyone* with *totally equal* access to a *completely open* discussion process would *ultimately agree upon* in a *totally unconstrained* way (free from all "distorting" influences) (see for instance Habermas 1990). At least this is what Habermas at one point *seemed* to be saying, and it is what his numerous exegetes have said he was in fact saying (see for instance McCarthy 1981 and Benhabib and Dallmayr 1990). As is, however, his custom, he himself has over the course of time qualified his remarks in ways that make it difficult to determine exactly what it is that he means (or meant). One thing that nonetheless remains clear is that what Knight called "rational consensus" cannot be reduced to unanimous agreement in any Habermersian sense of the term. There are a number of reasons for this.[18]

In the first place, the utopian notion of unanimous, uncoerced agreement (Habermas' "ideal speech situation") is, as Habermas himself recognizes, counterfactual – and is thus useless as a criterion determining the truth, in any given (real world) instance. In the second place, if it actually happened that everyone *were* in perfect agreement on this or that issue, discussion would have become pointless and would simply cease. This means, paradoxical as it might appear at first glance, that in fact there could no longer be said to be any "truth" of the matter, since the legitimacy of any belief's claim to be true is dependent upon the possibility of its being (re)confirmed in the face of challenges to it. As Knight recognized (anticipating Hans-Georg Gadamer), only where there is a *question* at issue can there be truth: "[T]ruth is the answer to a question; and, when any question is definitively answered, there is no longer any question, and no truth, in any significant meaning of the word" (Knight 1982, p. 353). It is only when an issue is open to dispute that it can be said that people are concerned about its being true or not – i.e., only in this case is it meaningful to speak about a "true opinion on the matter." As Mill had already said, speaking of what only later came to be called communicative rationality: "Complete liberty of contradicting and disproving our opinion, is the very condition which justifies us in assuming its truth for purposes of action." And as he went on to say: "The beliefs which we have most warrant for, have no safeguard to rest on, but a standing invitation to the whole world to prove them unfounded." This, he observed, is "the best that the existing state of human reason admits of" (Mill 1947, pp. 14, 21; Chapter 2, lines 137–39, 206–15). If a belief or opinion "is not fully, frequently, and fearlessly discussed," Mill insisted, "it will be held as a dead dogma, not a living truth" (Mill 1947, p. 34; Chapter 2, lines 230–32).[19]

Truth, therefore, can exist only when it is sought after or actively defended. Knight's view of truth is indeed, like Mill's, processual and not static: "To say the belief is free is to say that truth is inherently 'dynamic,' subject to change and actually growing and changing" (Knight 1982, pp. 468–69). Where there is no longer any possibility of reasoned disagreement (as in a state of perfect consensus), there can no longer be any truth. Political theorist Chantal Mouffe has remarked in this regard: "A healthy democratic process calls for a vibrant clash of political positions and an open conflict of interests. If such is missing, it can too easily be replaced by a confrontation between non-negotiable moral values and essentialist identities" (Mouffe 1993, p. 6).[20] Thus, as Clifford Geertz pertinently observes, progress in the pursuit of truth "is marked less by a perfection of consensus than by a refinement of debate" (Geertz 1973, p. 29). The crucial issue in determining how reasonable a discussion community is, is not the presence or absence of consensus and unanimity but rather *the manner* in which conflicts of opinion (which are surely to be expected in any free society) are dealt with on an on-going basis. The issue is not so much the actual beliefs ("truths") that people hold at any given time but rather the way in which they arrive at them and the way in which they struggle, amidst the diversity of opinion and the conflict of interpretations, to achieve some degree of general agreement sufficient to maintain the overall cohesion of the group in question (in any given intel-lectual discipline or, for that matter, in any given nation as a whole). In its pursuit of truth, a communicatively rational discussion community is indeed a form of democracy in that it is "a system of ruled open-endedness, or organized uncertainty."[21]

An analogy can be drawn between a communicatively rational society and a just society. In the same way that a society that merits the appellation "just" is not one in which *all* citizens can say at any given moment that they are fully content -- in that they feel that they have, as a matter of fact, received their "just desserts" or, when accused of infractions against the law, have been "accorded justice" (e.g., the legal verdict they would have liked in their case) – but is, rather, one in which the outcome was arrived at by "due process of law" (subject to appeal), so also a communicatively rational society is one which is not characterized by unanimity of opinion (consensus) but is rather one in which conflicts of opinions between individuals and groups are regulated or dealt with in a communicatively rational way, in accordance with the "due process" of argument and discussion. It is one in which those holding minority opinions always have the right freely to speak out and to appeal to a future common agreement.[22] The true mark of a civil society is neither objective unanimity nor its counterpart, subjective satisfaction on the part of all, but rather the open-endedness of the discussion process itself – "organized uncertainty." The one and only thing that citizens of a liberal-democratic, civil society can legitimately be expected to agree upon in the great majority is the preservation and betterment of the society itself.

This means that, in either a general democratic setting such as a municipal council or in a more restricted democratic setting such as an intellectual or academic community (which has its own rules as to "due process," i.e., its own rules as to "citizenship"), everyone has the right to a "due hearing," subject of course to democratic procedure (no individual who is not a recognized member of a group has the right to interrupt the procedures).[23] In addition, every member of a democratic group must have the right, when overridden by an opposing majority, to press forward with their views at a future date. If this right were not respected in the moral-cultural sphere, what we now know as science simply would not exist. Science is the realm not of unanimity, but of rationally mediated disagreement *par excellence*. That, so to speak, is precisely what, in the sixteenth and subsequent centuries, "science" was invented for, i.e., so as to allow free, inquiring individuals to arrive at general agreements not dictated by authority (e.g., the Inquisition) that, in their free conscience, they (as "rational individuals") could consider to be "true." It was "invented" so as to allow any qualified individual to challenge (without threat of personal harm) any given rational consensus. Without the challenge to consensus, there would be no such thing as "science."

Just as in political matters, so also in moral-cultural matters the important thing is not the "attainment of truth" (in any definitive sense) but the concernful cultivation of the "conversation of mankind." In other words, "truth" refers not to an ideal end-state but to a certain kind of process *in the here and now*, one marked above all by the democratic virtue of civility. In this respect, truth has much the same nature as does that other great desideratum: peace.

As in the case of truth, peace is more often than not viewed in terms of stasis rather than process: as an ideal goal to be achieved at some time in the future when peoples will have "overcome their differences" and will live together ever afterwards in harmony and happiness. However, just as truth, finally and fully attained, would in fact amount to the "death of understanding" (the termination of the discussion process), so likewise peace so conceived resembles nothing so much as the peace of the graveyard. The pacifists notwithstanding, peace does not mean the absence or cessation of conflicts and differences; as *realpolitik* theorists such as Henry Kissinger are right in reminding us, nation-states will always be motivated by "national self-interest," that is, by interests that often make for conflicts between them (witness the ever-renascent trade disputes between the United States and Canada, two nations that nevertheless share the "longest undefended border in the world"). During the Cold War era, for instance, Western pacificsts were thoroughly naive in thinking that nuclear disarmament (what they called for generally was *unilateral* disarmament) would have produced peace between the superpowers. Peace and the end of the Cold War only became a real possibility when Gorbachev, abandoning the traditional Soviet agenda based on the primacy of world-wide class struggle, proclaimed before the United Nations in December of 1988 his policy of "New Thinking" (*novoe myshlenie*) and his new-found adherence to "universal human rights" (a notion which, as we saw in Chapter 2, Marx had vehemently denounced as a bourgeois swindle). Peace is always a relative thing; it does not mean the elimination of all discord and hostility, but it can nevertheless be said to prevail when nations or peoples seek to deal with their differences by means of civilized discourse ("diplomacy") rather than by means of force (warfare or terrorism).[24] What is important in any given instance is whether the parties to a dispute have or have not committed themselves to (as we now say) the "peace process" – just as what is important in the truth-process is the ethical disposition ("good will") to understand others and to reach uncoerced agreements with them. In no process situation can any agreement ever be final, however, for it is a general characteristic of human affairs that no sooner have some problems been resolved than new ones arise.[25] What counts always is *the manner* in which problems or conflicts are dealt with. Conflict (of opinion, interest) is a fact of life. Only the most foolhardy of utopians would ever dream of banishing conflict from human affairs. What is important, liberals insist, is not the *elimination* of conflict but its *regulation* (or management), which is precisely what the procedures governing civil society in the cultural, political, and economic orders are designed to do. Peace, like truth, is a matter of communicative rationality and stands in opposition to arbitrary force. Peaceful communicative rationality is in a very important sense "rule-governed" – not of course in a instrumental-rational sense but in a sense that I shall attempt to elucidate below.

SPONTANEOUS ORDERS AND THE ORDER OF TRUTH

Since truth is not an end-state to be achieved at some time or other in the future but is instead of the nature of an on-going process, it is important to form a proper understanding of this process. The process, I have said, is not random or arbitrary but is "rule-governed." This is as true of the truth-process as it is of the processes characteristic of the political and economic orders of a civil society.[26] What needs to be determined in greater detail is the exact nature of the processes in question (such a determination constitutes in fact my overriding concern in this book). The most fundamental characteristic of all these processes is that they give rise to what F.A. Hayek very aptly referred to as *spontaneous orders.*

Spontaneous orders are what could be called "self-organizing or self-generating systems" (see Hayek 1973, p. 37). One writer describes this form of organization in the following way: "Self-organization ... refers to complex orders whose particular characteristics are *not* the intended outcome of actions by those who make up that order. Such orders arise when participants follow, consciously or unconsciously, rules capable of coordinating their interactions in patterns *too complex for them to grasp*" (diZerega 1992, p. 318). Unlike explicitly designed or "man-made" systems, the "logic" of spontaneous orders is not readily apparent and can in fact be discerned only by means of *interpretation* (hermeneutics), or what Hayek calls "reconstruction" (Hayek 1973, p. 38). A spontaneous order is therefore, as Hayek says, "abstract." In addition, because a spontaneous order is not the result of conscious planning, it cannot be said to serve any particular purpose or to aim at any specific end, except in the most general of senses, e.g., truth or justice. More precisely, the results (always provisional) of spontaneous interaction between individuals are not predictable in advance, and their rightness or appropriateness can be assessed only in terms of the degree to which the abstract rules operative in the order have been adhered to.

Perhaps the best way to clarify the meaning of a spontaneous order is to contrast it with a "non-spontaneous" one. No society can exist or long survive if it is not able, in one way or another, to generate cohesion among its members – in the moral-cultural order, the political order, and the economic order. There are, however, two fundamentally different, and altogether opposed, ways of going about the task of achieving cohesion: either by means of coercion or through reliance on the free ('spontaneous") association of individuals.[27] Two instances of coercive order as regards the moral-cultural sphere are, in the case of traditional societies, prescribed religion and, as regards the socialist societies of late modernity, state ideology. As regards the political sphere, coercion is synonymous with despotism, authoritarianism, or totalitarianism, while spontaneous ordering is synonymous with (liberal) democracy ("constitutional government").[28] In the economic sphere (in the case of modern, industrialized societies) coercion is synonymous with centralized economic planning (a "command economy"), while spontanenous ordering is synonymous with reliance on the mechanisms of free market exchange (a "market economy"). In a word, the central problem to be dealt with, in any sphere of society, is that of how *coordination* is achieved among its members, the overwhelming number of whom do not engage in face-to-face relations but who interact in highly complex social ways with others who are, and will ever remain to them, totally *anonymous* –

even though the actions of these anonymous others will impact on them in often important ways. The central problem of economics, for instance, is that of explaining how the activities of a myriad of, for the most part, mutually anonymous individual entities (persons and firms) come to be coordinated such that the economic needs of the society as a whole are met to some relatively acceptable degree.

The notion of spontaneous orders could easily be said to be the core notion in Hayek's work, whose general concern can be summed up as follows:

> How do social institutions work, through the filter of the human mind, to coordinate human affairs? . . . Hayek is concerned with the communicative function of social institutions in general. . . .The key question for the social theorist is how the various and diverse images of reality that individual minds develop could ever be coordinated to one another.
>
> (Bǫettke 1990b, pp. 61–9)

Hayek was one of the first of modern social theorists to attempt to give an account of social "wholes" in specifically (irreducibly) *social* terms, and he adopted the notion of spontaneous orders precisely in order to deal with what might be called the *social problem*. The problem is that of accounting for the existence of generalized, trans-subjective patterns of meaning that are the product of human *action* but are not the result of human *design*. Social or cultural institutions – such as, above all, language, a favorite example of Hayek's – are "spontaneous" orders in that they were never "planned" and cannot therefore adequately be accounted for in terms of isolated, atomistic individuals (no one ever set out to "invent" the English language). The language that one speaks and that affords one access to a universe of meaning is not one's own creation nor is it the creation of any number of individual minds – and yet, being the most human of all human traits, it is not a product of nature either. In order properly to conceptualize language or any other social institution of a complex sort, it is, as Hayek realized, necessary to have recourse to categories that are neither *subjective* (individualistic) nor *objective* (naturalistic). It is this unique realm of being that is neither subjective ("for itself") nor objective ("in itself") that Hegel was attempting to get at with his notion of "objective mind/spirit [*Geist*]" (a more ontologized version, so to speak, of Montesquieu's earlier notion of "*esprit général*"), and it is what more recently Merleau-Ponty was trying to articulate with his notion of an "interworld" and of a "logic within contingency" (see Madison 1993, pp. 32–8).

Hayek's notion of spontaneous orders is of the greatest philosophical interest from a postmodern or postmetaphysical point of view in that it represents a determined attempt to get beyond the Cartesian (i.e., modernist) categorical opposition of *subjective* (mind) versus *objective* (matter) that has dominated all of philosophical modernity. In fact, and without fully realizing the significance of what he was up to, Hayek like various postmodern thinkers after him was attempting to call into question that *oppositional* mode of thinking that runs throughout the entire metaphysical tradition. In Hayek's reading of him, Bernard Mandeville was one of the first to show the "way of escape" from a "conceptual scheme" that, as Hayek rightly observes, has prevailed for over two thousand years. The scheme in question is the dichotomy that the ancient Greeks drew between *nature (physis)* and *culture (nomos)* and which, according to Hayek, has been the source of "end-less confusion" (Hayek 1978, p. 253). The dichotomy between what is "natural" and what is "artificial," Hayek says, leaves no place for "any order which was the result of human actions but not of human design" (ibid., p. 254).[29] Social or cultural institutions are precisely such (rule-governed) orders, whose purpose it is to "bring it about that men's divergent interests are reconciled" (ibid., p. 260). In human affairs, language is obviously the coordinating mechanism *par excellence*. What is philosophically or method-ologically significant about the notion of spontaneous orders is that it provides the necessary alternative to the nature/culture opposition. As a means of achieving coordination, a spontaneous order, Hayek says (ibid., p. 260), is *neither* "natural" *nor* "artificial." Hermeneuticists would say that spontaneous orders of a social or cultural sort are neither subjective nor objective but are, rather, *intersubjective.* The realm of the intersubjective, as opposed to *either* the merely subjective *or* the merely objective, is pre-eminently the realm of hermeneutics.[30]

What we need more specifically to concern ourselves with at this point is the question as to how intersubjective coordination is achieved in the moral-cultural sphere of a civil society (i.e., how agreement as to what is generally to count as "true" and "good" is achieved by "spontaneous" and "rule-governed" means). Let us recall a remark of Knight's quoted earlier: "Men cannot live, as human beings, outside of *free* society, outside of association based on free agreement as to the nature of the society (meaning its constitu-tion and laws) and its activities, and free agreement and disagreement within this framework." (Knight 1982, p. 227). What this remark serves to point out is the all-importance of the "rules" (the "constitution and laws") and the overall framework (the "rules of the game") that allows disparate individuals to arrive at common agreements as to what is to count as true. There are, of course, all sorts of different kinds of "truths": scientific, philosophical, his-torical, and so on. The production of these different categories or "régimes" of truth (to borrow an expression from Michel Foucault) is the function of the different intellectual or scientific disciplines. An intellectual discipline is a rule-governed means of, as Charles Sanders Peirce would say, "fixating belief."

There are of course, as Peirce pointed out in his celebrated article of 1877, "The Fixation of Belief" (Peirce 1955) many different ways of "fixating" belief, but, as Peirce also pointed out, there is only one way (one mode of "inquiry") that is appropriate to the free pursuit of truth (to, that is, the moral-cultural order of a free or civil society). This is what, somewhat mis-leadingly, he called "science." The chief characteristic of the "scientific" way of fixating or arriving at beliefs ("truths") is that (unlike the methods of "tenacity," "authority," and the "a priori" [metaphysical] method) it is *non-arbitrary*. That is to say, only in the "scientific" method are the truths arrived at not a function of subjective whim; they are a function or direct result of the strict or rigorous application of the *method itself*.[31] In other words, "scien-tific" truth is essentially of a *procedural* nature: that is true – whatever it be – which is the "logical" outcome of a particular, rigorous *method of inquiry* (i.e., an inquiry operating in accordance with accepted "rules of evidence" or "proof").[32] As Peirce states: "The test of whether I am truly following the method [and thus the test of truth itself] is not an immediate appeal to my feelings and purposes, but, on the contrary, itself involves the application of the method" (Peirce 1955, p. 20). Truth, as I shall be arguing in what follows, is not a matter of feeling (either emotional [comfort] or intellectual [cer-tainty]) but is a matter of following the right "method." As in the case of liberal jurisprudence ("due process"), it is indeed a matter of *process*.

In part under the influence of Peirce, and under the influence as well of positivistic or neo-positivistic philosophers of science such as Karl Popper, science (i.e., the natural sciences) has in our culture come to be viewed as the paradigmatic (if not sole) means of achieving genuine (freely-arrived-at) truth. This is unfortunate,[33] and it is unfortunate as well that Jonathan Rauch, in his eloquent defense of academic freedom, should, in his otherwise well-argued book (Rauch 1993), have appealed to an outdated Popperian notion of science (which postulates the methodological superiority of the natural sciences over the humanities). It is unfortunate, since (freely-arrived-at) truth is not the exclusive property of the natural ("hard") sciences. As the postposi-tivistic (postmodern) philosopher of science, Stephen Toulmin, has strenu-ously insisted, between the natural sciences, on the one hand, and the human sciences and the humanities, on the other, there is a difference not of kind, but only of degree. "[T]he older, absolute division between the human and natural sciences," Toulmin insists, "has dismantled itself" (Toulmin 1982, p. 112). According to Toulmin, both the natural sciences and the human discip-lines are, at bottom, *interpretive or hermeneutical* in nature: "[T]he general cat-egories of hermeneutics can be applied just as well to the natural sciences as to the humanities." (ibid.)[34] Contrary to the myth of scientism rampant earlier in this century, the difference between the natural sciences and the human disciplines is not that the former are based on "hard evidence" while the latter are merely expressions of the whims of "scholars" (as opposed to serious-minded "researchers"). The mark of *all* recognized academic or intel-lectual disciplines is *rigor* and *rule-governed* inquiry, in the way in which Peirce would have understood this term. The humanities, for instance, Toulmin argues, are as "objective" in their own way as are the natural sciences, and the truths the practitioners of the human disciplines arrive at are no more "relative" than those arrived at by "scientists," the fact that there tends to exist a greater diversity of opinion among humanists than among scientists notwithstanding. This diversity of opinion is in fact something that is normal and fully rational, given the differing nature of the subject matter in question – human reality is infinitely more complex than natural reality. In the spirit of Frank Knight who argued the need to avoid "a false dichotomy between absolutism and relativism" (Knight 1982, p. 354), Toulmin states: "[I]t is a mistake to assume that the multiplicity of standpoints in the humanities implies that our choice of a critical standpoint has an inevitable subjectivity, which is absent in the case of the natural sciences" (Toulmin 1982, p. 109). What Gadamer says about art must be said of the humanities in general vis-à-vis the "sciences" (art being, as it were, from a positivist point of view, the "worse-case scenario"):

> Is there to be no knowledge in art? Does not the experience of art contain a certain claim to truth which is certainly different from that of science, but equally certainly is not inferior to it?
>
> (Gadamer 1975, p. 87)

Richard Rorty has also sought to eradicate the rigid demarcation line between what C. P. Snow referred to as the "two cultures." He writes:

> We would like to disabuse social scientists and humanists of the idea that there is something called "scientific status" which is a desirable goal. In our view, "truth" is a univocal term. It applies equally to the judgments of lawyers, anthropologists, physicists, philologists, and literary critics. There is no point in assigning degrees of "objectivity" or "hardness" to such disciplines. For the presence of unforced agreement in all of them gives us everything in the way of "objective truth" which one could possibly want: namely, intersubjective agreement.
>
> (Rorty 1987, p. 42)

In all the intellectual disciplines that populate the moral-cultural realm of a civil society, inquirers must, in accordance with the "rules of the game," engage in communicative rationality and must cogently *argue for* and give persuasive *reasons* for the positions they advocate, whatever their discipline. Naturally, these rules, i.e., the criteria as to what is to count as a rational argument, will vary from discipline to discipline. What all intellectual disciplines have in common, nonetheless, is that they generate agreements or truths in a *spontaneous* fashion, i.e., by means of free communication among a multitude of independent inquirers. To say that an order of truth is spontaneous is to say that it is the "logical," though nevertheless unpredictable or unforeseen, consequence of a free inquiry, i.e., one constrained by nothing other than the rules of inquiry itself. This exercise of communicative rationality is what Austrian School economists refer to as a "creative discovery procedure." In a genuine civil society, the moral-cultural order, the realm of truth, is a vast arena or "web of belief" (Quine) comprising a multitude of rule-governed, spontaneously generated orders.[35]

THE RULES OF RATIONALITY

Phenomenologically, pragmatically, or hermeneutically speaking, truth is always a matter of agreement among inquirers (not an "agreement" between an isolated mind and the so-called "objective" world),[36] but it does not follow from this that any sort of agreement whatsoever can legitimately lay claim to truth.[37] The sole operative criterion for the truth-value of agreements is *the manner* in which they are arrived at, namely, "spontaneously," in accordance with the dictates of communicative rationality. As Peirce would say, only agreements arrived at in a "scientific" manner are rational, and thus can count as true – in that only in this case is the outcome of the inquiry (the "truth" or belief arrived at) a function of the (procedural) application of *the method* itself. In other words, as I have argued, the truths that emerge spontaneously in this fashion are the result of a rule-governed mode of inquiry.

As I also mentioned, however, the term "rule-governed" must not be understood in an instrumental-rational sense. The "rules" of communicative rationality are not rules in the customary or "scientistic" sense of the term. That is to say, they are not formal procedures or algorithms that can be applied in a computer-like way, mechanically generating the sought-after conclusion. They are more like rough-and-ready "rules of thumb" that need at every moment in their "application" to be creatively interpreted, in much the same way that a judge must creatively interpret the law that he is called upon to "apply." The "rules of the game" of rational inquiry are not like the rules of a game in any ordinary sense, e.g., chess, in that they can never be unambiguously stated in an authoritative manual; as Hayek says: "rules in this sense exist and operate without being explicitly known to those who obey them" (Hayek 1973, p. 37). It is precisely because the rules of rationality are not rigid and cannot be laid out (as traditional philosophy of science sought to do) with any great degree of specificity that the results of their "application" cannot be predicted and are thus "spontaneous." As Hayek would say, the rules of rationality are *abstract rules.*[38]

Another way of expressing the matter would be to say that the rules of rationality, to the degree that they can be invoked, are expressive of a kind of practical understanding ("how to go about doing science") that itself can never be fully thematized or theorized. This is what the scientist and philosopher of science Michael Polanyi called "tacit knowledge." Tacit knowledge – the supreme guiding force in all rational inquiry – is "tacit" not simply because it has *not yet* been articulated but because it is quite simply, in any definitive and final sense, *inarticulable.* As Polanyi states: "The rules of [scientific] research cannot usefully be codified at all. Like the rules of all other higher arts, they are embodied in practice alone" (Polanyi 1962, p. 33). This is the case, Polanyi argues, even in regard to that supposedly most formalizable of all disciplines, mathematics: "[E]ven the most completely formalized logical operations must include an unformalized tacit coefficient" (Polanyi 1958, p. 257; see also p. 118).[39] Even in the most formal of disciplines, there is, Polanyi argues, an "irreducible residue" (ibid., p. 258) of tacit (nonformalizable) understanding. The matter can be expressed in another way by saying that all explicit understanding always presupposes a context or horizon of unthematized meaning or knowledge that can never, at any given time, be made fully explicit. We always "know" more than we are ever capable of knowing that we know. This, incidentally, is why, as Polanyi suggests, the program of "strong" Artifical Intelligence (as it is now called) is doomed to failure and, in fact, amounts to a fundamental *mis*understanding of human understanding: because it includes an irreducible "tacit coefficient," human understanding can never *in principle* be fully "decontextualized" in such a way as to be adequately expressed ("modeled") in the formal language of logic-machines, i.e., computers.[40]

This recognition of the tacit element in all understanding, it may be noted, is what serves to legitimate Toulmin's thesis to the effect that there is not, and cannot be, an essential difference, a difference in kind, between the natural sciences and the human disciplines.[41] What makes disciplines "scientific," and thus intellectually respectable (in that they are productive of "truth"), is not that one discipline, such as physics, employs "the scientific method" whereas another one, such as historiography, does not; for there is in fact no such thing as "the scientific method" - understood, as the logical postivists tended to do, as a purely formal procedure needing only to be applied in a quasi-mechanical way in order to generate "true knowledge." The scientistic myth of the scientific method is one thing that Polanyi sought throughout his writings to expose (as Paul Feyerabend was also subsequently to do in a most insistent fashion).[42]

There are, to be sure, genuine and significant differences between the natural sciences and the human sciences, but they lie elsewhere than in the supposed fact that the former are rigorously methodical whereas the latter are not. One crucial difference is that while both of these types of disciplines are, as Toulmin argued, interpretive, the human disciplines are *doubly interpretive* (a feature of the human sciences that Toulmin fails to note). They are doubly interpretive in that human beings, the object or subject matter of these disciplines, *are themselves* interpretive beings, i.e., ones which are continually engaged in a process of self-interpretation, long before the human scientist happens upon the scene. Although explanatory techniques of a formal, structural, functionalist, comparative, or other such sort have an important role to play in the human sciences, the task of these disciplines, *qua human* disciplines, is ultimately that of understanding various modes of human being-in-the-world, of interpreting the interpretations that people make of themselves.[43] This is a task the natural scientist is mercifully spared (the objects of the natural sciences are not "subjects" in their own right, and natural scientists need not, accordingly, busy themselves with thinking about what the objects of their study think about what they think about them), and it is what makes the human sciences to be, in some ways, even more intellectually demanding than the natural sciences. Social scientists, states biologist Richard Lewontin, "are asking about the most complex and difficult phenomena in the most complex and recalcitrant organisms, without that liberty to manipulate their objects of study which is enjoyed by natural scientists. In comparison, the task of the molecular biologist is trivial" (Lewontin 1995, p. 44). When practised in an intellectually conscientious manner, the human sciences are as rigorous in their own way as are the natural sciences, but achieving rigor in the human sciences often demands a greater effort than it does in the case of the natural sciences, since the human scientist must, by the very nature of the case, constantly be on his or her guard against the distorting influences of ideology (as Toulmin argues in his 1982 article cited above).[44]

There is, moreover, a curious phenomenon bedeviling work in the human sciences that is largely absent in the natural sciences; this is the phenomenon referred to as the "self-fulfilling prophecy" (or, equally well: the "self-falsifying prophecy"). Hermeneuticist Paul Ricoeur describes it in the following way:

> The essence of the phenomenon may be said to lie in the fact that if some situation is *defined* in a certain way, and the definition is *believed* to be real, then it is real in its consequences. . . . [The phenomenon] is rooted in the fact that men can become aware of what is thought or postulated about human reality, and this awareness can affect or influence it in a certain direction. The phenomenon is not found with respect to the world of non-human reality, for what we think about nature does not affect it in any sense, except in the purely technological one. But men are capable of self-consciousness, and thus can become aware of what is thought about them. Accordingly, the absence or presence of the capacity for self-consciousness on the part of that which is the object of study lies at the foundation of the fact that the phenomenon of 'self-fulfilling prophecy' is absent from our encounter with natural reality, and not quite so absent from our encounter with social reality.
>
> (Ricoeur 1979, p. 147)[45]

Unlike natural entities, human beings are sufficiently perverse and contrarian (due to the fact, no doubt, that they possess what metaphysicians call "free will") that, when they learn about them, they will often deliberately set out to falsify any scientific "predictions" made about them. In any event, what the social scientist, e.g., the economist, has to deal with is the way in which, in the social world, people are widely engaged in the mutually back-and-forth business of predicting other people's predictions (cf. John Maynard Keynes' famous analogy of the stock exchange with a beauty contest wherein each of the judges is seeking to predict the judgment of all the others). *Qua* inquirers, social scientists have a much rougher time of it than do natural scientists.[46]

What, at bottom, both the natural and the human sciences have in common is that the truths they produce are essentially *social* in nature (truth, as Frank Knight said, is "a social category").[47] The "pursuit of truth" is never, under any circumstances, a purely individual matter but always occurs in a social milieu.[48] The production of truth is a business carried on by, as Peirce would say, a "community of inquirers," a myriad of inquirers interacting in ways that more often than not are non-personal, "decentralized," and anonymous (i.e., non-face-to-face) – ways that, while being rule-governed, are not planned or controlled in a fully conscious manner by any individual or group of individuals. As Hayek says, these "orderly structures . . . are the product of the action of many men but are not the result of human design" (Hayek 1973, p. 37).[49] Just as in the case of the business world, the intellectual world, academe, is dominated throughout by the modern principle so emphasized by Adam Smith, that of *the division of labor*. While it has its drawbacks (at least in comparison with the old Renaissance ideal of the "universal man [scholar]"), it could not be otherwise – in, that is, a situation such as we have now where there is so much "knowledge" floating around (often in purely electronic form) that no individual could ever possibly get the "whole picture" (even as to what's going on in his or her own intellectual discipline). Spontaneous orders are intrinsically "polycentric."

What Polanyi says of mathematicians is true of inquirers in general, natural or human: they are "always guided by common standards which they enforce on each other by their professional consensus" (Polanyi 1958, p. 257). As Polanyi recognized and duly emphasized, an inquirer is an inquirer only as a member of an overarching *community* of inquirers: "Thus to accord validity to science – or to any other of the great domains of the mind – is to express a faith which can be upheld only within a community" (Polanyi 1964, p. 73). As economist Don Lavoie writes (with Polanyi and Gadamer, among others, in mind):

> [T]he growth of knowledge [is located not in] any explicit rules known by any single mind, but in the partly tacit judgments of, and the processes of discursive interaction among, the members of the scientific *community* [emphasis added]. The individual member of this community, whether a practising scientist or a philosopher or a historian of science, cannot possibly articulate a complete set of criteria for measuring one theory's advantages over another. The way this process works is by the contention among rival theories for the attention, the respect, and ultimately the support, of most members of the community of

scientists. The reasons for why scientists are swayed by one rival more than another are never listable in advance, but emerge in the process of communicative interaction itself, that is, in our mutual attempts to interpret and criticize one another.

(Lavoie 1989, pp. 584–85)

Summing up the literature on the subject, Lavoie remarks: "One implication of the hermeneutical view of knowledge . . . is that the problem of theory-choice, at its roots, is always a matter of whatever persuades open-minded but critical members of the scientific community" (ibid., p. 586).

When Polanyi speaks of a knowledge "which can be upheld only within a community," he is pointing to another aspect of the fact that, precisely because all understanding is essentially of a social nature, it always includes an important *tacit* dimension. The rules of rationality, as they apply to any given intellectual discipline, are, as I have argued, largely *praxial* in nature (rather than "theoretical"). They are, as many recent writers on science have emphasized, something that students learn "by osmosis," rather than by formal teaching. There is no possible way that, for example, physicists can be taught, in a purely formal manner, to be good physicists. This, as in any intellectual discipline, is something that can be learned only by long *apprenticeship*. One learns the ropes of one's discipline not by attending formal lectures but only by actual, "hands-on" *doing*. As Toulmin observes: "The apprentice scientist masters the current interpretive standpoint of a science in the course of being enculturated into the professional community of that science" (Toulmin 1982, p. 104).

This is a point that has been extensively remarked upon in the post-positivistic, hermeneutical philosophy of science inaugurated in large part by Thomas Kuhn.[50] The actual *practice* of science is more a matter of *doing* than *knowing*, of participating in an on-going conversation among like-minded inquirers whose inner resources (*ressorts*, springs or motives, as the French would say) are not fully known to any single participant in the conversation. Scientists do what they do, not because they adhere closely to some common manual on "the scientific method" taught to them in a formal setting, but because they have learned from their own science teachers, in a thoroughly praxial, inarticulate or tacit way, what was expected of them, a lesson that the brighter among them instinctively take to heart hoping, as they do, to be admitted into that particular community of inquirers; they do what they do simply because "that is the way it is done." There is nothing wrong with this. It is, in fact, the only way science can be done. Any intellectual discipline is a *social* affair, and the only rules of rationality it can appeal to (in an attempt to demonstrate its "truth-value") are those operative within a given, accredited community of inquirers.

The rules of rationality, in regard to any given discipline, are never fully formalizable, are culturally and socially "determined," but this does not mean that they are "arbitrary" and "relative." Actually, in human (as opposed to divine) affairs "relativity" is the rule, and so in the final analysis what counts is always the *relative* superiority of one belief over another. As one champion of the humanities has stated: "In our form of inquiry, which is creative and exploratory, there is no one right answer to a problem. In order to avoid claims that are simply arbitrary or subjective, these have to be tested against other opinions and other possible interpretations of the same material" (Simpson 1994, p. 6). The rules of rationality are precisely what enable us to determine with rigor (if not exactitude) that in any given instance and for all practical purposes one belief is (relatively) better ("truer") than another. As Mill rightly insisted: "There is no such thing as absolute certainty, but there is assurance sufficient for the purposes of human life" (Mill 1947, p. 19; Chapter 2, lines 127–29).

THE ETHICS OF COMMUNICATIVE RATIONALITY

The Republic of Science/Letters, centered as it is on the notion of a *community* of inquirers, has an ethics or a morality that is unique to it and particularly its own (just as, as we shall see in the following chapter, the political sphere has an ethics that is properly its own[51]). However, because intellectual work is based upon the (economic) principle of the division of labor, the morality that it invokes, and which is absolutely essential to its proper functioning, is not the old neighborly, Good Samaritan ("face-to-face") morality preached in our churches. Just as the rules of rational inquiry are not rules in the ordinary sense, so likewise the community of inquirers is not a community in any ordinary ("communitarian") sense. Unlike the latter, an intellectual community is for the most part characterized not by "proximity" but, as I have argued, by "anonymity," being, as it is, the spontaneous, unintended result of the interaction of a myriad of individuals who are often not directly aware of what their fellow researchers scattered throughout the world are up to, or who have only the sketchiest awareness of it. This means that the ethics or morality of communicative rationality is not, and cannot be, morality in the ordinary sense of the term, *individual morality*, i.e., a set of maxims whose purpose it is to regulate the direct dealings of individuals with one another in the everyday lifeworld. It is, so to speak, a *social morality* in that it resides not in the "good intentions" of the individual but in the rule-governed, social *practices* of a given intellectual or academic discipline. To know if someone is a "good" scientist, it is not necessary to know anything about their "psychology" or moral make-up; it is necessary only to know if they are playing by the "rules of the game." The ethics of communicative rationality constitutes, as it were, a *public* morality rather than a *private* one; it is a morality for which no special instruction or training is required, other than that which is praxially involved in mastering the rules of the game.

Here again there is a strict parallelism between the cultural and political orders of a civil society (see note 24 above). As the long tradition of civic or republican humanism has always insisted, a "republican" form of government requires for existence a "virtuous" citizenry. However, as late-eighteenth century liberals came to realize, "civic virtue" is qualitatively different from virtue in the traditional, "moralistic" sense of this term. As Tocqueville pointed out, following up on hints provided by Madison and other American constitutionalists, one need not be a "good person" in order to be a "good citizen."[52] The virtues of communicative rationality as it manifests itself in the intellectual sphere of human endeavor are in fact none other than the liberal virtues of a "civic society," namely: tolerance, reasonableness, a readiness to compromise, and a willingness to work out mutual agreements by means of discourse rather than by means of force. The ethics of communicative rationality (*Sprachethik*, hermeneutical ethics) rests on the realization that, as Paul Ricoeur has pointed out, violence and discourse are mutually exclusive and that once one has opted for discourse or discussion – "the search for agreement by means of language" – recourse to violence can no longer be (rationally) defended (Ricoeur 1979, p. 266).[53]

The supreme virtue or ethical imperative of communicative rationality is what I have called "reasonableness," and of this Rorty says:

> It names a set of moral virtues: tolerance, respect for the opinions of those around one, willingness to listen, reliance on persuasion rather than force. These are the virtues which members of a civilized society must possess if the society is to endure. In this sense of "rational," the word means something more like "civilized" [civil, in my terminology] than like "methodical." When so construed, the distinction between the rational and the irrational has nothing in particular to do with the difference between the arts and the sciences. On this construction, to be rational is simply to discuss any topic – religious, literary, or scientific – in a way which eschews dogmatism, defensiveness, and righteous indignation.
>
> (Rorty 1987, p. 40)

It may be noted that the hermeneutical notion of "good will" (the indispensable condition for arriving at genuine agreement) embodies the core precept of democratic pluralism: the other may possibly be right over against myself and thus must be accorded a freedom equal to my own. As Gadamer states: "[I]t belongs to the concept of reason, that one must always reckon with the possibility that the opposite conviction, whether in the individual or in the social order, could be correct" (Gadamer 1990b, p. 294). In a civil society, wherein the rights and liberties of all are mutually reinforcing, every single individual must be as equally free as any other to pursue the truth as he or she sees it, to express his or her views on the matter, and to solicit the accord of others – so long, that is, as each respects the freedom and the right of everyone else to do likewise.

63

This, of course, does not mean that everyone must be accorded "equal time to air their views" (as Habermas implies), only that they have a right not to be officially or arbitrarily censored; everyone must have an equal right to secure as great an audience for their views as possible, relying on their own devices (and depending on how many people are willing to listen to them). In any intellectual community (as in any civil society in general) there will always be those who command greater respect and attention than others, but this fact in no way violates the principle of the "equal freedom of all," what Mill would call "free and equal discussion" (Mill 1947, p. 10; Chapter 1, lines 378–79). There is all the world of difference between speaking from a position of *authority* (*auctoritas*) that has been earned and that is freely recognized by others and dominating the conversation from a position of *power* (*potestas*) ·deriving from factors extrinsic to the discussion process, such as race, sex, or social status. Unlike power, authority rightly understood is not coercive and has efficacy only to the degree to which it is freely acknowledged and willingly deferred to. Its only force is *moral* (see Sartori 1987, I, p. 188). Thus it is simplistic in the extreme to proclaim, as so many unthinking disciples of Foucault do, that "It's all a matter of power," of who "controls" the means of expression (a common complaint of both right-wingers and left-wingers, even though both have more than sufficient access to media of all sorts). As Gadamer has pointed out:

> [T]he essence of authority . . . is based ultimately, not on the subjection and abdication of reason, but on recognition and knowledge. . . . It rests on recognition and hence on an act of reason itself which, aware of its own limitations, accepts that others have better understanding. Authority in this sense, properly understood, has nothing to do with blind obedience to a command. Indeed, authority has nothing to do with obedience, but rather with knowledge.
>
> (Gadamer 1975, p. 248)

"I cannot accept," Gadamer says, "that reason and authority are abstract antitheses" (Gadamer 1976, p. 33).

"Authority," one could say, is the very essence of the process described above through which one masters the "rules of rationality" and becomes in one's own right a full-fledged member of an intellectual community, as Polanyi for one has noted:

> To learn by example is to submit to authority. You follow your master because you trust his manner of doing things even when you cannot analyse and account in detail for its effectiveness. By watching the master and emulating his efforts in the presence of his example, the apprentice unconsciously picks up the rules of the art, including those which are not explicitly known to the master himself. These hidden rules can be assimilated only by a person who surrenders himself to

that extent uncritically to the imitation of another. A society which wants to preserve a fund of personal knowledge must submit to tradition.

(Polanyi 1958, p. 53)

Authority is thus not a "power" concept, alien to the world of science (knowledge). It derives from the fact that knowledge is essentially social and from the fact that no isolated subject could ever "verify" for him or herself the entire fund of knowledge embedded in the tradition upon which he or she is continually drawing. As the interpretive economist Donald McCloskey says, quoting Gilbert Harman, "authoritative statements are ones we accept on behalf of some group, since learning about the world is a cooperative enterprise" (McCloskey 1994, p. 204). The moral-cultural order – the realm of truth – is like one immense cooperative or credit union.

While those in positions of (earned) authority in the Gadamerian sense will always be more readily listened to than those with less intellectual or moral authority (*ethos*, as the ancient rhetoricians would have said), this, in itself, in no way diminishes the "equal freedom of all" in the discursive community. (One of the chief functions in any discursive community is to ferret out "abuses of authority" of whatever sort; the equal right of every-one to challenge anyone else is as much a fundamental principle of the moral-cultural realm as it is of the political realm of a civil society.) Author-ity, in the proper sense of the term, is always freely acknowledged, whereas power, in the vulgar sense of the term, is at best only grudgingly acquiesced to.

The overarching value in the ethics of communicative rationality (as opposed to mere power plays which, admittedly, are ubiquitous in human life) is thus that of freedom. As Gadamer would say, no higher "principle of reason" is thinkable than that of the "freedom of all" (Gadamer 1981, p. 9).[54] Freedom of expression and of conscience is as crucial to the mainten-ance of a free community of inquirers as it is to a free society in general. Freedom as an overriding principle is in fact always "presupposed" whenever people seek to persuade one another by means of rational argument or deliberation. If anything approaches the status of an absolute value, it is the value of freedom, which cannot be compromised without the humanness of human beings itself being compromised.[55] As Mill observed, "freedom of opinion, and freedom of the expression of opinion" are necessary for the "mental well-being of mankind," and, as he further observed, "all their other well-being depends on this" (Mill 1947, p. 52; Chapter 2, lines 1433–35). Freedom is both the supreme human need and the supreme human right.

In arguing for freedom as the supreme value it is not at all necessary to appeal to metaphysical, theological, or other such "foundationalist" con-siderations of an arcane nature. Freedom of expression is a supreme human right – a "strategic" right – for the simple reason that without it no one can in

65

actual practice lay claim to or defend any other right, in any sphere of human endeavor. If, as Claude Lefort asserts, the supreme right is the right freely to claim rights, then freedom of expression is uncontestably the most vital human right of all. As James Madison observed some two hundred years ago: "[F]ree communication . . . has ever been justly deemed the only effectual guardian of every other right."[56]

FREEDOM UNDER SEIGE

I have argued that freedom is the supreme human right in that freedom of expression is the only real safeguard of all other rights. In ethical terms, freedom is the supreme value in that the legitimization of all other values depends on their being argued for in a rationally persuasive manner, i.e., by means of free discussion. Indeed, when values are not "justified" in this way, they cannot properly be said to be values at all; they are merely expressions of subjective wants and desires which, purely as such, cannot *rationally* compel the *free* assent of others. (To say "I want this" or "I like that" does not suffice to give oneself the moral or political *right* to having this or that.) For these reasons, the priority of freedom over other values is absolute; indeed, if any value can be said to be absolute, it is freedom. Freedom is absolute in that its status as a value is (rationally) unquestionable. As Gadamer has said with reference to Hegel's view of history as the history of the progress of freedom: "The principle of freedom is unimpugnable and irrevocable. It is no longer possible for anyone still to affirm the unfreedom of humanity. The principle that all are free never again can be shaken" (Gadamer 1981, p. 37).

It is a commonplace of our postmodern times to deny the existence of any absolute whatsoever. And, indeed, if the value of freedom can be said to be absolute, it is in a strictly nontraditional sense of that term. The concept of freedom is after all a relational concept and thus takes its meaning only from that which is other than it – just as, it might be pointed out, the notion of the "self" (the individual "bearer of rights") is itself a relational concept. As Chantal Mouffe rightly says: "[E]very identity is relational and . . . the condition of existence of every identity is the affirmation of a difference, the determination of an 'other' that is going to play a role of a 'constitutive outside'" (Mouffe 1993, p. 2). For a postmodern or hermeneutical liberalism, the self is not a "substance" in the traditional philosophical sense of the term, i.e., something existing "in itself" (the atomistic individual), something merely "given" or "ready-made." The self can exist for itself only in and by means of its relations to the "other."[57] The individual self is a social entity, just as the right to individual privacy is a social right. It is precisely because the self can "make" itself only through its interactions with other acting subjects that the right to freedom must be held to be absolute. Absent this right, the notion of "innate personal dignity" would be devoid of meaning.

Moreover, freedom can never be absolute in the sense of being unconditioned and without limits. Indeed, such a notion is unintelligible. One is and can be free only within limits, only in this or that respect and only to this or that degree. Freedom is essentially limited in that like all rights it is not "natural" (and thus potentially "absolute" in the metaphysical sense of the term) but is a human contrivance, the product of "actually existing" *civil society*. A product of legislation (a by-product, as it were, of the rule of law), freedom is always limited by law. This is to say that, its "absoluteness" notwithstanding, the actual meaning of the concept of freedom, in any particular instance, is always open to *interpretation*. What "freedom of expression" as guaranteed by the American Bill of Rights actually means, for instance, is something that can only in the last instance be determined by the Supreme Court of the United States – which is not to say that the Court's decisions at any given time can lay claim to absolute validity (the Court often makes mistakes which subsequently have to be corrected, previous interpretations then revealing themselves to have been *mis*interpretations). In short, as economist James Buchanan might say, freedom is only "a relatively absolute absolute."

That having been said, it is nonetheless crucial to insist on the priority of freedom over all other values. Even though it is itself "limited," the right to freedom is supreme in that, if it is to have any substantive meaning at all, it must take precedence over all other rights and must set limits to the way in which *they* are interpreted and the degree to which they are to be implemented (my right to free speech must always take precedence over your supposed right not to be offended). Consider, for instance, the value that democratic societies rightly attribute to *equality*. Ever since Tocqueville it has been widely accepted in political theory that even though equality (equality before the law, equality of rights, political equality) is a necessary component of democracy, the unrestrained pursuit of equality (equality of conditions or outcomes) can only be detrimental to freedom and must indeed result in the eventual destruction of any form of genuinely *liberal* democracy. Thus Agnes Heller and Ferenc Fehér, two expatriot Hungarian thinkers of the Left, argue that the principle of freedom takes precedence over the principle of equality and sets necessary limits to it. They write:

> Human beings are unique, in this sense they are not equal, they cannot and must not be equalized as far as the pursuit of happiness (the satisfaction of their multifarious needs) is concerned. The inequality, or, more precisely the uniqueness, of human beings is intrinsic in the very idea of negative freedom [freedom from coercion]. No principle applies to negative freedom except the principle of its recognition.

> The ultimate, absolute yardstick by which the justice or injustice of norms and rules can be measured, could then be formulated as follows: "equal freedom for all; equal life-chances for all". Not equality, but life

and freedom are the unconditional values of modernity. Equality is a conditional value in the sense that it needs to be related to the values of freedom and life in order to give it meaning. Equality in misery or in un-freedom, for instance, is of negative value.

(Heller and Fehér 1988, pp. 71, 125)

In the moral-cultural order the right to freedom translates as the freedom of expression and the freedom to engage in the rational exchange of opinions. And this freedom is "absolute" in that it has nothing to do with the actual "content" of these opinions (this is what the US Supreme Court has called the principle of "content neutrality"). Whether or not one's opinions are agreeable to one's discussion partners or to the general public matters not at all, so long as one operates in accordance with the rules of reasonable debate. The privileged locus of free discussion and reasonable debate has traditionally been the universities and academies of a civil society. The very *raison d'être* of a liberal education – the highest function of the university – is that of inculcating in people the ability to challenge established ideas and unexamined (though widely held) assumptions. In this, academic freedom is vital, for no one needs be guaranteed the freedom to express popular ideas; it is always and only the right to express unpopular views that needs at all costs to be defended.

The purpose of the free exchange of views in the university is that of enabling people to perceive that which is *questionable*, and for this it is necessary for academics to be independent of transient social attitudes. Academic freedom means nothing if it does not mean the right to be controversial. The ultimate purpose of a liberal education is the formation of free men and women, i.e., ones who have acquired the ability to appreciate the complexities of life and to be sensitive to the often fine nuances of difference between conflicting opinions, along with the ability to formulate a reasoned critique or defense of the ideas in question. There is no doubt that when conflicting views are freely aired, some people will feel offended or threatened by what they hear; this is naturally the case when one's basic values, beliefs, and assumptions are examined, challenged, and criticized. But that is precisely what university education is all about. The quest for truth is a dangerous business, and the learning process is necessarily disturbing. Education is not indoctrination.[58]

In recent times, however, a concerted attack has been mounted against the central role of the university by the advocates of "political correctness." As the Hon. John Sopinka, a justice of the Supreme Court of Canada, has stated:

In the last decade there has developed a phenomenon known as the demand for political correctness. Certain segments of society who are justifiably seeking equality for their particular interests have extended their demands so far that they threaten the freedom of others. They not

68

only criticize the expression of views that do not accord with their own but demand that contrary views be suppressed.

(Sopinka 1994, p. 13)

The principle animating the post-Marxist movement of political correctness is most definitely not freedom of speech but the supposed right of people – minorities always and only – not to be offended by opinions which they find – for whatever reason – to be disagreeable or "unwelcome," a principle that is diametrically opposed to the principle of freedom and which, if implemented, would destroy it. Mill's remark about his own times applies with even greater force to our own: "In our times, from the highest class of society down to the lowest, every one lives as under the eye of a hostile and dreaded censorship" (Mill 1947, p. 61; Chapter 3, lines 229–31). It is highly significant that this assult on liberty and on the freedom of conscience of individuals is conducted in the name of *equality*, the supreme value for most of those who choose to situate themselves on the Left. And thus another of Mill's remarks is uncannily appropriate: "Europe [and North America] . . . is decidedly advancing toward the Chinese ideal of making all people alike" (Mill 1947, p. 73; Chapter 3, lines 695–96).

Code words for this egalitarian assault on freedom are the "inclusive university" and "educational equity." Although the politically correct pursuit of "equalism" (as the post-Maoist Chinese now derisively call it) can, like the traditional socialist pursuit of equality, appeal to noble-sounding values, when translated into practice it is utterly destructive of the most noble value of all, the freedom of the individual. The sensitivity sessions now commonly mandated by the new logocrats or language police for the politically incorrect resemble nothing so much as "a kinder, more gentle" version of the old Maoist stress sessions and "political reeducation." This is nowhere more apparent than in the ubiquitous political attempts to outlaw "harassment."

The dangers that lurk behind most such attempts to institute anti-harassment codes are multiple and very serious indeed. The most obvious danger is that by defining, as they usually do, harassment to mean whatever anyone, for whatever reason, considers to be harassment (an affront to their "self-esteem"), just about anything and everything can qualify as such. When feelings are elevated to the status of rights, reason must necessarily go by the board. Even when attempts are made to forestall such excesses, most anti-harassment codes operate, as a matter of fact, on a principle which is altogether antithetical to the basic principle of liberal justice: the presumption of innocence. As the National Association of Scholars has stated: "Some of the sanctions now in force aim at thought reform [for supposed 'thought crime'], frequently through compulsory 'sensitivity training' programs. These programs often operate to humiliate those suspected of holding 'incorrect views.' They also frequently suggest that being white, male, or heterosexual constitutes a presumption of guilt. When *required* for faculty

69

and students, these programs constitute an assault on individual dignity and freedom."[59]

What, in accordance with their investigative mentality, the politically correct would construct for us is a new culture, a new culture of inquisition. As in the example at the University of New Hampshire cited on p. 30 (see note 15, Chapter 2), it is the person accused of harassment who must, at great cost to him or herself, prove the contrary (the negative) – even when the accusation is manifestly frivolous, or even vindictive. Even when anti-harassment codes attempt to spell out in detail what is proscribed language or behavior (and what, by implication, is OK), the unavoidable "gray" areas are so extensive that a chilling self-censorship invariably tends to settle in, one which is thoroughly inimical to free and open discussion (one is reminded here of the paranoid self-censorship rampant in the former socialist countries). As Alan Borovoy, head of the Canadian Civil Liberties Association, has warned: "One of the most critical dangers to freedom of speech is the existence of laws that impel us to look over our shoulders for engaging in normal democratic discourse." The ultimate casualty of enforced speech control is academic freedom itself. We are now, for instance, at the point where it is legislated that no reference is to be made in textbooks "which could be construed as unfavourable to any minority, no matter how factual or well established such references are."[60] In the politically correct movement, the very idea of liberal education is under siege. A fundamental liberal principle has been lost sight of, namely, that in a free society the only acceptable way of combating opinions or forms of speech to which one objects is not by banning them but by debating them. This is what the US Supreme Court has called the "bedrock principle" of freedom of speech. The principle maintains, in the words of Nadine Strossen, president of the American Civil Liberties Union, that "the appropriate response to speech with which one disagrees in a free society is not censorship but counterspeech – *more* speech, not *less*. Persuasion, not coercion, is the answer" (Strossen 1995, p. 41).

A superb example of politically correct antiliberalism carried to its extreme was the "Framework Regarding Prevention of Harassment and Discrimination in Ontario Universities" issued by the Ontario Minister of Education in the Fall of 1993. It would have required all Ontario universities to review and reform their existing policies in conformity with the extremely detailed (and altogether arbitrary) demands of the Ministry by March of the following year (in the event, there was such a concerted [and rather unexpected] reaction on the part of faculty associations throughout Ontario that the directive was later quietly shelved by the government).[61] Perhaps the most notable feature of this document (which was fully typical of the genre, which has become fairly common in the Western world) was the total absence of any reference to academic freedom and to the central role of the university.[62] The emphasis of the document was entirely in the opposite direction, that of speech regulation and thought control. If implemented it would most certainly have eviscerated academic freedom beyond all recognition. As one critic remarked at the time, "it threatens the very autonomy of the university, and is a document worthy of a totalitarian society" (Toro 1994, p. 15). "Totalitarian" is perhaps too strong a term; what we are dealing with here is a kind of Western-style "velvet totalitarianism," very widespread in today's Western world, and very "systemic" indeed (to use a favorite word of the PCers). In any event, the threat to academic freedom and to the role of the university itself was apparent in the very language of the document which, reminiscent of the Reagan administration's ill-conceived "war on drugs", stated that the "central goal" of the government was "zero tolerance" of harassment (very expansively defined). "Zero tolerance" is the language of repression, authoritarianism, and intimidation; it is not the language of reasonableness, justice, and rights. It is a language which effectively undermines the traditional liberal right to be presumed innocent until proven guilty (as was fully manifest in the DEA's "war on drugs").[63]

Language of this nature highlights a perhaps less apparent but no less insidious danger of all such "proactive" (to employ a PC buzz-word to be found in the Ontario document) attempts at social regulation/engineering. The language in which they are written is usually so vague and their rhetoric so lofty that the documents are subject to expansionary interpretations of the most unforeseeable sort (for an analysis of this phenomenon, see Lowi 1993). As the National Association of Scholars stated: "The criteria for identifying 'harassment' are often nebulous, allowing for expansive interpretations of its meaning" (see note 59 of this chapter, p. 229).

Just what, after all, is to count as making for a "negative (or poisoned) environment," and what exactly are to count as comments which are "unwelcome/unwanted, offensive, intimidating, hostile or inappropriate" (as the Ontario document puts it)? Surely it is not only a right but a duty for a professor to express views which, being unfamiliar to many students, are also likely, precisely because they are unfamiliar, to be "unwelcome/unwanted, offensive, intimidating, hostile or inappropriate" in the eyes of someone or other. In its "Reply" to the Ontario government's "Framework," the Canadian Association of University Teachers (CAUT) stated: "The words 'comfortable' or 'negative environment' should normally set off clear bells when they are applied to the classroom situation" (CAUT 1994, p. 14). As it functions in the zero tolerance agenda, "environment," as John Fekete points out, is "a totalitarian code word" (Fekete 1994, p. 320). The total "prevention" of any and all forms of "harassment" signals the total, censorious *control* of all forms of expression – and thus the total abolition of freedom of speech.

Learning how to object, with civility, to unwelcome opinions is precisely what a liberal education is all about. One has to learn how to say, summoning reasons to one's defense, "I disagree with that," rather than simply, "I find that offensive" (meaning: "I don't like what I'm hearing, since it goes against

71

the grain of what I've been accustomed to hearing").[64] Moreover, what exactly is to count as "systemic harassment/discrimination"? The bureaucratic definition – "policies, practices, procedures, actions or inactions, that appear neutral, but have an adverse impact" – is so ill-defined and so all-inclusive as to be practically useless (in, that is, any legal or juridical setting of a liberal sort; it is, however, such as to allow bureaucrats free reign in their interpretations of the directives).

Besides the fact that they themselves create a "negative environment" or a "chilly climate" for free discussion, the way most antiharassment codes are written is a guaranteed formula for bureaucratic arbitrariness (arbitrary government, *un régime de décrets*) – the long sought-after Shangri-La of bureaucrats. And it matters little whether the bureaucracy in question be that of the government or that of the university. For just as Ludwig von Mises observed that one cannot count on capitalists to defend "capitalism" (see Mises 1981, pp. 455–56), so likewise one cannot count on university officials to defend academic freedom and the autonomy of the univerity. As one postmodern academic observes in defending university autonomy (and the automony of the moral-cultural order):

> Unfortunately, most of the academic leadership of the contemporary university is virtual putty in the government's hands. The government is mixing the principles of managerialism and plebiscitary democracy in its efforts to uproot the culture and procedures of academic collegial governance [read "academic freedom"]. Inevitably, an academic leadership looking to the past for its erstwhile unquestioned scientific or scholarly authority is poorly placed to defend itself against this agenda. It is especially so when this leadership is sympathetic to the claims on justice in the university by marginalized groups such as women and Maori. . . .This provides a virtual vacuum within which the anti-academic requirements of governments for information rather than knowledge can make themselves felt.
>
> (Yeatman 1994, pp. 43–44)

As with power in general (as classical liberals never tired of pointing out), it is in the nature of bureaucracy to want continually to expand, and the social agenda insisted upon by the PCers furnishes it with a made-to-measure means of doing so. At the university level, attempts to police what is said (and even what is not said) and what is taught (or not taught) has resulted in the proliferation of mid-level PC administrators with little or no background in academic/scholarly experience and who are woefully unacquainted with the meaning and significance of academic freedom.

That antiharassment/discrimination policies of the sort described (amounting, to borrow a phrase from McCloskey, to "an appeal for a central planning of the intellectual marketplace" [McCloskey 1994, p. 320]) are divisive and counter-productive in the long run – in that they have for their ultimate effect to pit one minority group against another, giving licence to each to claim harassment at the hands of the other – is of no concern to the ideologically motivated politically correct.[65] In the meantime, the damage done can be quite extensive. Once the hard-won autonomy of the university has been surrendered to government mandated social engineering, it would no doubt be exceedingly difficult to regain it, as is always the case with lost liberties and as the arduous attempt to recreate civil societies in the former socialist countries so vividly demonstrates.

Three-quarters of a century of one of the greatest social fiascos in human history ("the road to Nowhere" [Erehwon]) do not seem to have dampened in the slightest the utopian aspirations of our would-be egalitarian reformers. One is led to wonder if there might not be something in the Christian doctrine of original sin after all and if human beings will ever learn to subordiate their own individual or group conceptions (usually self-serving) of what is "good" to what are in fact the universal demands for liberty and justice for all.

Although we may allow ourselves the hope that the current fad for political correctness will pass from the scene, the concerns and motivations which gave rise to this phenomenon most certainly will not. Intolerance has always and everywhere been the name of the human game, and it will most likely continue to be so for as long as the human race exists.[66] As Toulmin has observed: "Taking human history as a whole, heresy-hunting or intellectual conformism has been the rule, tolerance of free conceptual innovation the exception" (Toulmin 1972, p. 220). When intolerance is combined with ideological Messianism and revolutionist attempts to create a "virtuous" or "alternate" society, the mixture is potentially lethal, as we now fully know after three-quarters of a century of "really existing" Socialism. That knowledge will, however, undoubtedly not suffice to put to rest the ghosts of socialist thinking, which is as deeply ingrained in the human make-up as is the desire for justice itself. As Martin Malia observed in his masterful history of Socialism in Russia, "The socialist idea will surely be with us as long as inequality is, and that will be a very long time indeed" (Malia 1994, p. 514). All that we may reasonably hope for is that the desire for equality will continue to be tempered by an attachment to liberty and universal justice.

FREEDOM, A UNIVERSAL VALUE

That freedom is the supreme value is an idea that was first defended in Western academies and centers of liberal learning. As Jacques Ellul has observed:

> At the beginning of western history we find the awareness, the explanation, the proclamation of freedom as the meaning and goal of history. ... The West gave expression to what man – every man – was seeking.

The West turned the whole human project into a conscious, deliberate business. It set the goal and called it freedom, or, at a later date, individual freedom. It gave direction to all the forces that were working in obscure ways, and brought to light the value that gave history its meaning. Thereby, man became man.

(Ellul 1978, p. 17)

The thinkers Ellul is alluding to here not only proclaimed freedom to be the supreme value – the meaning and goal of history – they also asserted that it is a *universal* value. Ellul's text suggests two reasons for this line of argument, one of an empirical nature and the other of a more philosophical sort. The first is the claim that all human beings instinctively desire to be free (for Habermas the "human interest in autonomy and responsibility" is an "a priori" feature of human being [see Habermas 1971, p. 314]).[67] The second line of argument states that it is only by effectively being free and living in a free society that human beings can realize their own potentialities, can, in effect, become fully *human* (recall Knight's remark: "Men cannot live, as human beings, outside of *free* society"). In the case of human beings, the longing to be, *le désir d'être*, is at the same time the desire to be free, since it is only by being free that human beings can become, and be, who they truly are. The freedom and democracy movement sweeping across all the continents of the world today[68] would seem to lend universal confirmation to an idea that happened to be first put forward by a handful of Western thinkers. If freedom is a fundamental *human* right, it is necessarily universal.[69]

The overriding task facing humankind today, in an era of global civilization, is that of devising means of effectively *universalizing* (actually making it universal) the supreme value of freedom. As Jean-Paul Sartre, that great advocate of freedom, would say, there is most certainly a "human universality," but it is not something given; it has to be made (see Sartre 1973, p. 47). Freedom can no longer be the luxury of a few. Indeed, if, as I have argued, freedom, like all other human rights, entails *mutuality*, no one can desire freedom for themselves without at the same time desiring it for all others (as Sartre also pointed out; see ibid., p. 52). "Solidarity" means that the freedom of each is contingent upon the freedom of all. Thus, the "conscious, deliberate business" of all the peoples of the world today – which each must pursue in solidarity with others, yet each in its own way[70] – is above all the practical task of instituting and/or advancing civil society, in all its various aspects. And as a former Polish Solidarity activist reminds us, "Membership in civil society cannot be based only on moral rights; political and economic freedoms are also needed" (Krol 1994, p. 87). It is therefore to a consideration of political and economic rights that we must now turn.

4

THE POLITICAL ORDER

THE SPONTANEOUS ORDER OF THE DEMOCRATIC POLITY

In a civil society the political order is itself a spontaneous order, in ways in many respects similar to the moral-cultural order. It is surely not without significance in this regard that the terms that appear most suitable for characterizing the cultural order are themselves borrowed from the political order. Thus we speak of the "republic of science," the "commonwealth of letters," "intellectual democracy," and so on. The use of metaphors such as these (a metaphor is a transfer of meaning [*metapherein = transferre*] from one universe of discourse to another) points to a fundamental symbiotic relation between the two orders, since the metaphorical process (by means of which one understands one thing by likening it to some other thing) is itself a process of symbiosis.[1] "Symbiotic" is the opposite of "parasitic"; it refers to a relation of horizontal complementarity rather than vertical subordination. A symbiotic relation prevails when a mutually reinforcing commonality exists between two different or dissimilar things, e.g., biological organisms. What both the cultural and the political orders have fundamentally in common (whereby they reinforce one another) is that they are, both in their own way, spontaneous orders, as described in the preceding chapter.

Should we allow ourselves to be instructed by the logic of metaphorical predication (extending a metaphor in productive directions, the basic form of all human understanding [see Madison 1982]), we could gain an initial understanding of the political order by likening the rules of democracy to those of the moral-cultural order. This involves applying metaphors borrowed from the political realm "backwards": when a term (such as "republic") is used profitably in an area outside its "home" domain (politics), it picks up new connotations (in its application to the cultural realm), and these new connotations can be subsequently and profitably used to cast additional light on the domain of its origin. Following this procedure, therefore, we could say that the rules of democracy are like those of the cultural realm, in that they are purely abstract and procedural (as are, as we shall see in the

75

following chapter, the rules of economic democracy.) As in the case of the moral-cultural order, the political order of a civil society – democracy – does not exist or is not designed to serve any particular purpose or to achieve any specific goal (such as, for instance, a specific distribution of wealth among the citizenry). One political theorist observes: "A democracy is not established to pursue any particular purpose at all.... Democracy allows an indefinite and unpredictable number of positions to compete for public support" (diZerega 1989, p. 212). It is only in the most abstract of senses that the political order can be said to be goal-oriented, the goal here being what might be called the (socially) *good* or *just* – just as, analogically speaking, the goal of the cultural order is the (intellectually) *true* which, as we now know, is never of a substantive but always of a "processual" nature.

Thus, as diZerega observes: "What characterizes all spontaneous orders in social life is their *polycentricity*, wherein participants pursue their own purposes and interact through a system of mutual adjustments rather than by being coordinated in terms of a specifiable goal" (ibid., p. 209). As in the case of the cultural order, the political order of a civil society – a democracy – is "that abstract order of the whole which does not aim at the achievement of known particular results but is preserved as a means for assisting in the pursuit of a great variety of individual purposes" (ibid.). This is what Hayek calls "the spontaneous order of society" (Hayek 1976, pp. 5–6), of which he says:

> [T]hough the existence of a spontaneous order not made for a particular purpose cannot be properly said to have a purpose, it may yet be highly conducive to the achievement of many different individual purposes not known as a whole to any single person, or a relatively small group of persons [e.g., the government].
>
> (Hayek 1976, pp. 5–6)

Indeed, as Hayek also says, the advantages of spontaneous orders are twofold: "Knowledge that is used in it is that of all its members. Ends that it serves are the separate ends of those individuals, in all their variety and contrariness" (Hayek 1978, p. 183). The words "variety" and "contrariness" should clearly be emphasized in that the phenomena they designate are what serve principally to distinguish civil society from totalitarian society.

To say that the political order of a free society is not meant to serve any particular purpose is not to say that it does not have a basic *function* to perform, as does indeed the moral-cultural order. This is, of course, as in the case of all spontaneous orders, that of *coordination*. How can a multitude of disparate citizens, each with their own special and often conflicting interests, live together in relative peace and harmony in a *commonwealth* (*res publica*) wherein each, in the pursuit of his or her own interests, contributes nonetheless to the public interest (in medieval terminology: the common good)? This is the question to which liberal theory has always addressed itself and to

76

which the answer is unequivocal: *Civil Society*. Adam Seligman sums it up very well when he says:

> Two centuries after its origins in the Enlightenment, the idea of civil society is being revived to provide an answer to the question of how individuals can pursue their own interests while preserving the greater good of society and, similarly, how society can advance the interests of the individuals who comprise it.
>
> (Seligman 1992)

(For his part, Seligman is not terribly "sanguine," as he puts it, about the possibility of finding in the idea of civil society a means of resolving the age-old problem of reconciling private interests and the public good.[2] What I principally hope to show in what follows is that an approach to the issue in terms of Madisonian constitutionalism is quite adequate, on a conceptual level, for dealing with this problem, which, contrary to what many social theorists would have us believe, is by no means intractable.)

As it functions in the political sphere, the concept of civil society contrasts with both the socialist and the nationalist conceptions of society. The former seeks to achieve coordination by subordinating all things to the attainment of a particular goal or end-state of a utopian nature dictated by the state (socialist justice; "building Socialism"), whereas the latter attempts to create a commonality of interests by appealing to a mystical (and often mythical) past, a supposedly common ethnic origin (in the process it calls forth new inequalities and new exclusions, and thus new hostilities). In contrast, the notion of civil society is of a purely processual nature and operates without reference to either ideal end-states or mythical origins. What the "new politics of truth" (to borrow an expression from Michel Foucault; see Foucault 1980, p. 133) seeks to institutionalize is the realization that human rights are mutual rights and are thus dependent for their existence on effective procedures whereby the interests of each can, to at least a minimally tolerable degree, be reconciled with the interests of all. The politics of a civil society is one of reciprocity and mutual recognition, a willingness to engage in cooperative confrontation and to work out compromises and common agreements. As in the moral-cultural order, the only way this can be done, in such a way that the "equal liberty of all" is respected, is by means of free and open discussion, that is to say, by means of communicative rationality. As Frank Knight observed, "democracy ... is practically identical with discussion" (Knight 1982, p. 227).

This, it will be noted, is a properly *ethical* (though by no means, as we shall be seeing, moralistic) conception of politics. From a liberal point of view, the central problem of political theory, the problem of coordination, is not one of *control*, as empiricistic political scientists might say, but rather of *free, mutual agreement* as to what is to count as socially good and desirable. As Knight also observed:

With reference to the relation between science and philosophy, the supremely important matter is the danger that social problems will be viewed exclusively or primarily in scientific terms, and effort be directed to solving them by "the scientific method." A "scientific" approach to the study of society, from the standpoint of action, proceeds on the assumption that the problem is one of finding the given properties of the "material" with a view to its manipulation and use for the purposes of the knower as manipulator. . . . [T]his is the antithesis of the concept of democracy, or political freedom. And individual liberty must be the first principle of *rational political ethics* [emphasis added]. . . . [I]t is an implication of any public discussion of social problems . . . that they are "of right" to be solved by discussion, by all the parties concerned. The contrary principle, of one-sided control, is justified only to the extent that those subject to it are explicitly denied the full status of human beings. . . . In the right view of the problem it is a matter not of control but of arriving at a rational consensus.

(Knight, pp. 266–67)

Let us then consider in greater detail the main features or requirements of a political philosophy based on the principle of "discussion" or communicative rationality.

THE DISCUSSION/DELIBERATION COMMUNITY

In the history of political theory and practice, one attempt to articulate a politics of discussion stands out above all others. This is the philosophy of democratic governance embodied in the Constitution of the new American Republic of which James Madison was the chief architect. This was a truly remarkable attempt to create a functioning civil society, and, like all world-historical events (as Hegel would say), it merits careful scrutiny even today.

When they assembled in Philadelphia in the summer of 1787 to revise the unworkable "Articles of Confederation" (the Constitution of the first American Republic), the delegates to the constitutional convention were in common agreement that the only form of governance appropriate to the American situation was republican, i.e., one based on the principle of popular sovereignty. As Madison subsequently stated in *The Federalist* No. 49: "[T]he people are the only legitimate fountain of power, and it is from them that the constitutional charter, under which the several branches of government hold their power, is derived."[3] However, as they equally well realized, direct democracy, wherein the people governed themselves in assemblies open to all (the Athenian ideal, so to speak), was unworkable in a country as large as the United States (classical political theory, from Aristotle through Machiavelli, Montesquieu, and Rousseau was unanimous in asserting that

78

republican government is suitable only for small territories). The challenge they faced was, accordingly, that of devising a *representational* form of democracy in which those with delegated powers would nevertheless be held accountable to the population as a whole (see Hamilton, *The Federalist* No. 9). This is where Madison's genius revealed itself.

In opposition to the Anti-Federalists (i.e., those opposed to ratifying the Constitution proposed by the Philadelphia convention and who thought that the new federal govenment would not be sufficiently responsive – and close enough – to the wishes and sentiments of the people), Madison argued that the chief requirement of good and responsible government is not that the people's representatives should resemble the general population as much as possible. Madison was, in other words, arguing for a much more sophisticated conception of *representation*.[4] The function of government is not, or should not be, that of directly mirroring ("re-presenting," as it were) the transient passions momentarily agitating the public mind (an impossible task in any event, given the many "factions" among which the people of a large and diversified country will always find themselves divided). The function of republican or (as we would say today) democratic legislatures (Madison refered to this as "popular government") is not, as in the *anciens régimes* of Europe, that of transmitting the "will of the people" to a sovereign authority. Mere "representation" is not in itself a democratic notion, having as it does its origin in monarchical government (see Dahl 1989, p. 29). In the Madisonian view of things, the function of representational government is, in the absence of any higher authority, that of *articulating the popular will itself*, in a coherent and just fashion.

In other words, *the proper function of republican government is that of deliberation.* What "deliberation" means is that the laws passed by legislatures must issue from free and open debate, must explictly address themselves not primarily to separate interests but, above all, to the common good, and must be such that good (universalizable) *reasons* can be provided for them, ones for which the legislators will themselves be held *accountable* (i.e., able to *argue* for them and to defend them in a persuasively rational manner) to their constituents (in contrast, for instance to bureaucratic orders).[5] Governmental responsibility has to do with the ability of legislators to give rational, i.e., universalizable, justifications for their public decisions. And as Sunstein observes: "The [Madisonian] requirement that measures be justified rather than simply fought for has a disciplining effect on the sorts of measures that can be proposed and enacted. At the same time, the requirement will make it more likely that citizens and legislators will act for public-regarding reasons" (Sunstein 1993, p. 200).[6]

Undergirding Madison's defense of the new Constitution lay a profound insight: the process of democratic politics is, or should be, what I have already referred to as a "creative discovery procedure." If, as democratic or republican theory would have it, the people are indeed sovereign, then there must exist various forums in which the "sovereign will" (as Rousseau would have said) can be worked out and be made known (since it cannot be said to be known – or even to exist – until it has been articulated in an appropriately democratic manner). In the last analysis, this can only be done if (as Locke had already said) a civil society provides itself with a supreme legislative authority, operating in conformity to the rules of communicative rationality. As Madison wrote in *The Federalist*, No. 10:

> The effect of [the delegation of the government to a small number of citizens elected by the rest] is, on the one hand, to refine and enlarge the public views, by passing them through the medium of a chosen body of citizens, whose wisdom may best discern the true interest of their country, and whose patriotism and love of justice will be least likely to sacrifice it to temporary or partial considerations. Under such a regulation, it may well happen that the public voice, pronounced by the representatives of the people, will be more consonant to the public good than if pronounced by the people themselves, convened for the purpose.

Just as in economic matters (as we shall see in the following chapter) it cannot be assumed that people's tastes and preferences are at any given moment fully defined ("given") such that, in theory at least, a Central Planning Committee could, in a purely instrumental-calculative fashion, solve the "problem of coordination" as it arises in the economic realm, so likewise it cannot be assumed that in social-political matters citizens know exactly what it is they want – such that government could be turned over to a Board of Expert Administrators whose sole job would be that of collecting and collating ("aggregating") popular opinion (by means, for instance, of public opinion polls, interactive TV, or "electronic town hall meetings" à la Ross Perot).[7] People, either as economic agents or as citizens, are not Robinson Crusoes, atomistic individuals living separately on far-flung islands in the vast oceans of the world. Given the intersubjective nature of subjectivity itself, no one can be said truly to know exactly what it is that he or she thinks or, for that matter, even wants (especially when this concerns the common good) except by engaging in communicative rationality with other individuals. From a hermeneutical-philosophical point of view, people cannot be said to have opinions of their own until they have "tried them out on others" (and the nature and extent of the discussion community involved will often function to determine the "rightness" or "soundness" of the opinions in question). The entire *raison d'être* of "Madisonian republicanism"[8] was that government should be so devised ("contrived," as eighteenth-century writers were wont to say) so as to be able, structurally, to perform this "creative discovery procedure" and to serve as a supreme, overarching (beholden to no particular "factional" interest) forum of communicative rationality. As Sunstein very aptly observes in this regard: "[Madisonian] politics has, at the heart of its functions, the selection, evaluation, and shaping of preferences not simply their implementation." The presupposition involved here is of course that there is "something like a 'common good' or 'public interest' that is distinct from the aggregation of private preferences or utilities" (Sunstein 1993, p. 199).[9]

Madison's way of envisaging democracy for America represented a radical innovation in democratic theory. The idea of the deliberative republic as an institutionalization of communicative rationality is arguably the single most important development in the theory of democracy in modern political philosophy, even though its significance continues even to this day to go largely unappreciated. Unlike Madison, modern thinkers had (as, indeed, they continue to do) defined democracy as a regime designed to express or represent *the will of the people*. From Rousseau to Rawls, theorists of democracy have portrayed the problem of democracy as if it were the problem of aggregating the many separate wills of the individuals making up society in such a way as to arrive at the common or general will (reconciling in this way private interest and the public good). There are two major problems with this "will-centered" way of envisaging democracy, as Madison implicitly recognized.

The first problem is of a political nature. It is that of reconciling liberalism and democracy. Reliance on the notion of the general will, the "will of the people," or some such notion is quite simply incapable of guaranteeing that the democracy that prevails will be a *liberal* democracy. There is no intrinsic reason why the majority, or even the totality, of the citizenry should "will" liberal ("democratic") values. Democracy conceived of as an expression of the "general will" can equally well serve to underwrite populist (pseudo) democracy and cannot therefore provide an adequate theoretical basis with which to defend such liberal notions as civil liberties and human rights. This is reason enough to reject any theory of democracy whose centerpiece is the notion of the will.

The other problem with the traditional, will-centered way of formulating the problem of democracy is of a more philosophical sort, having to do with the very notion of human nature. As I argued above, there is, hermeneutically or epistemologically speaking, absolutely no justification for assuming that individuals have a well-defined "will" of their own prior to engaging in communicative rationality. In the words of Bernard Manin, "The free individual is not one who already knows absolutely what he wants, but one who has incomplete preferences and is trying by means of interior deliberation and dialogue with others to determine precisely what he does want" (Manin 1994, p. 197). The "problem of democracy" – how, as Rousseau put it, can the General Will be also *my* will? – will remain, as it has throughout all of modern times, intractable so long as it is assumed, as Manin says in his critique of Rousseau, that "individuals are already supposed to know what they want when they come to a public assembly to decide in common" (ibid., p. 190). The fact of the matter, as Manin points out, is that Rousseau's

81

citizens do not *deliberate* (see ibid., p. 191). Nor, Manin argues, do Rawls's individuals deliberate (as Aristotle and classical rhetoric would have understood this term); like *homo economicus* of neoclassical economics (as theorized for example in Rational Expectations Theory), they are mere "optimizing," calculating machines. What must be criticized in the theories of thinkers such as Rawls and Rousseau, Manin maintains, is "the assumption that individuals in society, in particular, those having to make a political decision, possess an already formed will, already know exactly what they want, and at most only need to apply their criteria of evaluation to the proposed solutions" (ibid., p. 193). And thus as Manin concludes, "We must affirm, at the risk of contradicting a long tradition, that legitimate law is the *result of general deliberation*, and not the *expression of the general will*" (ibid., p. 194).

This, I would argue, was precisely what Madison was seeking to "affirm" (to use Manin's term). Madison's great contribution to political philosophy was to have outlined a theory of democracy based not on the will but on *reason*.[10] Moreover, the view of reason with which he was working was not the traditional metaphysical conception of reason (still appealed to today by Rational Expectations Theory) according to which reason is a "faculty" of the "mind" for discovering "objective" or "demonstrable" truths. It was, rather, an Aristotelian-rhetorical view of reason, according to which rational deliberation consists in arriving at conclusions (agreements) that can be justified or argued for in a "persuasive" or communicatively rational ('reasonable") manner.[11] What is all-important in this view of rational deliberation[12] is not, as Manin says, the "predetermined will [of individuals] but the *process* by which they determine their will" (Manin 1994, p. 197, emphasis added). As we have seen in our discussion of the cultural order, and as we shall seek to show with regard to both the political and economic orders, the notion of process or procedure is absolutely crucial in determining the true meaning of democratic practice.

Madison's notion of "deliberative democracy" was, to be sure, an ideal (though by no means a utopian one). Although Madison's Constitution was in fact ratified, it never did function entirely in the way it was meant to, and the Anti-Federalists have had, in a way, their revenge. In the United States populist demands for more "direct democracy" – more referenda, limited terms in office, mandatory sentencing in judicial matters, and so on – have never abated. Indeed, a great many of the demands for direct democracy have been incorporated into the American political system, and this has had a decidedly negative effect on the first requirement of good government: stability and responsibility.[13] Like many others, American governments at both the state and federal levels find themselves increasingly incapable of governing, that is, of formulating a coherent and generally acceptable vision of the common good (the "vision thing," as President Bush referred to what he notably lacked). As Sunstein remarks, "We are far from Madison's deliberative democracy. Indeed, the evidence suggests that the factional

82

struggle that Madison sought to escape more closely captures politics as it is generally practiced" (Sunstein 1993, p. 190). In our supposedly "civilized," G-7 countries, politics is once more tending to degenerate into a Hobbesian "war of all against all," as Havel, the leader of a new, self-regenerating civil socity, pointed out (see Havel 1992d, and p. 33 of this volume). It is in any event now abundantly clear, as Tocqueville long ago pointed out, that the unrestrained pursuit of equality in either of its pernicious forms – equalism (equality of social conditions) or democratism (equal access to, or representation in, deliberative bodies) – is a pathology of the democratic body, which can remain healthy only if it counterbalances social welfare with individual liberties.

Madison's overriding concern in proposing the design for the constitution that he did was to cope with the dangers of "faction," which he defined as "a number of citizens, whether amounting to a majority or minority of the whole, who are united and actuated by some common impulse of passion, or of interest, adverse to the rights of other citizens, or to the permanent and aggregate interests of the community" (*The Federalist* No. 10, here and in what follows, unless otherwise indicated). His goal in this regard was that of setting up institutional means of *controlling* or *regulating* the pernicious effects of faction ("to break and control the violence of faction"), not that of *eliminating* faction altogether. To eliminate faction, Madison said, would necessitate either the complete elimination of liberty – liberty being, as he recognized, that which gives rise to differences of opinions in the first place ("different interests necessarily result from the liberty meant to be secured" [Madison 1984, p. 194]) – or "giving to every citizen the same opinions, the same passions, and the same interests." The latter option would amount to as utopian a project as the socialist one of creating a socially harmonious *homo sovieticus*, and Madison was nothing if he was not a firm opponent of political utopianism.[14]

Madison's opposition to direct democracy stemmed from his overriding concern to control the effects of "faction." Assiduous students of history that they were, it was the opinion of both Madison and Hamilton that the unrestrained or unmediated spirit of faction had always been the chief factor in the downfall of all previous democratic or self-governing ("republican") regimes. As Hamilton remarked in *The Federalist*, No. 9: "It is impossible to read the history of the petty republics of Greece and Italy without feeling sensations of horror and disgust at the distractions with which they were continually agitated, and at the rapid succession of revolutions by which they were kept in a state of perpetual vibration between the extremes of tyranny and anarchy." Or as Madison wrote in *The Federalist*, No. 10:

Hence it is that such democracies have ever been spectacles of turbulence and contention; have ever been found incompatible with personal security or the rights of property; and have in general been as short in their lives as they have been violent in their deaths. Theoretic politicians, who have patronized this species of government, have erroneously supposed that by reducing mankind to a perfect equality in their political rights, they would, at the same time, be perfectly equal and assimilated in their possessions, their opinions, and their passions.

And thus, as Madison also stated:

The friend of popular governments never finds himself so much alarmed for their character and fate, as when he contemplates their propensity to this dangerous vice. . . . The instability, injustice, and confusion introduced into the public councils, have, in truth, been the mortal diseases under which popular governments have every-where perished; as they continue to be the favorite and fruitful topics from which the adversaries to liberty derive their most specious declamations.[15]

His opposition to the anti-republicans ("the adversaries to liberty") notwith-standing, Madison freely admittted that the greatest danger menacing "popular government" was that of "faction," and, like liberal thinkers ever since, he realized full well that the most dangerous faction of all is that of "an interested and overbearing majority."[16] A "pure democracy" (mere majority rule), Madison declared, "can admit of no cure for mischiefs of faction." The most insidious form of tyranny is in fact the "tyranny of the majority" (a notion subsequently picked up and developed by Alexis de Tocqueville). In a "pure democracy" the concept of *human rights* (the rights of individuals and of minorities) would – given the natural tendency on the part of humans towards intolerance of dissenting opinions and towards "otherness" in general – tend readily to become an altogether meaningless concept. The only form of government appropriate to a civil society is thus that of representative or parliamentary democracy, not direct or "participa-tory" democracy. This is something that the citizens of the former socialist countries of Eastern Europe realized full well; the Easterners in this regard were altogether more theoretically sophisticated than our Western radicals who go on blithely calling for "greater democracy." The Easterners at least knew their Madison.[17] Alain Touraine, *doyen* of French sociology, sums up nicely the lessons of recent history when he states:

It is now impossible to speak of direct democracy, of people's power or even workers' control without immediately conjuring up the very real figure of the totalitarian party, with its authoritarian militants, the arrogant mediocrity of its petty bureaucrats, and the suffocatingly ponderous calls for the unity of people and nation.

(Touraine 1995, pp. 329–30)

John Stuart Mill had it perfectly right when, over a hundred years earlier, he stated that the "ideally best form of government will be found in some one or other variety of the Representative System" (Mill 1958, p. 36).

In addition to concerns of a practical nature of the sort mentioned above (the preservation of individual liberties and rights; stable, effective, and responsible government), the very widespread (and, one is tempted to say, unthinking) call for "more democracy" in our political institutions is worrisome for purely theoretical reasons. It betrays a lack of understanding of what genuine democratic "agreement" must actually be. Agreement in the political sphere can never be more than what it is in the cultural sphere; it can never mean consensus in the idealistic, Habermasian sense of the term. In political matters, all references to "unanimity" and "uniformity of interests" (as Madison would say) must be avoided, since these are recipes for either authoritarian or totalitarian government. A genuinely democratic civil society is characterized not so much by consensus (in the Rousseauian or Habermasian sense) as by dissent and dissensus (a "conflictual" state of affairs which is nevertheless regulated by a *procedural* consensus as to the "rules of the game" – the essence of party politics).[18] Paul Ricoeur expresses this point very well when, alluding to Claude Lefort, he says, "Democracy . . . is that regime which accepts its contradictions to the point of institutionalizing conflict" (Ricoeur 1991, p. 174). This is, to be sure, no utopic view of society, for it means, as Ricoeur also points out, that "Democracy is the regime for which the process of its own legitimation is always in flux and always in crisis" (ibid., p. 277).

From the point of view of political philosophy, the greatest defect in the idea of direct or "participatory" democracy is that it is the most direct (so to speak) expression of the "politics of the will" discussed above. A powerful siren call for many on both the Left and the Right, direct democracy – which must, in practice, reduce to plebiscitary, populist democracy (as Cronin [1989] points out) – is nevertheless the simulacrum of true democracy. In a book appropriately entitled *Democracy on Trial,* Jean Bethke Elshtain takes to task those proponents of "pure democracy" who advocate as a solution to the malaise of our present-day democracies a more direct expression of the people's will, by means for instance of instant plebiscites via interactive television ("televoting"). As she rightly points out, "plebiscitary majoritarianism is quite different from a democratic polity sustained by debate and judgment" (Elshtain 1995, p. 28). She goes on to say:

> The distinction between a democratic and a plebiscitary system is no idle one. In a plebiscitary system, the views of the majority can more easily swamp minority or unpopular views. Plebiscitarianism is compatible with authoritarian politics carried out under the guise of, or with the connivance of, majority opinion. That opinion can be registered

ritualistically, so there is no need for debate with one's fellow citizens on substantive questions. All that is required is a calculus of opinion.

(Elshtain 1995, p. 29)

The "deliberative republic" as advocated by Madison cannot be based, as Elshtain says, on a "compilation of opinions." What alone makes "genuine choice, hence democracy, possible," Elshtain points out, are those civic virtues Madisonian democracy was designed to promote, viz., "deliberation, reason, judgment, and shared goodwill" (ibid., p. 30).

Despite what some of its more enthusiastic apostles (the "cyber utopians") would have us believe (see for instance Grossman 1995), the new Electronic Age does not herald a qualitative change in the basic principles of democratic politics. While such things as the "information highway" have the potentiality of enlarging the public realm (by extending already-existing means of communication) and increasing democratic input into the workings of government, electronic interaction – which indeed makes something like direct democracy more feasible – can never dispense with the need for *deliberative politics*. (This includes the need for important decisions to be arrived at not by poll-taking but by select, democratically responsible committees.)[19] The smaller a community is, and the further down on the level of subsidiarity it is (the notion of subsidiarity will be discussed below), the more direct forms of democracy have a legitimate role to play, but even at the most basic level (e.g., New England town hall meetings), the will of the communal majority must always be subject to oversight and override by higher authority (the judiciary in particular), lest the rights of individuals and minorities be violated.

A democratic, civil society, being by nature pluralistic, is inevitably marked by what Mill called an "antagonism of opinion" or what Ricoeur calls "a conflict of interpretations." What nevertheless makes such a society *democratic* is the way in which these "differends" are dealt with, i.e., with civility. It is the civic virtue of reasoned debate and goodwill that the Madisonian system of government was explicitly designed to promote.

Although, like many other eighteenth-century thinkers, Madison was working out of the tradition of civic humanism (civic republicanism) and, accordingly, thought (rather uncritically) that good government was most likely to result from the deliberations of "enlightened statesmen ... whose wisdom may best discern the true interest of their country, and whose patriotism and love of justice will be least likely to sacrifice it to temporary or partial considerations" (*The Federalist*, No. 10) his theory of government was nevertheless based on a solid anthropology or philosophy of human nature. This is an anthropology which is perfectly in line with that defended by John Paul II (see p. 18) and which upholds the principle of human dignity. And as in the case of John Paul II, it is a distinctly non-socialist anthropology – without

86

being, for all that, a specifically "Christian anthropology." According to the Madisonian theory of human nature, human beings, while being neither intrinsically good nor intrinsically bad, are nevertheless capable of good government when, in good will and in a spirit of communicative rationality, they put their minds to it. As Madison wrote in *The Federalist*, No. 55: "As there is a degree of depravity in mankind which requires a certain degree of circumspection and distrust, so there are other qualities in human nature which justify a certain portion of esteem and confidence. Republican government presupposes the existence of these qualities in a higher degree than any other form." Alluding to Hobbes (and, one is tempted to say, anachronistically, to contemporary game theorists), Madison went on to say that this should not be taken to mean "that there is not sufficient virtue among men for self-government; and that nothing less than the chains of despotism can restrain them from destroying and devouring one another."[20] Madison was as distant from Hobbesian pessimism as he was from Rousseauian optimism (humans are neither angels nor beasts, he said). To borrow an expression from Alexander Hamilton, Madison was a "man disposed to view human nature as it is, without either flattering its virtues or exaggerating its vices" (*The Federalist*, No. 76). The purpose of "deliberative democracy," as Madison sought to institutionalize it in the American Constitution, is the altogether realistic and humanistic one of creating and cultivating the social/political *institutions* ("effectual procedures," as Madison referred to them in *The Federalist*, No. 57) which call forth from people, in the actual exercise of their lives in common, all the communicative rationality they are capable of. As Sunstein observes: "The structural provisions of the Constitution attempted to bring about public-spirited representation, to provide safeguards in its absence, and to ensure an important measure of popular control" (Sunstein 1993, p. 185) As he also says, "the structure of government should lead political actors to pursue a general public good" (ibid., p. 201).

Although, as I mentioned, Madison held on to some degree to the traditional view that good government is most likely to be expected from good ("virtuous," as the civic republicans would say) statesmen, he was under no illusions in this regard. "Enlightened statesmen," he said, "will not always be at the helm." Accordingly, the Constituion he helped to write was intended to operate under the assumption that "the spirit of party and faction [will be involved] in the necessary and ordinary operations of government." Thus, as I have attempted to point out, Madison did not wish to rely on "representatives whose enlightened views and virtuous sentiments render them superior to the local prejudices and to schemes of injustice"; rather, good government was to be assured in the last resort by "the greater obstacles opposed to the concert and accomplishment of the secret wishes of an unjust and interested majority." As Edmond Morgan has observed: "No constitutional device could offer complete protection against the ingenuity of human corruption; what a constitution had to do was make betrayal as difficult as possible" (Morgan 1993, p. 27; and see, more extensively, Morgan 1988).

In line with his altogether un-Rousseauian view of human nature, Madison, in accordance with his "policy of *supplying, by opposite and rival interests, the defect of better motives* (emphasis added)," stated in a much remarked upon text in *The Federalist*, No. 51:

> Ambition must be made to counteract ambition. The interest of the man must be connected with the constitutional rights of the place. It may be a reflection on human nature, that such devices should be necessary to control the abuses of government. But what is government itself, but the greatest of all reflections on human nature? If men were angels, no government would be necessary. If angels were to govern men, neither external nor internal controls on government would be necessary. In framing a government which is to be administered by men over men, the great difficulty lies in this: you must first enable the government to control the governed [this was the great lesson that Madison and the other framers of the Constitution of 1787 drew from the abysmal failure of the first American republic to function properly and effectively]; and in the next place oblige it to control itself. A dependence on the people is, no doubt, the primary control on the government; but experience has taught mankind the necessity of auxiliary precautions.

To put the matter in a more positive way, the function of politics in both the government sphere and the public sphere more generally should be that of encouraging a free and open deliberative process and a creative discovery procedure whereby the "people's will" is not simply "reflected" or "represented" but is actually *constituted*. Although he is among the ranks of those who today, uncritically and somewhat naively, call for greater "participatory" democracy, the institutionalist and neo-Marxist economist Geoffrey Hodgson is certainly on the right track when he asserts that "a crucial problem is to establish flexible and open institutions through which human needs can be articulated, clarified, evaluated and prioritized. . . . [It is] a matter of enhancing democracy within society so that this educative process can flourish" (Hodgson 1988, p. 252). This raises the whole question of the extent and function of the public realm in civil society, a question to which we must now turn.

THE PUBLIC REALM: PRIVATE INTERESTS AND THE PUBLIC GOOD

I take it as axiomatic that the only acceptable politics in the political realm of a civil society (excluding the bureaucracy, which necessarily operates mainly in accordance with the rules of instrumental rationality) is that of communicative rationality. To the degree that legislatures and governments in existing civil societies do not meet this requirement, they should be subject to "constitutional revolution," as Public Choice theorist James Buchanan would say (see Buchanan 1975). Government in a civil society is, however, only one part of the story. While national legislatures may be viewed as the highest forums (or courts of last resort) for the discussion of public/social issues, they are by no means the only ones – or even, given the postmodern information and communication revolutions, the most significant ones. While civil societies, where they exist, would be considerably enhanced were legislatures and parliamentary procedures reformed in order better to conform to the Madisonian ideal of deliberative government, the most significant area, in Western democracies above all, in which the forces of civil society are today most operative is *outside* the realm of government altogether.

Some decades ago social scientists came out with the theory that politics is simply a matter of elites vying for citizens' votes, citizens who otherwise remain inactive or purely passive in political matters. According to the "science model" (as Lindblom aptly refers to it [see Lindblom 1990, p. 223]), politics on the part of the general citizenry reduces to a matter of casting votes every once in a while in support of this or that "elite." This scientistic view (contrasting greatly with the earlier more liberal-philosophical view defended by Knight; see p. 78 above) was most famously articulated by Joseph Schumpeter in 1942. In his *Capitalism, Socialism and Democracy*, an immensely influential work, Schumpeter set out to debunk what he called the "classical doctrine of democracy" (based on such supposedly obsolete notions as the common good and the will of the people) and to substitute in its place a more "scientific" theory of democracy which he labelled "competition for political leadership." The "nutshell" definition of his new theory went as follows: "[T]he democratic method is that institutional arrangement for arriving at political decisions in which individuals acquire the power to decide by means of a competitive struggle for the people's vote" (Schumpeter 1976, p. 269). If this "empirical" definition does not altogether reduce the *public realm* to nothing more than the realm of *government*, it does nevertheless reduce the political aspects of the public realm to nothing more than occasional vote-casting.

Although Schumpeter's "updated" theory of democracy might well have been attractive to the new class of social scientists who were just then beginning to make their appearance on the public scene and although he had an altogether valid point in remarking (as I already have) that citizens' preferences must not be assumed to be given (such that they can simply be "represented"),[21] his "new" theory was nevertheless manifestly erroneous. And, in this particular matter, it must be said that the continued and on-going failure of "social science" to deal with the really important questions of social/political life has, of course, in no way interfered with the ability of social scientists to command government funding at the expense, and to the great detriment, of other forms of humanistic inquiry.

Whatever social/political "scientists" might, or might not, say, in a genuine civil society, politics, as it functions in the wider public realm, amounts to a great deal more than passively participating in election campaigns. In the United States, for instance, where a genuine civil society and its concomitant public realm has now existed for over two hundred years, one group which had immense effects on legislation was the women's movement for welfare reform active in the late nineteeth and early twentieth centuries, *even though at that time no woman had the right of vote.* Their voice was, nonetheless, distinctly heard in Congress (see Brinkley 1994).[22] What this fact points up is a most essential one: *in a civil society the public/ political realm is much wider than the realm of government per se.*[23] Perhaps, therefore, the term best suited to refer to the public realm of a civil society (including politics in the more narrow sense, i.e., government) is the old Aristotelian one: the *polity* (*politea*).

In a democratic polity one will find not only political parties vying for the vote (which they do, not just sporadically, as the "Schumpeterians" might say, but on an ongoing, continual basis – the only exception to this being miniscule parties, such as the Rhinoceros Party of Canada which usually puts a friendly beaver or caribou up for election and which only comes out of the woodwork when federal elections are called) but also a host of social movements trying, at every moment, to make themselves heard to both the government and society at large. Charter 77 in Czechoslovakia and Solidarity in Poland were only two of the more noteworthy of such social movements. The more developed a society is, politically and economically, the more one can expect (in accordance with the fundamental democratic principle of "freedom of association") a proliferation of different groups acting directly in (and on) the public realm.[24] These include professional associations such as the American Medical Association and demographic organizations such as the American Association of Retired Persons, business or producer associations, labor unions, farmers' lobbies, civic associations, church-related and other communal groups, grassroots movements of one sort or another (concentrating their efforts at the local, state, or federal level), recreational groups (such as the Sierra Club and the National Rifle Association), and a host of various interest-based, issue-oriented political action groups (environment, women's rights, gay rights, animal rights, consumer advocacy, prisoner rights, etc., etc.). In general, civil society comprehends just about every group organized around a social/ political goal or statement of principle. Citizens can be members of different groups at the same time,[25] and, in an electronic age, a wide range of means is available for "networking" both within and among groups.[26] This "social separation of powers," as Robert Dahl once called it (see Dahl 1956, p. 83), represents an immense, multivoiced, polycentric or "decentered" civic conversation, one which leaves its multiple impressions on the public realm and which inevitably, to one degree or another, resounds

90

in the halls of the houses of government. It also amounts to a kind of free-wheeling "political entrepreneurship" and a genuine creative discovery procedure.

Thus, the *public realm* of civil society includes, in addition to the government (the "state," as it is often, though erroneously, called) every group in civil society which, however organized or unorganized it might be, brings popular sentiment to bear on issues of common concern. Thus, purely "recreational" groups (to allude to Larry Diamond's unduly restricted definition of civil society referred to in Chapter 2), can, and in fact do, have a decided impact on political decision-making. One simply cannot say, as Diamond does, that because one's doings are merely "recreationally" or "spiritually" motivated they therefore do not fall under the rubric of "civil society." The "pro-Life," anti-abortion people are most assuredly motivated by purely "spiritual" concerns of a "private," religious nature; but who would dare to say that this particular group of people is not a most potent political force in civil society at the present time? In all things human, it is not motivation *per se* that is the supremely important factor; it is what people *do*. And, to a great extent, whatever their motivation for doing it might be (spiritual, recreational, etc.), what people do, is, in its effects and significance, *political*. In a civil society politics is an immensely great deal more than what professional politicians do. As Chantal Mouffe rightly observes: "[T]he political cannot be restricted to a certain type of institution, or envisaged as constituting a specific sphere or level of society. It must be conceived as a dimension that is inherent in every human society and that determines our very ontological condition" (Mouffe 1993, p. 3).[27]

The point I wish to make is that in the contemporary situation, and in the established democracies, the public realm of civil society has been so widened out that the governmental sphere (the political sphere, in the narrow sense of the term) now occupies but a small part of it. Government is, and will always be, the "court of last resort," but increasingly it is taking its deliberative bearings from discussions pursued in the wider realm of civil society.[28] This diffusion of the discussion process throughout civil society is perfectly in line with Madisonian republicanism. Like all liberals – and like his American contemporaries who had just fought a lengthy, bloody war in order to secure their own liberties – Madison, like Montesquieu before him and like liberals ever afterwards, was concerned with the issue of *power* and the question of how best to control its uses and abuses (this was a constant and overriding theme in his contributions to *The Federalist Papers*). The "solutions" to the abuse of power (and thus to the creation of responsible, deliberative government) that he built into his constitutional draft were multiform: they included above all the "separation of powers" between the legislative, executive, and judicial branches of government (a lesson he had learned from Montesquieu), as well as the separation of federal (national) from state (local) government,[29] and, above all, the *federal* system of government itself (his own unique contribution to political theory).[30] In a large, "federal" or "national" goverment, Madison argued, one could expect factions to multiply greatly. Far from being a cause for alarm, however, this proliferation of factions to be expected in any large country makes for the possibility of real (republican) democracy. As Madison stated: "Extend the sphere [of society], and you take in a greater variety of parties and interests; you make it less probable that a majority of the whole will have a common motive to invade the rights of other citizens; or if such a common motive exists, it will be more difficult for all who feel it to discover their own strength, and to act in unison with each other."

Madison returned to this theme in *The Federalist*, No. 51. "It is of great importance in a republic," he insisted, "not only to guard society against the oppression of its rulers, but to guard one part of society against the injustice of the other part." And there is, he argued, only one method for doing so consonant with a free or democratic society. He wrote:

> Whilst all authority in it [the federal republic] will be derived from and dependent on the society, the society itself will be broken into so many parts, interests and classes of citizens, that the rights of individuals, or of the minority, will be in little danger from interested combinations of the majority. In a free government the security for civil rights must be the same as that for religious rights. It consists in the one case in the multiplicity of interests, and in the other in the multiplicity of sects. The degree of security in both cases will depend on the number of interests and sects; and this may be presumed to depend on the extent of country and number of people comprehended under the same government.

In other words, Madison, like Tocqueville after him, was saying that there is really only one remedy to the problems to which democracy is incident, and this is quite simply more democracy – but of a kind compatible with representational, republican government: "In the extent and proper structure of the Union, therefore, we behold a republican remedy for the diseases most incident to republican government" (*The Federalist*, No. 10).[31]

Madison's proposed solution to the problem of reconciling democratic (majority) rule and the maintenance of civil liberties and human rights (on the part of individuals and minorities) was thus a reliance on *pluralism*, in terms of governmental organization and social structure.[32] It was his belief that although people are naturally prone to pursue their own interests, the pursuit of self-interest is not, in and of itself, inimical to the public good. In line with the philosophical anthropology to which he subscribed, he held that, given the appropriate governmental and social arrangements, people can display "sufficient virtue . . . for self-government." This is the problem of social synergy, of the reconciliation of private interest and the public good.

To paraphrase Madison, in a socialist paradise there would be no need for the institutions or structural arrangements of civil society, since people would be sufficiently other-regarding that they could be expected to respect the rights of others out of the generosity of their hearts; in a Hobbesian state of nature, in contrast, people would have no incentive to respect the liberties of others, since they would be so insecure in their own situation that it would be in their own narrow self-interest to pursue their interests howsoever they could, by hook or by crook, which would invariably be to the great detriment of the interests of others. The reason for instituting civil society is not the idealistic one of producing truly good people, in the moral or religious sense of the term; it is the altogether more realistic and more feasible one of, as Madison would say, "supplying by opposite and rival interests the defect of better motives." The reason for institutionalizing human rights in the form of civil society is to enable people to pursue their own interests and to work for the betterment of their condition in peace and tranquility and in a manner which allows everyone else to do likewise.[33]

One may legitimately expect that the public interest will prevail when people, pursuing their own interests, nevertheless respect the rights of others to do likewise, when indeed everyone realizes that rights are mutual and that freedom is indivisible. As Havel has insisted: "Human rights are universal and indivisible. Human freedom is also indivisible: if it is denied to anyone in the world, it is therefore denied, indirectly, to all people" (Havel, 1992b, p. 98). Although they are working mainly out of a Habermasian context, the views of Cohen and Arato regarding the new social movements, such as feminism and environmentalism, are basically Madisonian in that, unlike Seligman (1992) for instance, they view the emergence of these new movements not as a symptom of civil decay but, on the contrary, as dynamic elements contributing to a rejuvenated civil society (see Cohen and Arato 1992, as well as Arato and Cohen 1992).

When diverse groups pursue their own interests while at the same time respecting the right of others to do likewise, one can indeed expect that what Gadamer calls "social reason" will likely prevail (what in *The Federalist*, No. 10 Madison referred to as "the rules of justice and the rights of the minor party"). This is also what Gadamer refers to as "solidarity," the form of solidarity that is constitutive of civil society.

This form of solidarity is not, to be sure, solidarity as Socialism understood it; it is not *substantive* (everyone working in unison and altruistically with and for everyone else on commonly prescribed goals dictated by the state or an overbearing majority of PCers) but *procedural* (every one working for whatever they want to work for, separately or in free association with like-minded individuals, with nevertheless a respect for others to do likewise, so long as no one violates the rights of others in this regard and, in fact, actively

93

respects the rights of others to work for their own self-aggrandizement within an overarching recognition of universal human rights). A "substantive," communitarian understanding of solidarity and of the public good may be appropriate to small-scale communities, but it is a guaranteed recipe for tyranny in large-scale societies. The only common imperative in a civil society is the equal liberty of all to pursue their own interests, so long as they do so in a manner respectful of the rights and liberties of others. The Madisonian tactic in this regard is to rely on "the private interest of every individual" to be "a sentinel over the public rights" (see *The Federalist*, No. 51). Solidarity of this sort is, as a matter of fact, more likely to be realized when there exists throughout society a multiplicity of diverse "factions," since their very existence serves to thwart the emergence of mass movements of a populist and demagogic sort – the sort of thing that is most inimical to the maintenance of a *liberal* democracy.

The solidarity and social reason characteristic of civil society is perhaps best summed up in Kant's ingenious notion of "unsocial sociability" (see Kant, "Ideas for a Universal History", 1963a, pp. 15–17; here and in what follows). What Kant called "a lawful order of men" and "a civic society" results, he said, from the "antagonism" of men in society. Kant's view on this matter, paradoxical though it might at first appear, expresses a profound truth. Norberto Bobbio has in fact characterized Kant's notion of unsocial sociability as an "explosive judgment," "a judgment which might well be viewed as capturing the heart of liberal thinking" (Bobbio 1990, p. 23). By "antagonism" Kant meant: "The unsocial sociability of men, i.e., their propensity to enter into society, bound together with a mutual opposition which constantly threatens to break up the society" (Kant 1963a, pp. 15–17). Unsociability means that everyone wishes "to have everything go according to his own wish." Of course, as Kant recognized, everyone also knows that in this regard they can expect opposition from everyone else. But this is precisely what calls forth exertions on the part of individuals and which, accordingly, results in the advance of civilization. It is as though Kant had the socialist utopic view of social harmony in mind when he wrote:

> Without those in themselves unamiable characteristics of unsociability
> from which opposition springs – characteristics each man must find in
> his own selfish pretensions – all talents would remain hidden, unborn
> in an Arcadian shepherd's life, with all its concord, contentment, and
> mutual affection. Men, good-natured as the sheep they herd, would
> hardly reach a higher worth than their beasts; they would not fill the
> empty place in creation by achieving their end, which is rational nature.
> Thanks be to Nature, then, for the incompatibility, for heartless competitive vanity, for the insatiable desire to possess and to rule! Without

94

them, all the excellent natural capacities of humanity would forever sleep, undeveloped. . . . The natural urges to this, the sources of unsociableness and mutual opposition from which so many evils arise, drive men to new exertions of their forces and thus to the manifold development of their capacities.

(Kant 1963a, pp. 15–17)

Kant's point, in other words, was that when individuals are accorded the human right to develop freely and as best they can their own "abilities and talents" (as the *Déclaration des droits de l'homme* of 1789 put it), "opposition" and "unsociability" will arise,[34] but this unsociability is nevertheless of a positive, "social" sort in that in the long run it advances civilization and contributes, both spiritually and materially, to the overall common good and the well-being of humankind – what today's economists would call "social welfare." The society with the greatest freedom, Kant said, "is one in which there is mutual opposition among the members, together with the most exact definition of freedom and fixing of its limits so that it may be consistent with the freedom of others."[35] As Kant insisted, "All culture, art which adorns mankind, and the finest social order are fruits of unsociableness, which forces itself to discipline itself."

When Kant speaks of man's unsocial sociability as the means employed by "Nature" for the collective betterment of humanity (Kant speaks, in this regard, of "a secret mechanism of Nature"), one is reminded of nothing so much as the notion of the Invisible Hand put forward by one of his own contemporaries. The general well-being requires the solidarity of all, but this solidarity, Adam Smith argued, does not require that indivduals renounce their own interest and act instead out of "benevolence." In a passage become famous he wrote:

In civilized society [man] stands at all times in need of the cooperation and assistance of great multitudes, while his whole life is scarce sufficient to gain the friendship of a few persons. . . . [M]an has almost constant occasion for the help of his brethren, and it is in vain to expect it from their benevolence only. . . . It is not from the benevolence of the butcher, the brewer, or the baker, that we expect our dinner, but from their regard to their own interest. We address ourselves not to their humanity but to their self-love, and never talk to them of our own necessities but their advantages. Nobody but a beggar chuses to depend chiefly upon the benevolence of his fellow-citizens.

(Smith 1979, I, pp. 26–27)

As we shall see in greater detail in the following chapter, it is by means of the coordination made possible by the market economy of a civil society that, as Smith said, "every individual necessarily labours to render the annual revenue of the society [the common good in economic terms] as great as he

95

can" (Smith 1979, I, p. 456). Naturally, Smith observed, this need be no part of the individual's intentions. As Smith said: "He generally, indeed, neither intends to promote the publick interest, nor knows how much he is promoting it. . . . [H]e intends only his own security . . . and he is in this, as in many other cases, led by an invisible hand to promote an end which was no part of his intention" (ibid.).

The metaphor of the Invisible Hand has been much maligned, but it nevertheless aptly expresses what is fundamentally the case in this matter of social synergy: it is the actual (constitutional, so to speak) arrangement of civil society – what Kant called "a perfectly just civic constitution" – that brings about the desired result, not altruistic self-sacrifice on the part of its members. Madison, Kant, and Smith were in remarkable agreement on this matter (like liberals in general, they were cognizant of what Hegel was later to call the "cunning of reason"): provide the appropriate institutions that will guarantee to people their individual freedoms and rights, and people, in their own interest, will behave in what amounts to a socially cooperative way without any need for an overarching state to coordinate their activities.[36] In arguing for civil society on the basis of reason (and the cunning of reason), Madison, Kant, and Smith effected a decisive advance over earlier thought, that represented for instance by Adam Ferguson who in his famous essay on civil society of 1767 had sought to base civil society on the "moral sense," i.e., on a supposedly natural propensity in humans towards "affections of kindness and friendship" (Ferguson 1980, p. 35). In contrast to Ferguson and to the old tradition of civic humanism that he represented, Madison, Kant, and Smith sought to base the possibility of civil society not on "a benevolent heart" but on enlightened reason.[37]

The basic point that these three great thinkers of the Enlightenment were trying to make must not, however, be misconstrued. What each of them was attempting to argue, each in his own way, was that a decent regard for one's own interests need not be hostile to or incompatible with the good of society as a whole. Indeed, as we have seen, they maintained that the situation was just the opposite. It is important, nevertheless, to be clear as to what they were most definitely *not* saying. Let us consider the case of Adam Smith. An all-too-common misreading of Smith – by friends and foes alike – presents him as maintaining that vice is the source of all virtue and that selfishness should be given free reign – in the belief, clever or naive (as the case may be), that by means of some kind of miraculous "invisible hand" private selfishness will be transmogrified into public generosity. Adam Smith was, however, no Bernard Mandeville.

In his notorious *Fable of the Bees* (1714, 1724), Mandeville submitted that "public benefits" are nothing more than the by-product, as it were, of "private vices." Mandeville's infamous thesis was deliberately cynical and altogether amoral, if not downright "immoral" or "irreligious" (suggesting, as it did, that what is commonly held to be morality is itself nothing but the accidental by-product of immoral motivations, what Mandeville unhesitatingly called "evil") (Mandeville 1970). Smith, a professor of moral philosophy, was no such preacher of egoism (see Hayek 1978, p. 268). He absolutely refused to allow, without further clarification, that the egoistic pursuit of power and luxury ("conspicuous consumption," in Veblen's later words) is in the public interest. What, in his *Theory of Moral Sentiments* (1759), Smith objected to in Mandeville was the latter's "fallacy" of representing "every passion as wholly vicious, which is so in any degree" (Skinner 1989, p. 6). "The condition of human nature," Smith stated, "were peculiarly hard, if these affections, which, by the very nature of our being, ought frequently to influence our conduct, could upon no occasion appear virtuous, or deserve esteem and commendation from anybody" (Skinner 1989, pp. 6–7).[38]

If, however, Smith differed from Mandeville, he differed also not only from his contemprary, Adam Ferguson, but also from his predecessor and teacher at the University of Glasgow, Francis Hutcheson, who extolled the altruistic virtues of benevolence, sympathy, and fellow-feeling and who maintained that self-love "was a principle which could never be virtuous in any degree or in any direction" (Skinner 1989, p. 6). Somewhat like Rousseau who had enough good sense to distinguish between *amour de soi* (self-love) and *amour propre* (pride), Smith insisted that the pursuit of self-interest, while certainly not a virtue in the "moralistic" sense of the term (i.e., self-sacrifice or self-denial), is certainly no vice either (i.e., selfishness or avariciousness). What chiefly serves to distinguish the thesis advocated by Smith, Madison, and Kant from the provocative and paradoxical thesis put forward by Mandeville (extolling "pride and luxury") is a subtle but nevertheless highly significant point, the point being, as we have seen, that the public good is best served when the interactions between individuals are regulated by enlightened self-interest or what Tocqueville was to call "self-interest rightly understood." What the metaphor of the Invisible Hand (which of course Mandeville was clearly anticipating in his own rather outlandish way) was meant to express is the idea that the public good is actually the "unintended consequence" of the pursuit of individual self-interest; or, to state the matter more precisely, the public good will best be served if the *appropriate institutional (constitutional) framework* has been created, viz., one designed to provide individuals with the legal means of working for the betterment of their own condition and which grants them all the freedom and security necessary for this.[39] To express the matter another way, and in the most succinct of fashions, *self-interest* ("self-love," or better said perhaps, *self-esteem*)[40] is not to be equated with *selfishness* or *self-centeredness* (egoism). It is *neither* the case that humans are by nature antisocial ("*homo homini lupus*," as Hobbes said) *nor* that they have a natural and overriding sense of fellow-feeling ("benevolism," as eighteenth-century thinkers such as the second Earl of Shaftesbury termed it). By nature (as Aristotle would say), humans are social animals through and through ("man" in a presocietal state of nature is unimaginable; such a creature, as Aristotle said, would be either a god or a beast but would certainly not be human); but, as Kant said, this sociability, unlike that of ants or bees, is of a peculiar, "unsocial" sort – i.e., it is precisely *as (self-interested) individuals* that humans are social in nature.

One reason why, as I said, this is such an important point is that it can serve to counteract a widely held, yet altogether erroneous, belief, the belief, namely, that unlike the supposedly altruistic nature of Socialism, "capitalism" is a system based on greed and selfishness. For instance, one regularly hears it said that while it must be admitted that Socialism has now proven to be an economic fiasco and while it must be allowed that "capitalism" is the only realistically viable system (at least for the foreseeable future), the sad fact, nevertheless, is that we have to put up with a system which caters to hedonism and avariciousness ("possessive individualism"). In response to this line of talk, it has to be said that if, as what might be called the Enlightenment Thesis maintains,[41] it is just downright stupid to argue that in providing for one's own needs and those of one's family, i.e., acting out of self-interest, one is acting "selfishly," then it is equally inane to maintain that "capitalism" – that economic system whose entire *raison d'être* is that of maximizing the abilities of individuals to do just that – is itself an "immoral" system based upon selfishness. It would, in fact, be no exaggeration to say that, precisely because "capitalism" is an institutionalized system designed to encourage cooperation among individuals and a concern for the interest of others (the reason being that in a "capitalist" system one serves one's own interests best when one serves the interests of others, e.g., one's customers) and to discourage outrightly selfish, antisocial behavior (since such behavior is economically counter-productive), "capitalism" is itself a genuinely "ethical" economic arrangement. If, as Pascal said, humans are neither angels nor beasts but if, as Madison was later to add, they nevertheless have a portion of virtue sufficient to allow for democratic or republican government and, more generally, for a free, civil society, then it must also be said that, in the economic sphere, "capitalism" is that system which is best capable of bringing out what is best in human nature.

Since modern democracies ("polities") can only be *societies* and not *communities* (as I argued in Chapter 2), it must also be a basic right of citizens *not* to participate directly in the political/public realm and actively to align themselves with any particular "faction." An excessive fascination with the idea of the ancient Greek *polis* and the notion of participatory democracy it embodied (such as one finds in Hannah Arendt), can easily, in modern times, become a renewed formula for the "tyranny of the majority." In modern society, people should have the right to pursue happiness (which Jefferson listed along with life and liberty as a basic human right) in whatever strictly private ways they might choose; the happiness of citizens ought not to be equated with their active participation in the political realm. In her fascinating and insightful, yet highly tendentious, reading of the American Revolution, Arendt nevertheless equated Jefferson's "happiness" with "public happiness," with the ability (and, indeed, the obligation) for all citizens to participate actively in public affairs (see Arendt 1965, and 1968, pp. 143, 171). "Private happiness" was, in Arendt's usage, an almost pejorative term.[42] With her strong nostalgia for the communitarian *ethos* of the Greek *polis*, Arendt, it would seem, was unable to conceive of democracy other than according to the old "participatory" model which, as Madison and Hamilton had nevertheless attempted to point out, was a sure-fire recipe for failure.[43]

The error of those communitarian critics of liberalism such as Arendt or, more recently, Michael Sandel (see Sandel 1982) who harken back to the old idea of civic republicanism lies in thinking that the "public good" must somehow be *prior to* or *above and independent of* the particular interests of private individuals. As Madison, Kant, and Smith all tried to show, however, the public or common good in a free society respectful of individual rights is something that in a fully spontaneous fashion *emerges out of and is the result of* the actions of a multitude of separate and diverse individuals when these individuals operate in an institutional context designed to call forth civil behavior on their part. Although she proclaims her allegiance to the idea of "radical democracy," Chantal Mouffe perceives very well the shortcomings of all forms of communitarianism when she writes:

> [T]here is a real danger of returning to a premodern view of politics, which does not acknowledge the novelty of modern democracy and the crucial contribution of liberalism. The defense of pluralism, the idea of individual liberty, the separation of Church and State, the development of civil society – all are constitutive of modern democratic politics. They require that a distinction be made between the private and the public domains, the realm of morality and the realm of politics. Contrary to what some communitarians propose, a modern democratic political community cannot be organized around a single substantive idea of the common good. The recovery of a strong participatory idea of citizenship [an ideal Mouffe advocates, but does not do a great deal to clarify] should not be made at the cost of sacrificing individual liberty. This is the point where the communitarian critique of liberalism takes a dangerous conservative turn.
>
> (Mouffe 1993, p. 62)

To reject, as liberalism does, the notion of a "single substantive idea of the common good" is to reject the very notion that society ("community") is some kind of supra-individual entity, having a reality status superior to that of "mere" individuals. "Society" is simply the name for the (institutionalized) way in which individual subjects exist *inter*subjectively. As such, it cannot be said to have any *purpose* (or interest) of its own, or to serve any other purpose

99

than that of providing a framework within which its individual members can pursue their own individual or group interests.

It is almost as if Arendt, a refugee from Nazi Germany and subsequently a life-long "social pariah" (as she herself put it) and who was (perhaps for this reason) mesmerized by the siren calls of ancient, participatory democracy, had never paid sufficient heed to Benjamin Constant who had pointed out as long ago as 1819 that the "liberty of the moderns" is of a significantly different sort from the "liberty of the ancients" ('The Liberty of the Ancients Compared with that of the Moderns" in Constant 1988).[44] Whereas modern liberty includes both political liberty (the democratic right to participate in one way or another in public affairs) and civil liberty (the human right to pursue one's own life as one sees fit), ancient liberty was reduced to political liberty. This being the case, the ancients, Constant pointed out, "admitted as compatible with this collective freedom the complete subjection of the individual to the authority of the community. . . . Thus among the ancients the individual, almost always sovereign in public affairs, was a slave in all his private relations." (Constant 1988, p. 311). If individual or human rights, so valued by moderns, are to have any meaning, Constant went on to argue, individuals must not be forced to participate in public affairs. It is as if Constant were responding in advance to Arendt over the space of a century and a half when in his 1819 address he said:

> The exercise of political rights, therefore, offers us but a part of the pleasures that the ancients found in it, while at the same time the progress of civilization, the commercial tendency of the age, the communication amongst peoples, have infinitely multiplied and varied the means of personal happiness.
>
> It follows that we must be far more attached than the ancients to our individual independence. For the ancients when they sacrificed that independence to their political rights, sacrificed less to obtain more; while in making the same sacrifice, we would give more to obtain less.
>
> The aim of the ancients was the sharing of social power among the citizens of the same fatherland: this is what they called liberty. The aim of the moderns is the enjoyment of security in private pleasures; and they call liberty the guarantees accorded by institutions to these pleasures.
>
> (Constant 1988, pp. 316–17)

Constant's "freedom of the moderns" is what Isaiah Berlin has termed "negative freedom," the purpose of this form of freedom being to secure an "area within which the subject – a person or group of persons – is or should be left to do or be what he is able to do or be, without interference by other persons" (Berlin 1969, pp. 121–22). Of course, as Constant also pointed out (although this is – and quite typically – ignored by his present-day communitarian critics), while the modern conception of happiness cen-

100

ters around the notion of individual liberty, this makes political liberty no less important, since the latter serves as the guarantee of the former: "Individual liberty, I repeat, is the true modern liberty. Political liberty is its guarantee, consequently political liberty is indispensable" (Constant 1988, p. 323).

In modern times, Constant was in effect saying, people have better things to do – such as making a living and improving their own welfare ("happiness") and that of their families – than sitting around all day or all evening in political discussion sessions, listening to long-winded speeches about how best to run the public bodies of which they are members. Direct, "participatory" democracy is a recipe for tyranny, for a decided *un*representativity, since those who have nothing better to do than engage in endless political debates will always manage in the end to impose their will and individual agendas on those who have better things to do with their time (and when, as an economist would say, the "information costs" for full-time political activism are simply too high).[45] This, as Constant points out, is precisely the rationale for the sort of *representative* democracy that Madison had argued for ("Hence, Sirs, the need for the representative system" [ibid., p. 325]). Neither the Russian Soviets nor any other revolutionary "council system" (for which Arendt displayed such a fondness [see Arendt 1965, p. 250ff]) has ever proven that it can make for stable and effective government nor have any of them been able to survive for more than "a few days" (as Aristotle would say). In contrast, the Republic which Madison helped to constitute, based on the principle of democratic representation, has now endured for over two hundred years, which makes it the longest lived civil society in existence. The fact of the matter is that present-day advocates of civic humanism or republicanism who look askance at the commercial or "bourgeois" spirit and the "pursuit of self-interest" are, wittingly or no, extolling, along with the Renaissance celebration of public spiritedness, the premodern, warrior virtues of nobility, honor, and glory which form the cornerstone of the feudalistic ethic of chivalry. They appear to ignore the fact that a society founded upon virtues such as these cannot but be militaristic (as the ancient Greek and Renaissance Italian civic republics invariably were) and outwardly aggressive in its basic orientation.

In a modern democracy, people entrust the governance of the state or polity to elected representatives while retaining the political right to "act up" whenever they perceive that their individual rights and liberties are being violated by governments acting not out of a concern for the public good but out of purely sectarian and partisan interests. Of course, if some people's own personal happiness consists in being involved in politics on a daily basis, that is their right too, but it must not be such as to violate the rights of others who choose to pursue happiness in other ways. They want a right to say what they think is right when they feel the need to do so, but they don't necessarily want to stand around all day arguing for what they believe is right, and they equally don't want other citizens usurping this right of theirs. Politics, in the narrow sense of the term, is a job they have delegated to elected representatives, whom they hold accountable, as well as to various advocacy or watch-dog groups of which they are paid members or general beneficiaries. That, in our day and age, is what democracy is all about. In modern democracies, there is no call for opposing, as Arendt and other critics of "bourgeois" liberal society typically do, the *citizen* and the *consumer*.

THE ROLE OF GOVERNMENT IN CIVIL SOCIETY

In a civil society the political realm merges with the public realm, and the latter is a great deal more extensive than the sphere of government. As mentioned earlier (see Chapter 2, pp. 35–6), it has become customary to oppose civil society to the state, but, as I have argued, this is an unduly restrictive way of viewing the matter.[46] A democratic, civil society as described above *necessarily* calls forth a particular mode of government, this being representational (liberal) democracy. This is the only form of government that is fully compatible with the notions of civil society and human rights. In any other than a liberal polity, civil society will be stunted and human rights not fully respected. Moreover, when writers oppose civil society to the state, what they actually are referring to is not the State, in the proper sense of the term, but rather the "state apparatus," i.e., the government. In a democratic, civil society, government is by no means the same thing as the State.[47]

The liberal state, or, to be more precise, the liberal nation-state of modern times, is not a *de facto* collection of individuals holding political power ("the government"); it is, rather, a *de jure*, moral entity. It is, one could say in Hayekian terms, an abstract order, one of a very encompassing sort (Hayek refers to this as the Great Society). In the case of the United States, for instance, the State is the entire political and social set-up based on the principle of free association underwritten by the Constitution and allowing citizens, in all domains of civil society – political, cultural, economic – to pursue, either individually or collectively and in peace and security, their "happiness." In other words, the State is the Republic itself; it is that to which citizens pledge allegiance (unlike ordinary citizens, military personnel must also swear allegiance to the government). Whereas, at any given time, the government belongs, so to speak, to particular individuals (or political parties) – who invariably claim to be operating for the "common good" – the State, belonging as it does to everyone, belongs in fact to no one. It is indeed, as Cicero would say, public property, a *res populi* or *res publica*.[48] In order to highlight the difference between government and the State, one could say that while government is but one part of civil society, the State is, in a sense, coextensive with civil society.[49]

Since, as Frank Knight observed, people can be truly rational and free only by living in a rational and free society, the basic *raison d'être* of a liberal democratic State is to insure those rights that are the necessary condition for people to interact freely, in a communicatively rational manner. This is why Thomas Jefferson stated in the American Declaration of Independence that "to secure these rights, governments are instituted among men, deriving their just powers from the consent of the governed." And it is why he went on to say that "whenever any form of government becomes destructive of these ends, it is the right of the people to alter or abolish it." These rights will normally be listed in the Constitution of a liberal State in the form of a Bill or Charter of Rights; as Benjamin Constant stated in his *Principles of Politics* (1815): "[T]he constitution is the guarantee of people's liberty" (Constant 1988, p. 171). Being an instance of Basic or Fundamental Law, the Constitution not only sets up specific governmental arrangements and mandates governmental procedures, it also sets strict limits to the powers of government – so as, precisely, to insure the rights of individual citizens. For in the absence of constitutional guarantees of human rights and individual freedoms (and effective judicial means for enforcing them), the political liberty to participate in the democratic process would, as Constant realized, not be enough on its own to make individuals truly free, that is, to be *secure* in their liberty.[50]

The recognition of popular sovereignty, i.e., the recognition that the State belongs to "the people," and the concomitant principle of majority rule are not enough to guarantee the rights of individuals and minorities. In a participatory, direct democracy of the Athenian sort, "the people" would indeed be sovereign and all-powerful, but the notion of human rights and of the inviolable dignity of the individual, of each and every human person, would be without any substantive meaning. A regime of this sort would be a rule of might ("people's power"), not necessarily of right; when the "sovereign will" is determined by a simple majority, there can be no room for the autonomous forms of social self-organization that are crucial to civil society. The criterion of true democracy is the degree to which individuals and minorities are guaranteed rights and liberties that are not dependent on the mere will of the democratic majority (the government). As Lord Acton declared in the later part of the nineteenth century in his "History of Liberty in Antiquity," echoing as it were Constant: "The most certain test by which we judge a country is really free is the amount of security enjoyed by minorities" (Acton 1985, p. 7).[51]

Thus, although democratic rule is customarily defined as one in which sovereignty is invested in the people, it would be more correct to say, as Constant in fact did, that in a liberal-democratic nation-state sovereignty rightly belongs to *no one*, not even to the people themselves. In the chapter entitled "On the Sovereignty of the People" in his *Principles of Politics* Constant stated: "The abstract recognition of the sovereignty of the people does not in the least increase the amount of liberty given to individuals. If we attribute to that sovereignty an amplitude which it must not have, liberty may be lost notwithstanding that principle, or even through it." Objecting to Rousseau's ideal of participatory democracy (in Constant's opinion Rousseau's *Social Contract*, "so often invoked in favour of liberty, [was] the most formidable support for all kinds of despotism"), Constant insisted on the importance of "sheltering individuals from governments." For Constant the "important truth, the eternal principle" was: "The sovereignty of the people is not unlimited: it is on the contrary, circumscribed within the limits traced by justice and by the rights of individuals" (Constant 1988, pp. 175–83).[52]

As these remarks of Constant so forcefully illustrate, the traditional liberal view of the role of government in a constitutional democracy is that it should be strictly *limited*. Only if government is limited in its functions (by constitutional restraints) can individual and minority rights be effectively protected and only then can the multiple, free associations of civil society flourish. As the great American jurist Daniel Webster said of the Madisonian system of government:

> I have said that it is one principle of the American system, that the people limit their governments, National and State. They do so, but it is another principle, equally true and certain, and, according to my judgment of things, equally important, that the people often *limit themselves*. They set bounds to their own power. They have chosen to secure the institutions which they establish against the sudden impulses of mere majorities. All our institutions teem with instances of this. It was their great conservative principle, that in constituting forms of government, that they should secure what they had established against hasty changes by simple majorities.
>
> (cited in Hayek 1960, p. 447)

The principle of government Webster describes may indeed be called conservative, in that it is diametrically opposed to all forms of "revolutionism" (to be discussed in the following section). Freedom is something that is only achieved with difficulty and needs always to be painstakingly preserved ("conserved"). This "conservative" principle of politics has, however, nothing to do with conservatism in the customary political sense of the term and even less to do with laissez-fairism – with, that is to say, the doctrine of the "minimal state." As Frank Knight would say, "There is no implication of *laissez faire*" (Knight 1982, p. 240). A limited state is something altogether different from a minimal, "nightwatchman state," as advocated, for instance, by Robert Nozick (see Nozick 1974). According to this libertarian view of things, the role of the state is purely "negative" (providing for "law and order"; defending the supposedly "natural" right to property); in contrast, liberal theory (that of constitutional democracy) holds that while the powers of government should be strictly limited, the government does nevertheless have a *positive* role to play in society. In other words, the liberal State is not a "non-interventionist" state.[53] While the powers alloted to the government of a liberal State are limited, they are by no means "minimal"; within the sphere assigned to it, a liberal-democratic government can be extremely powerful indeed.

Despite what anti-state libertarians (right-wing anarchists, "anarcho-capitalists," as they sometimes call themselves) would have us believe, there is no reason, in principle, why government intervention, in and of itself, should be thought to be inimical to individual freedom in the realm of civil society. Indeed, if government is to perform its overriding constitutional task of protecting the rights of its citizens, it is under a moral obligation to intervene for this purpose in the workings of civil society when the situation calls for it. Government must, for instance, produce enabling legislation when this will help to make the rights and freedoms granted to citizens by the Constitution more effectively real.[54] Such, for instance, was the intent of the Civil Rights Act of 1964; without this interventionist measure on the part of the American government, Articles 14 and 15 of the US Constitution, dating back to 1868 and 1870 respectively (under the post-Lincoln administration) and granting full civil and human rights to those who had been formerly enslaved, would likely have continued to remain a dead letter.[55] Thus, as Knight says: "[T]here is occasion for intervention by the state or some other agency, without violating the principle of maximum freedom, but rather effecting its realization" (Knight 1982, p. 240). The basic liberal principle is, therefore: when government intervention in the workings of civil society serves either to protect or to enhance the rights and liberties of individuals, it is fully justified.

It is, of course, crucial in this regard that intervention on the part of government be in conformity with the fundamental liberal principle of the "equal liberty of all." It naturally goes without saying that, in the actual world in which we live, self-interested individuals will always seek to secure public support for their own purely private interests ("rent-seeking"), and it also goes without saying that they will always find public office holders, looking out for their own private interests as well (such as being reelected to office), ready to accommodate them. This is simply one aspect of the tendency towards corruption that is endemic to any and all forms of human governance, an undeniable and ineradicable fact of human existence. The criterion for legitimate government intervention in a liberal State is nevertheless clear: to be considered just, *intervention must serve the common good*.[56]

This is what the American constitutionalists referred to as "the general Welfare." Under this heading they listed items such as: the establishment of post offices and post roads (in order to provide for communication networks); the regulation of inter-state commerce; the establishment of uniform bankruptcy laws, the issuance of money and the regulation of the value thereof;[57] the establishment of standard weights and measures (in order to facilitate trade and economic development); copyright and patent laws ("to promote the Progress of Science and useful Arts"); military and militia powers (in order to secure "the common defense") (US Constitution, art. 1, sec. 8).

These are instances of what present-day economists call "public goods." Public goods are those things that are beneficial to the people and the nation as a whole (such as good roads and control of pollution) and which would not be provided, it is again supposed, if government did not intervene to do so. In a decidedly nonlibertarian fashion, Hayek writes in this regard: "[W]e find it unquestionable that in an advanced society government ought to use its power of raising funds by taxation to provide a number of services [Hayek refers to these as 'collective or public goods'] which for various reasons cannot be provided, or cannot be provided adequately, by the market" (Hayek 1979b, p. 41).

What all "public goods" (which can properly be called such) generally have in common is that they are of an "infrastructural" nature. The father of modern economics, Adam Smith, characterized these goods which it is the "duty" of the state to provide in the following way:

> that of erecting and maintaining those publick institutions and those publick works, which, though they may be in the highest degree advantageous to a great society, are, however, of such a nature, that the profit could never repay the expence [*sic*] to any individual or small number of individuals, and which it, therefore, cannot be expected that any individual or small number of individuals should erect or maintain.
>
> (Smith 1979, II, p. 723)

Infrastructural goods of this sort, Smith said, "are chiefly those for facilitating the commerce of the society, and those for promoting the instruction of the people." Of the latter he said: "The institutions for instruction are of two kinds; those for the education of the youth, and those for the instruction of people of all ages." These last remarks are instructive: Smith was in effect saying that infrastructual goods are of a dual nature – physical (such as "good roads, bridges, navigable canals, harbours, etc." [ibid., p. 724]) *as well as* intellectual or cultural. With the emergence of a global economy, we have in our times come to realize how exceedingly important it indeed is to stimulate the development not only of physical capital but, above all, of "human capital." This is because, given the "knowledge revolution," the latter has become the indispensable condition of the former [see in this regard Drucker 1993]).[58] Education (the development of "human capital") is now the supremely important public good in any country that would seek to maintain an economic "edge" in the global economy. This is something that John Paul II noted when in his 1991 encyclical he wrote: "Whereas at one time the decisive factor of production was *the land*, and later capital – understood as a total complex of the instruments of production – today the decisive factor is increasingly *man himself*, that is, his knowledge" (John Paul II 1991, §32).

Smith went on to say, however, that wherever possible the consumers of these public goods should contribute to defraying their costs.[59] Today we would speak of the need for "user fees" in order to control the cost of expensive public projects and social programs and in order to mitigate the "free rider" problem. Thus the principle which authorizes government intervention on behalf of the common good carries with it important caveats. The most important of these is that government intervention must always be assessed from an economic point of view. And a most important question that must always be addressed in this regard is: is government, in this or that particular instance, the best agent for providing this or that particular public good? There can be no fixed answer to this question since, as Smith would say, the answer will vary "in the different periods of society" (Smith 1979, II, p. 724). Depending on technological developments and the capacities of civil society, goods that at one time were assigned to government may, at another time, more economically be turned over to the "private sector." The list, so to speak, of government responsibilities is subject to on-going change. The general tendency of our times, given the great increase in the resources of civil society, is to "privatize" an increasing number of public goods and services (airlines, airports, seaports, railways, toll roads, telecommunications, etc.).[60] The general rule is that this should *always* be done, wherever and whenever it can be effectively done without harm to the "general welfare." As one writer remarks: "In practice, the best way to assist civil society is to encourage the privatization of cultural and social organizations" (Harik 1994, p. 56).

Another general rule is that government should only do (1) that which, from a public goods point of view, needs to be done and which, moreover, can be done in no other way and (2) that which it is fairly good at doing. Unfortunately (depending on how one views the matter), government, given the bureaucratic way in which it must necessarily operate, is not very good at doing a great many things. Generally speaking, government is terribly inept at doing anything which calls for entrepreneurial alertness and initiative, such as running an efficient, money-making business enterprise. One thing that government must nevertheless do, in the absence of effective competition, whatever its abilities for doing so, is to provide for "infrastructures." It can therefore be allowed that, under ordinary circumstances, government has an important role to play in an infrastructual way in facilitating commerce ("the economy"). In all such instances, however, government should not itself be directly involved in the production of economic goods (in the form of state-owned or nationalized industries). In the economic realm, bureaucrats can never substitute for entrepreneurs.[61] As Constant very aptly remarked, government intervention in what he called commerce "is almost always – and I do not know why I say almost – this intervention is indeed always a trouble

107

and embarrassment. . . . Every time governments pretend to do our own business, they do it more incompetently and expensively than we would" (Constant 1988, p. 315).[62] It is exceedingly difficult to imagine any sort of justification (other than purely ideological) for government to usurp the role and function of independent entrepreneurial agents, since the rule of (good) business is profit, and, if a particular business is profitable (and thus, from an economic point of view, viable), it can be assumed, as a law of economic science, that private agents will seize the opportunity (Nature abhors a vacuum). (In cases of businesses with high start-up costs and low initial returns on investment, government might, while remaining in its proper orb, choose to provide incentives to the enterprises in question, granting them, for instance, tax holidays.)

So far I have been discussing the *extent* of legitimate government intervention in society. A matter of equal importance is the *form* this intervention, when legitimate, should take. As one economist aptly observes: "It is not government intervention itself that is the problem, but rather the form of the intervention" (Varian 1993, p. 556). The general rule in this regard is that when national governments (nation-states) do retain responsibility for the provision of various public goods, they should always, as much as possible and wherever feasible, delegate this responsibility to lower levels of government (state or provincial, municipal, and even neighborhood), as well as to autonomous, non-governmental organizations such as volunteer, non-profit associations. As one feminist writer observes, what is called for is a

> shift away from centralized, formal, rational-bureaucratic types of decision-making in the direction of context-responsive, organic and decentralized types of decision-making. While there has to be a macro-polity framing and guiding what happens within it, much of this system is better conceptualized as a series of interconnected polities, some local, some regional, some interregional, to use spatial metaphors.
> (Yeatman 1994, p. 89)

In a democratic civil society – and in order to arrest or retard the cancerous growth of a distant, monolithic, and unresponsive bureaucracy whose interests, by the nature of the case, are at odds with those of an autonomous civil society[63] – government should always be as close to the people as possible. In Catholic social doctrine this is what is called the *principle of subsidiarity*. In his encyclical letter, *Centesimus Annus*, addressed, exceptionally, not only to the episcopate but to "all men and women of good will," John Paul II formulated the principle of subsidiarity in the following way:

> [A] community of a higher order should not interfere in the internal life of a community of a lower order, depriving the latter of its functions,

but rather should support it in case of need and help to coordinate its activity with the activities of the rest of society, always with a view to the common good.

(John Paul II 1991, §48)[64]

Emphasizing the need to cultivate volunteer work on the local level, the Pope went on to censor the modern Welfare State for its bureaucratic insensitivity in this regard:

By intervening directly and depriving [civil] society of its responsibility, the Social Assistance State leads to a loss of human energies and an inordinate increase of public agencies, which are dominated more by bureaucratic ways of thinking than by concern for serving their clients, and which are accompanied by an enormous increase in spending.

(John Paul II, 1991, §98)[65]

The ultimate form of the Social Assistance State was well exemplified by the Soviet Union; under the Soviet "social contract" (on this see Harding 1993, p. 171), people surrendered their democratic freedoms and rights to a monopolistic party-state in exchange for the provision of social security – thereby making themselves over into political serfs.

According to Michael Novak, the Catholic principle of subsidiarity can be traced to Abraham Lincoln (Novak 1993, p. 76); as Lincoln pointed out, "You cannot help men permanently by doing for them what they could and should do for themselves." Were the principle of subsidiarity adhered to, Novak says, "government programs would be aimed at strengthening civil society rather than eroding it" (ibid., p. 165). Unfortunately, even after what one would have thought would have been a true "wake-up call" delivered by the revolutions of 1989 in Eastern Europe, the message did not seem to get through to some Western governments. Thus, for instance, while, as I pointed out in the previous chapter, the Government of Ontario attempted in 1993 in the name of "equity" to abolish university autonomy, that same government introduced in the legislature the following year, in the name of "ease of access," a bill ("The Long-Term Care Act") which aimed at centralizing all long-term health care in the hands of the government bureaucracy and which – altogether intentionally – aimed also at eliminating from the public realm the great majority of privately run health care organizations (what the Government derisively referred to as the "private sector"). As the president of the Catholic Charities of the Archdiocese of Toronto said at the time, the net result of this interventionist legislation would be to dry up the millions of dollars and volunteer work that are currently, without any government support or encouragement, expended, by a multitude of charitable contributors, on long-term health care. And as a spokesperson for the Saint Elizabeth Visiting Nurses Association of Ontario declared: "We believe this bill ... will signal the end of charitable, community based agencies."[66] The move by the Government of Ontario was a blatant, heavy-handed attempt to absorb the autonomous public realm of civil society into the purely political, i.e., governmental, sphere. And, like all such moves, it was economically irrational and fiscally irresponsible in that its net effect would be, in the words of John Paul II, "an enormous increase in [government] spending." The socialist ideal – well described by Tocqueville when he prophesied over a century and a half ago that the new tyranny would be that of a benevolent government, concernedly looking out for every need of its citizens, but which would also want to assure for itself the exclusive responsibility for satsifying these needs (see Tocqueville 1961, II, pp. 4, 6) – obviously lives on.

Having described the legitimate *extent* and *form* of government intervention in society, it remains only to articulate the *purpose* of government in this regard. Although the point to be made is implicit in much of what I have said above, it merits being singled out for special mention. While, from a strictly empirical point of view, it is necessary (as Hobbes well knew) for any government to *control* the governed, a liberal democratic government (despite what uncritical disciples of Foucault might say) is much more than a mere "control mechanism," an apparatus for the exercise of "power" (although, at the minimum, it is most certainly that).[67] The overriding principle of "republican" or liberal democratic government can be formulated as follows: the ultimate purpose of government (and governmental intervention) is not *control* but *cultivation*.

This distinction, borrowed from Hayek, is crucially important. Don Lavoie, an Austrian School economist in the Hayekian tradition, expresses the matter well when he writes:

> Hayek's term "cultivation" is useful to suggest that when we understand a complex order's general principles of operation we may be able to cultivate conditions in which that order can best operate. Attempts to directly control the detailed operation of such complex processes as scientific discovery, political discourse, industrial organization, or the distribution and level of employment, have failed, but this does not mean that we need to give up trying to improve on the workings of these processes. What we need to do is cultivate more appropriate conditions within which these uncontrollable processes are more likely to yield the kinds of beneficial results we desire.
>
> (Lavoie 1988, p. 1)

As Hayek always insisted, large-scale human orders are not the sort of thing that can be managed so as to achieve *specific end-results*. Attempts at "social engineering," such as the one undertaken on a gigantic scale by the Soviets, are doomed to failure in the long run and can only contribute to the bringing into being of a technocratic, totalitarian state. The conclusion to be drawn (from, for instance, the failed Soviet experiment) is not, however, the one that libertarian laissez-fairists would have us draw. With the aid of general theories as to the logic of social orders, Hayek maintained, we can make changes to the macro-order (the institutional structure of the order in question) and, in this way, increase the likelihood that beneficial results will predominate over disadvantageous ones. Or as Hayek put it, by devising appropriate frameworks of a general sort having to do, for instance, with the definition of property rights, we can encourage the exercise of individual freedom and initiative, thereby making possible a general increase in the level of benefits to society as a whole, be these material or cultural, a by-product of the marketplace of goods or the marketplace of ideas. As a general rule, when we are dealing with self-ordering, spontaneous structures, "we can create the conditions under which they will operate, but we cannot determine what will happen to any particular element" (Hayek 1988, p. 83). Thus, although complex social orders may be "spontaneous" and "self-organizing," this does not mean that human reason cannot contribute in a positive way to their further development (see Madison 1990, pp. 104–5). And thus government intervention in the workings of civil society – in the pursuit of justice[68] – is fully justified when it operates in the manner described above.

The cultivation of the autonomous formations of civil society continues, in fact, to be as urgent a task in the West, whatever this or that retrograde Western government might think, as it most obviously is the task of the newly liberated countries of Eastern Europe.

In summary, the role of government in a civil society (the political sphere in the narrow sense of the term) is, by way of intervention in society, to do everyting that is incumbent upon it to do by way of furthering the public good. This is, as a matter of fact, the *only* role that a constitutionally established and regulated democracy (the liberal State) allows its government. At the same time, this constitutional allowance imposes upon the government, thus empowered, a most sacred obligation: in furthering the public good, the government (or "state") must recognize all those autonomous groupings of civil society which, in numerous spheres of life, can often perform the tasks government would willingly assign itself better than government itself can – and government must, accordingly, delegate its own state power to them, thereby empowering civil society to take over all those functions which it is supremely capable of handling.[69] The fundamental meaning of civil society is that individuals, either on their own or in voluntary association, must have the unquestioned and sacrosanct right to act freely in their own interests, either individual or collective, either self-regarding or charitably altruistic, without government interference or obstruction. That is what "human rights" is all about, and when such rights prevail throughout society in actual practice – when spontaneous orders are allowed freely to spring up and

111

develop among the citizenry – the net result (though it might often take a more or less long "shake-out" period) is usually a great enhancement of the "general welfare." That, as the historical and comparative record clearly shows, is an undeniable fact of free, civic life. The most well-to-do countries in the world enjoying the highest "quality of life" are, on the whole, those which permit the freest expressions of civic spirit. And civic spirit, when it is allowed to operate, does not, it should be most clearly noted, impose any costs on the (already greatly over-burdened) national treasury. That, in the financially strapped times of the 1990s, is a feature of civil society that governments should not under any circumstance be allowed to ignore. For those governments which do choose to ignore the lesson of the times, Jefferson's declaration of human rights in 1776 should be as pertinent a warning now as it ever was:

> [W]henever any form of government becomes destructive of these ends [human rights: life, liberty, and the pursuit of happiness], it is the right of the people to alter or abolish it, & to institute new government, laying it's [sic] foundation on such principles, & organizing it's powers in such form, as to them shall seem most likely to effect their safety & happiness.
>
> (citing Jefferson's original draft; see Jefferson 1984, p. 19)

THE CIVIC CULTURE OF A DEMOCRATIC REGIME

Democratic institutions of a Madisonian sort have as their purpose the cultivation of a democratic way of being or *ethos*, what Hegel referred to as *Sittlichkeit*, i.e., a particular form of social life or culture. For no democracy, however artfully contrived, can either flourish or long endure unless it is supported and sustained by, as Montesquieu would say, the *moeurs* of a people, unless, that is to say, it is solidly rooted in social practices. Democracy, Jean Bethke Elshtain points out, "is about not only constitutions, rules, public accountability, and deliberation but also about everyday life, habits, and dispositions" (Elshtain 1995, p. 55). Democracy, she says, is "an ethos, a spirit, a way of responding, and a way of conducting oneself" (ibid., p. 80). Yet another writer observes:

> Democratic governments function poorly, if at all, in the absence of certain explicit and implicit cultural practices and assumptions. A number of attitudes must be first ingrained in the social order, such as a certain degree of individualism, public-spiritedness, respect for and tolerance of others, and acceptance of winning and losing according to "the rules of the game." Indeed, a major reason for the emphasis placed on civil society is the belief that a democratic system of government planted in a hostile and alien culture is not likely to survive, let

alone prosper. . . . In the long run . . . a democratic government needs a democratic political culture, and vice versa.

(Harik 1994, pp. 43, 56)[70]

Thus democracy is not just a matter of certain political arrangements; it is above all a matter of a certain kind of *political culture*. As the editor of the Egyptian journal, *Civil Society*, has stated: "Unless they are rooted in a democratic political culture (which presupposes a vibrant and free civil society), even the most brilliantly designed democratic procedures and institutions can be all too easily undermined or hollowed out by nondemocratic forces" (Khalifa 1995, p. 162).

A good illustration of how civic virtues are required on the part of the citizenry if a democratic regime is to function properly is provided by the attempt to build a civil society in Russia. As the longtime anti-Stalinist, Fyodor Burlatsky, stated in the last days of the Soviet regime:

We are faced with a paradox. We must democratize power in order to democratize society, but in order to democratize power we need a democratic society. . . .Even though Soviet society is ridding itself of Stalinism and stagnation, those decades of experience have left deep scars. Look at the lack of tolerance, even among educated political people. Too many of them don't know how to live with an opponent. They want to deprive him of the right to speak, destroy him, or put him in a concentration camp. Tolerance of pluralism, the ability to understand another person's interests and viewpoints, are true signs of a democratic culture.

(in Cohen and Heuvel 1989, p. 195)

The attitude ingrained in Soviet society that needs to be overcome, Burlatsky said, is: "If two people are arguing, one must strangle the other – then everything will be okay" (ibid., p. 196). Or as Yevgeny Yevtushenko very nicely put it: "We still don't know the art of insulting each other politely – the art of polemics" (ibid., p. 276).[71] If developing "a democratic political culture," as Burlatsky refers to it, is the prime requirement of a newly emerging civil society such as Russia, the question as to how to cultivate such a culture in this land so new to democracy is, as a matter of fact, equally germane to the question as to how civil societies in the West can continue to be maintained, for the dynamics of civil society are, in each and every instance, invariably the same.

The democratic *ethos* or way of life is the diametrical opposite of the "culture of violence" that prevailed in Mao's communist China (see Mirsky 1994, p. 24) and amounts to a kind public morality. This is a morality or an ethics of communicative rationality similar to the one that characterizes the moral-cultural order (see Chapter 3, pp. 62–6). It is, as I said of the latter, a *social* morality, and it is to be looked for not in the "good intentions" of individuals but rather in the rule-governed, social *practices* of a given area of

113

human endeavor. The "ethics of politics" is not the same thing as the "ethics of politicians." What is important in this morality is not so much the good-ness of people's inner motivations as the rightness of their public behavior. What Tocqueville said of democracy in America as he observed it in the 1830s went straight to the heart of the matter. The Americans, he said, are not "a virtuous people" in the moralistic sense of the term, and yet, as he also said, they are free and self-governing. How can this be, he asked, given that, as civic humanism had always maintained, a republican way of life (self-governance) requires that a people be "virtuous"? The lesson Tocqueville drew was a properly Madisonian one: what is important in the matter of civic virtue is not so much the "cause" as the "effect." If, for whatever reason, people exercise moderation in their demands and restraint in their mutual dealings, this is really all that matters. For civic virtue to prevail, it is not necessary, Tocqueville said, that people set their self-interest aside; all that is required is that they act out of "calculated personal interest" (see Madison 1986, p. 120).

To put the matter another way, the existence of a civic or democratic culture depends on everyone realizing that rights are a matter, as I have said, of "mutuality" and thus that their own rights and freedoms are best secured when the rights and freedoms of all others are as well. As Yakovlev so nicely said, one must learn to resist the temptation of sending those with whom one disagrees off to Siberia, since when this attitude is widespread one can be fairly sure that at some point or other one will find oneself exiled to Siberia (see note 71 of this chapter, p. 243). For civic culture to prevail and for the common good to be respected, it suffices, as Tocqueville would say, that everyone act out of "self-interest rightly understood." A reference to the economic realm may serve to illustrate the point. There is a great incentive for business people to act "ethically" when they are permitted (by means of the appropriate legal system) to look to their own long-term interests. While large, windfall profits are to be had from "ripping off" consumers and doing business in a hit-and-run or fly-by-night fashion, and while the temptation to engage in this sort of unscrupulous (and even criminal) activity is great in situations such as prevailed in Eastern Europe after the collapse of Socialism and before a civil market economy could be fully developed, when, however, a stable legal order has been instituted and the interests of business people and entrepreneurs are fully protected, it is in their long-term interest (the long-term maximization of profit) to act with restraint and in a way which actually best serves the interests of their clients or customers (see in this regard Kornai 1990).

What is all-important in this matter is the time horizon of agents, be they economic or political. Adam Przeworski makes this point in addressing the "puzzle" as to why people should comply with "the democratic interplay" when this often generates, at any given time, winners and losers: why shouldn't people subvert the democratic process when it generates such results? The survival prospects of democracy are nevertheless better than a cynic (a game-theoretical social scientist, for instance) might think when one actually understands the role of democratic institutions. Przeworski writes:

> Democratic institutions render an intertemporal character to political conflicts. They offer a long time horizon to political actors; they allow them to think about the future rather than be concerned exclusively with present outcomes. . . . Political forces comply with present defeats because they believe that the institutional framework that organizes the democratic competition will permit them to advance their interests in the future.
>
> (Przeworski 1991, p. 19)

The essence of a democratic civil society, one could say, is *proceduralism*. Goodwill sufficient enough for the maintenance of a democratic culture – which always requires *loyalty* on the part of its members – will likely be forthcoming when people are made to realize, through the actual practice of democracy, that what is in their own best interest is not this or that particular end-result, at any given moment, but the existence of an on-going process which guarantees to them the right freely to work towards that which they desire. The essence of constitutionally mandated proceduralism is that, as a contractarian theorist such as James Buchanan observes, it allows the members of a civil society to work for reforms in the social structure and to do so by means of "a process that preserves orderly measures for making futher changes which are now unpredictable but which may be desired in the future" (Buchanan 1977, p. 115). As Mouffe very correctly observes:

> The identification with those rules of civil intercourse [prescribing norms of conduct to be subscribed to in seeking self-chosen satisfactions and in performing self-chosen actions] creates a common political identity among persons otherwise engaged in many different enterprises. This modern form of political community is held together not by a substantive idea of the common good but by a common bond, a public concern. It is therefore a community without a definite shape or a definite identity and in continuous re-enactment.
>
> (Mouffe 1993, p. 67)[72]

What is crucial to democracy is not, as I argued previously, that the "people's will" be fully expressed at any given moment; it is rather the democratic *process* itself, i.e., the process of on-going *deliberation*. In the political realm, just as in the cultural realm, the true, the right, or the just is not, Habermas notwithstanding, what – even in an "ideal speech situation" – everyone would be in agreement upon. In what is undoubtedly a reference to Habermas, Mouffe writes: "[I]t is important to abandon the myth of a transparent

115

society, reconciled with itself, for that kind of fantasy leads to totalitarianism" (Mouffe 1993, p. 18). In a democratic society the "truth" is nothing other than the democratic process itself, whose *raison d'être* is not the *elimination* of conflict but rather its *control* or mediation (there is no reason why, in principle, there should be an incompatibility, or even conflict, between the notions of individual rights and the common good). Having grasped the true meaning of our postmodern times, Luis Guastavino, a senior member of the Chilean communist Party, said after the revolutions of 1989 (and was duly expelled from the Party for saying so): "I don't believe in total truth anymore. There's just one truth today, and that's democracy" (see Christian 1990, p. 5).

Democracy is not a matter of unanimity and the absence of conflict; it is a matter rather of "civility within conflict," and this sort of civility is (and can only be) the product of proceduralism. This is, once again, what principally serves to distinguish liberal, civic democracy from Socialism. Liberal democracy is premised on the belief that since "the good life" (like truth itself) is never to be fully and finally attained, procedures allowing for continual selfcorrection and for challenges to the general consensus are all-important, whereas Socialism, in its drive to construct the perfect society, tends to ignore the importance of democratic procedures altogether, its belief being that the end justifies the means. As Malia writes: "In the dynamic world of reality things either go up or they go down, but they never remain stationary. Yet the whole Soviet system was predicated on attaining 'Socialism' and then staying there, as if that were the end of history" (Malia 1994, p. 365). The basic trait unique to liberal or constitutional democracy is that it is *not* organized around a substantive – and unchallengeable – notion of the common good, one which must necessarily preempt the separate interests of individuals.[73]

Unlike Socialism, there is only one way that democracy can be brought into being and can be maintained, and this is by means of democratic procedures.[74] As Havel writes:

> I don't know whether directness, truth, and the democratic spirit will succeed. But I do know how *not* to succeed, which is by choosing means that contradict the ends. As we know from history, that is the best way to eliminate the very ends we set out to achieve.
>
> In other words, if there is to be any chance at all of success, there is only one way to strive for decency, reason, responsibility, sincerity, civility, and tolerance, and this is decently reasonably, responsibly, sincerely, civilly, and tolerantly.
>
> (Havel 1992b, pp. 7–8)

A most important factor in this regard is one which Cohen and Arato have emphazied in their detailed study of civil society. With the example of Eastern Europe in mind, they have stressed the importance of the notion of *self-limitation* as it applies to social movements (see Cohen and Arato 1992). If the revolutions (or "refolutions," in Garton Ash's appropriate neologism, combining "reform" and "revolution") of 1989 were successful in bringing democracy to Eastern Europe, one of the major reasons for their success was that they were peaceful, self-limiting, "velvet" revolutions.[75] They were not armed "liberation movements" which, as the historical record demonstrates almost without exception, invariably, when they are successful, end up by establishing a tyranny of their own. These revolutions were in fact not revolutions at all in the traditional, modernist sense of the term, and it may indeed be hoped that they in fact signaled the end of *revolutionism*.[76] By this I mean the utopian belief that a better, "alternative" (as Claude Lefort would say) society can be brought into being by a violent overthrow of the established order and a usurpation of political power. Contemplating the new politics of human rights and the struggles of numerous groups in this regard, Claude Lefort – already in 1980 – made the following prescient observations:

> Whatever their affinities and convergences, they are not dominated by the image of an agent of history, a People-as-One, and they reject the hypothesis that right will be achieved in reality. So we must resolve to abandon the idea of a politics ["revolutionism," as Lefort refers to it] that would compress collective aspirations in the model of an alternative society, or, what amounts to the same thing, the idea of a politics that would stand over the world in which we live and allow it to be struck by the thunderbolts of the Last Judgment.
>
> (Lefort 1986, p. 266)[77]

This is precisely what the East Europeans "resolved" to do, and what they in fact did do. As another French political scientist has observed:

> In fact, 1989 brought to a close the era of revolutions precisely by its rejection of the idea of violence as a midwife for the birth of a new society. The revolutions of 1989 were unique in history because none of these claimed to bear within itself a new societal "project." With no new social utopia, there is little reason to fear the combination of virtue and terror typical of past revolutions.
>
> (Rupnik 1995, p. 62)

Subsequent to the velvet revolutions of 1989, one Czech participant in these events noted how their "specifically post-totalitarian feature" was "a healthy distrust of all uniquely correct solutions" (Bednář 1994, p. 4). Conscious of the historically novel character of the revolutions (or refolutions) of 1989, Miroslav Bednář, a Czech philosopher who had been denied the right to practice his discipline under the communist regime, observes:

The mainly non-violent democratic revolutions in Eastern Europe are, from the viewpoint of political theory, in their typology and revolutionary development events which deserve the greatest attention. The bicentenary celebration of the French Revolution brought about an end to the era of revolutions in the French manner, which had been the revolutionary paradigm for modern times. In other words, the Central European revolutions of 1989 – with the partial exception of Romania – meant the end of violent revolutions which logically culminated in terror.

(Bednář 1994, p. 136)

Another common denominator of these nonviolent, "postmodern" revolutions that Bednář emphasizes is that they were carried out by non-party organizations in which "elementary citizenship is applied" (ibid., p. 136). "These types of free associations for political action," Bednář writes, "are a clear expression of elementary civil action: it is politics in the original sense of the word." What, in Bednář's estimation, was truly novel about these free citizens' associations was that they were "horizontally" organized and that, in addition, they were animated by a healthy mistrust of "any kind of one-and-only correct solution as the way to salvation" (ibid., p. 136). In other words, they were "self-limiting," and, according to Bednář, this marked "a possible beginning for a new European political tradition of authentic civic life, in which party machines and their coalitions would not play a decisive role" (ibid., p. 137). Echoing, as it were, this view, one Western observer has stated that the invention of self-limiting (constitutional) revolutions "has emerged as perhaps the greatest gift of twentieth-century politics to future generations" and "is perhaps the most dramatic step forward in the political broadening of the constitutionalist tradition" (Sołtan 1993, p. 79). As Sołtan points out (ibid., p. 91), the goal of self-limiting social movements (which he sees as having more democratic promise than participatory democracy) is to change institutions, not necessarily to participate directly in the decision-making activities of government itself.

The crucial thing to be noted in this regard is that the single most important factor contributing to the Great Transformations of 1989 in the countries of Eastern Europe was the prior existence in these countries of social movements whose principal trait was their commitment to, and extensive engagement in, communicative rationality. These spontaneous and multifarious groupings served above all to give a voice to the hitherto voiceless. Moreover, the degree to which, in each of the different countries, transformation in the direction of liberal democracy was successful (e.g., Poland and Hungary versus Romania and Bulgaria) was itself a function of (or correlated with) the degree to which the practice of communicative rationality had already been developed (in regard to both of these points, see Chilton 1994).[78]

One of the things postmodernism accordingly stands for is the rejection of revolutionism, of Marxist-type confrontational politics, and one figure who, considerably in advance of his time, contributed in an important way to the eventual demise of the revolutionist myth was Albert Camus. In his book, *The Rebel* (*L'homme revolté*, originally published in 1951 at a time when Marxism all but dominated the intellectual scene in France), Camus argued that rebellion should never be allowed to degenerate into revolution. In the act of rebellion, Camus maintained, people assert their human worth in solidarity with others (the massive street demonstrations in Leipzig leading up to the collapse of the East German regime were a fine example of rebellion in Camus' sense of the term). Rebellion, Camus maintained, is a demand for justice and the reciprocal recognition of individual liberties. Because of this, rebellion is necessarily self-limiting. In contrast, revolution is anything but self-limiting; it celebrates unrestrained violence in the pursuit of its seemingly noble but altogether utopian goals. The net result is not that of bringing into being a more humane society but rather a society which, in point of fact, amounts to the institutionalization of the violence of man against man. The politics of revolutionary regimes is the politics of exclusion, one in which dissent is stifled and individual lives are marginalized. The revolution that Camus was talking about was of course the one idealized by his fellow intellectuals of the period, the Russian Revolution. As Camus stated:

> For a far-off justice [the Marxist-Leninist doctrine] legitimates injustice during the whole of history. . . . It makes injustice, crime and lies acceptable by the promise of a miracle. Yet more production and more power, uninterrupted work, incessant sorrow, permanent war and a time will come when the serfdom prevailing throughout the total Empire will wondrously be changed into its opposite: free leisure in a universal republic. The pseudo revolutionary mystification has now found its formula: All freedom must be killed off in order to conquer the Empire, and the Empire will one day be freedom.
>
> (Camus 1951 p. 287)

It would be interesting to compare Camus' last remark with Havel's observation a quarter-century later on how living under a "revolutionist" regime amounts to living in hypocrisy and lies: "government by bureaucracy is called popular government; the working class is enslaved in the name of the working class; the complete degradation of the individual is presented as his or her ultimate liberation" (Havel 1995, p. 30). In any event, the important thing to note is that revolutions of the modernist sort generate fanaticism, uncompromising partisanship, and terror; they are incapable of producing the reasonableness, civililty, and trust that are the necessary conditions of a democratic civil society. Alain Touraine sums up the matter well:

The revolutionary attitude does not encourage democracy. Rather than defining a social conflict amenable to political solutions or reforms, it posits the existence of insurmountable political contradictions and the need to overthrow and eliminate adversaries. It therefore dreams of a socially and politically homogeneous society, and takes the view that its social adversaries have betrayed the people and the nation. A truly social conflict, in contrast, is always limited, and it is when the limits disappear that social movements give way to political counter-cultures or violence.

(Touraine 1995, pp. 331–32)

I have just alluded to the notion of *trust*. Socialist regimes, as numerous commentators have noted, are characterized by an all-pervasive mistrust (see for instance Seligman 1992, pp. 180–81), such that face-to-face primary groups become "a substitute for civil society rather than an integral part of it." Thus as Richard Rose rightly says: "Trust is a necessary condition for both civil society and democracy" (Rose 1994, pp. 22, 18).[79] A self-organizing or self-regulating society can function only if its members share a kind of generalized trust, believing that others are as committed as they are to pursuing their interests in accordance with the rules of the game and a mutual recognition of rights. Trust, as has always been recognized, is a matter of mutuality. William James put the basic philosophical point as well as anyone when he wrote:

A social organism of any sort whatever, large or small, is what it is because each member proceeds to his own duty with a trust that the other members will simultaneously do theirs. Wherever a desired result is achieved by the co-operation of many independent persons, its existence as a fact is a pure consequence of the precursive faith in one another of those immediately concerned. A government, an army, a commercial system, a ship, a college, an athletic team, all exist on this condition, without which not only is nothing achieved, but nothing is even attempted.

(James 1956, p. 24)

The interesting thing to note in this regard is that the trust that is necessary for a viable civil society is, so to speak, not of a "*gemeinschaftlich*" but, rather, of a "*gesellschaftlich*" nature; it is located on the overall institutional level of social anonymity and is not so much psychological ("subjective") as it is social ("objective"). Even though the trust characteristic of modern, large-scale civil societies is of an abstract, generalized sort, it is nevertheless no less a matter of mutuality than is the sort of trust to be found in small, face-to-face communities. In regard, in particular, to the relation between citizens and their government, trust is a function of the assurance on the part of the citizenry that government will operate within its constitutional limits, in such a manner as to promote the common good.[80]

Generally speaking, trust is something that is forthcoming when the various anonymous orders of social cooperation operate in a spontaneous and rational fashion. Although the workings of such orders produce outcomes that, at any particular point in time, are uncertain and unpredictable, they nonetheless give rise to a kind of long-term social stability ("predictability"), and they are thereby such as to generate confidence on the part of the general citizenry. A kind of diffuse trust is thereby brought into being by reason of the reciprocity and mutual dependence ("solidarity") that is created by the social division of labor wherein, as Hegel said:

> The selfish end in its actualization, conditioned in this way by universality, establishes a system of all-round interdependence, so that the subsistence and welfare of the individual and his rightful existence are interwoven with, and grounded on, the subsistence, welfare, and rights of all, and have actuality and security only in this context.
>
> (Hegel 1991, §183)[81]

As in the matter of social trust, so more generally the participation of individuals in the various orders of cooperation in civil society amounts to a genuine learning experience, a kind of civic *paideia*. What people learn in this respect – in actual *praxis* – is not a set of theoretically inculcated, abstract doctrines (as in the case of the indoctrination so crucial to the ideological party-state) but rather a kind of *habitus* or practical ability. Citizens learn this vital, lifeworld lesson in democratic civility in much the same way that, as I attempted to point out in Chapter 3, students learn the ins and outs of communicative rationality in regard to any particular intellectual discipline. This is a function, as I argued, not of merely formal education but of praxial enculturation into the disciplinary practices and procedures in question. The lesson that participation in civil society brings with it is a lesson of a similar sort: it is a lesson in what Aristotle called practical reason (*phronesis*) and what I have been calling communicative rationality. This is a lesson that in 1989 the Chinese knew they had to learn but which they were nonetheless denied the occasion to learn in the proper, praxial manner. Civil society is, in the words of a former Chinese government official, one of the leaders in the Tiananmen demonstrations of 1989 and now an expatriot, one in which "the power of reason" is "brought into full play" (Yan 1992, p. 121). As Yan realized, the essence of civil society consists in the ability "to make maximum use of people's enthusiasm, their spirit of creativity, and their initative" (ibid., p. 207).

What Michael Novak says of economic transactions – which, in a free society, most definitely call for creativity and initiative – applies to all forms of social interaction: "Practical intelligence is infused into economic transactions in every corner of society by persons employing their own practical intelligence to the maximum degree possible. Social systems differ in their openness to the practical intelligence of individuals" (Novak 1989, p. 93). Assuming that this is indeed the case, the question arises (as Novak puts it): "Through which concept of order can such openness be maximized?" The answer to this question that I am proposing is: through a concept of spontaneous orders in the cultural, political, and economic spheres of human understanding and agency. A hermeneutical political theory aims above all at clarifying the conditions for the "maximization" of the exercise of practical reason or communicative rationality. As Richard Bernstein has said, Gadamer's philosophical hermeneutics confronts us with "a practical task":

> to foster the type of dialogical communities in which *phronesis* [practical reason, communicative rationality] becomes a living reality and where citizens can actually assume what Gadamer tells us is their "noblest task" – "decision-making according to one's own responsibility – instead of conceding that task to the expert"
>
> (Bernstein 1983, p. 159)

Thus as Mouffe recognizes: "Gadamer's philosophical hermeneutics ... offers us a number of important ways of thinking about the construction of the political subject" (Mouffe 1993, p. 17).

The necessary condition for civil society is, as Havel has continually emphasized, civility, and civility is a product of reasonableness, of people behaving in a reasonable fashion. The ability to behave in a reasonable (and self-limiting) fashion is, in turn, something that people invariably learn when in all spheres of civil society – cultural, political, economic – they are allowed maximum responsibility for organizing their own lives and are granted the constitutional right to pursue their own well-being ("happiness") in free association with others, for what this teaches them is that in the long run their own interests are best served and their own rights best protected when, in a spirit of reciprocity, they respect the rights of others to pursue their own interests in a like fashion. Maximizing as it does people's capacities for social reason, for communicative rationality, the liberal State is the most rational of all human regimes, fitting as it does Eric Weil's description: "The regime that requires reason from all and from everyone is thus the reasonable regime *par excellence*" (Weil 1971, p. 172).

My basic point is, therefore, twofold: it is essential to a healthy civil society that social movements and other groups be "self-limiting," i.e., reasonable, and it can, moreover, be expected that they will be such when they learn, through actual experience, that their own rights are best protected when they, like everyone else, respect the rights of all others. The norms or values necessary for maintaining civil society and the social cohesiveness necessary for this form of social self-organization emerge out of democratic *praxis* itself.

122

A people which has learned to manage their collective affairs in a communicatively rational way, maximizing thereby their collective welfare in all realms of civil society, has every reason to be proud of themselves, of their civic republic. Herein lies the true meaning of *patriotism* in a postmodern, global civilization, at the very time when nation-states are losing a great deal of the sovereignty they traditionally enjoyed (this is due in large part to free trade agreements and the coordinating arrangements that these arrangements necessarily call forth).[82] True patriotism, in any event, has nothing to do with ethnocentric nationalism (which would best be described by its French term, chauvinism). (One reason for the spread of virulent nationalism – always of an exclusionary sort and more often than not in the form of anti-Americanism – throughout many of the more backward countries of the world is that the people in these countries have nothing much they can be justly proud of in regard to the workings of civil society of either a political, cultural, or economic sort.) True patriotism is based on pride of *citizenship* and not on ethnic or other such communitarian commonalities or affiliations (this distinction corresponds in a rough way to Michael Ignatieff's distinction between "civic nationalism" and "ethnic nationalism" [see Ignatieff 1993]). Citizenship has everything to do with participating, in one's own freely chosen way, in all those spontaneous orders which contribute to the common good; it has nothing to do with gaining self-esteem by identifying with a particular ethnic, racial, religious, or other such community. And citizenship in this sense is not opposed to universalism or cosmopolitanism. As Enlightenment thinkers rightly insisted, one can have a true love for one's own country only if one is willing, in a spirit of universal reciprocity, to accord due respect to all others (see Lepenies 1993, p. 24). There does in fact exist a kind of global solidarity amongst the citizens of different liberal democracies or nation-states, which is not only not at odds with but is actually a function of the calm patriotism they severally have in their own civil republics.

THE POLITY AND THE ECONOMY

Just as, in a civil society, the cultural realm is independent of the political realm, so likewise is the economic realm. But just as a free civil society demands a particular kind of political arrangement (as I have argued in this chapter), so likewise (it could be argued) it demands a particular kind of economic arrangement. This is what is generally referred to as a "market economy." This fact (having to do with the logic of social orders) has not always been recognized by social theorists. The noted American political theorist, Charles E. Lindblom, for instance, long an opponent like so many of his left-leaning colleagues of "capitalism," stated in 1977: "The large, private corporation fits oddly into democratic theory. Indeed it does not fit" (Lindblom 1977, p. 356). In 1990, however, the same Lindblom was to be found singing the praises of "the market" and arguing that one of the best examples of communicative rationality in practice (what he would call mutual adjustment in the social inquiry process) was "the market system" (see Linblom 1990, pp 241, 245).[83] This, in itself, was a measure of how far Western social science had evolved in the meantime (due largely, no doubt, to the upheavals in Eastern Europe and the Soviet Union). As Malia has observed:

> With hardly any soul-searching Western and Third World socialist parties suddenly dropped their advocacy of such measures [as centralized planning and nationalization]. At the same time, in the wake of 1989–1991, and almost overnight and without debate, there emerged an astonishing worldwide consensus that the market and private property were indispensable features of any functioning economy; that they were indeed the basis of constitutional democracy and the rule of law; and that this amalgam constituted the natural order of civilized modernity.
>
> (Malia 1994, pp. 514–15)[84]

The "natural order of civilized modernity" is none other than what Adam Smith had long before called the "system of natural liberty."

Although, like a vast number of others, Lindblom had discovered the communicatively rational values of the market, he nevertheless stated that social science "has not much generalized from market to other areas." The truth of the matter is that while "social science" may not have done so, hermeneutical theory most definitely has. Now that the myth as to the possibility of a "third way" between "capitalism" (the market economy) and Socialism has finally been put to rest, it is necessary to deal in detail with the question as to what sort of market economy – generally recognized now to be the most rational of all economic systems – is compatible with, and indeed demanded by, representative democracy. What is the relation between political democracy and economic democracy? What indeed *is* economic democracy? Those are the questions to which we must now turn.

5

THE ECONOMIC ORDER

DEMOCRACY AND THE MARKET

What is the relation between the political order and the economic order in a civil society? What sort of economic arrangement ("system") does a democratic regime call for? Treatment of these questions has been greatly facilitated by the demise of Socialism, of which one author says:

> [M]y generation is the last that can reasonably place faith, and commitment, in the particular blueprint that congealed in Europe between 1848 and 1891: "rational administration of things to satisfy human needs," socialism. Today, as market-oriented reforms sweep the countries that have experienced "socialism on earth," this vision is no longer credible.
>
> (Przeworski 1991, p. 100)[1]

Przeworski is fully representative of the great majority of left-leaning political theorists subsequent to the revolutions of 1989. While he is critical of neoliberalism and supports that position generally referred to as "social democracy," he is under no illusions that this constitutes, in economic terms, any kind of "third way" between a free market economy (based on the right to private property) and a socialist, centrally controlled or planned economy (based on the idea of the public ownership or control of the means of production). "Social democracy" does not designate some kind of supposed alternative to the basic institutions of liberal democracy – including that of a market economy.

Other left-leaning writers whom I have had occasion to cite, such as Jean Cohen, Andrew Arato, and Chantal Mouffe, all of whom could generally be grouped under the label "social democrat" (whether this be their preferred designation or not; perhaps the most appropriate generic term would be "neoleftist," since they generally view their task as that of combating neoliberalism) are of a like mind. As a general rule, they all support the basic principles as well as the core institutions of liberal democracy. Unlike the communitarians, they are committed to such liberal democratic principles as

125

the separation of Church and State, the private and the public realms, private morality and public morality (justice), and, above all, a constitutional defense (such as Constant called for) of the rights of the individual, i.e., human rights. They also recognize that the market system in the economic realm is the only appropriate system for a free, democratic society. However, coming as they do out of an "anticapitalist" background, one thing that they also generally have in common is a profound distrust of the workings of a free market (a trait common to most members or affiliates of the Frankfurt School).

Thus, for instance, because the medium of communication in the realm of a market economy is *money*, thinkers like Arato and Cohen automatically assume that, money being the crass and impersonal thing that it supposedly is (I shall argue later in this chapter that money is essentially a social and intersubjective phenomenon and a medium of communicative rationality), the economic sphere is dominated by instrumental rationality – and power – rather than by communicative rationality (see for instance Arato and Cohen 1992, p. 205; and see also Cohen 1990). This assumption is, however, quite erroneous, as we shall see in the following section. Thus the call on the part of neoleftists such as these for introducing "communicative action" into economic institutions, i.e., for "democratizing" them (see Arato and Cohen 1992, p. 213), is equally misplaced, is, indeed, totally irrelevant and mis-guided.[2] To the degree that it is allowed to operate in accordance with the logic proper to it, the economic realm of a free, civil society is *already* a realm of free, communicative action and interaction. If this is indeed the case (as I hope to show that it is), the call on the part of the neoleftists for "social control" over the economy would have as disastrous an effect in the eco-nomic realm as "social control" over the state (i.e., participatory democracy) would have in the political realm (as I argued in the preceding chapter). One cannot, without contradiction, embrace political liberalism, as Chantal Mouffe for instance does, and at the same time continue to ride the old anticapitalist bandwagon and oppose economic liberalism.[3] Political liberal-ism and economic liberalism go together and are altogether inseparable; citizens cannot be truly free unless they are free economically as well as politically. Freedom, as Havel says, is indivisible.

Calls for "economic democracy" in the market place on the part of neoleftists who seem to have not the slightest appreciation for the way in which a free market economy actually does work are thus, in my estimation, not only inappropriate but also pernicious (in subsequent sections of this chapter I shall consider in more detail the relations that obtain between the political and the economic realms of a civil society). While, after the demise of Socialism, the former Marxist, or *marxisant*, theorists have now endorsed, if only grudgingly, the principle of a market economy, they have done so in ways which reveal a profound misunderstanding of how this "system" actu-ally works.[4] Although, as I shall be arguing (as I have throughout this book),

126

there are profound commonalities between the logics proper to the cultural, political, and economic realms (they are all, each in regard to each other, "synergic" in that they are all forms of communicative rationality), there are nonetheless important differences between them. These differences are altogether ignored by the post-Marxists. Continuing to operate under a kind of "holistic" (totalizing) mentality – their discovery of the virtues of liberal pluralism notwithstanding – they would impose on the economic realm criteria that are appropriate only to the political realm, confusing and confounding in the process the roles of *citizen* on the one hand and *consumer* or *worker* on the other (an error that is as common to them as, it should be noted, it is to numerous libertarian defenders of free enterprise; I shall return to this question in the final section of this chapter).[5]

Thus, at the very moment when the virtues of a free market economy have been recognized by all open-minded political/social thinkers, there persists a great deal of misunderstanding – on all sides – as to what "the market" is and how it functions and, accordingly, as to what legitimately and properly (and feasibly) can or cannot be done by way of "intervention" in it. Thus the effort of this chapter must, for the most part, be restricted to elucidating some of the more important features of the logic of market economics.

A market economy is what is usually referred to as "capitalism." The latter is, in my opinion, a most unfortunate term and one which I personally find distasteful, given its ideological overload, although I suppose we simply have to learn to live with it. It is interesting in this regard that the Catholic Church under the pontificate of John Paul II has learned how to do so, the negative connotations of the term notwithstanding. Throughout all of its modern history, the Catholic Church as represented by the Vatican was notably hostile not only to "liberalism" but to "capitalism" as well.[6] As Michael Novak has pointed out, however (see Novak 1993), the 1991 encyclical of John Paul II, *Centesimus Annus*, represented a noteworthy advance (as Novak would say) in the social teaching of the church. Conscious of the fact that the new forms of modern society and the new forms of property and labor bring with them "the hope of new freedoms" but alert also to "the threat of new forms of injustice and servitude" (John Paul II 1991, §4), the Pope continued to be critical of the "consumer society" (ibid., §19). That notwithstanding, the Pontiff put forth a revised assessment of "capitalism" in the light of the revolutions of 1989 and the demise of Socialism. Of the latter he wrote: "[T]he historical experience of socialist countries has sadly demonstrated that collectivism does not do away with alienation but rather increases it, adding to it a lack of basic necessities and economic inefficiency" (ibid., §41). He then went on to raise the inevitable question: "[C]an it perhaps be said that, after the failure of Communism, capitalism is the victorious social system, and that capitalism should be the goal of the countries now making efforts to rebuild their economy and society? Is this the model which ought to be proposed to the countries of the Third World which are searching for the path to true economic and civil progress?" (ibid., §42). For readers familiar with this Pope's past pronouncements as well as with the traditional social teaching of the church, John Paul's answer had an element of genuine surprise to it. He said:

> The answer is obviously complex. If by "capitalism" is meant an economic system which recognizes the fundamental and positive role of business, the market, private property and the resulting responsibility for the means of production, as well as free human creativity in the economic sector, then the answer is certainly in the affirmative, even though it would perhaps be more appropriate to speak of a "business economy," "market economy" or simply "free economy."
>
> (John Paul II 1991, §42)

Elsewhere in his encyclical the Pope made this endorsement of "capitalism" more specific. For instance: "The modern *business economy* has positive aspects. Its basis is human freedom exercised in the economic field, just as it is exercised in many other fields. Economic activity is indeed but one sector in a great variety of human activities, and like every other sector, it includes the right to freedom, as well as the duty of making responsible use of freedom" (ibid., §32). And: "It would appear that, on the level of individual nations and of international relations, *the free market* is the most efficient instrument for utilizing resources and effectively responding to needs" (ibid., §34).

The last remark raises an interesting point that I shall return to in an appendix to this book wherein I shall address the issue of human rights and international justice. As regards the preceding statement on the Pope's part, it is of the greatest relevance to my central argument in this book. To rephrase it somewhat: the economic sphere is one sector of civil society. The idea of civil society is itself based on the notion of human rights (a civil society is nothing other than a society which, throughout, is coherently organized around the idea of human rights). Therefore, an indispensable condition for the existence of a full-fledged civil society is that human agents be accorded as much freedom in the economic "sector" as they are in the moral-cultural and political realms. Respect for the intrinsic dignity of the human person demands as much. Respecting the dignity of persons means respecting their right to exercise to the fullest their innate intelligence and creative abilities. In the economic realm, *entrepreneurship* is one vital aspect of human creativity, as the Pope recognized. Thus as John Paul also says: "Man fulfils himself by using his intelligence and freedom. In so doing he utilizes the things of this world as objects and instruments and makes them his own. The foundation of the right to private initiative and ownership is to be found in this activity" (John Paul II 1991, §43).

128

In light of the discussion of social solidarity in the preceding chapter, it is interesting to note as well how the Pope observes that in working for themselves people also, at the same time, work not only for their own sake "but also *for others* and *with others*" – and contribute, in this way, to "a progressively expanding chain of solidarity." A final note in this regard concerns the notion of "market Socialism": assuming that this term is not an oxymoron pure and simple, "market Socialism" (a notion that I shall analyze in greater detail in a subsequent section of this chapter) would, in any event, be incompatible with free enterprise, since, by definition, it would allow for only a narrow range of economic arrangements (favoring, for instance, small-scale cooperatives and prohibiting those large-scale, publicly owned corporations that are anathema to many leftists, neo- or other); it is indeed hard to imagine how any such regime would not want to maintain control over (in Lenin's words) "the commanding heights of the economy." Market Socialism would, therefore, *a priori*, be incompatible with the freedom of economic agents who must, among other things, have access to the freest of banking and financial systems available. (Although there is no clear consensus in the scientific literature as to why it should be the case, and in spite of the fact that in most Western democracies cooperatives are actually encouraged by the legal set-up, it is nevertheless a fact that the form of economic organization that citizens most prefer when allowed a choice in the matter is not the cooperative, worker-owned enterprise but rather the publicly owned, joint stock company.)

Given everything that has been said up to this point, it is obvious that the chief task facing us in this chapter is that of forming a proper understanding of just exactly what a *free market economy* is. It is only when one understands the *principles* of market economics that one can meaningfully "critique" this form of social self-organization (a condition which is plainly not met by many leftist critics of "capitalism"). Frank Knight made a highly pertinent, and most noteworthy, remark in this regard:

We must always keep in mind the relations between the ethical and mechanical aspects of the critical discussion of the economic system. In so far as undesirable results are due to obstructions or interference of a frictional character in the workings of the organization machinery, the correct social policy will be to remove these or to supplement the natural tendencies of the system itself. In so far as these natural tendencies are wrong, the effort must be to find and substitute some entirely different machinery for performing the right function in the right way. There is much confusion in the popular mind on this point: critics of enterprise economy who do not have a fair understanding of how the machinery works cannot tell whether to criticize it because it doesn't work according to the theory or because it does.

(Knight 1982, p. 57)

The important thing to note in this context, and at the outset, is that just as a socialist system – defined as "common ownership of the means of production, distribution, and exchange," in the words of the British Labour Party – has a logic peculiarly its own and which is everywhere the same, so also does the economic "system" of a democratic civil society.[7] As Morton J. Peck observes: "[A] market economy has a certain logic and obeys certain rules whether the economy is located in Latin America, Asia, or Eastern Europe" (Peck and Richardson 1991, p. 15). There is, however, a profound difference between the two "logics." The crucial difference lies in the fact that while the logic of a socialist regime is homogeneous (totalitarian) throughout all the sectors of society, in a civil society each "sector" has its own logic (even though, as I have argued, these different logics are complementary or synergetic in regard to one another). The main task of this chapter will accordingly be that of elucidating the logic of the "capitalist" system. A couple of parenthetical remarks are nevertheless in order at this point: the "capitalist" system is in fact, as we shall see in the following section, not a "system" at all, and "capitalism" is not the best term for referring to the system. As Braudel has pointed out (1982, p. 237), the term "capitalism" is of recent vintage, having emerged only in the early years of this century, and, as Hayek has noted (1988, p. 237), it is "negatively loaded," suggesting as it does that the system in question is designed to serve the special interests of "capitalists" and is thus based on the "exploitation" of the "working class." A more appropriate – and time-honored – name for the "system" in question would be the one used by both Frank Knight and John Paul II: the enterprise economy.

By way of concluding these opening remarks, it may be noted that the *theoretical* task that this chapter assigns itself is not without *practical* relevance. As Janos Kornai very pertinently observes, what one might refer to as "actually existing capitalism" contains, throughout the Western world and like implanted embryos of alien monsters, what Marx referred to as the "germs of Socialism."[8] It is to be hoped that a proper understanding of the logic of the market economy will enable us to uncover and extirpate these germs or seeds before they have the time fully to sprout, overwhelming in their wild profusion the garden, so painstakingly cultivated over so many generations, of civilized society.

Whereas in previous chapters we talked, metaphorically, about "the market place of ideas," we must now analyze *the market place* in its own most proper sense. Just as the common good in the moral-cultural realm is the free market place of ideas (e.g., academic freedom), and just as the common good in the public/political realm is a free market place of ideas of a somewhat similar nature (whose concern is not the "true" but the "just"), so likewise the common good in the economic realm is the market place pure and simple.[9] No developed economy can exist without functioning markets of all sorts (for the exchange and, above all, the valuation of goods and services of every conceivable sort, as well, most importantly, for the financial instruments necessary for dealings and participation in the former). The ancient Greeks called their market place the *agora*. Even though the Greek ideal of participatory democracy is as unfeasible (or undesirable) now as it was then, the Greek institution of the *agora* is as pertinent an institution now as it ever was. For in the free space of the *agora* the Greeks not only traded goods and services of all sorts, they also exchanged ideas of all sorts (the *agora* was a favorite hang-out for the Sophists, the first entrepreneurial class of free-inquiring intellectuals and practitioners of communicative rationality in the history of the world),[10] and, of course in the *agora* ordinary Greek citizens discussed important matters of public policy. Just as happens today, in any free, civil society. No free society can exist without a free and open *agora*.

As I mentioned in Chapter 2, the central problem that has to be dealt with in regard to all three orders of civil society is the problem of *coordination*: how is it that out of the free actions on the part of a multitude of disparate and often unrelated individuals a discernible and well-defined order emerges (or is maintained) that is nevertheless not the result of conscious design or planning on the part of anyone in particular? In regard to the economic order, as Steven Horwitz observes, "the main fact to be explained . . . is how actors with *different* expectations and knowledge are able to coordinate their behavior despite such differences and despite the anonymity inherent in markets" (Horwitz 1994b, p. 20).

The theory of spontaneous orders as worked out by Hayek and other Austrian economists is an attempt to resolve this problem and, in regard to what concerns us in this chapter, to provide an answer to what could be called "the economic question." Institutional economist Geoffrey Hodgson has formulated this question in the following way:

> Since the rise of capitalism, social theory has been faced with a set of questions which mainstream economists have preferred to ignore. How is it that a complex society with extensive market relations and a high degree of competition can stay together and not disintegrate in the war of each against all? Why does a sufficient measure of social solidarity exist in a society where the bonds of tradition are weakened, where the variety of different occupations and vested interests is increased, and people are encouraged to look first and foremost to their own self-interest? What, in these circumstances, prevents society from ruinous schism or collapse, and promotes a degree of integration in a highly differentiated system?
>
> (Hodgson 1988, p. 156)

An examination of the logic of market processes should enable us to resolve these questions.

THE SPONTANEOUS ORDER OF THE MARKET

I indicated that in this chapter we would consider the market place in the proper, literal sense of the term. That is not quite correct. Whereas in so-called "primitive" societies as well as in the Middle Ages in Western Europe when capitalism was in its nascent stage the "market" had a literal meaning, referring to an actual, physical place (*place*, in the French sense of the word) in which goods and services were traded (often, as in the *fêtes foraines* of medieval towns, only once a year), that is no longer the case in modern, highly developed societies. To be sure, markets of the traditional sort continue to exist in the form, for instance, of flea markets and farmers' produce markets (although, it must be admitted, in our times the latter often draw upon wholesalers to "top up" the supply of produce that they offer to consumers and which they themselves are not capable of bringing to market, at any given time or other). The (modern) fact of the matter is that markets have become increasingly *immaterial* and *invisible*. Indeed, the most important market of all in the emerging global economy, the market in capital and financial instruments, exists nowhere in particular and has no physical substrate, being located as it is in the diaphanous realm of cyberspace.[11] The point that I wish to make is that in order to understand "the capitalist system" it is of the utmost importance to realize that "the market" is not a place or a static entity but is, rather, a dynamic *process* – or, to be more exact, a whole ensemble of such processes ("millions of disaggregated micromarkets" [Aslund 1994, p. 68]). The study of the market *economy* is nothing other than the study of market *processes*.

What, then, is the nature of these processes? In accordance with what sort of rationality or logic do they operate? Przeworski, whom I quoted above in connection with the demise of Socialism, quite fittingly remarks on how "the very notion that any decentralized social system can function in an orderly way still baffles the imagination of many socialist critics of capitalism" (Przeworski 1991, p. 105). Ever since Marx, socialists have spoken of the "anarchy of the market" (cf. Alexander Yakovlev in 1988: "Of course, in conditions of private property and social antagonism, the market is, inevitably, pregnant with crises, wrecks and numerous adverse implications for the working people" [Yakovlev 1988, p. 66]). Thus, as one Marx scholar observes: "Genuine Communists . . . have always seen the market as synonymous with economic anarchy, as a total surrender of human beings to blind, uncontrollable, quasi-natural forces. Hence the Communist ideal of human liberation presupposed the destruction of the spontaneous order of the market and its replacement by conscious, rational planning" (Walicki 1989, p. 365; see also Walicki 1988). (It may be noted that, like the socialist critics of capitalism Przeworski speaks of, post-Marxist critics of academic freedom have no more of an idea as to how the market place of ideas generates its products ["truths"] than they have as to how the market place

132

of goods and services does, which is, of course, by a process of ordered anarchy.)

That a socialist, planned economy would be more rational, in the purely instrumentalist sense of the term, than a self-coordinating market is undeniable. However, on the basis of the empirical evidence that is now available, it is also undeniable that such an economy is an unworkable pipe-dream. It is interesting that while Przeworski fully concedes this point, he nevertheless continues to maintain, along with the Marxists, that capitalism is *irrational*.[12] Why is this? A moment's reflection on the reasons for Przeworski saying what he does may put us in a better position for understanding the logic of market processes.

Without going into the details of what is a highly complex and hotly debated issue in the fundamentals of economic theory, the key notion in this matter is that of *general equilibrium*. Przeworski can claim, and rightly so from his point of view, that capitalism is irrational in that it does not, as an actually existing system, meet the requirements for "rationality" (optimality) as laid down by main line, neoclassical economic science. That is to say, markets never actually, as a matter of fact, do what according to standard theory they're supposed to do, namely, "clear." They never reach an equilibrium point wherein supply perfectly conforms with demand and the productive forces (as Marx would say) are utilized to their maximum and most efficient potential.[13] Przeworski says that according to the "capitalist blueprint" itself, i.e., the definition of capitalism defended by neoclassical supporters of the system, capitalism is a failure – or, better said perhaps, is not the fully rational system its defenders make it out to be. I believe that Przeworski is perfectly right on this score. If "capitalism" is defined in the way mainstream economic science defines it – in terms of equilibrium – it is indeed irrational. In response to Przeworski, however, I would want to insist that the notion of equilibrium is not the appropriate conceptual tool for understanding market processes (what Przeworski aptly refers to as "collective rationality") in the first place. (This is another reason for my dislike of the word "capitalism"; in the way economic science defines it, "capitalism" fails, in my estimation, to refer adequately to the real world phenomenon of market processes.)

Within the cultural order of ideas, those specifically having to do with economic matters, encouraging developments are, however, underway. A number of younger representatives of the "Austrian" school of economics have not hesitated to call into question the very notion of equilibrium – in many ways the most sacrosanct dogma of mainstream economic science (see Mirowski 1989). Their reason for doing so is a properly hermeneutical one, their goal being that of working out theoretical instruments better adapted to capturing the meaning of the real world ("lifeworld") economic *praxis* of economic agents engaged in the daily workings of a market economy. It is their conviction (as it was that of Frank Knight who, as far back as the 1940s, declared that "the need is for an interpretative study [*verstehende Wissenschaft*] which, however, would need to go far beyond any possible boundaries of economics and should include the humanities as well as the entire field of the social disciplines" [Knight 1956, p. 177]) that economic science has for too long been dominated by positivistic, "objectivistic,"[14] and excessively rationalistic concepts and methodologies bearing no real resemblance to what goes on in the real world populated by flesh and blood economic actors. Economic agents are not mere "factors of production" (or consumption) but are, as Kierkegaard might say, actually existing persons. The "Austrian" concern for "real world" economics is of the sort shared by Nobel prize-winning economist Ronald Coarse who has criticized what he calls "blackboard economics" and who has insisted that the acting human being is not *homo economicus* (a purely imaginary, bloodless entity), i.e., is not the mere "utility maximizer" neoclassical economics has made him out to be: "[T]he rational utility maximizer of economic theory bears no resemblance to the man on the Clapham bus or, indeed, to any man (or any women) on any bus" (Coarse 1988, pp. 19, 3–4). "Much of modern economics," the neo-Austrians for their part insist, "is trapped in an ahistorical equilibrium world unable to render intelligible the purposive action of human beings in the real world" (Boettke et al. 1994, p. 70).[15] As yet another writer observes: "[E]quilibrium theory is bound to eliminate central features of real life, at least as far as it is not in a position to give an adequate picture of what is going on in market processes. In other words, equilibrium theory excludes *real time* and *human creativity* from its investigation" (Fehl 1994, pp. 198–99; see also Madison 1994c). In short, as Steven Horwitz points out: "The deterministic utility maximization equations of general equilibrium theory deny any scope for the 'subject'" (Horwitz 1994b, p. 20).

It is worth noting in this regard how the scientistic notion of equilibrium in the economic order corresponds perfectly to the Habermasian notions of consensus and unanimity in the cultural and political orders. This suggests that the notion of equilibrium is as inappropriate in the economic order of a free society as the other notions are in their respective orders. It is indeed odd that in an attempt to make sense of real world processes of an economic, cultural, or political sort, writers such as Habermas should have recourse to theoretical constructs that describe a situation that would prevail *only if the processes in question no longer existed*! Just as Habermasian consensus describes a state of affairs in which the pursuit of truth has come to an end – the "death of understanding" – so likewise, as Prychitko observes, "general equilibrium spells the end of time, uncertainty, and human action" (Prychitko 1993a, p. 373) – the end, in sum, of economic activity itself.[16] In opposition to this end-state way of thinking, the neo-Austrians seek to view the market process as an ordering process of an "evolutionary" sort (analogous to the inquiry process analyzed in Chapter 3). And as they point out, no biologist would ever say that evolutionary processes are best understood

134

when viewed in the light of ideal end states (i.e., in static terms). Thus, as they say, "the evolutionary process in economics does not refer to an end-state [equilibrium], but instead explains how creativity leads to complexity, while retaining a sufficient degree of coordination to make the complexity beneficial" (Boettke, Horwitz, and Prychitko 1994, p. 66). The important thing is that the market economy be conceived of not in terms of *stasis* but in terms of *process*. As Ulrich Fehl states: "If . . . the spontaneous order of the market cannot . . . be illustrated by the final state of a process, that is, an equilibrium state, it has to be brought into close connection with the ongoing market process itself; that is, we have to look for an order, *sui generis*, referring to the process *as a process*" (Fehl 1994, p. 200; emphasis added).

The general point that this discussion of the notion of equilibrium was meant to make is that the market economy can be said to be irrational only to the extent that one entertains an overly *rationalistic* conception of rationality, one which in fact reduces reason to mere instrumental, means-end (utility maximizing) rationality.[17] It is no doubt not without irony that in this regard both the Marxists and the anti-Marxist defenders of "capitalism" are agreed on what a capitalist system should be, at least in principle. Neither I nor the latest generation of Austrian economists share this common assumption, however, and we are therefore calling for new paradigms in economic thinking. What might happen, for instance, if we broke away from the mainstream, neoclassical paradigm (which Habermas, for one, continues to adhere to, viewing "the economy" as simply a "sub-system" run according to "steering-mechanisms" and the dictates of purely instrumental rationality)? If we were to abandon "the standard perfect competition analysis upon which most neoclassical economists base their defense of capitalism" (Lavoie 1995, p. 124), how might we then attempt to conceptualize market processes (which, it must always be remembered, is only a shorthand way of referring to the complex array of activities on the part of all those multitudinous individuals who, when their freedom and dignity as creative beings is recognized, engage in all sorts of multifarious interactions of a totally unpredictable sort)? Perhaps the best way of getting a handle on this issue would be to address the question of *money*. Although leftist intellectuals usually profess a disdain for money, they also know that money plays a vital role in any developed economy.[18] Why does money play such an important role? Indeed, what exactly is money?[19]

In previous ages money was a tangible, material sort of thing (having an "intrinsic" value of its own): pieces of gold or tobacco leaves. Gold, tobacco, and other such material entities have now, however, become mere "commodities" whose value is continually reassessed in purely monetary terms on the various commodity markets of the world. Money itself no longer has anything "material" about it. Given the immensely complicated forms of credit and finance that modern banking and financial institutions have developed (and the workings of which they themselves only very vaguely understand), it is in fact impossible to say exactly what money is (is it M1, M2, M3, or what?). While economic science may not be in a position to tell us exactly *what* money is, or how best to calculate the amount of it there is in circulation, we nevertheless now know very well what money *does*, what its *function* is (which may indeed be its true "essence"). The more advanced an economy is, the more it relies upon money or monetary credits (as opposed to barter, the direct exchange of one concrete value for another). And the more diversified and complex the banking and other financial institutions of an economy are, the more money itself is diversified into all sorts of intangible and immaterial forms (which can only be very vaguely kept track of by highly sophisticated [and no doubt also, highly unreliable] accounting techniques). Unlike gold or any other thing-like commodity, money is not the sort of thing that could be the exclusive possession of private individuals, as isolated atomistic subjects. The miser who hoards his money under a mattress is not only not contributing to the common good – which he would do if he deposited his money in a bank, from where it would be reinvested in profitable enterprises – he is undermining his own private welfare as well. For money, unlike gold or some other material substance, is, in its very essence, *intersubjective* and cannot be kept out of general circulation without losing in value. As Simmel stated in *The Philosophy of Money*, first published in 1900: "Money is entirely a social institution and quite meaningless if restricted to one individual" (Simmel 1990, p. 162).[20] The value of money is in no way an intrinsic property of it; whatever particular value a money or currency might command is a function of the valuations that individual economic agents place upon it. As one eighteenth-century writer, J.M. Dominguez, had already observed: "The value of money, undoubtedly, is like the value of everything under the sun: it is determined in accordance with the price which they [the people] are willing to assign" (see Chafuen 1986, p. 81).

This brings us to the crucial point. Now that money has pretty well been divested of all its traditional material substrates (in regard to all the advanced economies of the world, the value that is freely attached to various national currencies, such as the dollar or the yen, is above all a function not, as was the case in former times, of the amount of "territory" that a nation-state commands or of the amount of "natural resources" it may possess but of the "human capital" of the country in question), it is becoming apparent that money is not a material but, as the Germans would say, a *geistig* sort of thing. Money is a thoroughly *human* thing, and its function is that of facilitating human transactions and interactions, i.e., the conversation of the market place. *The essence of money, it could therefore be said, lies entirely in its communicative value.* As Simmel put it, "money is involved in the general development which in every domain of life and in every sense strives to dissolve substance into free-floating processes" (Simmel 1990, p. 168). Money must be understood not metaphysically (in terms of "substance") but hermeneutically (in terms of communicative processes). Money is most properly what it is only to the degree that it is a vital

136

component in "the conversation of mankind." (This is why, when various conversationalists in the business or economic world lose faith – trust – in this or that national currency, that currency plummets in value.)

When in a free market system (i.e., one based not on coercion but on free, mutually voluntary exchange),[21] I offer to someone a certain amount of money for this or that good or service, I am in effect engaging in an argument of a communicatively rational sort. I am saying to that other person: "I think it is in your best interests, as it is in mine, that you take from me this or that amount of money in exchange for this or that good or service. I'm sure you'll agree, if you think about it." Monetary transactions are of a communicatively rational nature; they are not, as neoleftists naively think, purely utilitarian and instrumentalist. Monetary transactions are one extremely important way in which citizens of a civil society carry on their society-constituting interactions with one another.

It may be noted in passing that the "just" price for any good or service is not something that any central planner (or any right-minded social philosopher) could ever decide in an *a priori* fashion, based on their own personal scale of values. The "just price" can, in principle, be arrived at only by autonomous individuals in the course of their intersubjective dealings and in the context of the free discussions in the market. That agreement as to price which is freely arrived at in this manner is, by definition, the "just" price (this is the only truly meaningful, empirically relevant definition there can be of it). In his encyclical letter John Paul II referred to a "just price" as one "mutually agreed upon through free bargaining" (John Paul II 1991, §32). In defining the just price in this way, the Pope was harkening back to ideas first articulated by the "School of Salamanca," a group of fifteenth- and sixteenth-century Spanish Scholastics. In opposition to standard medieval theory and in line with their generally nominalist, anti-essentialist orientation, these Scholastics argued against the traditional objective or substance theory of value and the notion that the value of a good or of money is something intrinsic to it (*bonitas intrinseca*) (Pribram 1983, pp. 20–30). There is, they maintained, no *objective* way to establish the "just price," since value in exchange depends on value in use (as Ludwig von Mises was later to say, "The concept of a 'just' or 'fair' price [in any purely 'objective' sense of the term] is devoid of any scientific meaning" [Mises 1963, p. 332]). Utility and thus value (as measured by price [see Chafuen 1986, p. 97]), Luis de Molina (1535–1600) stated, "depends on the relative appreciation which each man has for the use of the good . . . and on the fact that some men wanted to grant it value" (Chafuen 1994, p. 488).[22] Eclipsed by later objectivist or "substantialist" (essentialist) theories of value (such as the labor theory of value espoused by Marx [see Pribram 1983, p. 254]), these insights into, as Simmel would say, the functional and communicative nature of value were to be reaffirmed in the latter part of the nineteenth century by the "subjectivist" revolution brought about by Carl Menger and the Austrian School of economics: "In effect, the Schoolmen were the forerunners of the late nineteenth-century economists who 'discovered' the subjective theory of value" (Chafuen 1986, p. 103).

That the rationality of the market place is that of communicative rationality is something that Adam Smith also sought to emphasize. In his lectures in moral philosophy at the University of Edinburgh he stated:

> If we should enquire into the principle in the human mind on which this disposition of trucking [economic exchange] is founded, it is clearly on the natural inclination every one has to persuade. The offering of a shilling, which to us appears to have so plain and simple a meaning, is in reality offering an argument to persuade one to do so and so as it is for his interest. Men always endeavour to persuade others to be of their opinion even when the matter is of no consequence to them.
>
> (Smith 1978, p. 352)

Smith returned to this point in *The Wealth of Nations*. A student of classical rhetoric and, thus, of communicative rationality, Smith referred here as well to the human "propensity to truck, barter, and exchange one thing for another" of which he said: "Whether this propensity be one of those original principles in human nature, of which no further account can be given; or whether, as seems more probable, it be the necessary consequence of the faculties of reason and speech, it belongs not to our present subject to enquire" (Smith 1979 I, p. 250). Whether or not this belonged to Smith's enquiry, it most definitely does belong to ours. As a professor of classical rhetoric, Smith had every reason to believe that humans are economic creatures, engaging, as no other animal species does, in "trucking, bartering, and exchanging" *precisely because* they are beings possessing the "faculties of reason and speech," what the Greeks (Isocrates in particular) called the *logos*, i.e., the "faculty" of communicative rationality.

A free market economy is, therefore, best viewed not as Habermas and other Frankfurters do, as an instrumental "steering-mechanism," but rather as a free-floating, open-ended *conversation* in the Gadamerian sense of the term. Economic interactions and transactions constitute a genuine form of *dialogue*, even if, as in the case of modern, large-scale economies, one's dialogical partners remain largely anonymous (but, as we saw in Chapter 3, the situation is no different in the case of the community of inquirers). The animating principle of a market economy is basically the same as the one at the center of the cultural order. As one writer expresses this core principle: "It is persuasion, not coercion and manipulation, that characterizes the proper relationship of one life to another" (Palmer 1987, p. 12). (Where coercion and manipulation do exist in any particular market economy, this can usually be attributed to a failing due to exogenous causes [often involving a violation of human rights] of the system to function properly and is a proper object of government intervention.)[23] Appealing to the hermeneutical notion of conversation, Tom G. Palmer writes:

> A free market economy is a kind of grand conversation, made possible by man's faculties of reason and speech [Palmer is here alluding to Smith]. The market is not, however, merely a very efficient device for integrating disparate bits of economic data, as many neoclassical economists consider it. It is not simply an information collating system. Rather, it is a forum for *persuasion*. Persuasion is an essential element in our understanding of the market process because the preferences of suppliers and consumers are not [as main line economic theory assumes them to be] merely *data* (simply the Latin term for "givens") to be input into a vast calculating mechanism, thereby yielding a fully determinate result that was implicit initially. Instead, the market exchange process is better illuminated by the light cast by rhetoric, the art of persuasion (and one of Gadamer's favorite examples of a process not reducible to explicitly articulated rules).
>
> (Palmer 1987, p. 103)[24]

Prychitko is even more explicit on this point. At the risk of citational overload, I nonetheless cite his observations, since they are very much to the point. Prychitko writes:

> [S]pontaneous formed market institutions are *not* the result of atomistic individuals responding to a given array of prices, but the result of individuals already involved in truly dialogical relationships. Trade journals, industry studies, marketing agreements, business lunches, conference calls, higgling and haggling, the interpretation of accounts and so on are all part of the grand conversation of the market place. . . . To deny the spontaneous outcomes of voluntary dialogue – to abolish the market institutions of price and monetary calculation – seems to me to deny dialogue's epistemological relevance in a complex social setting.
>
> (Prychitko 1988, pp. 137, 138–39)

When Prychitko speaks about "dialogue's epistemological relevance," he is alluding to what Austrian economists generally refer to as "the knowledge problem in economic coordination."[25] This problem is, of course, the most fundamental problem of all: how in a free market system do a myriad of economic agents, acting purely in response to immediate considerations and without for the most part any direct knowledge of the plans and interests of other economic agents, manage nevertheless to coordinate their activities such that, on the whole, everyone (the economy as a whole) is served? How is it, for instance, that whenever I need a new supply of milk, I can go to any corner store and find it, in the form of either 1%, 2% or 5% milk fat, readily available in the cooler section? The answer to this problem – one which socialist planners were never adequately able to deal with (milk, like all other consumer items, had always to be rationed, in one form or another) – is actually, in one sense, of the utmost simplicity. In a free market economy, just about everything that market participants need to know is conveyed to them directly by *monetary prices*.

Money is not a physical entity but, like any language, a *semiotic* entity.[26] Money is that particular semiotic system in which humans, in their capacity of economic agents, express (in terms of prices) the value that they attach to various things (see Menger 1976, p. 173). Simmel put the point in the following way: "In this sense, money has been defined as 'abstract value.' As a visible object, money is the substance that embodies abstract economic value, in a similar fashion to the sound of words which is an acoustic-physiological occurrence but has significance for us only through the representation that it bears or symbolizes" (Simmel 1990, p. 120). This has to do with what Austrian economists refer to as the "subjective theory of value." The core principle of this theory was stated in the following way by Carl Menger in 1871: "[V]alue is nothing inherent in goods and . . . it is not a property of goods. . . . [N]ot only the *nature* but also the *measure* of value is subjective. Goods always have value *to* certain economizing individuals and the value is also *determined* only by these individuals" (Menger 1976, pp. 145–46). The "subjective" theory of value is in fact a phenomenological theory of value, i.e., one which focuses on the role of the acting subject; it maintains that, as Mises later stated, the "ultimate source of the determination of prices is the value judgments of the consumers. . . . It is ultimately always the subjective value judgments of individuals that determine the formation of prices" (Mises 1963, pp. 331–32). Or as Simmel said: "Economic value consists in the exchange relationship of objects according to our subjective reaction to them" (Simmel 1990, p. 130).

Money, I said, is a semiotic system. A semiotic or sign system, such as a natural language, e.g., French or English, is a system of differential values in which the individual units or values, e.g., words, have meaning not in themselves but only in relation to one another; the value ("meaning") of a word, for instance, is, in any given language, a function of its exchangeability with regard to other words (this is why we have thesauruses or *dictionaires de synonymes*). Being a pure system of differential relations ("diacriticality," as the Swiss linguist Ferdinand de Saussure would say), a semiotic system thus serves to express relationships between things (as humans perceive them). As Simmel wrote:

> The philosophical significance of money is that it represents within the practical world the most certain image and the clearest embodiment of the formula of all being, according to which things receive their meaning through each other, and have their being determined by their mutual relations. . . . [M]oney represents pure interaction in its purest form; it makes comprehensible the most abstract concept; it is an

individual thing whose essential significance is to reach beyond indi-
vidualities. Thus money is the adequate expression of the relationship
of man to the world, which can only be grasped in single and concrete
instances, yet only really conceived when the singular becomes the
embodiment of the living mental process which interweaves all singu-
larities and, in this fashion, creates reality. . . .The significance of
money . . . [is] that it expresses the relativity of objects of demand
through which they become economic values. . . .[I]t is nothing but a
pure form of exchangeability.

(Simmel 1990, pp. 128)

When the relative value of goods and services is expressed in monetary
terms (in the form of prices), this allows for that particular semiosis or
communication process that is nothing other than the market process itself.
As in other communicative processes wherein participants seek to work out
mutual agreements, the market process is a process of mutual adjustment. As
Boettke says: "The nature of the dialogical process of the market begins with
the face-to-face relations of the buyer and seller, but that relationship provides signals by way of the establishment of exchange ratios which guide
thousands of anonymous actors to coordinate their actions one to another"
(Boettke 1990c, p. 37). Thus, when in a free pricing market there is not
enough milk on the market to meet consumer demand such that consumers
are competing for what limited supply of it there is, retailers, in what is then a
seller's market, will raise the price of milk (in accordance with the law of
supply and demand [the more dollars there are competing for scarce goods,
the more those goods will rise in price]); this raising of prices on the part of
retailers will, however, send out a clear and distinct message to dairy farmers,
the message being that they can themselves make more money by producing more milk; the increased production of milk that then results will in
turn result in lower unit prices of milk on the retail market (given, once
again, the law of supply and demand); the net result will be that consumers
will have all the milk they desire, at the most reasonable price. Thus as
Boettke also says: "Focus must be placed upon the communicative function
of the market system within disequilibrium and how that system utilizes the
scattered bits and pieces of knowledge throughout the economic system to
coordinate the diverse expectations and plans that exist on the economic
scene" (Boeltke 1990c, p. 38). (It should go without saying that this mutual
adjustment process by means of free-floating monetary prices cannot be
expected to work where there are "rigidities" built into the market, due for
instance to government-controlled marketing boards or various forms of
government-licensed monopoly.)

What this means is that a market or self-regulating economy is unique in
that prices, as established by the give-and-take of free trade, communicate
essential information to economic actors, telling them in effect how best to

allocate their limited resources in order to achieve maximum economic gain. As Lavoie says,

> A price is not just a number. It is an indicator of the relative scarcity of some particular good or service of whose unspecified qualities and attributes we are only subsidiarily aware . . . .[P]rices act as an economical summary of information by allowing decision-makers to respond to changes in relative scarcities without knowing the causes of such changes.
>
> (Lavoie 1995, p. 131)[27]

To speak of the "language of prices" is therefore no mere metaphor: prices do indeed communicate vital economic information and thus constitute a kind of semiotic code. Prices are indeed, in the economic realm, the most efficient medium of communicative rationality. As Przeworski notes: "The fact is that the only practicable mechanism we know today by which people can inform each other about their needs and their capacities is the price mechanism" (Przeworski 1991, p. 118).

It is of the utmost importance to note that the rationality of pricing mechanisms is altogether different from technological-instrumental rationality, i.e., the form of rationality according to which both Marxists and neo-classical defenders of capitalism seek to understand the "capitalist system." It is a different form of rationality in that the economic meanings embodied in prices, which is to say the knowledge that prices communicate about the saleability of commodities and other valuations attached to them by consumers, are not "theoretical" but "practical." That is, they are inextricably embodied in economic *praxis* itself and are thus (like the various forms of "tacit knowledge" described in Chapter 3) never fully thematizable. What we have to deal with here is a kind of "local knowledge" that cannot be "universalized," that is, expressed in overarching, algorithm-type formulas.[28] The key question for economic analysis thus becomes, in the words of Don Lavoie, "How . . . does a genuinely competitive system manage to make use of knowledge that its own participants cannot even articulate" (Lavoie 1995, p. 116)?

To sum up the discussion so far: hermeneutics views the market process as a conversation aiming at "agreement" and conducted in the language of prices. The function of monetary prices is that of communicating amongst the members of society the innumerable bits and pieces of knowledge possessed by separate individuals, often in a merely tacit form, thereby enabling participants in the market process to coordinate their activities in a spontaneous fashion. Money serves in this way to make possible a self-coordinating economic *community*. It should go without saying, however, that a genuine economic conversation can exist only when it is free from extra-market constraints on prices themselves (i.e., only if prices are determined in the very course of voluntary market transactions and not by government fiat) and only if there is no attempt to determine in advance the outcome of the conversation (just as is the case, *mutatis mutandis*, for arriving at truth in the cultural order). As Gadamer would say, in a genuine conversation (one that "guarantees truth") "no one knows what will 'come out'" (see Gadamer 1975, pp. 447 and 345).[29] A vibrant economy can no more be "planned" than can be the conversation of the cultural order. There is in fact in this regard a most interesting parallelism between the cultural and economic orders. Just as the new, politically correct radicals agitate for an intellectual regime that would be such as, in advance, to allow for only "correct" opinions (e.g., those which are not "demeaning" towards women or racial minorities) to be expressed – by means of speech codes spelling out what may and what may not be said (see Fekete 1994) – so likewise the socialist ideal was a system of planning that would make possible a *pre-coordination* of economic activity by determining "an equilibrium configuration of prices in advance of any actual production activity" (Lavoie 1995, p. 118). Needless to say, mind-sets such as these ignore totally the "trial-and-error" process that is indispensable for the creative discovery process as it operates in either the cultural or the economic realms, i.e., as regards the discovery of either truth or true value.

The basic reason why in the economic realm the conversation conducted in the form of prices must be given free reign is that the knowledge that monetary prices convey *does not preexist the act of communicative discovery itself.* This is the case, phenomenological hermeneutics maintains, in all instances of the creative discovery process. The languages of prices does not merely "express" preexisting economic knowledge, any more than language in general merely "expresses" or "transmits" a fully-formed and preexisting thought, as the leading French phenomenologist, Maurice Merleau-Ponty, most notably argued (see Merleau-Ponty 1962, as well as Madison 1981). The kind of knowledge that entrepreneurs pick up on, for instance, does not, unlike merely technological information, preexist the "application" that entrepreneurs put it to.[30] Entrepreneurship is a prime instance of the "creative discovery procedure"; creative entrepreneurship is, as Mises emphasized, the key factor in determining ("discovering") the correct or "just price" of things – which means of course that, contrary to standard theory, "There is nothing automatic or mechanical in the operation of the market" (Mises 1963, p. 335).

Thus, although I said above that a socialist, planned economy would be the most rational of economies, that was not quite correct – even though I did qualify my remark with the phrase "in the purely instrumental sense of the term." In "pure" theory and in a world in which people acted in a purely (instrumentally) rational fashion (as envisioned for instance by Rational Expectations Theory), Socialism might well be the best of all economic systems, but Socialism is manifestly not the best of systems when one takes into account (and where theory must be adapted to) the real world of human beings – beings who, as is manifestly the case, have only limited and finite understanding and who, as Frank Knight pointed out, must continually cope

143

with *risk* and *uncertainty* (Knight 1921) or what Austrian economists call "radical ignorance." In an imperfect world such as this, central planning is absolutely, *theoretically* impossible, and for one simple reason: the "knowledge" that planners would have to take account of in order to do their planning simply does not exist! As Hayek argued in the famous "socialist calculation debate" of the 1930s (see Lavoie 1985b and Vaughn 1994), central planning runs up not merely against an immense technical problem (collecting all the knowledge or "information" necessary to coordinate an economy in such a way that all producers' and consumers' demands are met), it is impossible as a matter of principle, the reason being that the knowledge that would have to be collected is, to a very large extent, of a merely tacit or practical nature (as described in Chapter 3). Thus the important thing to note is that the price system is not only a transmitter of decentralized knowledge (as economists now generally recognize) but that, as Hayek also insisted, this knowledge is largely of an *inarticulate* sort (see Lavoie 1995).[31] As Merleau-Ponty would say, it is a form of "embodied" knowledge which can never be fully "thematized"; the free play of prices in a market economy amounts to a kind of "*spontanéité enseignante.*" To put the matter another way, the knowledge in question is a kind of knowledge that is generated *only in the actual process of free market transactions*. James Buchanan, a student of Knight's at the University of Chicago, states in this regard:

> I want to argue that the "order" of the market emerges *only* from the *process* of voluntary exchange among the participating individuals. The "order" is, itself, defined as the outcome of the *process* that generates it. The "it," the allocation-distribution result, does not, and cannot, exist independently of the trading process. Absent this process, there is and can be no "order". . . . From this it follows that it is *logically impossible* for an omniscient designer to know, unless, of course, we are to preclude individual freedom of will.
>
> (Buchanan 1982, p. 5)

Just as the only conceivable way in which a planned economy (or an "equilibrium" economy as envisaged by neoclassical economists) could work would be, as Buchanan says, if economic agents were *not* free, autonomous subjects, so it is also the case not only that planning cannot employ the tacit knoweledge embedded in market transactions but that central planning would, as one scholar points out, "also probably destroy [this tacit knowledge] in the attempt to articulate it in an explicit manner" (Bellarmy 1994, p. 345).

The communicative function of market processes is, nevertheless, subject (as in the case of all things human) to various pathologies – which means that it often does not work the way it should according to the theory outlined above. Commenting on Hayek's view of money as a communicative medium and the price system as a communication network facilitating economic coordination, two market economists observe that "The use of money, while greatly facilitating economic coordination, contains an inherent potential for discoordination" (Garrison and Kirzner 1989, p. 129). In this regard, one of the most serious pathological conditions of the body politic is monetary *inflation*. This particular disease is so serious that when an analogous situation occurs in the cultural realm, we speak, metaphorically, of linguistic inflation, a development whereby concepts (such as democracy, liberty, or equality) progressively lose greatly in semantic value or decidable meaning (see for instance the usage of terms such as "harassment" or "affirmative action" in the hands of the politically correct or, more ominously, the use of the word "democracy" by regimes such as North Korea and the former East Germany). Linguistic inflation is a very dangerous phenomenon, since when things go wrong with language, it can be expected that they will also go wrong with the world which we construct by means of language. This is because, as the hermeneutical philosopher Charles Taylor observes, there is no rigid distinction "between social reality and the language of description of that reality." "The language is constitutive of the reality," Taylor says, "is essential to its being the kind of reality it is" (Taylor 1985, p. 34). Given the relation of symbiosis, which is to say, the relation of metaphoricity that prevails between the various orders of civil society, to speak of linguistic inflation is not to have recourse to a "mere" metaphor. Inflation, be it linguistic or monetary, is a pathological disorder of social reason, a disorder of the very first order.

The inflation in the economic realm I am speaking of does not have to do with normal cost of living increases resulting from increases in the price of this or that particular good due, for instance, to unexpected shortages (such as when inclement weather devastates the coffee crop in Brazil). Inflation of this kind is always, however often it occurs, a one-time sort of thing, and it is something that any healthy economy can usually cope with (in the 1970s Japan managed to deal with the gigantic hike in oil prices dictated by OPEC in such a way as to keep its products, automobiles in particular, generally competitive). As Steven Horwitz observes, alluding to the "standard text-book definition" of inflation as "a rise in the general level of prices," price rises due to non-monetary causes (such as shortages) are

> not inflationary because the higher prices are simply accurately reflecting the increased relative scarcity of a factor of production. Making such knowledge available through price changes is precisely what markets are supposed to do according to Austrians, and these price changes should not be thought of as inflationary any more than an efficiently-generated decline in prices should be seen as a problematic deflationary trend.
> (Horwitz 1994a, p. 402)

The truly insidious form of inflation is not anything nearly so banal; it is inflation of a chronic and systemic sort which is caused by continued increases in the money supply (the expansion of credit) that are not matched by increases in productivity. Even when it does not reach hyper proportions (as it did in Russia at the end of the Soviet regime, causing a breakdown in the economy and a reversion to a primitive barter system), inflation of a government-produced sort is always destructive. Attempts to stimulate the economy (employment in particular) by inflating the money supply, a policy aggressively argued for by socialists such as J. K. Galbraith, are invariably counterproductive in the long run and are a recipe for social disaster (the only regime capable of running a country devastated by inflation being a socialist, command economy, which is precisely what Galbraith and his fellow socialists seem still to desire most ardently). While inflation is often in the short-term interests of particular groups such as manufacturers, the automobile and housing industries, and labor unions, it is not in the short-term interest of numerous other groups in society (e.g., bond holders and those living off fixed incomes), and it is most definitely not in the *long-term* interest of society as a whole, since, among other things, it contributes to financial instability and a boom-and-bust economy (see Batemareo 1994).

The reason why inflation is so pernicious is that it thoroughly distorts the conversation of the market place. As various Austrian economists have pointed out, if – as a mere hypothesis – all prices were to inflate at the same rate all across the board, there would be no problem; everything would then retain the same relative value in relation to everything else. This, however, never happens.[32] Because of the complex interdependencies in the market and the differential rate at which increases in prices work themselves through the system, in times of chronic inflation no economic actor can any longer be sure of what any particular price increase means or what lesson it is trying to convey. A great deal of noise and static is introduced into the channels of communication, and prices can no longer perform their essential function, which is that of transmitting knowledge about *relative* changes in the real value of goods (values, being of a diacritical nature and a function of people's sliding "preference schedules," are always relative, never absolute): "The main effect of inflation is the way in which it alters the structure of relative prices" (Horwitz 1994a, p. 403). This serves to undermine the coordinative cohesion – the solidarity – of the economic community, destroying thereby the *trust* that is so vital to the economy of a civil society. When it is allowed to go unrestrained, inflation destroys the very bases of the self-regulating, communicative mechanisms of the market: "The importance of these relative price changes is that they undermine the process by which prices facilitate the social use of knowledge" (ibid., p. 403).[33]

What is particularly pernicious about inflation is that, while it seriously undermines the public good in the way just described, it is nevertheless in the interests (the private good) of those who control the government to allow it to occur, since inflation is a form of hidden taxation and a means whereby governments can avoid facing up to the need to control their expenditures (to the degree that the national currency is allowed to inflate, to that degree the national government will not have to pay back its obligations). And there is yet another reason why chronic inflation is such an insidious disease of the body politic: it encourages the growth of government along with its inherent desire to interfere in all manner and form in society, in such a way as to work directly against the autonomous formations of civil society. As Hayek has pointed out:

> It is no accident that inflationary policies are generally advocated by those who want more government control – though, unfortunately, not by them alone. The increased dependence of the individual upon government which inflation produces and the demand for more government action to which this leads may for the socialist be an argument in its favor. Those who wish to preserve freedom should recognize, however, that inflation is probably the most important single factor in that vicious circle wherein one kind of government action makes more and more government control necessary. For this reason, all those who wish to stop the drift toward increasing government control should concentrate their efforts on monetary policy.
>
> (Hayek 1960, pp. 338–39)

Speaking of the importance of maintaining a stable currency, Oakeshott says that "this belongs to the political economy of freedom needs no argument: inflation is the mother of servitude" (Oakeshott 1962, p. 58).

Inflation undermines trust, and trust is the vital element in a market economy, just as it is in the other spheres of civil society. The reason why trust is so vital to civil society is that trust is one of the prime means by which people cope with *uncertainty* (a ubiquitous, "existential" feature of human life), and civil society is, in regard to the workings of all the various spontaneous orders it comprises, a matter of "organized uncertainty." As Simmel observed in this regard:

> Without the general trust that people have in each other, society itself would disintegrate [a phenomenon that actually occurred in the last days of the Soviet Union], for very few relationships are based entirely upon what is known with certainty about another person, and very few relationships would endure if trust were not as strong as, or stronger than, rational proof or personal observation. In the same way, money transactions would collapse without trust.
>
> (Simmel 1990, pp. 178–79)

When trust is lacking, social solidarity does indeed break down and people revert to what is worst in their nature: hatred, greed, envy, resentment, and the rapacious pursuit of self-interest, narrowly conceived. Thus, as Adam

147

Smith would say, a market economy presupposes the existence in the general population of certain "moral sentiments." The important thing about a free monetary order is that it is itself a moral and civilizing force in that, as Frankel says in speaking of Simmel, money "facilitates the development of an ever widening circle of economic interdependence [i.e., solidarity] based on the dispersion of trust" (Frankel 1977, p. 14). Thus the development of money conceived of as a social institution is not only, as Hayek pointed out, *comparable* to the development of a moral code, *it is itself* a most significant development in social morality. Just as, as Montesquieu pointed out, *fear* is the "principle" of despotic regimes, so similarly *trust* is, as it were, the organizational principle of regimes based not on coercion (e.g., central planning) but on the moral value of freedom.

A free market economy can indeed function properly only so long as, like the other orders of civil society, it is informed by the ethics or norms of communicative rationality. This is an ethic of mutuality and reciprocity: "The market," Frank Knight pointed out, "rests on the ethical principle of mutuality with each party respecting the equal freedom and rights of others" (Knight 1982, p. 449). Unlike the socialist ethic, however, the free market ethic of mutuality and reciprocity does not require that everyone be *de facto* equals, be equal in respect to their material conditions. "Symmetric reciprocity, as the main constitutive element of modern society," Agnes Heller observes, "does not exclude a hierarchy resulting from the division of labour" (Heller 1990, p. 148). Moreover, it is an ethic which, in promoting good will and civil communication, serves also to reconcile private interests and the common good. Unlike the socialist, communitarian ethic, it does not require self-sacrifice and "benevolence" on the part of economic actors; like representative democracy, it is (as Mill would say) an order designed for people as they are, or are speedily capable of becoming.[34] There is, in any event, no more reason for thinking that individual "competitiveness" and social harmony stand irreconcilably opposed in the economic realm than for thinking that they stand so opposed in the political or cultural realms. Kant's observations on man's "unsocial sociability" (see Chapter 4) are as pertinent to the economic realm as they are to any other sphere of human existence.

Addressing, as it were, the charge of immorality ("possessive individualism") routinely brought against capitalism, Frank Knight made the following pertinent observations:

> The theoretically ideal market is described in terms of "perfect competition." This is a most unfortunate term since psychological competition or emulation is not involved and is in fact inconsistent with economic motives. A free market means simply provision for effective intercommunication, so that every man as buyer or seller (or potentially one or the other) is in a position to offer terms of exchange to every other, and any pair are free to agree on the most favorable terms

acceptable to both parties. A free market will establish a price, uniform of all, on every good or service, with the general result that all parties will specialize in production in the manner and degree which secures for each the greatest advantage compatible with the free consent of all. The market rests on the ethical principle of mutuality with each party respecting the equal freedom and rights of others.

(Knight 1982, pp. 448–49; see also pp. 428–29)

Hegel, who knew his Adam Smith, made much the same point in speaking of the "dependence and reciprocity" of all upon all in civil society: "[I]n providing for himself, the individual in civil society is also acting for others" (Hegel 1991, §255; see also §199). More recently, Michael Novak has sought in many of his writings to highlight the ethical dimensions and presuppositions of democratic capitalism. He writes for instance:

Ironically, a society supposedly based upon competitive individualism and possessiveness seems to favor in its citizens forms of generosity, truth, extroversion, and reliance on the good faith of others. Meanwhile, existing socialist societies seem to narrow the circles of trust, as groups competing for the same allocations run afoul of each other's interests. Collectivism pits man against man. A system which encourages each to seek first his own interests yields liberty and receives in return loyalty and love.

(Novak 1982, p. 226)

The last word on this subject is, however, perhaps best left to a former socialist. As Alexander Yakovlev states: "Morality is an integral part of the culture of the commodity society; they are founded on the same principle, which is freedom of choice. Attempts to reject simple morals in the name of some higher communist morality led to disastrous consequences" (Yakovlev 1993, p. 88).[35]

To sum up once again: the form of economy befitting civil society (in fact, the only form of economy compatible with it) is the free market economy. In line with my "inclusive" definition of civil society (see Chapter 2, pp. 35–6), I do not (unlike White 1994, for example) view the economic realm as something outside of civil society, as simply one of its "foundations" or as something in which it is merely "embedded." Under conditions of economic modernity (or postmodernity), a free market economy is an integral part of what is meant when one speaks of "civil society" (as opposed, for instance, to a totalitarian society); no society can fully qualify as "civil" except to the degree that the economic dealings of the citizenry are animated by the principle of communicative rationality as it applies to the market place. It is no accident that the currently much discussed issue of "democratization" (to be considered in more detail in the appendix to this book) invariably involves discussion of the transition to democracy *and* the market.

149

As to the market or enterprise economy itself, it is best conceptualized not as a *system*, in the scientific or physicalistic sense of the term, but as a *self-organizing* or *spontaneous order* of human cooperation. By that I mean that the relation between the "units" of the order (economic actors) are not mechanistic cause-and-effect relations, as in the case of physical systems. Economics is not, or should not be thought to be, a kind of social physics, a Newtonian mechanics of human affairs. To apply, in an unrestricted way, mechanistic or physicalistic (scientistic) categories to human affairs is altogether inappropriate, since the proper object of economics is, or should be, human action, and what is distinctive about the latter is that it is both *meaningful* and *creative*. Since the proper object of economics is human reality and since the realm of human affairs is the realm of freedom, economics is not a natural-science type discipline but, as Carl Menger said, an "ethical" science having to do with "the ethical world," the realm of human or "ethical phenomena" (see Menger 1985, p. 58). To conceive of the economic order as a physicalistic system would be to commit the error of "mechanomorphism."[36] It must be admitted, however, that throughout all of its history main line, neoclassical economics, in its attempt to make of itself a "hard science," has been a victim of "physics envy" (Mirowski 1989) and has sought in the most slavish of ways to model itself after physics, i.e., the study of inanimate matter.[37]

What is involved here is a philosophical issue of the most fundamental sort, an issue in the theory of knowledge or human understanding (i.e., hermeneutics). The old positivist notion that everything that can be understood can be understood properly only by means of concepts borrowed from the study of nature (physics in particular) must be rejected (see my remarks on the postpositivistic philosophy of science in Chapter 3). As hermeneutics has always insisted, human reality has its own unique characteristics. It is thus unfortunate that someone like Habermas should accept main line economic theory without question, since he has in other respects shown himself to be a perceptive critic of positivism. It is indeed ironic in this regard that Habermas furnishes one of the best descriptions of a free market economy when (in a different context, to be sure) he speaks of "a communication community existing under constraints toward cooperation"; the market economy is indeed nothing other than one of those "intersubjective life-contexts" in which, as Habermas says, communicative reason is embodied (see Habermas 1987, p. 40). It is for basic philosophical reasons having to do with the nature of human agency (ones of which Habermas himself is perfectly well aware when it comes to matters other than economics) that "planning," either of the centralized sort characteristic of Socialism or of the more flexible, macroeconomic sort defended by Keynesianism (cf. Habermas' notion of "steering-mechanisms") is to be rejected.[38] Thus, as Don Lavoie succinctly states: "In short, the whole case against Planning . . . is rooted in a critique of objectivist theories of knowledge" (Lavoie 1985a, p. 57).

Although the free market of a civil society is self-regulating and autono-mous (and thus cannot be "planned"), it is not for all that "sovereign," by which I mean that it does not, and cannot, exist in a cultural/legal/political vacuum. As in the case of the other orders of civil society, there are relations of dependence and interdependence between the economic order and other orders, the political order in particular. It is therefore to a consideration of the role of the state in the economy that we must now turn.

THE ROLE OF THE STATE IN THE ECONOMY

Just as many leftists think they are making a telling criticism of "capitalism" when they point out that a market economy fails to achieve the equilibrium in terms of which neoclassical economics erroneously attempts to con-ceptualize it, so likewise a great many leftists believe that they are pointing up a fatal flaw in the capitalist system when they observe that, contrary to *laissez-faire* or libertarian theory, a market economy cannot function prop-erly without "state intervention." Alluding to this criticism, Przeworksi remarks: "I think it can be dismissed with a 'So what?'" (1991, p. 113). Even though this particular leftist criticism is indeed irrelevant, I do not myself propose to dismiss it quite so abruptly. For in order properly to understand the market economy, it is of the utmost importance to understand the sense in which and the degree to which such an economy is dependent on the political order. Addressing the issue of the role of the state in the economic order, John Paul II makes the following pertinent observations:

> Economic activity, especially the activity of a market economy, cannot be conducted in an institutional, juridical or political vacuum. On the contrary, it presupposes sure guarantees of individual freedom and private property, as well as a stable currency and efficent public ser-vices. Hence the principal task of the State is to guarantee this security, so that those who work and produce can enjoy the fruits of their labours and thus feel encouraged to work efficiently and honestly.
>
> (John Paul II 1991, §48)

This is an excellent way of putting the matter. It is indeed the function of a constitutional or liberal State to guarantee the rights of its citizens. These rights are not only civil and political but economic as well. Basic economic rights are, as the Pope observes, the right to exercise one's creative abilities (the right to work), the right to enjoy the fruits of one's labor, and the right to be secure in one's possessions. These rights cannot exist in the absence of the appropriate legal framework (as the countries of Eastern Europe readily learned in their attempt to create market economies).

It is one of the great myths of *laissez-fairism* that a healthy market econ-omy can come into being and flourish in the absence of positive action on the part of the political order. One of the more unfortunate things about the libertarian ideology is the way it provides a ready-made strawman for leftist critics of the market economy who, as Oakeshott says, have no trouble ridiculing it "when they have nothing better to say." As Oakeshott goes on to remark:

> As every schoolboy used to know, if effective competition is to exist it can do so only by virtue of a legal system which promotes it. . . . To know that unregulated competition is a chimera, to know that to regulate competition is not the same thing as to interfere with the operation of competitive controls, and to know the difference between these two activities, is the beginning of the political economy of freedom.
>
> (Oakeshott 1962, p. 55)

Economic activity is, as Adam Smith observed, one of the most characteristically human of all human activities. That particular economic institution referred to as the free market is, in turn, not only the most efficient form of economic exhange yet devised, it is also the most humane of economic arrangements, incorporating as it does a respect for fundamental human rights. However, like all things human, it needs to be carefully cultivated in order to exist and to prosper. As Hayek explicitly stated in his *Road to Serfdom*, often erroneously taken as an apology for *laissez-faire* capitalism:

> An effective competitive system needs an intelligently designed and continuously adjusted legal framework as much as any other. Even the most essential prerequisite of its proper functioning, prevention of fraud and deception (including exploitation of ignorance), provides a great and by no means yet fully accomplished object of legislative activity.
>
> (Hayek 1944, p. 39)

In the absence of laws and regulations whose purpose is that of guaranteeing the "security" of economic agents, the kind of market that would tend to prevail would not be a freely coordinating market but, as the Russians would say, a *mafiya* controlled market.[39] As in the case of both the cultural and political orders of a civil society, there is no contradiction involved in maintaining that while the market is a *spontaneous* order it is also one which requires *diligent cultivation*. Kornai observes in this regard:

> The market coordination of the developed countries emerged spontaneously, but each step in its development was supported by legislation and legal practice. There are a great many refined legal regulations to protect decentralized private transactions, enforce the observance of contracts, ensure fair competition, remove the obstacles to free entry, provide orderly ways of "exit," and defend the rights of debtors and creditors.
>
> (Kornai 1992, p. 452)[40]

152

Knight expressed the matter in his customarily succinct manner when he said: "The main function of government in the modern world is to provide and enforce a framework of rules for securing freedom, and the conditions necessary for effective freedom in economic life. This means that either politics or economics can be regarded as a sub-division of the other" (Knight 1982, pp. 242–43).

In economic matters the single most important human right that it is the supreme function of the State to ensure is the right to private ownership of property. The State ensures this right when, through its political organs, it passes legislation spelling out property rights. Throughout the history of political thought, from Aristotle onwards, the right to property has been argued for in various ways, the most noted of which being no doubt the attempt on the part of John Locke to argue that this is a most basic, "natural" right of man. In line, however, with the "anti-essentialist" and "postmetaphysical" approach that I have been taking throughout this book, I shall engage in no such argument.[41] In a postmodern age the notion of "natural rights" is philosophically naive and unpersuasive in that (as is fully evident in the case of Locke) it presupposes a metaphysical view of the universe of a theological (onto-theological), and thus highly culture-relative, sort (any theological view of the universe will be persuasive only to those belonging to particular religious traditions). In addition, an appeal to "natural" rights suggests that rights belong to people as isolated individuals, but this is not the case. As I have argued previously, human rights are "rational" rights and belong to people only to the degree that they are rational beings, i.e., beings who are essentially social/political animals. It is not man in the state of nature who possesses rights, it is only man in civil society, as Knight insisted.[42] Like the right to privacy discussed in Chapter 3, the right to private property is a *social* right (which means, of course, that property rights will vary somewhat from one civil society to another).[43] That society is the most humane which, by means of judicious legislation, accords to individuals the right freely to develop themselves, along with the rights to autonomy, privacy, and property necessary for this. And, as we have had ample occasion to see, the benefits that accrue to individuals thereby also contribute to the overall common good.[44] Thus, while it is often said that the economic realm is the realm of purely private dealings (between individual and individual) and thus, as some would say, for this reason falls outside the realm of civil society, this is not at all the case. The institution of private property (and the free interactions that this allows for between private individuals) goes to make up one of the most vital *public* realms of civil society. The market is indeed a kind of public forum or *agora* in which individuals can best and most freely realize what is social in their nature. A market economy, it should always be remembered, is an economy mediated by money, and as Simmel pointed out with the utmost clarity, money is an essentially *social* (intersubjective) sort of thing (money, he said "is the essence of the relation of the contracting parties to the whole social group" [Simmel 1990, p. 179]). Don Lavoie underscores this point as well when he remarks: "It is interesting that the Greek word *agora*, which means a marketplace, connotes . . . values of openness and publicness. Despite our modern language of the private sector, markets are essentially communicative processes that need to take place in public. Thus, the secrecy required in black markets is one of the key reasons they do not work very effectively" (Lavoie 1992, p. 445, n. 16). To the degree that one participates in a money economy, to that degree one is involved in one great, intersubjective, and immensely complex "web of significance." As Simmel would say, monetary exchanges in a market economy are a form of social coordination and solidarity of the most highly developed sort.

A less metaphysical way of arguing for the right to property than by appealing to the dubious notion of "natural" rights would be that adopted by John Paul II in his 1991 encyclical. The right to private property, the Pope in effect argued, must be granted to people if their freedom and dignity is fully to be respected and if they are to be "empowered" to pursue their own economic wellbeing ("This right, which is fundamental for the autonomy and development of the person, has always been defended by the Church up to our own day" [John Paul II 1991, §30]). If, as I argued in Chapter 3, freedom is a supreme value, the right to private ownership of property must be held to be a fundamental right, for without this right freedom is severely curtailed. As Hegel would say, the right to private ownership is what enables people to transform the things of nature through creative work and to confer value on them; as such, it is the most concrete expression (realization) of human freedom. "Since I give my will existence through property, property must also have the determination of being this specific entity, of being mine. This is the important doctrine of the necessity of *private property*" (Hegel 1991, §46). Property is the "first reality of my freedom" (ibid., §41). "Not until he has property," Hegel stated, "does the person exist as reason" (ibid., §41). Property is essential for the realization of one's "talents and abilities," for self-realization, and thus for the dignity of the human person.

Where the right to private property does not exist, everyone must work for the state, and no one can be in control of his or her own destiny. The former Soviet Union and the former socialist countries of the world always granted their "citizens" the "right" to full employment, but this was a right they enjoyed only so long as they worked exactly where and how the government told them they should (if they had any objections to the particular job "allocation mechanism" operative in their case, they were packed off to work in the labor camps of Siberia where, while they were definitely "employed," they nonetheless received even less in the way of remuneration).[45] In any event, a less metaphysical argument for private property than the one based on so-called natural rights is available now that a general consensus exists as to the overall desirability of market arrangements – now that, as Václav Havel puts it, it is generally realized that "the only economic system that works is a market economy, in which everything belongs to someone" (Havel 1992b, p. 62).

The argument would go as follows. All economic systems, even the most primitive, are based on property arrangements of one sort or another. A socialist system, for instance, cannot exist unless the main form of property is that of public or collective ownership of the means of production. A market economy has its own exigencies, and the logic of the system requires that the right to private property be fully respected. As Janos Kornai, who as a Hungarian economist was formerly an advocate of that hybrid form of economy referred to as market Socialism, says, it is a matter of "affinity." Just as certain chemicals have an affinity for combining with other chemicals, so, Kornai says, the situation is metaphorically the same "in political economy as well: certain property forms are capable of combining with certain coordination mechanisms. There is also a contrary phenomenon: some property forms cannot associate naturally, without force, with some coordination mechanism or other" (Kornai 1992, p. 477). And thus as Kornai further observes: "There is a close affinity between private ownership and the market mechanisms." Spelling out this affinity in greater detail he writes:

A private enterprise is autonomous by definition: the property rights belong to a private individual or group of individuals. So self-evidently, these autonomous economic units enter into contracts with each other voluntarily, without orders from above. This ownership-based autonomy requires decentralized coordination.

(Kornai 1992, p. 447)[46]

As Kornai points out, one cannot, under pain of logical contradiction, sub-scribe to the idea of a market economy without also, at the same time, recognizing the right to private property. A free market economy simply cannot function properly if individuals are not free to engage in economic transactions on a decentered and mutually voluntary basis, which is to say of course, if they are not free to own and dispose of ("alienate," as economists would say) property as they see fit, within the confines of the law. Quite simply, as Peter Berger states, "There can be no effective market economy without private ownership of the means of production" (Berger 1986, p. 190).

Echoing, as it were, a prominent theme in the writings of Václav Havel and other Czech reformers, economist James A. Dorn observes in this regard:

When the rights associated with private ownership are protected by law, owners will bear responsibility for the uses of their property; they will capture the rewards from efficient use and incur the losses from ineffi-cient use. The linkage between private property and individual responsibility is an important element of private ownership; it provides private owners with an incentive to search for new opportunities for mutually beneficial exchange. Private property, therefore, extends the range of market activity and is essential for a free market price system.

(Dorn 1994, p. 443)

A market economy, as we have seen, is one based on free pricing mechanisms. The important thing to note in this connection is that the "price mechanism" cannot work in the absence of the institution of private property, as Don Lavoie makes abundantly clear:

Private ownership makes possible a social learning process that takes place by embodying knowledge into the price system. The competitive market process gives rise to prices that reflect knowledge about consumer demands and alternative production possibilities, so that prices approximately reflect the relative scarcities of different goods and services. These scarcity-indicating prices then, through the use of profit-and-loss accounting, inform individual decision makers about the relative costs of alternative projects. Thus, more cost-effective alternatives can be found. Profits tell market participants where to find opportunities to improve social coordination, and losses direct them away from unpromising alternatives. Prices act as communicative aids for separated consumers and producers, allowing them to bring their actions into closer harmony with one another.

(Lavoie 1992, pp. 444–45)

Succinctly put, property rights "provide a solution-mechanism for the knowledge problem" (Kamath 1994, p. 127).

To defend the right to property along lines such as these amounts to a rejection of the thesis put forward a number of years ago by Robert Dahl, one which long exerted a pernicious effect on attempts to conceptualize in an appropriate way the relation between the political and the economic orders. "Private ownership," Dahl proclaimed, "is neither a necessary nor a sufficient condition for a pluralistic social order and hence for public contestation and polyarchy [democracy]" (Dahl 1971, p. 61). Recent scholarship of a more serious nature (such as the work of Kornai on socialist economies) is fairly unanimous in rejecting the idea that, as Dahl would have it (having like many others at the time the "Yugoslav Model" in mind), genuine competition is compatible with "social ownership" of the means of production and that a society organized in this way could be "decentralized" and democratic. Given the logic of systems, about which a great deal is now known, a "decentralized" socialist economy (such as was sought after by various "reform communists") is not an "ideal type" (the notion of "ideal types" will be analyzed in what follows). It is, rather, the name for a logically inconsistent and unstable state of affairs which must, of necessity, collapse at some point or other and be replaced by either a genuinely free economy (based on private ownership) or an outright command economy.

The situation has greatly changed since the time when Dahl made his pronouncement. After the demise of Socialism leftist critics of capitalism now generally concede the legitimacy, and even the necessity, of the right to private property. However, they often combine this admission with suggestions that the best economy would nonetheless be a "mixed economy" in which the state would continue to be the major player. How does it stand with this reasoning? Is a "mixed economy" the long sought-after "third way"?

I argued above that although a market economy is "spontaneous" in its workings, it will nevertheless not work the way it's supposed to work in the absence of an appropriate legal-political framework. It is in this sense – and in this sense alone – that the economic order is dependent upon the political order. And, as I also mentioned, that this is the case is demonstrated *a contrario* by the great difficulties that former socialist countries of Eastern Europe experienced in creating functioning market economies in the absence of the proper legal framework having to do with property rights, the law of contracts, tort, taxation, bankruptcy and so on. "East European and Soviet experience since 1990 teaches," as one economist remarks, "that, contrary to earlier assumptions, capitalism does not just happen when people are left alone" (Prybyla 1994, p. 75). While the emerging markets in these countries could have been said to be free in that they were no longer directly controlled by the state, the freedom that for the most part characterized them was a kind of Wild West, anarchic freedom, *une liberté sauvage*, in which there was a great incentive to engage in predatory economic activity and in which mafia-type entrepreneurs rapidly managed to corner a lion's share of the market.[47] In a situation such as this private entrepreneurship consisted mainly in making a "quick buck" and contributed little to the common good. These newly liberated markets were largely and most noticeably *uncivil*.[48] What is therefore crucial from the point of view of political economy is not simply that a free market be *allowed* to exist but that this market be explicitly *designed* to be, in the words of Richard Rose, a *civil market economy* (see Rose 1992).

One of the most instructive attempts in the annals of the history of economic theory and practice to create, *ab novo* as it were, a spontaneously ordered, civil market economy on the rubble of a socialist-type economy was that undertaken by the Ordo group of liberal economists in post-World War II West Germany. At a time when socialist ways of thinking were still in vogue and when Germany itself was under an Allied occupation that had imposed a state-controlled system of economic planning and distribution on the impoverished, war-torn country, a dedicated group of neoliberals, including economics minister Ludwig Erhard, concluded that the only sort of economic system capable of bringing prosperity to Germany was the spontaneous order of the market as advocated by, among others, F.A. Hayek.[49] The task this group set itself was that of working out an *economic constitution* (*Wirtschaftsverfassung*) that would be in conformity to the overall logic of a civil society. As Wilhelm Roepke, one of the leading members of the original Ordo group, said, it is "a question of social and economic philosophy and the corresponding total economic order" (see Bernholz 1989, p. 208). This was, as Ordo theorist Hans Willgerodt observes, a thoroughgoing attempt "to find an economic and social framework that would encourage both a productive economy and personal freedom in a socially-balanced order" (Willgerodt 1976, p. 65).

Another of the original Ordo-liberals, Alfred Müller-Armack, called the new social-economic order (*Wirtschaftsordnung*) a "social market economy," *Soziale Marktwirtschaft*. "The central thrust [of the 'social market economy']," one neoliberal observes,

> was the need to create, in an environment of general political freedom, a situation of economic freedom for the individual within the rule of law. As its advocates saw the problem, both intellectually and through their own experience, this could be achieved neither by central planning nor by *laissez-faire*. . . . The system must be "guided", by way of the provision of an "economic constitution" provided by the state.
>
> (Wiseman 1989, p. 161)

Although the radical reforms instituted under Erhard's long-term economic administration unfolded in stages, immediately upon the stabilization of the German currency (with the creation of a new deutsche mark replacing the worthless reichs mark) and the lifting of most price controls in 1948 shortages disappeared almost overnight and the German economy began its dramatic and long-uninterruped expansion. What followed the freeing of prices was, as Hayek says, "in fact a more determined and conscious effort to maintain a free-market economy in Germany than in any other country" (Hayek 1992, p. 194). The result of this experiment in free market economics is what came to be called the *Wirtschaftswunder*, the German Economic Miracle.[50]

"Miracle" is perhaps not the best word, however. As Roepke always sought to remind people, the miracle was no "miracle" at all but simply "the predictable result of the application of sound economic principles" (Roepke 1987, p. viii). Be that as it may, the "miracle" would continue to unfold from 1948 to about 1970 – as long, that is, as the order as originally conceived was preserved intact. (As an increasing number of state-welfare measures were grafted on to the system in the 1970s, the German economy began to go into a progressive slow-down [see Barry 1987, ch. 7, and Hamm 1989]). In its original version, however, the "social market economy" had nothing in common with what later reform socialists in Eastern Europe would mean by the term. The word "social" was meant to indicate that the market economy that was to be instituted – as pure a market economy as possible – was nevertheless to be an *integral* part of civil society as a whole (dovetailing with the cultural and political orders appropriate to a free society) and that the *raison d'être* of this economy was the promotion of the common good. The German social market economy was indeed a civil market economy based on the principle of private property[51] and decentralized coordination with the state playing an extremely important but nonetheless only indirect, "cultivating," role.[52] The post-war Germans realized full well that the bringing into being of the spontaneous order of a *civil* market economy requires, paradoxical though it might sound, careful *planning*. This is what has been called the "orthodox paradox," i.e., "the need to increase state capacity in order ultimately to shrink the scope of the state's economic intervention" (Armijo et al. 1994, p. 172). Of the German experiment in liberalization Willgerodt observes: "[T]he rules of conduct in a market economy could not and cannot be left entirely at the mercy of market agents, whose own self-interest would often encourage them to harm the new system" (Willgerodt 1976, p.75) – a fact of life that was borne out in the postsocialist, *un*civil market economies of Eastern Europe.

If the virtues of a free market economy are to be defended, such a defense (as the Germans knew full well) can only be provided by the State, by, that is, the collective and enlightened will of a democratic people; no such defense will ever be forthcoming from "capitalists," left to their own devices. Left to their own devices, capitalists (often backed up by solidly entrenched labor unions) will invariably demand monopoly privileges and protectionist measures from government. Even though he is something of a cult hero for libertarians of the most extreme sort, Ludwig von Mises grasped this fact of human life perfectly well when he wrote:

> Entrepreneurs ["capitalists"] ... have absolutely no special interest in fighting Socialism and socialization as such. ... It is not to be expected that entrepreneurs or any other particular group in the community should, out of self-interest, necessarily make the general principles of well-being the maxim of their own procedure. It is not the business of entrepreneurs to lead the political fight against Socialism; all that concerns them is to adjust themselves and their enterprises to the situations created by the measures directed towards socialization, so that they will make the greatest profit possible under the conditions prevailing.
>
> It follows, therefore that neither associations of entrepreneurs, nor those organizations in which the entrepreneurs' support counts, are inclined to fight on principles against Socialism. ... To fight on principle for the maintenance of an economy based on private property is not part of the programme of organized entrepreneurs. ...
>
> Thus there are no individuals and no classes whose particular

159

interest would lead them to support Capitalism as such. The policy of Liberalism is the policy of the common good, the policy of subjecting particular interests to the public welfare – a process that demands from the individual not so much a renunciation of his own interest, as a perception of the harmony of individual interests. There are, therefore, no individuals and no groups whose interest would ultimately be better guarded by Socialism than by a society based on private ownership of the means of production.

(Mises 1981, pp. 455–56)

Mises is uttering here a profound if usually ignored truth: the institution of private property and the free market economy is designed to serve the interests not of a minority ("the capitalists") but of society as a whole. The free market economy is a common good (which means that "free entry" into the market is, in a civil society, a fundamental human right, a question to which I shall return in the following section). A fundamental concern of the Ordo-liberals (given their memories of earlier tendencies in the German economy towards cartelization and monopoly and the way in which this arrangement [based on an autarkic hostility towards foreign trade] facilitated the National Socialist take-over of the economy) was to create a system that would encourage both free trade and open competition. This is not an unimportant issue. For all the follies that the United States Free Trade Commission has engaged in, it is a fact that the State must keep an eye out for fair trade practices. This is because established "capitalists" have, by the nature of the beast, an incentive to collude rather than to compete, as Adam Smith pointed out over two hundred years ago: "People of the same trade seldom meet together, even for merriment and diversion, but the conversation ends in a conspiracy against the publick, or in some contrivance to raise prices" (Smith 1979, vol. I, p. 145). While inflation may be a disease inflicted on the body politic by government and which, therefore, only constitutional measures can ultimately control, unfair business practices are something that the government, in a regime which upholds free enterprise, is itself constitutionally charged with dealing with. (How to insure that the government will exercise its constitutionally mandated, yet strictly limited, responsibilities in this regard in a fair and equitable fashion is one of the overriding problems of our times.)

In this respect the "economic constitutionalism" of the German Ordo-liberals paralleled Madisonian constitutionalism, the purpose of which, as we have seen, was to control the abuses of political power. As one commentator notes, "structural parallels exist between the political constitution on the one hand and free trade on the other" (Möschel 1989, p. 150). In both cases, this writer says:

> The common point should be regarded as being the problem of power. Just as it is the first task of a political constitution to tie governmental power to the law, so it is the first task of an economic constitution to

solve the problem of economic power. . . .[T]he proposed response suggests a substantive separation of powers in the state's relations with society and within society itself.

(Möschel 1989, pp. 151–52)

Both economically and politically, the chief concern of the Freiburg school of Ordo-liberals was the containment of power in the interests of individual autonomy (Streit 1994, p. 510). Speaking of Franz Böhm's notion of economic constitutionalism, one economic historian remarks:

This reflects the recognition that the rules governing private autonomy in a market system and those securing the control of its use through competition have to be considered as complementary in view of the basic conflict between freedom and power. The structure of the economic constitution corresponds to the political constitution of a government under the law (*Rechtsstaat*): on the one hand, autonomy is granted to those who are entrusted to make laws and to govern, but since, on the other hand, autonomy tends to provide opportunities to exercise power, a sophisticated combination of checks and balances is required to prevent an arbitrary use of power.

(Streit 1994, p. 512)

Throughout modern times the formulation of a full-fledged theory of economic liberalism has lagged behind the working-out of a theory of political liberalism, but if by the late eighteenth century the time was ripe for actively designing a liberal polity by means of political constitutionalism, the mid-twentieth century, when socialist ways of thinking were beginning to be put into question, was surely a most appropriate time for formulating a fully developed economic constitutionalism, and this is precisely what the German Ordo-liberals did.

In order to ensure an economic separation of powers and to prevent arbitrary interventions in the economy, ones determined not by economic rationality but by political expediency – the purpose of this constitutional measure being that of securing the economic liberties of the citizenry – the basic constitutional principle of the social market economy was that intervention on the part of the state should, as much as possible, be *marktkonform*, i.e., should operate in conformity with the logic of market processes, in such a way as neither to distort the market nor to impede its functioning.[53] Like the political order devised by Madison, the economic order devised by the Ordo-liberals was a *deliberate* attempt to promote the *spontaneous* ordering of civil society.[54]

The German experiment in economic constitutionalism is highly instructive because it indicates that there is in fact no "third way" between a market economy and a planned economy. It was this mythical third way that reform socialists such as Gorbachev and Aganbegyan vainly sought to pursue under the heading "market socialism" ("plan-cum-market") and that post-Marxian socialists in the West continue naively to advocate, referring to it as a "mixed economy" – something like a Dr. Panglossian "best of all possible worlds" combining all that is supposedly best in Socialism and "capitalism." Logically speaking, however, there is no such thing as a "mixed economy." To be sure, mixed economies do exist in reality, but this is only because in reality everything is always mixed up to some degree or another (witness, for instance, Canada which, although it is in fact a republic and governs itself in a purely republican fashion, is nevertheless, technically speaking, a monarchy presided over by the Queen of Canada, a monarch who is a non-resident in the country she supposedly rules over since her main job is that of being Queen of England). In a market economy, problems (such as "externalities") will inevitably arise whose costs cannot be fully "internalized" and which accordingly cannot be dealt with by purely market mechanisms, just as in a command economy markets will – out of sheer necessity – usually be tolerated to some degree or other. Each system has its own dominant logic, however, which it is the task of interpretation (hermeneutics) to make evident.

Although any actually existing economy is always of a more or less mixed sort, we must nevertheless have recourse to what Max Weber called "ideal types" if we are to understand and deal successfully with the complexities of the real world. We need to have recourse to "essences" in the phenomenological sense of the term because, as Merleau-Ponty said, "our existence is too tightly held in the world to be able to know itself as such at the moment of its involvement, and . . . it requires the field of ideality in order to become acquainted with and to prevail over its facticity (Merleau-Ponty 1962, p. xv). Although Menger, the originator of Austrian economics, admitted "quite unreservedly that *real* phenomena are not exactly typical" and that there "are no strict types in empirical reality" (Menger 1985, pp. 214, 57), he nevertheless stressed (in 1883) the methodological importance of having recourse to ideal types. He referred to these as "strict types" or "strictly typical phenomena of a definite kind," and he opposed these ideal types to what he called "real types" ("actual regularities"), types of a merely empirical sort. The notion of ideal types as reformulated in the 1920s by phenomenologist Alfred Schutz in an attempt to provide what he perceived to be the necessary underpinnings to Austrian economics is especially relevant in this regard (for a dicussion of Schutz's views in this regard and his relations with the Austrian school of economics, see Prendergast 1986 and Ebeling 1987). The only way by means of which we can grasp the logic of human affairs, i.e., discern *meaningful patterns* of human action, is by means of what Schutz called "typification." The social world is itself, as one commentator remarks in speaking of Schutz's views, "an intricate web of intersubjective typifications that emerge, are institutionalized through repeated social actions of various forms and are modified and changed as actors assign new meanings to their

162

actions and objects" (Ebeling 1987, p. 56; see also Ebeling 1986). According to Schutz and Austrian economists such as Ludwig von Mises, the form-ation of ideal types (such as that of "the stock broker") is what enables anonymous individuals productively to coordinate their activities.

In addition, the construction of ideal types or interpretive constructs is what enables social analysts (hermeneuts) to grasp the logic at work in any given social set-up. As Schutz observed:

> The thought objects constructed by the social scientists refer to and are founded upon the thought objects constructed by the common-sense thought of man living his everyday life among his fellow men. Thus, the constructs used by the social scientists are, so to speak, constructs of the second degree, namely constructs of the constructs made by the actors on the social scene, whose behavior the scientist observes and tries to explain.
>
> (Schutz 1962, p. 6)

In formulating their "second-order" hermeneutical or interpretive constructs, social scientists will often be obliged to reinterpret the self-interpretations of lifeworld actors themselves, since the meaningful consequences of human action are very often not the ones consciously intended by these actors. As one hermeneutical economist observes:

> The economist, in fact, often performs an important service by show-ing that the effects of agents' plans were different from those which were intended by the agents. Interpretive economics is interested pre-cisely in the process by which unintended consequences emerge and affect future plans and outcomes. The requirement that an understand-ing of agents' plans be included in economic analysis means that the economists' explanation of unintended consequences must be related to the agents' perspective.... [Typification] suggests that instead of collecting isolated impressions about economic events, the interpretive economist investigates *social* patterns that define the conceptual frameworks within which agents make their plans. The inclusion of the agents' intersubjective context in economic theorizing clearly distinguishes the hermeneutical-based, interpretive approach from positivist methodology.
>
> (Rector 1990, pp. 225–26)

Just as, as Mises said, "typification" enables economic actors in the everyday lifeworld to form *expectations* of what their fellow (though largely anonym-ous) actors are likely to do in any particular situation, thereby facilitating market interactions, so likewise viewing empirical reality through the medium of ideal types enables social analysts to make *predictions* as to the kind of results likely ("typically") to be generated by a particular type of social arrangement.

163

I hasten to add, however, that since in a human science like economics we are dealing with free human agency and not deterministic, cause-and-effect natural occurrences, "prediction" must be understood not in a physicalistic sense but rather in Hayek's non-scientistic sense of the term, i.e., as mere "pattern predictions" (see Hayek 1978, Chapter 2).[55] It would therefore be more appropriate to speak of the ability of theory to *anticipate* outcomes rather than to *predict* them. As Mises very nicely put it, ideal types enable "acting man" to be "the historian of the future" (Mises 1957, p. 322; cited in Ebeling 1994, p. 52). Thus the fact that a good theory has anticipatory or predictive value has itself important public policy implications. A good theory can instruct us as to what kind of interventions in the empirical arrangement in question are likely to produce beneficial results and what kinds of interventions are, on the contrary, likely to produce undesirable, counterproductive results, given the logic of the system in question. This means that hermeneutical analysis is such as to enable us to exert *control* (in, to be sure, Hayek's merely "cultivating" sense) over social outcomes, allowing us thereby, as free agents, to assume responsibility for our own destinies.[56]

One of the founders of the Freiburg School of Ordo-liberalism, Walter Eucken (described by Hayek as "probably the most serious thinker in the realm of social philosophy produced by Germany in the last hundred years" [Hayek 1992, p. 189]), who was strongly influenced by phenomenology and by Edumund Husserl's notion of "phenomenological reduction," characterized what I have referred to as an ideal type, as an "isolating abstraction" or an "abstraction of significant salient features." An "abstraction" of this sort is not, in Eucken's terms, a "generalizing abstraction" which merely isolates a number of features common to many phenomena; it is not a generalizing induction (in the way in which British empiricism understood this), a search for statistical regularities, but is, as Husserl would say, "essential intuition" of a phenomenological sort (*Wesenschau*). The purpose of abstraction or "typification" of this sort is, so to speak, to zero in on certain recurrent elementary forms (ideal types) in economic life. For Eucken the market or exchange economy and the planned or centrally directed economy are two such ideal types, two basic forms of economic organization having their own distinctive logics (see Streit 1994, pp. 510–11). In contrast, a "mixed economy" is not an ideal type in its own right but rather an unstable combination of elements borrowed from these two quite distinct ideal types. Just as different types of political regimes are, as Montesquieu pointed out, animated by different "principles" which determine what they essentially are, so likewise are different types of economic systems. Kornai's notion of "affinity" is once again highly relevant in this context. As Kornai points out:

> Classical socialism is a coherent system, among other reasons because there is an affinity between public ownership and bureaucratic

coordination; these elements in the system are organically connected and reinforce each other. Capitalism is likewise a coherent system, because there is an affinity between private property and market coordination, which are also organically connected and reinforce each other. The attempts to realize market socialism, on the other hand, produce an incoherent system, in which there are elements which repel each other: the dominance of public ownership and the operation of the market are not compatible.

(Kornai 1992, p. 500)

In other words, as Kornai also notes, the logics of the two economic systems in question (spontaneous coordination versus bureaucratic coordination) are mutually exclusive.[57] Planning and market cannot exist side by side, so to speak, in a perfect "mix." One principle or the other must invariably predominate at the expense of the other. As Kornai futher observes:

The conception of a semideregulated ["mixed"] economy is based on the premise that bureaucratic and market coordination can be combined in any proportion, let us say, in a ratio of fifty-fifty. Experience suggests this premise is mistaken. Lively operation of the market is compatible with a measure of state intervention, so long as it does not interpose too often in the processes taking place when the parties to the market reach free agreement. But bureaucratic intervention can attain a critical mass that destroys the market's vitality. That critical mass is certainly exceeded by the million interventions in the public sector of the [socialist] reform economy.

(Kornai 1992, p. 504)

Or as Giovanni Sartori puts it: "A breaking point is reached at which the market is destroyed as an efficient mechanism for determining costs and prices (for the productive economy as a whole)....[T]he issue ultimately boils down to the alternative market versus nonmarket" (Sartori 1987, II, pp. 401–02).

With, like Kornai, the "problem of economic order" ("systems") in mind, Wilhelm Roepke stated in 1957 that the pursuit of what he called "fiscal socialism" (Welfare State Socialism) inevitably brings about a situation where "quantity finally changes to quality," i.e., what results is the destruction of the market economy itself (Roepke 1987, p. 7). On the other side of the ledger, so to speak, in the case of countries seeking to implement liberal reforms, it is not enough in order to create genuine markets merely to *allow* "pluralism in the development of forms of property" (Aganbegyan 1988, p. 75). John D. Sullivan, executive director of the Center for International Enterprise, observes: "[W]hile it is often assumed that the existence of a private sector is proof that a country enjoys a market economy, deeper consideration reveals that the growth of the market economy requires more than just the retreat of government" (Sullivan 1994, p. 149).[58] So long as public or state ownership is not reduced to a relatively small proportion of the whole and private ownership does not become the *dominant* economic form, no real markets can be expected to emerge. In other words, a healthy pluralism (as regards, in this case, different forms of property ownership) can exist only in an overall order which is not socialist but liberal. The great naïveté of the Soviet reformers was to think that economic freedom and democracy – as reflected in open markets – can be brought into being and a "diversity of forms of property ownership" can spring up while at the same time the "basis of Socialist society [public ownership of the means of production] remains immutable" (Yakovlev 1988, p. 42). Speaking of the Chinese attempt to create a mixed economy, Jan Prybyla echoes the views of Kornai when he writes:

[F]or an economic system to function properly, that is, in the interest of the material welfare of the people who live and make their living within it, it must comprise a minimum critical mass of integrated, compatible, internally consistent, interrelated, and interacting ideas and institutions that together constitute an identifiable organism. The integration, compatibility, and so on, need not (perhaps should not) be total – there can be borrowings and transplants from other systems – but there has to be a minimum mass of clearly dominant, related institutions and ideas that give the system structural harmony and internal logic. Two-tier property rights and two-track prices [as in China] do not seem to fulfill this condition, and are clearly a transitional phenomenon. Sooner or later, one of the two tiers or tracks has to become dominant.

(Prybyla 1994, p. 84)

There is a lesson to be had from the universal failure of attempts in Eastern Europe to create a hybrid economy called "market socialism,"[59] and there is in this failure something that, as Garton Ash would say, the West can learn from the East. Market mechanisms can work properly and can contribute to a vibrant economy and the general well-being only so long as the "capitalist" principle of private ownership predominates and state intervention is kept to a minimum.[60] Were, however, the economies of Western nations to become so "mixed" that the public sector came to dominate the system as a whole, nothing less than the kind of revolutions that occurred in the East would be necessary to redress the balance.[61] Thus, the German attempt to create a civil market economy in the late 1940s is such as to furnish an economic maxim for the governance of societies that aspire to be civil as well as for societies that seek to remain free: State intervention should be both limited and indirect and should always seek to operate as much as possible in a manner that is *marktkonform.*

166

DEMOCRATIC CAPITALISM AND SOCIAL JUSTICE

If, as the German example clearly demonstrates, the economic realm is dependent upon the political realm, it could equally well be argued that the survival of liberal democracy is dependent upon the maintenance of a free economy. Democracy and the market are inseparable; the fate of the one is in direct correlation with the fate of the other. As Mario Vargas Llosa, candidate for president in the Peruvian elections of 1990, has said: "Economic freedom is the counterpart of political freedom, and only when the two are united – two sides of a single coin – can they really function" (Vargas Llosa 1989, p. xx). As I have argued, there is no "third way" between Socialism and "capitalism," i.e., between a system based on public ownership of the factors of production and one based on the right to private property. The idea of a third way is a logical chimera. In terms of ideal types, the "Swedish model," for instance, which seems to be what most people have in mind when they speak wistfully of a "third way," is no such thing; the Swedish economy is as capitalistic as they come (see, for instance, Gray 1993). To be sure, in this century the Swedes managed to create one of the most extensive of Welfare States imaginable (which, however, in the 1990s they proceeded to trim back), but this had nothing to do with economics; it was a political matter pure and simple (Sweden's Welfare State was funded by means of high taxes levied on a free and [in comparison with the U.S.] relatively unregulated market economy). Thus, as Peter Berger notes, viewing Sweden as an instance of "democratic socialism" "confuses the organization of the economy with the scope of the welfare state" (Berger 1986, p. 248, n. 3).

In addition to arguing against the notion of a "third way," I have also argued that "capitalism" as I have characterized it in the preceding pages (the German Social Market Economy functioning as a kind of paradigm in this regard) is in no way synonymous with *laissez-faire*. An enterprise economy, while being an ideal type, is not for all that a "pure" type (such as would be, in theory at least, an unalloyed *laissez-faire* economy).[62] Precisely *qua* ideal type, an enterprise economy is dependent in its very being – even in a relatively "unmixed" form – on the political order, which is why the analysis of an economy such as this falls under the heading of "political economy." A civil market economy presupposes, as I have argued, a legal-political framework, and it is irrelevant whether such a framework be the result of deliberate design, as in the case of the German Social Market Economy, or of the gradual evolution of common law practices, as in the case of Anglo-American capitalism.[63]

When people (e.g., those who call themselves "social democrats") speak of a "third way," what it seems they principally have in mind is the *Welfare State*. The Welfare State is supposedly the means for achieving what is customarily referred to as *social justice*. Accordingly, it is with a consideration of these related issues that I shall conclude this chapter.

In particular, I propose to argue for a conception of social justice that dissociates it from the notion of the Welfare State, linking it up, in contrast, with the normal workings of democratic capitalism. Two basic issues are involved in any critique of what could be called "welfarism": (1) the question as to its empirical feasibility and (2) the question as to its moral desirability. The first issue can, for the purposes at hand, be dealt with rather summarily. As the financial crises that confronted various liberal democratic Welfare States with full force in the 1990s clearly demonstrated, a full-fledged Welfare State is simply too costly to be maintained; no market economy can indefinitely bear the costs imposed upon it by the extensive (and ever-escalating) "entitlements" that welfare governments grant to their citizenry. Indeed, as these governments are increasingly beginning to realize, conventional, means-tested welfare, by a kind of perverse, built-in logic, tends to generate an ever-increasing welfare dependency; it does so by altering the behavior of welfare recipients, by creating disincentives for self-reliance, and by contributing to the break-down of the family (see *The Economist*, June 10, 1995, pp. 52–3). It could be argued, moreover, that systematic attempts to *redistribute* wealth ("social justice" in the "welfare" sense of the term) have proven to be largely inefficacious in any event (the only notable effect being the unintended one of severely weakening the economy itself (i.e., killing off the goose that lays the golden eggs).[64]

These are empirical considerations. The more serious argument against welfarism is of a moral or ethical nature: even if welfarism were empirically (economically) feasible, it would still be morally undesirable. To put the argument in its most succinct form, welfarism is quite simply incompatible with the principle of human dignity, and thus with the very idea of civil society. The reason for this is that welfarism, as it has traditionally been conceived, operates under the assumption that, in the words of the late-nineteenth-century socialist and welfare advocate, L. T. Hobhouse, government is, or ought to be, the general "over-parent" of the citizenry (see Hobhouse 1974, p. 115). This is *paternalism* of the most invidious sort imaginable. The net result of more than a century of welfare activism has been, as Alexis de Tocqueville predicted that it would be over a century and a half ago, to produce a dispirited population dependent upon a "tutelary power" which works for the people's happiness, but which "wants to be the sole judge and arbiter of this" (see Tocqueville 1961, II, 4, 6). Such a government, Tocqueville said, "does not at all tyrannize; it hinders, it inhibits, it restricts, it enervates, it extinguishes, it stupifies." By its very nature, the paternalistic Welfare State (*l'Etat providence*, as it is aptly called in French) robs people of their autonomy, and thus their dignity, which is why, as we saw in Chapter 4, John Paul II condemned this particular means of attempting to realize social justice. "By intervening directly and depriving society of its responsibility," he said, "the Social Assistance State leads to a loss of human energies and an inordinate increase of public agencies, which are dominated

168

more by bureaucratic ways of thinking than by concern for serving their clients, and which are accompanied by an enormous increase in spending" (John Paul II 1991, §48). The views of John Paul II are echoed by Jean Bethke Elshtain: "When professionals move in on communities to 'solve a problem,' what happens is that people grow weaker, not stronger, for their 'needs' are authoritatively defined by sources outside themselves" (Elshtain 1995, pp. 17–18). This point is also argued by the feminist writer Anna Yeatman (1994). (It may also be noted that this is where the principle of *subsidiarity* discussed in the preceding chapter comes in.) Even leftists have largely conceded the validity of criticisms such as these. Cohen and Arato, for instance, point out how the Welfare State has reduced the role of the free citizen to that of a passive client. And thus, as they state, "a whole model of directed social change associated with the term 'socialism' has become obsolete."[65]

The question of social justice cannot be divorced from the question of social (public) morality. How could anyone not of a servile mentality ever think that they have a "right," are "entitled," to live at the expense of someone else? In a free society the funds needed to pay for "entitlements" are not created by the government acting as an agent of divine providence and deputized to perform the miracle of the loaves and fishes but come from taxes paid by those citizens who do provide for themselves and their families and who in so doing contribute to the common good. In a civil society it is not the case that "society owes one a living," since in a societal organization such as this there is in fact no such entity as Society – there are only citizens who, through their political representatives, freely consent to tax themselves in order to come to the aid of the more unfortunate among them. This is an act of public charity on their part, not a "duty" dictated by a "right" on the part of the recipients of public aid. The very notion that "society" has an "obligation" to provide everyone with unearned benefits such as housing, subsidized food, free health care, child care, and job security is the hallmark of patrimonialism and was the defining trait of State Socialism. It is a formula designed to transform the needy into the greedy – "The communist regime pledged to take care of everyone, and wound up teaching everyone to be an egoist" (Smolar 1994, p. 82) – and is quite simply incompatible with the public morality of reciprocity upon which a civil society depends for its very existence. As Elshtain remarks,

> a bureaucratic top-heavy state that numbers among its tasks defining populations by their "needs" and targeting them for various policies based on assumptions about such needs, really cannot help moving in the direction of a "social engineering" that exists in tension with democratic freedom, civic society, and individual liberty.
>
> (Elshtain 1995, p. 20)

169

Under welfarism the State *qua* republic of free and equal citizens bound together by a mutual respect of rights and freedoms ceases to exist, becoming, in the words of that nineteenth-century critic of Socialism, Frédéric Bastiat, "the great fiction by which everybody tries to live at the expense of everybody else."

If the Welfare State is a counterproductive means for achieving social justice, what is the alternative? Indeed, how must one conceive of social justice if the welfarist, redistributive model has, as Cohen and Arato concede, indeed become obsolete? An answer to these questions is readily available if it is indeed the case (as I have argued throughout this book) that the three principal orders of civil society are synergetic and are animated, each in its own way, by the principle of communicative rationality. For what this means is that the democratic principle is central to each of the three orders. Social justice must be linked up with the concept of economic democracy.

However, as I stated at the beginning of this chapter, democracy in the economic realm cannot mean the exact same thing that it does in the political realm. "Workplace democracy," in which workers are equated with citizens and which would allow workers to vote on how the company they work for is to be run, violates the first principle of a market economy, that of the private ownership of property. Those who do not have a share in the ownership of a business enterprise cannot legitimately lay claim to a determining voice in how it is run. Workplace democracy, as leftists conceive of it (on the model of political citizenship) is contrary to the logic of a market economy. A business firm is not a polity, and one does not participate in it by means of political representation. The right to free association is, of course, central to all three orders of civil society, and thus the right of workers to advance their interests by joining labor unions must be held to be a fundamental economic right. This right cannot, however, mean the right to participate on an equal footing in managerial decisions, which must remain the right of the owners of business or their representatives. Referring to the German Codetermination Law (*Mitbestimmungsgesetz*) of 1976 which granted representation to workers on the supervisory boards of business firms, one analyst remarks: "The result is a labour market which today probably conforms less with a market economy than was the case in the early years of the social market economy" (Kloten 1989, p. 84). Contrary to what one specialist in labor studies advocates in calling for "industrial democracy," and with the German practice of codetermination foremost in mind, labor policy should indeed be viewed in economic, *not* political "imagery"; forums for discussion between labor and management should precisely *not* be decision making arenas (see Roy Adams, 1993, pp. 4, 13).[66] While the economic realm has important links with the political realm, economics is not politics and should not be politicized – any more than the cultural realm should be politicized. One lesson that can (or should) be learned from the failure of market socialism is that the logic of a market economy is subverted when attempts are made to

170

introduce into it the kind of decision procedures proper only to the political realm.[67] In the new, more entrepreneurial corporate culture now emerging, what is called for is not the introduction of an outmoded and rigid political model of representation but the working out of a more flexible (post-Fordian) corporate culture built around enhanced communication between production teams and various levels of management.

Moreover, because the "corporatism" (the tripartite monopoly on social/economic policy by big government, big unions, and big business) favored by policy advocates like Adams amounts to setting up a kind of equality between select *interest groups*, it is actually at odds with the democratic principle, i.e., the equality of individual *citizens* – and is thus hostile to the very idea of civil society.[68] Economist Don Lavoie suggests an alternative, non-politicized way in which – in a free, civil society – democratic principles might be "extended throughout society and into the very production process of the economy" (Lavoie 1992, p. 436). Lavoie is in agreement with Marx on at least this point: "Democracy should apply to all of our lives and should not be narrowly conceived as a form of government" (ibid., p. 440). However, in reflecting on the failure of socialist ideals regarding economic democracy, he maintains that Socialism "led to disaster because it had concluded that market institutions were essentially incompatible with democratic values and needed to be replaced by a democratically determined central plan" (ibid., p. 437). The analogy that Lavoie for his part wishes to draw between the political and the economic realms rests on the fact that, as he sees it, democracy has not so much to do with mere voting as it does with "the extent to which the prevailing attitudes of the participants are conducive to genuine dialogue" (ibid., p. 439). He spells out what he means by this in greater detail in a subsequent article:

> We must not reduce our understanding of democracy to a view of the form of government which allows periodic elections. We should recognize, rather, that for a society to be democratic it is neither necessary nor sufficient for it to be ruled by a particular form of government. More important than whether the government permits regular elections is the issue of whether all the other institutions of human interaction are imbued with a democratic spirit, with an open political culture.
>
> What are the qualities of the political culture which characterize liberalism? What I think we should mean by democracy is the distinctive kind of *openness* in society which the Soviet system crushed, and which began to recover under the banner of *glasnost*. . . .
>
> It seems to me that this openness and publicness, not some particular theory of how to elect the personnel of government, is the essence of democracy. Like the market, a democratic polity exhibits a kind of distributed intelligence [Lavoie elsewhere refers to this as "social

171

intelligence"], not representable by any single organization which may claim to act on society's behalf. Democracy is not a quality of the conscious will of a representative organization that has been legitimized by the public, but a quality of the discursive process of the distributed wills of the public itself.

(Lavoie 1993, pp. 110–11)

Inquiring into the "core meaning" of democracy and into exactly what it is that makes a culture, a government, and a market place democratic, Lavoie writes:

We know democratic behavior when we see it close-up in the way people conduct themselves in discussions when they take both their subject matter and one another seriously, and when they seek mutual understanding. Democracy, then, can be usefully defined as that set of attitudes conducive to mutual understanding and an open-ended process of dialogue.

(Lavoie 1992, p. 440)

In line with general hermeneutical theory, Lavoie maintains that "a good conversation is in many ways the model of what we mean by democracy" (ibid.). Given the need for the various orders of a democratic, civil society to complement and mutually reinforce one another, the key question becomes: "Can democratic values shape not only the way we exchange words with one another, but also the way we exhange goods and services?" (ibid., p. 436)

Applying the hermeneutical-dialogical model to the economic realm, Lavoie concludes that the kind of communication that characterizes a free market economy (and that I analyzed earlier in this chapter) is an extension of democracy conceived of as *open conversation*. The key word here is "open." When applied to economic matters, openness of communication – *glasnost*, democracy – translates into "the principle of free entry in markets" (ibid., p. 445).[69] Thus, as Lavoie concludes, "open markets should be seen as the very embodiment of democratic values" (ibid., p. 450). The opposing notion defended by socialist critics of the market economy, the notion, namely, that markets can only be democratic if they are subject to the direct control of a democratic *government*, is, as Lavoie observes, "a throwback to pre-democratic thinking" (ibid., p. 451).[70]

Just as the democratic forms of civil society have as their philosophical basis the notion of fundamental human rights, so, more particularly, the notion of economic democracy rests on the notion of economic rights. The *raison d'être* of economic rights, like that of human rights in general, is to safeguard the dignity of the human person. What makes individuals deserving of respect is that they are autonomous beings who should be allowed to forge their own destinies. Not to be a free person responsible for one's own destiny is to be a *slave*, i.e., a being whose autonomy is denied, who is without

172

rights, and who cannot accordingly claim due respect. If justice is defined as granting to people what is their due, and if one's due is what one has a right to, then justice basically amounts to respecting the fundamental human rights of individuals. Thus, as Madison stated, government is instituted to protect "the various rights of individuals ... that alone is a *just* government which *impartially* secures to every man whatever is his *own*."[71] What, more specifically, is referred to as social justice amounts to an active respect for the economic rights of individuals. How might these rights best be conceived?

If, as I have argued, a civil society is based on the notion of fundamental human rights, and if a market economy is the kind of economy most befitting a civil society, and if, yet in addition, the principle of market economics is private ownership of property, it follows that economic rights must, in some general sense, revolve around the right (the freedom) to acquire and dispose of property. To be more specific, what Lavoie refers to as "freedom of economic action" boils down to what could be called the *right to work*. By this term I do not mean what is often meant by it in the United States, viz., the right not to have to join a labor union in order to have a job.[72] By "right to work" I mean what economists such as Lavoie mean when they speak of "the principle of free entry in markets." "Free entry" means that artificial barriers should not be erected which prevent or hinder individuals from pursuing any line of economic activity for which they believe they have a talent and from which they believe they can gain a decent living and can improve their wellbeing.[73] It was precisely this right that Adam Smith was effectively arguing for when in *The Wealth of Nations* he attacked monopolistic practices, just as it is the right that the German neoliberals were arguing for when in their post-war economic constitution they sought energetically to promote open competition. It is also the right that John Paul II defends when he speaks of "human rights to private initiative, to ownership of property and to freedom in the economic sector" (John Paul II 1991, §24). The basis of the "business economy," the Pope stated, is human freedom exercised in the economic field, just as it is exercised in other fields. "Economic activity," he went on to say, "is indeed but one sector in a great variety of human activities, and like every other sector, it includes the right to freedom, as well as the duty of making responsible use of freedom" (ibid., §32). Since the Roman Pontiff has provided us with one of the most eloquent defenses of these rights and freedoms, it is worth considering his views on the matter in a bit more detail.

Like his predecessors, John Paul maintains, in conformity with the philosophical anthropology he defends, that a crucial area in which the human person fulfils him or herself is *work*: "Work ... belongs to the vocation of every person; indeed, man expresses and fulfils himself by working" (ibid., §6). By means of work, humans creatively transform both their natural

173

and human environments and, in the process, as the Pope says, develop "important virtues ... such as diligence, industriousness, prudence in undertaking reasonable risks, reliability and fidelity in interpersonal relationships, as well as courage in carrying out decisions which are difficult and painful but necessary, both for the overall working of a business and in meeting possible setbacks" (ibid., §32). Any defense of human dignity must accordingly involve a defense of the freedom or right to work. Or as the Pope says: "The foundation of the right to private initiative and ownership is to be found in this activity [work]. ... The obligation to earn one's bread by the sweat of one's brow also presumes the right to do so" (ibid., §43). As the Pope describes it, what I am referring to as the "right to work" is nothing other than the right of each and every individual freely to realize his or her own potentialities through personal initiative and creative enterprise – and the right, as well, to benefit from the fruits of one's own labor (which, as the Pope points out, is always realized in concert with other free agents). The core economic right is the right to freedom of action in the economic sphere.

In the course of his discussion of economic matters, John Paul also mentions that the right to work cannot be directly ensured by the State – unless, that is, "it controlled every aspect of economic life and restricted the free initiative of individuals" (John Paul II 1991, §48). What the Pope means by "right to work" in this context is that, as I have argued, the proper role of the state is an indirect one: "[T]he State has a duty to sustain business activities by creating conditions which will ensure job opportunities, by stimulating those activities where they are lacking or by supporting them in moments of crisis" (ibid.). In other words, the right to work does not and cannot mean the "right" to be guaranteed a job by the state. This is an important point which I would like to develop further by drawing a distinction between *rights* and *entitlements*.

As the Pope himself recognizes, it is the function of the State to guarantee the rights of its citizens. If, however, welfarism is to be avoided (since its ultimate effect is to destroy the right to freedom itself by making of its citizens wards of the state and, indeed, by transforming them from citizens into mere clients), it is crucially important that the notion of rights not be misconstrued. There is indeed at the present time an immense amount of confusion as to what goes to make up that sub-set of human rights referred to as "economic rights." It is sometimes difficult to detect any significant difference between Western statements of economic rights and those that were to be found in the constitutions of the former socialist countries. Thus we often hear it said that economic or social rights include the "right" to a job (guaranteed by the government), the "right" to free health care, the "right" to paid holidays, the "right" to subsidized housing, and so on. Strictly speaking, however, these are not rights at all but rather entitlements – which, accordingly, a democractic society, through regular political means, may or may not choose to make available to its members, and with whatever limitations it may deem appropriate. Indeed, a fundamental role of financial prudence which merits being constitutionally "entrenched" is that welfare expenditures of whatever sort – as opposed to some forms of capital investment – should never be allowed to exceed the ability to cover them out of current accounts: funding welfare by means of deficit spending is a guaranteed recipe for the financial ruin of any state, just as any household would be ruined were it to finance its discretionary spending on an on-going basis by means of borrowed money.

A right in the proper or basic sense of the term, i.e., a human right, is something "negative," whereas entitlements are "positive." In other words, entitlements confer special privileges (and have direct monetary value), whereas rights prohibit discrimination (and confer no special material benefit on their beneficiaries). Thus, for instance, the right to free speech means that neither the state nor society may restrict my freedom to express the truth as I see it; it does not mean that either the state or society must provide me with the physical or financial means for publicizing my views. The right to free movement and emigration does not mean that the state has an obligation to provide me with free transportation to wherever I should happen to like to go. Similarly, the economic right to work does not mean that the government owes me a job; it means, rather, as I have argued, that the government may *not* prevent me from pursuing my own well-being as best I see fit (within, naturally, the confines of the law). The fundamental human right to "property" is the right freely to acquire property (i.e., wealth) through one's own creative efforts; it is not, for instance, the "right" to a government-guaranteed income. When Jefferson listed "the pursuit of happiness" as a fundamental, unalienable right, the word "pursuit" was all-important: everyone has, or should have, the right to pursue happiness; no one has the "right" actually to be made happy. If government does have an obligation to ensure the rights of the citizenry, it is the "negative" one of seeing to it that they are not violated (which itself, as I mentioned in Chapter 4, often calls for positive action on the part of the state).[74]

One of the chief functions of a constitution is to list the basic freedoms and rights of the citizenry.[75] This suggests a useful pragmatic test for determining what is and what is not a human right in the proper sense of the term: fundamental human rights are those rights, and those rights only, which qualify for inclusion in the Fundamental Law of the land. *And only those rights so qualify which can be enforced by constitutional means*, in particular by recourse to the judiciary, and whose guarantee is in a sense *absolute*. This is the case with traditional civil and political rights, but it is not the case with the so-called "economic rights" of the sort mentioned above (the right to housing, social security, free medical services, food, etc.). "Rights" of the latter sort are strictly *relative*, in that they are wholly dependent for their effective existence upon the financial resources available at any given time in any given society. Human rights are constitutionally guaranteed rights, whereas "rights"

175

of a more "positive" sort are legislated entitlements. Thus, for instance, those rights enumerated by Madison in the American Bill of Rights are not "entitlements" but, rather, *immunities*, i.e., guarantees against government intrusion into the workings of civil society (see Elshtain 1995, p. 15).

A constitition (guaranteeing fundamental rights) is crucial for the existence of civil society. And for a constitution to be both meaningful and workable it must not be overloaded with utopian goals which may be unrealizable or realizable only to a relative degree. Thus, as one constitutional scholar writes:

> [B]ecause constitutions must be capable of generating fulfilled expectations [if they are to have any real force at all], their content should not be obscured with unrealizable utopian provisions. This is a problem for the authors of new constitutions for Eastern Europe and the republics of the former USSR, who seem determined to extend the Communist tradition of overloading constitutions with statements of aspirations that no state can meet. . . . Constitutions ought to avoid vague lists of utopian policy goals that are beyond the capacity of the state to realize, and they ought to focus instead on the minimal institutions and rights that are sufficient to ensure society's ability to coordinate for the realization of policy goals as expressed through such agencies as democratic elections.
>
> (Ordeshook 1993, pp. 206–7)

From the point of view of the logic of constitutionalism, entitlements must not be confused with or placed at the same level as rights in the proper sense of the term. As yet another constitutional scholar states:

> A constitution that protects both liberties and entitlements is incoherent and very difficult to interpret. It seeks to accomplish two diametrically opposite goals. Moreover, guarantees of entitlements in a constitution that provides for judicial review will jeopardize the judiciary's protection of liberty. To enforce entitlements, the judiciary might mandate imposition of taxation and spending, and neither the people nor the legislature would be able to control this power. The judiciary would be given control over important fiscal decisions. Taxing the people and spending the receipts are peculiarly legislative powers, stemming from the idea that only the people, acting on their own or through their representatives, are entitled to decide how they will utilize their own funds.
>
> (Siegan 1994, p. 66)[76]

In other words, the inclusion of entitlements in a constitution not only gives rise to "rent-seeking" (see Chapter 4), it also subverts the very foundations of liberal democracy (such as the separation of powers). Welfarism is a recipe not for social justice but for *social corruption* and is destructive of civil society itself. Indeed, as a corollary to the fundamental law of liberal political theory to the effect that "power corrupts," one could formulate a law of economic life asserting that the more highly an economy is state-regulated, the more corruption will tend to spread throughout all segments of society.[77] A civil society cannot be a Welfare State, and economic rights of a constitutional or "human" sort must be limited to the rights to property and to work as described above.[78]

Does this mean that a civil society cannot legitimately provide assistance to the poorest and worse-off of its members? Whatever might be the position adopted by the more extreme advocates of *laissez-faire* in this regard, no such conclusion follows from the logic of a civil market economy. The situation is, in fact, the opposite. What Catholic social teaching refers to under the heading "preferential option for the poor" – the principle according to which the true test of any society is the way in which it deals with the poorest of its members – can be argued for in terms of market economics (or, as Peter Berger puts it, this moral principle "can readily be translated from the language of Christian ethics to that of the social sciences. . . . [It] translates itself to an option for capitalist development strategies" [Berger 1986, pp. 132, 139]).

One thing that this means is that dismantling the patrimonial Welfare State need not in any way entail dismantling the state itself, reducing it to a *laissez-faire* "minimal state," a merciless "survival of the fittest." Jean Bethke Elshtain expresses the matter well when she writes:

> Please note well: This argument behind "ending welfare as we know it," when it comes from the direction of a civil society, is not about grinding the faces of the poor into dust from a lack of compassion. Rather, it is about how welfare professionalizes care and counsel and turns citizens into clients.
>
> (Elshtain 1995, p. 17)[79]

As a matter of fact, doing away with unnecessary and unproductive state interventionism (the "megastate") can contribute to a stronger and more effective (though leaner) state and to a gain in efficiency in legitimate public service agencies and programs. As one social analyst rightly observes (with the example of the hitherto grossly overextended state apparatuses of Latin American countries principally in mind):

> In the long run, dismantling its interventionist apparatus will strengthen the state. Focusing on indispensable public tasks, shedding discretionary economic interventions that are a magnet for special interests and corruption, and establishing a more sound fiscal situation should all help promote the emergence of a more focused and effective public sector.
>
> (Naim 1994, p. 39)

*

Democracy must work from the bottom up, or it cannot work at all (this is why what is crucial for democracy is the existence of a democratic culture or *ethos*, not simply formal mechanisms such as the vote). This is true not only of political democracy; it is true of economic democracy as well. For the tree of democracy – the liberty tree – to flourish, its roots must be nourished. As Alexander Yakovlev stated early on in the Soviet attempt at reform: "Glasnost, like democracy, should first of all exist at the local level. . . .[T]he strength of any phenomenon lies in its roots" (Yakovlev 1988, p. 40). This is where the "preferential option for the poor" comes in. An option such as this can be justified in terms of the logic of democratic capitalism if it can be shown that it does not involve redistributive measures appropriate only to a Welfare State (robbing the rich and industrious in order to benefit the poor and indolent)[80] but, on the contrary, is a means for contributing to the common economic good and is, in this way, in the general interest – or, as John Paul II puts it, "is never exclusive or discriminatory towards other groups" (John Paul II 1991, §57).[81]

Capitalism, as Marx said, is a "mode of production"; it is a mode of production based on the principle of the private ownership of the means of production and on free market exchange.[82] Adam Smith's great insight (to which Marx remained oblivious) was that in a capitalist or free market system, i.e., a system based on voluntary exchange, the parties to an exchange derive mutual benefit (otherwise, the exchange would not freely occur).[83] When these free exchanges multiply, the benefits proliferate and spread throughout society, the net result being a general increase in "the wealth of nations." In game-theoretic terms capitalism is a win-win form of activity, whereas the pre-capitalist, mercantilist system in which nations sought to export as much and import as little as possible, seeking in this way to accumulate wealth (gold and silver) at the expense of other nations, was a win-lose activity.[84] Mercantilism was in effect a means for *redistributing* existing wealth, whereas capitalism is a means for *creating* new wealth (as Hernando de Soto has pointed out [1989], mercantilism – not capitalism – is the system that prevailed in Latin America where policies of import substitution and extensive state intervention in the national economy were pursued well into the 1980s). Under mercantilism, Smith argued, the larger part of the population, the laborers, are disadvantaged, since such a system works to keep prices high and wages low, whereas in what he called the "system of natural liberty" or what we today call "capitalism" the poor, Smith said, would be the chief beneficiaries, since such a system works in the opposite direction, lowering prices and raising wages (see Himmelfarb 1985, p. 51).

In a free market economy wealth-creation is not a zero-sum game, and winners in this game are not "exploiters." If, in a market economy, some people succeed in getting rich, it is because they provide goods or services that other people value (entrepreneurship, the Pope says, is "the ability to

178

perceive the needs of others and to satisfy them" [John Paul II 1991, §32]). In marshalling the productive forces necessary for producing these goods and services, they also contribute to increased economic activity and the GDP (e.g., through the creation of new jobs). Speaking of the modern (or "postmodern") capitalist economy (based on "know-how, technology and skill"), the Pope says:

> Organizing such a productive effort, planning its duration in time, making sure that it corresponds in a positive way to the demands which it must satisfy, and taking the necessary risks – all this . . . is a source of wealth in today's society. In this way, the *role* of disciplined and creative *human work* and, as an essential part of that work, *initiative and entrepreneurial ability* becomes increasingly evident and decisive.
>
> (John Paul II 1991, §32)

Thus, in a free market economy private interest and the public good are not antithetical. The situation is indeed just the opposite; the entrepreneurial pursuit of private profit serves to enhance the general welfare.

Central to liberal theory has always been the notion of the "common good," inherited from medieval political philosophy (Thomas Aquinas in particular). Herein lies the chief difference between liberalism and libertarianism (*laissez-fairism*); the notion of the common good (as something more, conceptually speaking, than merely the statistical aggregate of private goods) is utterly foreign to libertarianism's conceptual schemas. If liberals have always defended the market, it is not because it "maximizes" the "utilities" of individuals, atomistically conceived ("possessive individualsm"), but because it was and is their belief that a system designed, so to speak, to allow individuals the greatest extent of freedom possible in their mutual dealings will invariably promote the good of society as a whole. The core principle of liberal economics is, as we have seen, the right to (private) property, and for liberalism the ultimate *raison d'être* of private property is that it is that system which contributes the most to the common good. If I insist on this point, it is in order to emphasize an equally important point (which again serves to differentiate liberalism from libertarianism). From the liberal rationale for private property it follows as a kind of direct corollary that tax revenues may legitimately be used, by way of a supplement to the workings of the market, to aid those who, in the short run, are not in a position to benefit from or to participate in market-generated prosperity. As one political historian observes:

> While liberals historically have defended individual rights to property, they have done so in large part because of the contribution of such rights to the preservation and prosperity of all; in those cases where prosperity came only in the long run or only to a majority, a liberal

theory of property has required the use of the government to guarantee some level of welfare to those who in the short run have not
benefited.

(Horne 1994, p. 428)[85]

Freedom of economic activity is a common good even though some will
invariably put this freedom to better use and will draw greater profit from it
than will others, and the common good itself will be enhanced the more
democratic an economy is, i.e., the greater the number of people there are
who are able actively to participate in it and are free to exercise their entrepreneurial skills. Just as, through participating actively in the global economy,
less developed countries can become economically productive and amass
wealth, and just as this improvement in their economic condition is in the
interest of the advanced industrial nations of the world since it contributes
to a global increase in economic activity from which they themselves can
benefit, so likewise the more the poorer members of society are able to
become productive economic agents, the more society as a whole benefits. It
is therefore in the interests of all citizens of a civil society that both the state
and private organizations should actively promote "free entry" and the "right
to work" on the part of the less well-off. As Michael Novak states: "An
activist government must design its laws, politics, and financial dealings in
ways that encourage *citizens* to become activists on their own behalf" (Novak
1993, p. 191). Measures taken in this regard (such as, for instance, enhanced
educational opportunities, job training programs or access to credit and
venture capital), while amounting to a "preferential option for the poor," are
nevertheless in the general interest and contribute to the general welfare by
increasing the amount of "social capital" (or "social intelligence"), thereby
making for a more vibrant economy in general.

When it is the state – acting not as an "over-parent" but as a catalyst – that
provides enabling measures of this sort, it must obviously do so by means of
taxation (assuming that it does not resort to deficit spending), but taxation in
this instance is just and fair and is not redistributive in nature in that the
monies collected from the more well-to-do members of society are used to
cultivate the very system that has enabled them to acquire their wealth in the
first place. Taxation for this purpose promotes the general welfare as much
as it does when used to provide for the common defense. Taxes of this sort
could be likened to the dues everyone is expected to pay in order to belong to
organizations from which they draw tangible benefit. The view of Thomas
Aquinas on the nature of (just) law can be applied to tax laws. According to
St. Thomas, an unjust law is no law at all (Aquinas 1945, *Summa Theologiae*,
I–II, qu. 95, art. 2). Just laws are ones which promote the common good, but,
in order to be considered just, the burdens they impose on individuals for
the sake of the common good must be in accordance with "an equality
of proportion." If (like a progressive income tax) they fail to impose

180

"proportionate burdens," they also fail the test of justice (*Summa Theologiae*, I–II, qu. 96, art. 4). Q.E.D.

What in the final analysis "preferential option for the poor" means is that, as Novak writes:

> The poor should be approached as creators of wealth. They should be assisted in their efforts to make themselves asset-producers rather than mere consumers. The revolution needed in the welfare system – now a dependency-maintaining Socialism – is to transform it into an asset-building system. . . . In this way, government programs would be aimed at strengthening civil society rather than eroding it. For the poor and the vulnerable, government assistance is no doubt necessary; but *how* this assistance is designed is more important than either its existence or its size. The first maxim of medicine, *"Do no harm,"* should also be the first maxim of government assistance. A profound revolution in the conception of welfare is needed: to view the poor as creative, not as dependents; as agents of their own destiny, not as serfs.
>
> (Novak 1993, pp. 164–65)

Even if, for argument's sake, measures of this "enabling" sort were to cost as much, in terms of budgetary outlays, as welfare of the traditional, "disabling" sort, they would still be significantly less costly if one were to calculate costs as economists do: as forgone benefits (what Menger's disciple, Friedrich von Wieser, termed "opportunity costs"). By forgoing the contributions that the poor and unemployed could otherwise make to the economy, a society which does not adopt a preferential option for the poor pays a high price in terms of lost productivity – and is jeopardizing its competitiveness in the global economy.[86] Measures taken to enable the poor to become productive economic agents should be viewed as a form of investment in "infrastructure" described in the preceding chapter – as a means, therefore, of promoting the general welfare. The more productive everyone is in a market economy, the more everyone benefits, and the more the common good is served.

Democracy in the economic realm of civil society – market democracy – is a formula not only for prosperity, it is equally well a formula for both freedom and social justice.

APPENDIX

ON CIVIL SOCIETY AND INTERNATIONAL JUSTICE

What lessons might the discussion of civil society in the preceding pages have to offer as regards the currently much discussed issue of international justice? Can the concept of civil society as I have outlined it in this book be "internationalized"? I believe that it can; indeed, I believe that the notions of civil society and human rights provide a framework that is at once the most appropriate and the most fruitful for considering the two most important topics on the global agenda today: *democratization* and *development*. The surest means for achieving both democratization and development, I wish to argue, is the formation of civil societies world-wide.

I am not of course referring to anything like a "global civil society." Despite calls in the past for something like a World Government, no such entity is discernible on the horizon, and no alternative paradigm of a workable sort to that of the nation-state is ready to hand. As things now stand, that undoubtedly is a good thing, since it is hard to see how something like a supranational megastate (a kind of glorified United Nations) could be anything but tyranny on a global scale, the all-pervasive rule of a remote and irresponsible (and highly inefficient) bureaucracy. At the present time, and no doubt for quite a long time to come, the struggle for democracy and human rights will be best waged within the context of specific nation-states, i.e., actually existing state entities. What these struggles will amount to, whether or not this be their express intent, is an attempt on the part of their inhabitants to make of these states genuine civil societies. Whether or not these states were arbitrarily set up in the first place and are ethnically diverse and "artificial" (as in the case of much of Africa) is a matter of little importance. Nationalism is not the issue.

It is of course true, as I have already remarked, that the rapidly increasing trend towards economic globalization spells the end of "national sovereignty" as it has traditionally been conceived and practiced. And that too is a good thing, since the weakening of the paradigm of the nation-state, the key political paradigm of the modern era, provides an opportunity for conceptualizing in an appropriately *post*-modern way the increasing interdependence of the nations of the world. The new world order that we may legitimately hope for can only be based on the solidarity of a multitude of free, yet interdependent and mutually reinforcing civil societies.[1]

Subsequent to the end of the Cold War, a new world order is indeed emerging, however cloaked in obscurity its features may still be. One prominent feature is nevertheless already apparent: the end of East–West confrontation signals a transformation of North–South relations, i.e., relations between developed and underdeveloped countries, now politely termed less-developed countries (LDCs). With the disappearance of the "second" world, relations between the West and the "third" world are changing accordingly. Gone is the time when the countries of the former third world could play off one superpower against the other in a bid for hand-outs in the form of no-strings-attached foreign aid. International development will no longer be fixated on the issue of foreign aid; indeed, foreign aid (i.e., state-to-state income transfers) is fast becoming a thing of the past (the developmental alternative to foreign aid is discussed below). Foreign aid simply does not "work." Or as Alan Waters, former chief economist for the US Agency for International Development (USAID), has stated:

> Foreign aid is inherently bad. It retards the process of economic growth and the accumulation of wealth (the only means of escape from poverty and degradation); it weakens the coordinating effect of the market process; it pulls entrepreneurship and intellectual capital into non-productive and administrative activities; it creates a moral ethical tone which denies the hard task of wealth creation. Foreign aid makes it possible for . . . societies to transfer wealth from the poor [the general populace] to the rich [the rulers of third world countries and their hanger-ons].
>
> (see Osterfeld 1994, p. 201)

Foreign aid and a "global redistribution of wealth" are notions that are as bankrupt internationally as are, nationally, the notions of income redistribution and the Welfare State (as I argued in Chapter 5). What the end of the Cold War signals as regards international development is the need for, as Gorbachev might say, a "new thinking."

The old, atavistic notion that the well-being of the well-to-do is gained at the expense of the not-so-well-off is no more valid internationally than it is nationally (as, again, I argued in Chapter 5). The spectacular development of the Newly Industrialized Countries (NICs) of East Asia – South Korea, Taiwan, Hong Kong, and Singapore, as well as, more recently, Thailand, Malaysia, and Indonesia – over the course of the last few decades should be enough to dispel decisively that myth of "third-worldism" so very fashionable in the 1960s and 1970s, viz., so-called Dependency Theory. According to this myth, the world capitalist economy (the "center") creates a debilitating dependency for third world countries (the "periphery") and serves to perpetuate their poverty. "A central element in all of this is that the root causes of underdevelopment are sought *outside* the national societies, in the workings of the international capitalist system" (Berger 1986, p. 125). In reality, the *dependencia* myth ignores two important facts. The first is one that P. T. Bauer, an economist who has written extensively on developmental issues, has emphasized:

> Far from the West having caused the poverty in the Third World, contact with the West has been the principal agent of material progress there. The materially more advanced societies and regions of the Third World are those with which the West established the most numerous, diversified and extensive contacts: the cash-crop producing areas and entrepôt ports of South-East Asia, West Africa and Latin America; the mineral-producing areas of Africa and the Middle East; and cities and ports throughout Asia, Africa, the Caribbean and Latin America. The level of material achievement usually diminishes as one moves away from the foci of Western impact. The poorest and most backward people have few or no external contacts; witness the aborigines, pygmies and desert peoples.
>
> (Bauer 1981, p. 70; see also Bauer 1984 and Bauer 1991)

The second fact that is irresponsibly overlooked by advocates of third-worldism and "liberation theologians" roaming the countryside of Latin American and the alleyways of its shanty towns preaching the Gospel According to St. Marx is that the root causes of underdevelopment in these countries are to be sought not outside but *inside* the countries in question. Mario Vargas Llosa, the world-renowned novelist, and Hernando de Soto, a Peruvian businessman turned social activist, make this point in regard to Peru in particular and Latin America more generally (see de Soto 1989; see also Rohter 1987 and Lewis 1984). They point out how the lack of development in Latin America is due not to a capitalist economy but rather to the *lack* of such an economy. Before the "new thinking" began to take hold in Latin America in the 1980s, an economy such as Peru's was mainly not capitalist at all but rather "mercantil-ist," i.e., *pre*capitalist. Writing in the mid-1980s when dependency theory was still in vogue among members of the leftist intelligentsia both "Southern" and "Northern," the Catholic scholar Michael Novak remarked:

> Latin American economies are not capitalist but *pre*-capitalist. They are heavily burdened by traditionalist state bureaucracies, which dominate the economy. To have markets, private property, and a private sphere is *traditional*, not in itself capitalist. Capitalist economies go beyond traditionalist economies in setting limits upon state activities in the economic sphere; in their attention to educa-tion, invention, and creativity; in the public virtues they nourish; and in the balance they try to strike between the political system and the economic sys-tem. . . . Latin America has not yet passed from a pre-capitalist, traditionalist system to a capitalist system. . . .
>
> An empirical study of dependency, in short, does *not* show that the destiny of Latin America depends more upon external factors than upon internal changes in Latin American law and practice. On the contrary, Latin American institutions and practices discriminate against capitalist activities among the poor, and dis-courage internal investment and internal invention even among the affluent. . . . In Latin America, the law excludes the vast majority from free capitalist activities. Latin America continues in ancient habits of dependency because self-reliance and personal dynamism are shackled. Breaking these bonds would liberate the economic talents of the poor. Given its abundance of natural resources, Latin America would then become one of the most prosperous continents on earth.
>
> (Novak 1986, pp. 46, 139, 140)

Vargas Llosa, who ran as a candidate for the Peruvian presidency in 1990 in a bid to oust the corrupt administration of Alan Garcia Pérez, for his part writes:

> One of the most widely accepted myths about Latin America is that our back-wardness results from the principles of economic laissez-faire adopted in almost all our constitutions when we achieved independence from Spain and Portugal early in the last century. According to this myth, the opening of our economies to market forces made us easy prey to imperialists, whose voracious business practices brought about the inequities between rich and poor.
>
> After their exhaustive study of Peru's black market, Hernando de Soto and his institute [the Institute for Liberty and Democracy] conclude that Peru – as well as other Latin American countries and probably the majority of third-world

185

nations – never had a market economy. . . .De Soto uses the word "mercantilist" to describe Peru's economic system. By mercantilism, he means a bureaucratized state that favors the "redistribution" of wealth over the production of wealth.

(Vargas Llosa 1987, pp, 42, 47)

In a situation such as this, the solution to developmental problems is not less capitalism but *more capitalism* and more free trade.[2] The key to development and the creation of industries that are both competitive and profitable – and which accordingly contribute directly to the "common good," i.e., the promotion of social justice – lies in turning not inwards (autarky) but outwards, towards the global capitalist economy. "*Dependencia*" is nothing more than a mantra for, as Marx might say, those "false consciousnesses" that desire to effectuate a magical transformation of vice into virtue (yet another instance of the "cult of the victim" discussed in Chapter 2).

As in the case of the Marxism from which it draws its inspiration, dependency theory and liberation theology were blissfully ignorant of, as Adam Smith would say, the "nature and causes of the wealth of nations." Novak observes:

> In Marxist analysis (which has as its precondition the successful creation of wealth by a capitalist society, which it despises), affluence is simply taken for granted and poverty is said to be caused solely by exploitation. Marxist analysis says nothing about creating new wealth, about invention, about entrepreneurship. Its assumption is that wealth creation is a zero-sum game, that my poverty is someone else's fault, and that its cure is to expropriate the expropriators. Dependency theory has been invented to apply this myth to pre-capitalist lands, whose residual widespread poverty . . . is said to be caused by others – chiefly, by the United States.

(Novak 1986, p. 28; see also Novak 1984)

Just as a symbolic moment leading up to the end of the Cold War was furnished by Ronald Reagan when in 1987 he called upon Gorbachev to "tear down" the Berlin Wall (see Chapter 1), so likewise a highly symbolic moment heralding the birth of the new thinking in regard to international justice and the global economy was Reagan's performance at the North–South Summit at Cancun, Mexico, in 1981. The summit, with wide representation from both "North" and "South," had been convened for the purpose of launching the long-discussed New International Economic Order – an ambitious program long advocated by leftists everywhere designed to close the gap between rich and poor nations by means of a global redistribution of wealth on a truly massive scale. But as Michael Manley, former socialist prime minister of Jamaica, observes, the whole idea "was formally buried at the supposed moment of its birth":

> Ronald Reagan, who had just been elected, killed it with a smile. He smiled at Julius Nyerere. He smiled at Jose Lopez-Portillo, the president of Mexico. He smiled at all of us and just said no. In two days, 20 years of international struggle went up in smoke. Everyone packed up and left Cancun, confessed of their powerlessness, admonished and discharged with a smile.

(Manley 1992, p. E4)[3]

186

APPENDIX

Manley is himself highly symbolic of the new, transformed thinking that began to take hold in the 1980s, even before the end of the Cold War. What contributes to Manley's symbolic stature is his own thoroughgoing personal transformation. Before becoming in his second round in office (1989–1992) a leading advocate of the market economy and economic liberalization in developing countries, he was, during his first terms (1972–1980), an outsopken advocate of third-worldism and "dirigiste dogma" (Lal 1985) and an ardent proponent of the New International Economic Order which called for political management of the world economy – in effect, a kind of global command economy; he was, in his own words, a "pal of Fidel Castro who preached the state control of the economy and said that Jamaican millionaires could go to Miami." What however Manley learned from his ill-fated experiments in state control over the economy was that the "nationalist and statist approach" simply does not work. For at least two reasons, as Manley points out. In the first instance, you cannot manage an economy on a long-term basis by appealing to social patriotism (Manley calls this the "Guevarist myth," after Cuba's Che Guevara); if they are to perform efficiently, economic agents must have a real (economic) interest ("an equity stake or a profit motive") in the success of their enterprises. Second, it is not possible neatly to combine a socialist economy and a market economy; the elements of the former will inevitably tend to drive out the latter (as Jamaicans learned much to their chagrin). What Manley came to realize is that, as I argued in Chapter 5, there is a *logic of systems*, and this logic cannot be violated with impunity. There is no "third way."

Confronted with the collapse of the Jamaican economy brought on by state interventionism (i.e., confronted by, as he says, "reality"), Manley "began to appreciate a deeper truth about development":

> You can't circumvent the market economy. If you want a really dynamic, effective economy, the only thing you can do is to pursue the market logic completely. Whole hog, not halfway.
>
> This means you have to divest what was brought under state control. You must liberalize foreign exchange controls. You must eliminate subsidies and price controls. You must expose the economy to the shock of competition, knowing full well that you will lose some of what you built up in order to create a leaner but more enduring process of development.
>
> (Manley 1992, p. E4)

In light of the "preferential option for the poor" discussed in Chapter 5, it is to be noted that Manley, a life-long trade unionist and member of Socialist International, embraced unreservedly the logic of market economics *precisely because* it seemed to him to offer the best prospects for improving the lot of the poorest of Jamaicans. "There is no way to eradicate poverty," Manley states, "if you resist the logic of capitalism." "Ending poverty," he also says, "is essentially a matter of creating access to the savings that have resulted from productive activity" (ibid.). This is another way of saying that the best way to combat poverty is by effectively guaranteeing what in Chapter 5 I argued is the basic human right in the economic sphere, namely, the right of "free entry." Economic democracy and economic liberalization go hand in hand. Together, they are a formula for increased economic prosperity, even in the poorest of countries. (A formula, it must be emphasized, not a miracle solution; the path to development is a long and arduous one which holds out the promise of success only for those who have the courage of their convictions and are steadfast in their commitment to freedom.)[4]

Just as the logic of the market economy is, as I have argued (and despite what *dirigiste* Japanese bureaucrats might think), everywhere the same, so likewise the formula for economic well-being is everywhere the same. Or as Manley says: "There is no reality to grand plans aimed at equalizing North and South. There are only [nation-]states doing their small part in a decentralized fashion to hook up with a dispersed global economy" (ibid.). [5] Manley's message to his colleagues in other LDCs is that they have much more to learn from Adam Smith than from Karl Marx.

Even if there exists no "grand plan" for achieving international justice by purely political means, there is nonetheless, to use Manley's term, a *logic* to development. Those countries which resist this logic will, as Manley says, "be washed away in the tide of history driven by technological change" (ibid.). "Where history is going," he says, is in the direction of "a global market economy". Hooking up in a decentralized fashion with this dispersed global economy is the route to development; resisting it by the old politics of autarky (e.g., import-substitution) is a guaranteed formula for stagnation and even (as in the case of sub-Saharan Africa, Nkrumah's Ghana being a noteworthy example) regression. In the new world order there will not be three "worlds" but only one world, a world in which countries at various levels of development interact in a multitude of diverse and mutually beneficial ways. The development model that largely prevailed from the 1950s to the 1980s and that was characterized by nondemocratic, authoritarian *dirigisme* and social engineering aimed at "modernization" has indeed been washed away by the tide of history. A prime example was Nyerere's Tanzania, for many years the Western world's favorite third-world socialist experiment (christened *Ujamaa* by Nyerere), a highly subsidized one which was kept going only thanks to massive transfusions of foreign aid.[6] All that decades of nationalistic/socialistic isolationism has brought those countries that practiced it is worsening poverty, massive budget deficits, mounting debts, a crippling reliance on foreign aid, and social and bureaucratic corruption of the most extreme and all-pervasive sort. In the newly emerging world order, the speed and thoroughness with which countries are able to embrace free trade and effect the necessary economic and political liberalization measures will determine the pace of their development.

A great amount of ink has been spilled over the question as to what reformers should concentrate on first, democratization ("*glasnost*") or economic liberalization ("*perestroika*"). Like Aristotle's old question as to which comes first, the chicken or the egg, the question is not only intractable (advocates for the priority of either approach can cite any amount of merely empirical or historical data to buttress their case), it is also perhaps *beside the point*. The fact of the matter is that, as Minxin Pei observes: "The most notable trend in global political and economic development since the early 1980s has been the surge of [both] political democratization and market-oriented reforms, first in the developing countries and then in communist states" (Pei 1994a, p. 90). Real, sustainable development must, by the nature of the case (as I hope to indicate), involve both economic (market) and political (democratic) elements. As Robert A. Scalapino, director of the Institute of East Asian Studies at Berkeley, observes: "One cannot encourage innovative, productive economic citizens while keeping them politically mute" (Scalapino 1989, p. 78).

Consider, for instance, the case of those economically stagnant countries that for decades have been victimized by socialist-style interventionism but which, for one reason or another, are suddenly caught up in the great "third wave" of democratic transitions. This is the case with most Latin American countries as well as a number of African states. If, after the introduction of a democratic regime, the economic inequities and injustices that have been allowed to build up over decades of economic mismanagement and patrimonial exploitation are not rapidly addressed, it is only to be expected that, in the absence of perceptible improvement in their lot, people will soon lose faith in the much vaunted virtues of democracy and will fall prey to a new authoritarianism of a populist sort. Thus, making these countries "safe for democracy" requires that *economic reforms* follow swift upon the heels of political transformation. However – and this is the important thing to note – in order fully to be implemented, economic reforms require in turn an expansion and deepening of *democracy*, i.e., not merely the introduction of formal democratic procedures such as free elections but, beyond that, the creation of genuine civil society. Economic liberalization and political democratization are mutually reinforcing. "Democratization and market-oriented economic reform clearly coexist in practice in a number of countries today. We need to know more about how they coexist in theory" (Armijo et al. 1994, p. 174). Let us then look at the matter in a bit more detail.

The economic reforms that are called for by what is sometimes referred to as the New Policy Agenda are basically of two sorts and are, as it were, sequential in nature. The first sort of reform is one that, in order to work at all, needs (as I argued in Chapters 1 and 5) to be undertaken as thoroughly and as rapidly as possible (see also Aslund 1994). The immediate concern of any newly emergent democracy should be *macroeconomic stabilization* (see in this regard Nelson 1990 and Haggard and Kaufman 1992). This involves fiscal and monetary measures designed to eliminate soft budget contraints (budget deficits) and inflation (mostly a consequence of the former); lifting price controls and eliminating subsidies; dismantling trade barriers; devaluing the (usually overvalued) national currency and instituting full currency convertibility, by means for instance of currency control boards (eliminating foreign exchange controls). These kinds of stabilization measures can be successfully undertaken by authoritarian regimes (e.g., Pinochet's Chile, a model widely appealed to), and, indeed, it is often argued (by, for instance, apologists of Chinese-style neoauthoritarianism and "East Asian exceptionalism" [see Pei 1994a]) that this is precisely one reason why economic reform should precede political (democratic) reform. The reason that is usually cited in support of the "transitional incompatibility" thesis is that reforms of this sort invariably create a great deal of socio-economic dislocation and impose severe hardships on large segments of the populace, which could therefore be expected to reject them if they had the democratic means of doing so. There is an undeniable truth to this argument. Macroeconomic reform can be extremely painful – which is precisely why, when these reforms are undertaken by democratic regimes, they should be implemented as rapidly as possible, during the period of "extraordinary politics" when the new regime is still in its "honeymoon" stage and disposes of a significant amount of political "capital." There is, however, another side to the story. (And, as I shall indicate in a moment, there is a democratic means of coping with the threat that radical economic reform poses to the survival of democratic regimes.)

It could equally well be argued that, whatever competitive advantage authoritarian regimes enjoy over democratic regimes in the short term in having a free hand to undertake macroeconomic reforms ("shock therapy"), these reforms themselves cannot, in the long run, be expected to bear fruit unless they are followed up by reforms of another sort: long-term, on-going *institutional (microeconomic) reform*. Reforms of the latter sort necessarily call for, and are productive of, increased *democratization*. As one specialist in international relations pointedly observes:

> What an authoritarian regime clearly cannot manage without fundamentally changing its character is the second stage of reform. This stage consists of institutional changes such as the development of stock markets; the liberalization of labor markets; the revamping of social security, social services, and retirement systems; large-scale privatizations, especially of state banks; the restructuring of state enterprises; the encouragement of competition within the domestic private sector; and the establishment of a coherent regulatory framework.
>
> (Barkey 1995, p. 114)

The important thing to note is that (economic) reforms of the latter sort, ones which are crucial for bringing into being a genuine civil market economy, are reforms that have *political* consequences. *Their net result is the creation of civil society.* "Such second-stage tasks," Barkey observes, "entail a major transfer of power from the state to civil society – a civil society that is weak or nonexistent in authoritarian states" (ibid., p. 114). Thus, as Barkey goes on to say: "[E]very step that an authoritarian regime takes along the path of the second stage of reform limits its direct control over individuals and groups and is thus a nail in its own coffin.... If real competition is allowed ... then both an efficiently functioning market and a vigorous democracy are a good bet to emerge" (ibid., p. 114).

Once an option has been made in favor of *development* – which requires full-scale market-oriented reform – the cards are stacked in favor of *democracy*. As is so often the case in human affairs, there is at work here a kind of "ruse of reason" or "invisible hand." Effective economic reform consists, as was mentioned, of two stages; these could be labelled the "authoritarian" and the "democratic." Shock therapy type reforms are authoritarian in nature, even when practiced by democratic regimes (they are, as it were, reforms that are "decreed" and are effected by central governments and technocratic elites). By themselves, however, they are not sufficient to produce an effectively functioning market economy, as the case of Eastern Europe and Russia in particular so vividly demonstrates. The logic of successful economic reform requires implementation of the second stage of democratic reforms, i.e., a transfer of power from the state to society and the institution of civil society. The reason for this is quite simply that, unless this happens, those privileged elements in society that were formerly in positions of power and that benefited from the *status quo ante* (bureaucrats, party activists, managers and workers in state-owned enterprises [SOEs], a bourgeoisie parasitical on government patronage, etc.) will use their positions of on-going privilege to engage in rent-seeking and will co-opt whatever economic benefits are produced by the first stage of economic reform (by, for instance, exporting their capital to Switzerland); the sort of corruption endemic to state-controlled economies will once again become the name of the game.[7] This in turn will subvert the whole process of economic liberalization, which must then inevitably falter. The much hoped-for economic "take-off" will fail fully to materialize. Speaking of postcommunist societies, former Polish finance minister Leszek Balcerowicz observes: "[B]y channelling entrepreneurial and managerial energies into rent seeking and corruption rather than the search for greater efficiency, nonradical programs that avoid liberalization destroy the prospects for economic development" (Balcerowicz 1994, p. 84). Like a person riding a bicycle, economic liberalization is a dynamic process that must continue to unfold lest it stall and collapse (this is the danger that, after close to twenty years of incremental reform, now threatens China which has yet to bite the bullet and engage in a serious effort at privatizing its inefficient SOEs whose soft budget constraints are a major factor contributing to China's galloping inflation). Thus, as far as economic reform and the institution of a market economy is concerned, it is, as Michael Manley would say, whole hog or nothing. Or as Joan M. Nelson, a specialist in international development, states: "A strong case can be made that largely market economies and open and competitive political systems, once both become established, are mutually reinforcing" (Nelson 1994, p. 61). By the logic of things, development calls forth democracy, and democracy serves as an on-going guarantee of development.

This talk about the logic of reform and the ruses of reason is not as abstract as it might seem. I mentioned above that one of the most serious threats to effective and sustained reform in a newly emergent democracy is the resistance that can be expected from those hitherto marginalized sectors of society (e.g., peasants and the lower middle classes, the "working poor") – now however enfranchised – upon whom will fall especially hard the costs of macroeconomic stabilization (e.g., the elimination of subsidies) and institutional restructuring (e.g., widespread unemployment due to the closing down of unprofitable SOEs). There is no quick fix to this unfortunate situation; as Nelson observes, the costs of economic reform are immediately felt whereas the benefits come only gradually (see Nelson 1994, p. 53) The experience of Latin American countries that have pursued developmental and democratizing reforms suggests that only years of sustained economic growth can begin to eliminate longstanding and widespread poverty. However, as the case of Latin America also demonstrates, there are interim measures that can be adopted by democratic governments to ease the pain of transition and cushion the effects of adjustment. The interesting thing to note is that these measures, while serving an important economic function, serve also as one of the best ways for promoting – by means of a kind of invisible hand put to work at a basic level of social dynamics – the spread of democratic institutions and the formation of civil society.

I am alluding here to the "social fund" or "safety net" programs that a number of Latin American (and other) countries have instituted – with a greater or lesser degree of success – in order to deal with the problems of adjustment. These are government-funded programs designed to alleviate the social cost of market-oriented reforms suffered by the more marginalized sectors of society. As illustrated perhaps best of all by Bolivia's Emergency Social Fund instituted in 1986, these programs work best when they are (1) demand-based and (2) non-political or non-partisan (see Graham 1995). Their purpose is not to provide welfare hand-outs, for, as Aristotle rightly pointed out long ago, aid of this sort "is like water poured into a leaky cask" (Aristotle 1941, *Politics*, 1320a32). Their purpose is rather that of making funds available to local community and nongovernmental organizations for the purpose of instituting projects that are likely to be self-sustaining and that have the potential of contributing to lasting poverty alleviation (i.e., projects of an "infrastructural" nature). Their purpose is to help the poor help themselves and to inculcate lessons of "empowerment" that are so utterly crucial for any long-term improvement in the lot of the poor. The great merit of compensatory programs such as these is that, by funding projects that are locally originated and locally administered, they encourage initiative and responsiblity at the local level and, in this way, contribute to development of grass-roots democracy. As

191

APPENDIX

Carol Graham writes: "[E]ncouraging the poor to participate in addressing their own problems and exercise their political voice can give these marginalized members of society a stake *in both economic reform and the democratic system*" (Graham 1995, p. 143; emphasis added). Measures of this sort can, as she says, "amplify the *political voice* as well as the economic potential of previously marginalized groups, thereby expanding the democratic political process." Given the appropriate institutional incentives, democracy and development are indeed fully compatible.

The challenges confronting those countries that opt for genuine development are daunting. It is no easy task to turn things around and undo the systematic damage wrought by decades of misguided, counterproductive policies.[8] "The main difficulty in reforming state-socialist economies," Minxin Pei observes, "has less to do with the level of development per se than with the level of misdevelopment" (Pei 1994a, p. 97). Once socialist-style practices have taken root, they are, like corrupt practices in general, extremely difficult to extirpate, as the poor record to date of half-hearted attempts at liberalization in countries such as India and Egypt (one of the major, on-going recipients of U.S. foreign aid) vividly demonstrate. (According to one World Bank official, Egypt remains largely a "Soviet-style command economy" [see Elon 1995, p. 34]; in India, the Soviet model enthusiastically imitated for some forty years has only recently been called into question.)[9] Socialism always results in the creation of extensive, high-handed bureaucracies,[10] and bureaucracies are one of the greatest sources of entrenched resistance to any program aimed at economic reform – especially when, as in India, they have been co-opted by powerful unions which have nothing to gain, and everything to lose, from successful reforms aimed at promoting economic efficiency. (Upon his election to the presidency in July of 1994, Ukraine's Leonid Kuchma quipped that probably the only way to get radical reform going would be to fire all the bureaucrats.) Speaking of Asian economies, Scalapino observes: "One of the effects of the commitment to socialism, irrespective of the degree of success or failure, was the rapid emergence of a larger, more powerful bureaucratic class. Far from breaking with the colonial tradition, the new leaders in this respect fortified it" (Scalapino 1989, p. 46). The dismantling of inflated bureaucracies is one of the most important, but also most difficult, tasks that reform-minded governments must confront. It is in any event one of the chief reforms called for by any genuinely "postcolonial" agenda.

One country that, through sheer political will, has embraced the new thinking and has begun to make a turnaround is Argentina. What is particularly interesting about Argentina's case is that at the beginning of this century it was one of the world's ten richest countries with a per capita income close to that of Western Europe and at least four times higher than Japan's (Chirot 1994, p. 270). By the 1980s, however, after years of populist Socialism under Juan Peron and subsequent military dictatorships which sought to implement an ideology of nationalistic autarky, Argentina had been turned into something of an economic basket case, a country riddled with corruption and plagued by capital flight, massive indebtedness, and rampant inflation[11] (during the same time, at the opposite end of the hemisphere, Canada had passed from being an underdeveloped country, lagging far behind Argentina, to being a select member of the club of rich nations, the G-7). If Carlos Menem (along with his superbly competent finance minister, Domingo Cavallo) was so remarkably successful in initiating radical economic reform during his first term in office in the early 1990s, one major reason accounting for his success was no doubt because he could count on an earlier tradition in that country of liberal democracy and on the liberated forces of a basically sound civil society. The situation is otherwise in the case of India and Africa.[12] Indeed, sub-Saharan Africa offers something like a "worst-case scenario" of the difficulties that confront those countries which today, and after decades of ill-fated socialist-paternalist experimentation, would seek to charter a new course towards democracy and development. Postcolonial Africa has fared even worse than India, which since independence has pursued the "socialist path to development" and which accordingly has performed extremely poorly, achieving only minimal economic growth (dubbed the "Hindu rate of growth" by Indian economist Raj Krishna). On the whole, Africa has not achieved even that. As one writer observes:

> With a handful of exceptions, the postcolonial state in Africa has been largely antidevelopmental. Parasitic, rent-seeking, and inept, it has been simultaneously very coercive and extremely weak, forced to prey on the economy and civil society – with devastating effect – just to survive. The bureaucracy's effectiveness has typically been undermined by a patrimonial logic, in which state assets are routinely plundered for the political advantage of the regime, and state-society relations have been characterized by clientelism rather than citizenship. The state, powerless to elicit respect or loyalty from the populace, has typically used threats and coercion to achieve minimal – usually passive – acquiescence.
>
> (van de Walle 1995, p. 132)

Postcolonial African states have for the most part been nothing more than huge patronage machines permeated to an utterly mind-boggling degree by corruption, cronyism, and embezzlement ("Swiss bank account Socialism").

In a situation such as this, the only way of overcoming societal stagnation is by pursuing a reform program such as that adopted by Zambia subsequent to its turn to democracy in 1991, i.e., a program aimed simultaneously at democratization and market-oriented reform. No amount of authoritarian-led economic liberalization is likely to have any significant effect in countries plagued by a long history of political and social corruption (Bauer aptly refers to these regimes as "kleptocracies");[13] in their case, democratization is a developmental *sine qua non*. Democratization can work, however, only if it is combined with a thorough-going attempt at fostering the development of the autonomous forces of civil society, and this requires a total commitment to creating a civil market economy. As Minxin Pei remarks, "[T]he growth and expansion of market forces are the only way to rebuild a civil society – and its pluralistic social institutions, which are the foundations of modern democracy" (Pei 1994b, p. 71).

The single most vital element in the development of true democracy (as opposed to democracy of a merely formalistic [e.g., plebiscite] sort) is the development of civil society. The development of civil society requires, in turn, the unequivocal recognition and implementation of *human rights* of a civil and political sort. This is the meaning of *liberal democracy*, to which there exists no meaningful alternative: "[H]uman rights standards . . . require a particular type of 'liberal' regime, which may be institutionalized in various forms, but only within a relatively narrow range of variation" (Howard and Donnelly 1989, p. 66). Just as there is a logic of market economics which, despite its many variants, is everywhere the same (see Chapter 5), so likewise there is a logic of democracy which is everywhere the same, even though this universal logic, in order to be effective, must (as Montesquieu well knew) always be adapted to the particularities of time and place.[14] The logic of liberal (or constitutional) democracy and the enterprise economy is everywhere the same, and no country or region of the world is *unique*, although each is *different* from all others, in this or that respect (whence the need for "interpretation" in the "application" of liberal principles). Political and economic principles as defined by liberal theory are, like the laws of nature, universal, and there is no room in human affairs for "exceptionalism." As late-eighteenth century liberals liked to say in their Enlightenment attempt to formulate the basic principles of what Tocqueville called "*une nouvelle science de la politique*," like causes everywhere produce like effects. Granting "exceptions" to the liberal principle of universal human rights amounts to according a licence to the whimsies of authoritarian governance, be it totalitarian, autocratic, or populist. As Aung San Suu Kyi, Fang Lizhi, and other champions of human rights in the "third world" have cogently argued, there is no such thing as an "Asian" democracy essentially different from "Western," liberal democracy. Nor, it may be added, is there any such thing as a generically specific "African" democracy, as a figure as prominent and influential as Adebayo Adedeji, former undersecretary-general and executive secretary of the Economic Commission for Africa of the United Nations, would nonetheless have us believe.

Although Adedeji is altogether within his rights in criticizing the structural adjustment programs (SAPs) long-proposed to African countries as a solution to their economic woes by institutions such as the World Bank and the International Monetary Fund (IMF), he is right for the wrong reasons. These programs, whose chief purpose was macroeconomic stabilization as described above, were inadequate (and largely ineffectual) not because they relied on "models derived from the experience of Western Europe and North America" (Adedeji 1994, p. 120) – the implication being that they were "eurocentric"; they were inadequate for the simple reason that they were much too narrowly focused. They addressed themselves to economic issues all too narrowly conceived (e.g., current accounts deficits) and to non-democratically backed governments rather than to broader, institutional issues of a socio-political, infrastructural sort, i.e., issues having to do with the formation of civil society – which, as I argued above, is the *sine qua non* for long-term economic liberalization and developmental take-off.[15] One thing in particular that in the past these programs crucially ignored was the issue of Good Government, i.e., *glasnost* and democratization, that has now become part and parcel of the New Policy Agenda. In short, these programs were both "unrealistic" and "impractical." In contrast, Adedeji's "alternative for Africa" – as he calls it – errs on the side of utopianism. Adedeji's scenario is, in the words of Thomas Callaghty, a political scientist specializing in African affairs, "a redemptive, utopian one increasingly popular among Africa's well-educated elites. It seizes on the very weaknesses of the African neighborhood as a tool for freeing the continent from external economic and political control so that African peoples may institute true participatory democracy and equitable development" (Callaghty 1994, p. 135).

Sub-Saharan Africa is, by all accounts, the most backward part of the world at the present time.[16] It is most certainly not the case, however, that Africa has become, as Adedeji claims, "the hapless victim of a massive failure to understand the nature of its problems" (Adedeji 1994, p. 120). Actually, the problems are pretty well understood, and the way of resolving them is fairly evident, though by no means easy to implement. There is no facile solution to Africa's long-standing problems, ones, moreover, which, as in the case also of India, have been largely self-inflicted, albeit often with the advice and encouragement of Western leftist intellectuals (oil-rich Congo [Brazzaville] which formally became a Marxist state in 1970 after a coup by Captain Marien Ngouabi and which subsequently proceeded to squander its wealth being a case in point). Adedeji is therefore altogether right in asserting that "the continent needs fundamental structural change and transformation, not just tinkering at the margins" (ibid., p. 121). And he is also right in thinking that this change and transformation must be made to occur above all on the community level. He is altogether wrong, however, in thinking that true democracy means "participatory" democracy (see Chapter 4), as well as in thinking that development can come from Africa turning inwards, cultivating ancient, ethno-specific traditions (ones which in this day and age, even in Africa where passengers in interurban buses can have their fantasies stimulated by watching televised reruns of "Dallas," are largely irrelevant to present-day social dynamics), ignoring the process of economic globalization going on everywhere else in the world. The laws of economics and the maxims of sound fiscal and monetary policy are the same for Africans as they are for all the other peoples of the world. Blackness or *négritude* cannot, as if by the wave of a magic wand, dispense Africans from these universal laws. For latecomers to development, it is especially important, as Scalapino points out, to "abandon autarky and seek entry into regional and global market networks, thereby acquiring the capital, technology, and skills necessary to accelerate the developmental process" (Scalapino 1989, pp. 113–14). For regimes that in the past have invested heavily in nationalistic pride and self-sufficiency, internationalization (*kokousaika*, as the Japanese call it) and economic liberalization may be a bitter pill to have to swallow, but no other medicine will do the job – certainly not the ersatz medicine prescribed by afrocentrics like Adedeji.[17]

Adedeji is especially in error when he suggests that the solution to Africa's problems lies in a revival of its "traditional, local institutions":

> [I]nstead of copying Western systems, why can we not transform our own traditional, local institutions into modern local governments? After all, these traditional systems still wax strong. Why can we not devise a new system of political organization based on our traditional political societies and associations instead of mimicking the Western model of divisive political parties? Africans are past masters in consultation, consensus, and consent. Our traditions abhor exclusion. Consequently, there is no sanctioned and institutionalized opposition in our traditional system of governance. Traditionally, politics for us has never been a zero-sum game. Why can we not find a way of bringing these values into the transformation of our political economy?
>
> (Adedeji 1994, p. 126)

Scenarios such as Adedeji's convey, as Callaghty says, "a powerful image of an aggrieved community escaping from an evil external world that is attempting to carry out a capitalist-imperialist plot to keep Africa down" (Callaghty 1994, p. 140).[18]

In attacking the "Northern model of democracy" and in appealing (in a way reminiscent of the autocrats in Beijing) to Africa's supposedly "unique characteristics" (which would allow it to dispense with "divisive political parties"), Adedeji comes across as an African version of Singapore's patriarchal champion of the "Asian" way to development, Lee Kuan Yew. Adedeji would have us believe that Africans can build democracy and achieve economic growth by ignoring that crucial element of democracy that "Northerners" so long strove for, viz., the proclamation and institutionalization of fundamental human rights and freedoms of a civil and political sort.

APPENDIX

As Jean Baechler stated some time ago in seeking an explanation as to why it was in Western Europe that spectacular, sustained economic growth was first achieved – the so-called "European miracle": "The first condition for the maximization of economic efficiency is the liberation of civil society with respect to the state" (Baechler 1975, p. 77; cited in Raico 1994, p. 38). What excuse can there be for those who are not prepared to learn from the experience, both positive and negative, of others? Adedeji's "alternative for Africa," based on a nostalgic call for a return to a largely imagined past (and which in no way addresses the social havoc wrought in most African countries by years of military or one-party rule – all in the name of "communal spirit" and "social harmony"), has all the earmarkings of a formula for *de-development*, to borrow an expression from Rhoda Howard, a Canadian scholar specializing in African affairs. "Contrary to the received left collectivist viewpoint," Howard writes, "civil and political rights and the rule of law are necessary prerequisites to the successful attainment of economic democracy and equality" (Howard 1992b, p. 10). And as she rightly observes, "Citizen action within a liberal capitalist society appears so far to be the best approach to attaining the full set of human rights." Whence she concludes that "the radical capitalist agenda may turn out, in the medium to long term, to be the best approach to development in Africa" (ibid., p. 14). To put the matter another way, Adedeji's anti-Western "alternative for Africa" would predictably produce the same disastrous results in Africa as Nehru's attempt to create in India "a new civilization, radically different from the present capitalist order" did in that country (see Kamath 1994, p. 95).

Not all – or even the greater part – of Africa's problems can, as Adedeji insinuates, be attributed to the legacy of Western colonialism (unless by "Western colonialism" is meant the seduction of African elites by Western Marxism [cf. Guinea's Sékou Touré's program of "Marxism in African clothes"]), and it is more than doubtful that solutions to its problems are to be had by stigmatizing Western "individualism" in the name of overlooked, pristine communal values of a traditionalist sort. One would think that any self-respecting African would want to agree, as regards themselves, with the sentiments voiced by Aung San Suu Kyi, leader of the democratic opposition in Burma: "The proposition [put forward by the current Burmese dictatorship] that the Burmese are not fit to enjoy as many rights and privileges as [Western] democratic countries is insulting" (Suu Kyi 1992, p. 11).[19] Appeals to "cultural integrity" or "national culture" amount, for the most part, wherever they are uttered, to nothing more than a call for a renewed form of patrimonialism and paternalistic government (see Suu Kyi 1995, p. 14).[20] The antiliberal "politics of ethnicity" (yet another "alternative" to what Adedeji calls the Western idea of "divisive political parties") practiced by African leaders such as Kenya's Daniel Arap Moi is nothing more than a recipe for political backwardness and economic stagnation. As Axelle Kabou, a Cameroonian sociologist, has recently had the courage to state: "The Africa of nationalisms has exhausted its resources." Kabou's work is, in the words of Howard French, "one of several works by African intellectuals deploring the glorification of the past by Africans in everything from poetry to political science" (French 1994, p. E3). Kabou, according to French, argues that:

In post-independence Africa ... the political use of négritude which celebrates blackness, helped feed dictatorships like that of Zaire's Mobuto Sese Seko with its jackboot ideology of "authenticity" that outlawed Western business suits and

196

Christian names, and expropriated, then bled to death foreign-owned businesses in the cause of national sovereignty.

(French 1994, p. E3)

The rejection on the part of Adedeji of universal values and standards, and afrocentric stances such as his which seek to discover in Africa's backwardness the germs of its own self-generated salvation are actually a prime element in reinforcing, in an altogether perverse way, what Peter Anyang' Nyong'o of the African Academy of Sciences in Nairobi says are "the views of many Westerners who think that Africans are basically backward and cannot be judged on the basis of any universal standard" (Anyang' Nyong'o 1992, p. 94). Are not Africans *human* beings, like all other such? And, as human beings, do they not desire what all human beings most ardently desire, viz., recognition of their freedom and dignity as beings endowed with fundamental moral rights to self-determination? Rights which it is the express purpose of "Western," liberal democracy to ensure?

> The truth is that Africans, like all other human beings, want justice, equity, transparency, responsibility, and accountability. They want respect and human dignity. They want a decent life and an opportunity to feed, shelter, and clothe their families. . . . They want to create a strong civil society that can hold its leaders accountable and responsible, as well as sustain mechanisms of governance which ensure the security of the people rather than the security of Heads of States and a small group of supporters and opportunists who surround them.
> This is the type of democracy millions of Africans are striving for.

(Anon. 1994, p. 185)

Wilful ignorance of the "Western model" and a quixotic search for an "alternative" to rights-based, liberal democracy can only prove detrimental to the cause of democracy and development in Africa. Writes Howard:

> Repression of basic civil and political rights has detrimental consequences for economic development. If the only human rights available to Africans during the last three decades had been those traditionally associated with the rule of law and freedom of expression, development might well have made more progress because people would have been able to articulate their complaints, make officials aware of their concerns, and talk to and organize with each other. . . .
> [B]asic civil and political rights must be protected if the current populist thrust in Africa is to be transformed into a stable democratic political system with the potential for fair and equitable economic reform. Individual rights to freedom of expression, embodied in freedom of speech, press and association, underpin political democracy; without them, political democracy is a meaningless exercise.

(Howard 1992b, p. 8)

The rejection of universal values in general and the "Northern model" of individual human rights in particular, one is tempted to say, can only make experiments in "African" democracy a meaningless exercise. And, in terms of development forgone, a very costly one at that.[21]

"[I]t now may be taken as an established fact that there can be no authentic development without democracy." So writes Honoré Koffi Guie (1993, p. 122), and by democracy he means liberal democracy. Guie is an Ivorian scholar and a leading activist in GERDDES-Africa (Groupe d'études et de recherches sur la démocratie et le développement économique et social), a nonpartisan, nongovernmental organization dedicated to the creation of "a true civil society" and the promotion of "universal ideals with the goal of assisting the cause of human rights and democracy" in francophone Africa (ibid., p. 120). On the interdependence of democracy and development Guie remarks:

> If once there might have been uncertainty about the relationship between democracy and development, today the case is clear-cut: it is possible to have economic growth under a dictatorial regime, but genuine development – the kind that is measured in terms of full human well-being – cannot exist without democracy. In every instance, economic advances can be consolidated and made durable only by a responsible populace.
>
> (Guie 1993, p. 122)

"Genuine development," as Guie rightly observes, is conditional upon the development of a "responsible populace" (a populace which are wards of a social Welfare State cannot, by definition, be "responsible"). Neither real development nor real democracy is possible in the absence of a thriving civil society. As I argued in Chapter 5, the only way of building real democracy is by working from the ground up. Or as Rhoda Howard puts it, "rights must be wrested from below" (Howard 1992b, p. 8). No amount of what Adedeji refers to as "long-term economic planning" (Adedeji 1994, p. 123) (by whom? one wonders) will translate into socio-economic progress so long as governments do not do their utmost to allow, and indeed to encourage, individuals to pursue and to assume responsibility for their own well-being, either on their own or in voluntary association with other like-minded individuals. The absolutely crucial element in economic advance is, as Guie says, "a responsible populace," i.e., a populace that is permitted to assume responsibility for *its own* fate. This is the basic reason why "development planning" must be rejected; it is absolutely incompatible with civil society, i.e., the "self-organization of society," since *by definition* it is an attempt on the part of the state to direct or "rationally control" not only its own affairs but also those of the nation – society – as a whole.

It is because economic advance is contingent upon a populace assuming responsibility for its own affairs that I stated at the outset that it is in the context of the nation-state that the struggle for democracy is best waged. (This is not to say that international assistance is irrelevant – far from it, as I shall indicate in the following section.) "[E]conomic prosperity," Howard correctly observes, "now will depend on internally, not externally, generated change" (Howard 1992b, p. 11). Neither Africans nor any other peoples can be expected to reap the rewards of development so long as they continue to subscribe to some form of the dependency thesis and and luxuriate in blaming their woes on others. From its origins earlier in this century in Marxist-corporatist thinking, dependency theory, as Daniel Chirot observes, became "more than a mere economic argument":

> Its political and social ramifications suited nationalists perfectly because they blamed most of the economic and social ills of the nation on foreign intervention. Was there poverty? That was because foreign interests were milking the nation dry. Were some local entrepreneurs becoming rich? That was proof that

they had sold out to foreign interests. Was labor repressed? That was because foreign investors wanted labor costs kept down, and they were using local elites to enforce their will. Was foreign capital flowing in? That was to better rob and weaken the nation. Was it flowing out? That was proof that the imperialists were exporting their profits and not investing.

(Chirot 1994, p. 250)

The merely reactive mindset of the "victim" – expressive of nothing more than envy and *ressentiment* and superbly adept at discovering anywhere and everywhere but within itself the reasons for its own failures, and which accordingly demands "proactive" measures to compensate for them – is not conducive to self-improvement. One of the great good fortunes of South Africa was to have jettisoned a nationalist and racist ideology and to have embarked on the path of democratization only after the whole ideology of third-worldism had pretty much run its course. Nelson Mandela articulates well the "new thinking" in this regard when he says: "Africa has long traversed a mindset that seeks to heap all blame on the past [i.e., colonialism] and on others. The era of renaissance we are entering is, and should be, based on our own efforts as Africans to change Africa's conditions for the better" (*The Economist*, May 20, 1995, survey 4).

Democratization and development are not only compatible, they are "synergetic," mutually reinforcing. And the motor that drives both is the dynamism that is unleashed when the many autonomous groupings of an active and articulate civil society are allowed to flourish. From the point of view of Austrian economics (as discussed in Chapter 5), development cannot adequately be understood by means of the static allocation approach favored by mainline, neoclassical economics and cannot adequately be measured in objective, quantifiable terms as growth in per capita real income (the approach long favored by USAID, the IMF, and the World Bank under the direction of Robert McNamara and his whiz kids). Development is not, contrary to what Jawaharlal Nehru asserted in 1960, "a matter of mathematics" (Kamath 1994, p. 97), nor is prosperity something that can be "engineered." Development is not something that can be "planned" but is rather the name for a *social process* of a *spontaneous* sort (as described in Chapters 3, 4, and 5) that occurs when individual agents are free to interact in a communicatively rational way in their pursuit of the "good life." As such it is a function of the innumerable, unquantifiable *institutional* variables – social, legal, political, as well as economic (see Bauer 1972) – that serve to facilitate the process of communication and coordination among individuals – what Hayek calls "synergetic collaboration" (Hayek 1988, p. 80).[22] "It is this coordination, in combination with the increasing complexity and creativity it brings, that constitutes economic growth and increasing economic order" (Horwitz 1994c, p. 213). Just as the freer and more democratic the cultural order in any given civil society is, the greater amount of truth ("knowledge") it will produce, and just as the freer and more democratic its political order is, the more justice it will produce, so also the freer and more democratic its economic order is, the more prosperity it will produce. Development cannot be "controlled" by *governments*, but, by means of judicious *governance*, it most definitely can be "cultivated."

The single most important factor in democratization and development, and the key to both, is the entrepreneurial spirit on the part of individuals and groups as it manifests itself in all the realms of civil society – social-cultural, political, and economic. The crucial factor in achieving sustainable development is the development of civil society and the liberation of what economist Don Lavoie would call "social intelligence" on a large scale (see Chapter 5). Economic development is basically a matter not of quantitative, linear growth ("more of the same") but of *change*, of abandoning old ways of doing things and finding new ways of doing them better, as well as discovering altogether new and more profitable things to do – and entrepreneurship is the absolutely key element in this process. Howard notes in this regard:

> What is needed is release of internal economic motors and relief from inefficient economic controls. These inefficient controls are sometimes imposed in response to populist calls for more national jurisdiction over the economy. Yet they usually have the effect of benefiting a small elite, and they undermine the entrepreneurial capacity that is at the heart of a development strategy that uses local resources.
>
> (Howard 1992b, pp. 11–12)

Just as democracy must be built from the ground up, so also the people of every nation must build it for themselves; no one else (and no amount of foreign aid) can do it for them. "Intelligent *domestic* economic policy," economist Melvyn Krauss states, "is an essential ingredient for economic prosperity in Third World countries" (Krauss 1983, p. 3). Efforts to build a politically and economically democratic culture *from within and from below* are well illustrated by the Civic Alliance in Mexico that was initially called into being by the 1994 presidential elections. This was a coalition that embraced hundreds of nongovernment organizations (NGOs), labor unions, and social movements and that was highly successful in stimulating the growth of a civic spirit of initiative and responsibility (see Quezada 1995). As this example demonstrates, what is especially important for both democratization and development is the role played by NGOs of all sorts (of which GERDDES-Africa and de Soto's Institute for Liberty and Democracy in Lima are prime examples). Indeed, it could no doubt be said that NGOs and various community-based groups are the best vehicle for fostering the local initiative that is so utterly crucial for both democratization and development.[23]

By promoting, as Michael Novak would say, a "capacity to form associations for the sake of improving the community" (Novak 1993, p. 187), NGOs are also, it may be noted, the single most important means of promoting *social justice*. "As a virtue, social justice is the capacity to cooperate with others . . . in achieving ends that benefit society either in part or as a whole" (ibid., p. 191). Unlike legal justice, social justice, as Novak rightly insists, is not something doled out by the state: "Social justice is, properly, a form of free association" (ibid., p. 233). *Social justice, it could in fact be said, is synonymous with the promotion of civil society.*

Although the various nations of the world no longer have any other option but that of helping themselves, no nation, like no man, is an island unto itself – especially in the era of the global economy. Self-responsibility does not, or should not, mean autarkic self-reliance – what the North Koreans call *juche*. Although, as I mentioned, *foreign aid* no longer has any significant role to play in international development,[24] what could be termed *foreign assistance* does have a role to play, one which in fact will be of ever increasing significance. As John Paul II observed in his 1991 encyclical, *Centesimus Annus*:

> Just as there is a collective responsibility for avoiding war, so there is a collective responsibility for promoting development. Just as within individual societies it is

200

possible and right to organize a solid economy which will direct the functioning of the market to the common good, so too there is a similar need for adequate interventions on the international level.

(John Paul II 1991, §52)

Let us therefore, by way of conclusion, focus more directly on the issue of *international justice*.

As I indicated in Chapter 4, self-interest is not necessarily the same thing as selfishness. The unique trait of the enterprise or market economy, i.e., one based on the principle of voluntary exchange for mutual benefit, is that it harnesses private interest to the service of the public good. And it does so by means of *incentives* built into the very structure of free trade; unlike socialist systems, a "capitalist" economy does not have to rely on "benevolence" and does not have to appeal to a morality of self-sacrificing altruism (the "Guevarist myth"). "Whatever the motives of individuals," Novak notes, "the result is that each member of society is taught by markets to pay due regard to the wants and needs of others" (Novak 1986, pp. 214–15). In order to function effectively, however, the political economy of democratic capitalism must grant to *all* its citizens fundamental human rights of a cultural, political, and economic nature. The only truly effective way of promoting social justice is by promoting the development of civil society and human rights.

The formula for achieving international justice is no different. Just as it is in the interest of the members of any given society to respect the freedoms and rights of their fellow citizens since, as Novak says, "the capacity to form associations" is the key to achieving "ends that benefit society either in part or as a whole," so also it is in the interests of the citizens of one nation to promote the political and economic welfare of the citizens of other nations since, as I mentioned in the conclusion to Chapter 5, in a "capitalist" set-up everyone tends to benefit from the increased well-being of all others. Global democratic capitalism is not a zero-sum game of wealth redistribution but a positive-sum game of wealth creation. By playing their parts in this game, all parties are led to develop, in a mutually beneficial manner, their own "comparative advantages" (as Adam Smith pointed out long ago).

As I have argued in the course of this book, the fact of the matter is that rights are mutual and freedom is indivisible. No one can legitimately desire freedom for him or herself without also desiring it for all others. Freedom, like rights, is a matter of mutuality and reciprocity. Even businesspeople preoccupied with their "bottom lines" are coming to realize that their own private interests are best served when they do their part to further human rights and the rule of law in those countries in which they do business. This is a lesson that McDonald's learned when in 1994 the Chinese communist government, in the absence of political-economic rights and the rule of law in China, violated with impunity a twenty-year lease with the company and evicted it from the biggest of its worldwide restaurants near Tiananmen Square in order to make way for a development of its own. The corruption (e.g., bribes and kick-backs in order to obtain contracts) that is endemic to nondemocratic regimes imposes high transaction costs on companies seeking to do business in them. Their own strictly private interest would be best served were they, as responsible world citizens, to do what is within their power to lend support to the worldwide freedom and democracy movement. Business firms not only have an understandable interest in the economic health of the countries in which they operate, they also have, whether or not they are enlightened enough to realize it, a real interest in the political and social health of these countries. Businesses have both short-term and long-term interests. When they look beyond their next quarterly or yearly statement, they will discover that democracy, the rule of law, and respect for human rights are good for business and that it is in their long-term interest to do what is within their power to promote them. In the case of China, for example, it is in the supreme interest of transnational corporations which have invested heavily there that the country succeed in making an orderly transition to democracy. In any event, at a time when groups in civil society opposed to environmental degradation or abusive child labor can focus glaring public attention on them, corporations concerned about their reputations and desirous to avoid alienating their customers have no choice but to behave as good citizens. As writers for *The Economist* recognize, "behaving like good corporate citizens makes eminent business sense" (*The Economist* survey 15, June 24, 1995).

Thus, there is, as Adam Smith said in his *Theory of Moral Sentiments*, a kind of "invisible hand" at work in human affairs which serves to turn the "natural selfishness and rapacity" of the rich to the benefit of the poor (see Smith 1982, p. 184). It is thanks to this invisible hand that the desire which is natural to everyone to "better their own condition" (see Smith 1982, p. 50) works, in a "system of natural liberty," to secure the betterment of all. Summing up the philosophy of Stoicism which was so influential in his thinking, Smith writes:

> Man . . . ought to regard himself, not as something separated and detached, but as a citizen of the world, a member of the vast commonwealth of nature. To the interest of this great community, he ought at all times to be willing that his own little interest should be sacrificed. . . . We should view ourselves, not in the light in which our own selfish passions are apt to place us, but in the light of which any other citizen of the world would view us. What befalls ourselves we should regard as what befalls our neighbour, or, what comes to the same thing, as our neighbour regards what befalls us.
>
> (Smith 1982, pp. 140–41)

Where Smith diverged from Stoicism was in maintaining that world citizenship is neither hostile to nor incompatible with (requiring the "sacrifice" of) the attachments that people everywhere feel to themselves, their friends, and their countries (see Smith 1982, p. 292).

Those who desire freedom and prosperity for themselves have a moral responsibility to support, in the words of John Paul II, "interventions on the international level" designed to promote human rights worldwide. These "interventions" are likely to be most successful in promoting democracy and development when they themselves operate "democratically," i.e., when they are undertaken not by national governments but by institutions operating at arm's length from government, such as the National Endowment for Democracy in the U.S. and Canada's International Centre for Human Rights and Democratic Development, and by various citizens' groups and other private organizations of a cultural, commercial, religious, or professional (e.g., academic) nature. The appropriate motto for international development is no longer, "More control by the state," but rather, "More power to the people."

Foreign aid of the traditional sort – and "development economics" in general – is not the most effective way of promoting either democracy or development, since by its very nature it is premised on the assumption that national governments are the best vehicle for achieving progress. All the empirical evidence accumulated over the past several decades indicates that this is most definitely not the case. Indeed, in Africa as well as elsewhere the state has over the years become the greatest enemy of progress. Governments of LDCs that adopt the principles of Good Government – government that is responsible and answerable to the citizenry and that seeks not to *direct* but to *liberate* the energies and enterprise of their citizens and which leaves them free to pursue happiness in their own self-chosen ways – will, by reason of the moral leadership they can exert when they put their minds to it, continue to have a very important role to play in social and economic development (and will continue to require some degree of foreign aid – preferably multilateral – in order to do so).[25] They are, however, no substitute for the forces of vibrant and pluralistic civil societies. As Aristotle pointed out over two millenia ago in his defense of democracy, "as a feast to which all the guests contribute is better than a banquet furnished by a single man, so a multitude is better judge of many things than any individual" (Aristotle 1941, *Politics*, 1286a30). Or as Nicolas van de Walle says of present-day Africa, foreign "aid tends to provide merely symptomatic relief" (van de Walle 1995, p. 134). Moreover, and more importantly, "aid dependence makes governments less accountable to domestic constituencies and obscures the nature of the economic choices that societies need to make." In any event, grandiose industrial projects (which would indeed require vast amounts of foreign aid since no sane private sector "capitalist" would consider investing money in them) are neither necessary nor feasible in Africa and many other regions of the world in their present state of (de)development. Given their particular factor-endowment, i.e., capital-poor, labor-rich, it is economically absurd for these countries to concentrate on capital-intensive industries such as steel, heavy equipment, petrochemicals, etc. to the detriment of the production of labor-intensive goods such as textiles, wearing apparel, footwear, etc. in which they enjoy a comparative advantage. What is above all required, and what is fully workable, are small-scale projects (often, as in China, agriculture-related) that directly benefit local communities, and these can be instituted by NGOs and, as regards somewhat more ambitious undertakings, the private sector by foreign direct investment – indeed, this is the very best way of instituting them.

Morever, since a reliance on foreign aid has become one of the stigmas of highly indebted third world governments (the "global South"),[26] continued over-reliance on it can only serve to perpetuate myths of third-worldism and justify the new tag of "neocolonialism" levelled by those "remnants of the Bandung attitude" (in the words of France's former ambassaor to the UN, Jean-Bernard Mérimée, speaking of the now-defunct Nonaligned Movement [see Crossette 1994]) which continue to resist inquiries into their on-going human rights abuses. In a situation of nationalistic frustration and *ressentiment* such as this, foreign assistance works best when it by-passes these governments as much as possible and operates "horizontally," in a direct people-to-people fashion – what Václav Havel calls "people-to-people solidarity" (Havel 1995, p. 37).

Another reason why foreign assistance is preferable to foreign aid in the case of countries attempting the difficult transition to democracy has to do with the different incentive effects of the two. Foreign aid to governments eases the pressure on them to effectuate the radical economic reforms called for (there is no reason why they should voluntarily reform themselves), whereas foreign assistance has just the opposite effect.

Foreign assistance has a positive incentive effect on governments in that it serves to drive home to them the realization that private capital in the form of foreign direct investment will not be forthcoming unless and until they eliminate the corrupt government practices that have an adverse effect on the creation of a full-fledged civil market economy. Foreign assistance can in this way act as a major stimulus for both political and economic democratization.

In any event, properly designed foreign aid/assistance is not – should not be – a matter of transferring *income* or wealth[27] but of transferring *prosperity*, i.e., the ability to create wealth on one's own. "The essence of the economic development problem," Melvyn Krauss writes, "is the transfer of prosperity (i.e., the transfer of the ability to produce adequate amounts of real income) from the advanced countries to the less developed ones" (Krauss 1983, p. 109). To prove effective, such aid/assistance must rely to the greatest possible degree on "private sector" participation, given the "comparative advantage" that the private sector clearly has in *creating* wealth, in contrast, as Krauss says, to the comparative advantage that government has in merely *transferring* (i.e., squandering) it.

The best form of foreign assistance is that which, in encouraging the growth of the multitudinous formations of civil society, is instrumental in facilitating what Minxin Pei calls "societal takeovers" (see Pei 1992), i.e., transfers of ultimate power from the state to society (as Pei has shown, China's astounding economic growth beginning in the 1980s was in direct correlation to the degree of autonomy achieved in that country by the forces of civil society [see Pei 1994b]).[28] In the final analysis, this form of foreign assistance can only be the product of the innumerable groupings and institutions of civil society in both the advanced and the developing world, a product of their acting in concert and targeting their efforts at what Honoré Koffi Guie calls "*les forces vives de la nation*," i.e., civil society. "The principles of democracy," Guie states, "are universal principles." Thus, as he also says, the struggle to implement these principles "all over the world" speaks to "a solidarity that transcends all considerations of race, color, or nationality" (Guie 1993, p. 129).

What is international justice? It is the solidarity of all those working, in voluntary civic association, to promote the cause of liberty, human rights, and democracy worldwide. When these efforts succeed, economic development inevitably follows, just as surely as day follows upon night.

NOTES

INTRODUCTION

1 *Journal of Democracy* 6, no. 3 (July), p. 185.

1 THE IDEA OF CIVIL SOCIETY

1 Even before Sweden's Social Democrats went down to electoral defeat, finance minister Kjell-Olaf Feldt candidly remarked: "The market economy's facility for change and development and therefore economic growth has done more to eliminate poverty and 'the exploitation of the working class' than any political intervention in the market's system of distribution" (as cited in Lipset 1991, p. 191).

Adam Przworski, who styles himself as a "social democrat," nevertheless concedes that there is no "third way," no alternative to a market economy. He writes:

> What was it that collapsed in Eastern Europe? "Communism" is a neutral answer to this question, since it is a label that has no more advocates. But was it not socialism? Many of those who believe that there can be no socialism without democracy contend that the system that failed in Eastern Europe was perhaps Stalinism, statism, bureaucracy, or communism, but not socialism. Yet I fear that the historical lesson is more radical, that what died in Eastern Europe is the very idea of rationally administering things to satisfy human needs [the socialist ideal *par excellence*] – the feasibility of implementing public ownership of productive resources through centralized command; the very project of basing a society on disinterested cooperation – the possibility of dissociating social contributions from individual rewards. If the only ideas about a new social order originate today from the Right, it is because the socialist project – the project that was forged in Western Europe between 1848 and 1981 and that had animated social movements all over the world since then – failed, in the East and in the West. True, the values of political democracy and of social justice continue to guide social democrats such as myself, but social democracy is a program to mitigate the effects of private owernership and market allocation, not an alternative project of society.
>
> (Przeworski 1991, p. 7)

2 See Madison 1994c; this text was composed in 1990, about a year before the 1991 coup attempt against Gorbachev, at a time when the field of "Sovietologists" was

largely dominated by writers (such as Stephen Cohen) supportive of Gorbachev's reform efforts, and before it was generally realized that *perestroika* had proven to be a grandiose failure. Reflecting on the situation that prevailed under Gorbachev – and which he was one of the relatively few to correctly diagnose at the time – Martin Malia pointedly observes how in fact Gorbachev

> was a Reform Communist who had never understood the structural limitations of reform imposed by the nature of the system. So he rashly pursued restructuring to the point where he had irreparably "destructured" the system and then drew back when it was too late to stop the forces he had conjured up. So, like the sorcerer's apprentice, he would spend the rest of his time in power trying to ride the deluge he had unleashed.
>
> (Malia 1994, p. 480; see also p. 446)

For a critical discussion of so-called "revisionist" (pro-Soviet) Sovietology, see Laqueur 1994.

3 For background documentation on the Shatalin Plan, see Peck and Richardson 1991.

4 For an interesting, and well-intentioned, attempt to combine the incompatible, i.e., Socialism and capitalism, see Aganbegyan 1989. Aganbegyan was, for a time, one of Gorbachev's chief economic advisors. Acknowledging the absurdity of the idea of "market socialism" and expressing regret for the demise of the Five-Hundred-Day Play, Alexander Yakovlev, who had been one of Gorbachev's closest collaborators, states:

> It was not realized in time that efforts to conceive of the economic situation and its prospects based on such Soviet economic categories as "expenditures," "self-financing," "cost-accounting system," and so on were theoretically and psychologically reminiscent of the economic criteria of stagnation. It was the same as if in foreign policy there were calls for "humanizing nuclear confrontation," or "civilizing ways of conducting atomic wars," or something like it
>
> (Yakovlev 1993)

Political scientist Lincoln Allison observes in this regard:

> In considering the relations between capitalism and democracy, it is important to start by abolishing any myth and euphemisms which still exist about "social markets" or about the possible "economic liberalization" of socialist structures. . . . [T]he post-communist experience precisely confirms a truth which we might have derived a priori, that there can be no true hybrid; the benefits of markets do not occur unless they include capital markets, allowing finance to move to its most efficient location and real estate to be accumulated. . . . If you try to create some liberalization on an essentially non-capitalist basis, you must create price distortions and corruption.
>
> (Allison 1994, pp. 20–1)

5 See also Ash 1989 p. 316: "One message of Poland and Hungary today was summed up for me by a leading activist of Hungary's opposition Free Democrats: 'We say there is no third way. There is no credible alternative between Western capitalism and Eastern socialism.'"

6 This is not to say that a society operating according to the dictates of a market economy may not use a portion of the wealth generated by such an economy to fund social programs that are highly desired by the citizenry. It is important to note, however, that this is precisely not a question of *economics* (as if we were

talking about something other than a market or "capitalist" system) but of *politics*. Chapters 4 and 5 of this book will examine in more detail the "welfare issue" as it relates to the notion of a civil or social (*not* socialist) market economy (*soziale Marktwirtschaft*). At this point it may simply be noted that the concept of civil society is incompatible with that of the Welfare State.

7 Note that "rational" does not mean "rationalized" (which is precisely what a centrally planned economy always seeks, but inevitably fails, to be). The notion central to this entire work is that of "communicative rationality," a notion that we shall begin to explore in detail in Chapter 3.

8 All these measures are part and parcel of the logic of reform; they are interlinked and synergetic. See Balcerowicz (1994, p. 82) for a succinct statement summing up these interlinkages.

9 On the transition to a market economy, see also Kornai 1990 and Milanovic 1989. For a diagnosis of Gorbachev's failure as a reformer, see Aslund 1992. Boris Yeltsin summed up well the inherent absurdity of Gorbachev's attempts at reform when he said: "He wanted to combine things that cannot be combined – to marry a hedgehog and a grass snake – communism and a market economy, public-property ownership and private-property ownership, the multi-party system and the Communist Party with its monopoly of power. But these things are incompatible" (cited in Aslund 1992, p. 80).

See also Yakovlev's remark: "He [Gorbachev] tried to reconcile the irreconcil-able: democracy and centralized government, the market and state-controlled trade, different factions in the Party, and many other things. He believed for too long that the Party could be a constructive force" (Yakovlev 1993, pp. 227–28).

Even though he is no champion of neoliberalism, José Maria Maravall, minister of education and science in Spain's social democratic government in the 1980s (which oversaw Spain's transition to political democracy and a market economy), recognizes that when "a window of opportunity for reform" suddenly appears (as it did in 1989),

> it is important to act quickly. In general, reforms are best initiated after a new government takes power, when the ruling party is still united, public confidence is high, and the national mood is hopeful. Reforms that are radical and launched early, rather than gradual and undertaken late, have the greatest chance of success – except in the case where considerable political pedagogy is required for society to accept that costly reforms are necessary
> (Maravall 1994, pp. 23–4)

10 For a follow-up assessment of Russia's transition to a market economy, see Aslund 1994 and 1995.

11 A few years later, in early 1994, political scientist Peter Reddaway had however to observe: "Russia is caught in a no-man's-land between the old 'admistrative-command' system [a Soviet euphemism for "totalitarian," a term which could not be uttered in Russia until near the very end of the régime] and an as yet unattained market" (Reddaway 1994, p. 14). The horrendous problem confronting an emerging civil society, such as that in Russia, is well characterized by Ash in the following terms: "that peculiar post-Communist mixture of enterprise, organized crime, ex-nomenklatura, corruption, and politics" (Ash 1994, p. 20).

12 See *Journal of Democracy* 6, no. 3 (July, 1995), pp. 190–91.

13 Apart from a small number of die-hards, 1989 in the West saw the full fruition of a trend of thinking that had begun to take hold on a increasingly large scale around about 1980: the disappearance from the intellectual (and political) scene of social-ists in the traditional sense of the term, i.e., advocates of the "public ownership of

the means of production." (At its party congress in 1989, the British Labour Party finally jettisoned its traditional call for public ownership of the means of production, a move which didn't prevent it from going on to lose a general election [that of 1992].) Those who formerly would have willingly accepted the label "socialist" now preferred, as a general rule, to be called "social democrats." This was not, as in the case of some of the ex-Communist Parties in the East, a change of merely cosmetic significance. Although they still had problems coming to terms with the structural requirements of a market economy (which they now endorsed, albeit with reservations), although, that is, they had problems with the notion of economic liberalism (continuing to advocate in its place a vague notion of "economic democracy"), Western leftists now, as a general rule, fully endorsed the classical principles of political ("bourgeois," as the Marxists had formerly called it) liberalism.

14 This is what became known as the "socialist calculation debate"; in it Mises and Hayek found themselves pitted against Oskar Lange, who in the eyes of the general pubic appeared to have carried the day. For an examination of the debate, see Lavoie 1985b.

15 As Lebowitz makes clear (see Lebowitz 1991).

16 See also p. 105:

> Take a more or less representative sample of politically aware persons [in Czechoslovakia]. Stir under pressure for two days. And what do you get? The same fundamental Western, European model: parliamentary democracy; the rule of law, market economy. And if you made the same experiment in Warsaw or Budapest I wager you would get the same basic result. This is no Third Way. It is not "socialism with a human face." It is the idea of "normality" that seems to be sweeping triumphantly across the world.
>
> (Ash 1990, p. 105)

For a critical analysis of the idea of "market socialism," see Lavoie 1985a.

17 For remarks on the relation between social democracy and the Welfare State, on the one hand, and bureaucratism, on the other, see Dahrendorf 1988, pp. 129–36, 166–67. Dahrendorf also states: "The choice between freedom and serfdom is stark and clear, and it offers no halfway house for those weaker souls who would like to avoid making up their minds" (Dahrendorf 1990, p. 62).

18 It was with undeniable prescience that, a number of years ago, Giovanni Sartori stated:

> Those who are still advocating a greater democratic liberty [i.e., socialist egalitarianism] at the expense of the despised liberal liberty, are no longer in the forefront of progress. They resemble much more a rearguard that is fighting the previous war than a vanguard that is facing the new enemy and present-day trends.
>
> (Sartori 1979, p. 310)

19 As soon as, in 1989, the socialist governments of Eastern Europe hesitated – thanks to Gorbachev and his "New Thinking" (the "Sinatra Doctrine": "I had it my way" [as misquoted by Gennady Gerasimov], which replaced the Brezhnev doctrine of "socialist solidarity") – to resort to terror, they collapsed, one and all, like so many houses of cards.

20 Speaking of the "message" of the revolutions of 1989, Ash remarks:

> [T]here is a whole kaleidoscope of new parties, programmes and trends, and it is little short of impudence to subsume them in one "message". Yet if you

look at what these diverse parties are really saying about the basic questions of politics, economics, law and international relations, there is a remarkable underlying consensus. In politics they are all saying: there is no "socialist democracy," there is only democracy. And by democracy they mean multi-party, parliamentary democracy as practised in contemporary Western, Northern and Southern Europe. They are all saying: there is no "socialist legality", there is only legality. And by that they mean the rule of law, guaranteed by the constitutionally anchored independence of the judiciary. They are all saying, and for the left this is perhaps the most important statement: there is no "socialist economics", there is only economics. And economics means not a socialist market economy but a social market economy. Not Ota Sik but Ludwig Erhard. Of course there are grave differences in these countries between, for example, Freidmanites and Hayekites. A good word might even be heard for Keynes. But the general direction is absolutely plain: towards an economy whose basic engine of growth is the market, with extensive private ownership of the means of production, distribution and exchange.

(Ash 1990, p. 151)

Although Havel is certainly somewhat to the "left" (or is that now the "right"? – in any event, not a pure Hayekean) of Václav Klaus, former finance minister of Czechoslovakia and subsequently prime minister of the Czech Republic, he is nonetheless a good example of the "consensus" Ash speaks of, in that he has expressed his unequivocal support for the idea of a market economy, as, in Ash's words, the "basic engine of growth":

Though my heart may be left of center, I have always known that the only economic system that works is a market economy, in which everything belongs to someone – which means that someone is responsible for everything. It is a system in which complete independence and plurality of economic entities exist within a legal framework, and its workings are guided chiefly by the laws of the marketplace. This is the only natural economy, the only kind that makes sense, the only one that can lead to prosperity, because it is the only one that reflects the nature of life itself. The essence of life is infinitely and mysteriously multiform, and therefore it cannot be contained or planned for, in its fullness and variability, by any central intelligence [this, it may be noted, is a "pure" Hayekean statement].

The attempt to unite all economic entities under the authority of a single monstrous owner, the state, and to subject all economic life to one central voice of reason that deems itself more clever than life itself, is an attempt against life itself. It is an extreme expression of the hubris of modern man, who thinks that he understands the world completely – that he is at the apex of creation and is therefore competent to run the whole world; who claims that his own brain is the highest form of organized matter, and has not noticed that there is a structure infinitely more complex, of which he himself is merely a tiny part: that is, nature, the universe, the order of Being.

Communist economics was born of an arrogant, utopian rationality that elevated itself above all else. When realized in practice, this utopian rationality began to liquidate everything that did not fit, that exceeded its plans or disrupted them. Censorship, the terror, and concentration camps are consequences of the same historical phenomenon that produced the collapsing centralized economy we inherited from Communism. In fact, they are two dimensions of the same error that began with this ideological illusion, this

209

pseudo-scientific utopia, this loss of a sense of the enigma of life, and lack of humility before the mysterious order of Being, thus turning away from moral imperatives "from above" and thus from human conscience.

(Havel 1992b, pp. 62–3)

Havel goes on to argue (on page 67) that "it is a great mistake to think that the marketplace and morality are mutually exclusive. Precisely the opposite is true: the marketplace can work only if it has its own morality." An important point to which I shall want to return.

21 Even that staunch conservative, Richard Nixon, proclaimed at the time of his presidency, "We are all Keynesians now."

22 By "revolutionism" I mean that particularly modernist conception of revolution that emerged from the French Revolution and was consolidated in the Bolshevik Revolution of 1917, namely, the violent overthow of an established political and social order, followed by a period of "revolutionary justice," i.e., systematic terror (absolutely necessary, as both Lenin and Mao instinctively knew, if the Great Utopia is ever to be realized). The revolutions of 1989 were of an altogether different sort (as exemplified most fully in the Czech "velvet revolution"). In their rejection of organized violence and their appeal to reasonableness, they were, indeed, genuinely "postmodern." Even in its failure, the Chinese Democracy Movement and the Tiananmen demonstrations earlier in 1989 were a model for this new kind of postmodern revolution. As Yan Jiaqui, a leader of the post-Tiananmen Front for a Democratic China founded in Paris in August of 1989, observed: "The Democracy Movement was characterized by one outstanding feature: demonstrators used only peaceful, rational, and nonviolent means to try to achieve their goals" ('Han Minzhu" 1990, p. vii).

In his 1991 encyclical, *Centesimus Annus*, John Paul II noted this unique feature of the revolutions of 1989:

> [W]orthy of emphasis is the fact that the fall of this kind of "bloc" or empire was accomplished almost everywhere by means of peaceful protest, using only the weapons of truth and justice. While Marxism held that only by exacerbating social conflicts was it possible to resolve them through violent confrontation, the protests which led to the collapse of Marxism tenaciously insisted on trying every avenue of negotiation, dialogue, and witness to the truth, appealing to the conscience of the adversary and seeking to reawaken in him a sense of shared human dignity.

(John Paul II 1991, §43)

The alternative to the modernist politics of revolutionism is a postmodern politics of communicative rationality, a subject to be discussed in Chapter 4.

23 According to Havel, the task of the new postmodern politics of civility is that of promoting "an atmosphere of tolerant solidarity and unity in diversity based on mutual respect, genuine pluralism and parallelism" (Havel 1992a).

24 One of the interesting features of Tocqueville's study is the way in which it extensively documents how the French monarchy was ever increasingly incompatible with the idea of a civil society. Actually, one of Tocqueville's main theses in this book is that the destruction of a functioning civil society on the part of the *ancien régime* was one of the major factors paving the way for the ruthlessness and incivility manifested in the course of the French Revolution (see, for instance, Tocqueville 1955 p. 206).

25 This is the question of *justice*. And the question of justice has always been *the* basic question or problem in political philosophy. Although Hayek was (as usual) excessive in his rejection of the notion of "social justice" – "justice" being, by

definition, as he rightly pointed out, "social" (see Hayek 1976) – he did (as usual) have a valid point to make. "Justice," under any liberal reading of the term, cannot mean robbing the well-off in order to give to the poor (a policy that benefits mainly the redistributors of such funds, i.e., politicians, whose overriding public policy concern is the more narrowly private one of getting reelected). Such a policy, which is that of the Welfare State, is not only an unjustifiable attack on those who do provide for themselves and have some monetary reserves, it is also, in its practice, totally demeaning for those who are the (voiceless) recipients of this form of government loot (and there is no way to avoid this consequence – short of ideologically inculcating in people the belief that they have the "right" to anything they want or deem proper, even though they know quite well that they have not made the slightest personal effort to attain it – (a belief which, try as hard as some would like, nonetheless goes against the grain of human nature). As I shall argue in Chapter 5, the idea of a civil society (based on the idea of the equal human dignity of all) is thoroughly incompatible with the modern notion of the Welfare State. And yet the problem persists; the notion of "social justice" cannot be simply dismissed with a Hayekean magic wand. As James Madison, perhaps the most reasonable of all liberals, remarked: "It [justice] ever has been and ever will be pursued until it be obtained, or until liberty be lost in the pursuit" (James Madison N.D., no. 51).

As opposed to all other forms of modern governance, totalitarianism and authoritarianism in particular, civil society can only exist (and survive) if it embodies a form of (social) justice recognizable, in principle, by all. As Cicero had already pointed out, a civil society or, as he called it, a *res publica* (or *res populi*) is "not any collection of human beings brought together in any sort of way, but an assemblage [association, *societas*] of people in large numbers associated in an agreement with respect to justice and a partnership for the common good" (Cicero 1977, bk. I, ch. xxv).

26 The moral dimensions of the idea of civil society is also a theme that Seligman (1992) emphasizes throughout his book.

27 Kant goes on to characterize such a society as "the society with the greatest freedom. Such a society is one in which there is a mutual opposition and fixing of its limits so that it may be consistent with the freedom of others" (Kant 1963, p. 30). This has to do with Kant's notion of the "unsocial sociability" of human beings, a most important notion to which we shall return in Chapters 4 and 5.

28 According to Rorty, "The existence of human rights has as much or as little relevance as the question of the existence of God. I think both have equally little relevance" (Rorty 1985, p. 220).

29 In *Nedelya*, no. 26 (1988); cited in Brezinski 1989, p. 34.

30 As Hannah Arendt pointed out in her classic study of totalitarianism, the totalitarian State is one in name only. In totalitarian societies the State is essentially nothing more than a façade that hides the real chains of command which are secretive and carefully hidden from public view and inspection; as Arendt said: "Totalitarianism in power uses the state as its outward facade, to represent the country in the nontotalitarian world" (Arendt 1973, p. 420).

When Gorbachev (bowing, as it were, to the unsolicited and long-standing advice of Solzhenitsyn in his *Letter to the Soviet Leaders* [1974]) separated State from Party in 1990 and accorded the former its own autonomy, this effectively announced the impending death of the Party and its puppet state (i.e., the Soviet Union).

31 To describe the Soviet *nomenklatura* as a "mafia" involves not the slightest bit of exaggeration, as David Remnick has clearly demonstrated (Remnick 1993; see also Malia 1994, pp. 368–70). Alexander Yakovlev refers to the former USSR as "the

past criminal Party-state mafia" (Yakovlev 1993, p. 66). For an in-depth study of the culture of crime in postcommunist Russia, see Handelman 1995.

32 If the Leninist model of Socialism was grossly inefficient economically, it was nevertheless, as Peter Berger observed in the mid-1980s, "marvelously efficient" in political terms, that is, "not only in terms of maintaining the material privilege of the political elite but more importantly in securing its monopoly of power." As he went on to say:

> The way of life of this elite (the *nomenklatura*, as it is known in the Soviet Union) has been described in great detail – a small structure of privileged and powerful people, far removed from the grubbiness of the masses, provided with exclusive stores, apartments, and vacation resorts, and associating mainly with each other. The Soviet model is perfectly suited to the vested interests of this elite – and of any other group seeking to become such an elite. This fact goes a long way toward explaining why the Soviet model of socialism, despite its glaring weaknesses in terms of economic development, continues to be very attractive to actual and would-be elites in countries far beyond the reach of Soviet armies.
>
> (Berger 1986, p. 180)

The fact that by the mid-1990s all the major leftist guerrilla groups operating in Colombia for the last several decades had, despite their earlier allegiance to Marxist ideology, become nothing more than criminal organizations out for plunder and profit lends weight to Berger's earlier observations (see Brooke 1995).

33 By 1989 it had become obvious to an increasingly large number of people that modernity had culminated in equally – if differently – dismal states of affairs in both East and West: state-Socialism in the one, state-welfarism in the other.

34 On p. 259 Lefort (1986) writes: "Under totalitarianism it is clear that human rights are annulled and that by struggling to get them recognized the dissidents are attacking the political foundation of the system."

35 The appeal to human rights was also a central feature of the Chinese Freedom and Democracy Movement in 1989. For a representative sampling of texts from this period, see "Han Minzhu" 1990.

36 Prototypes of this sort of postmodern revolution, which, while being (unavoidably) confrontational, nonetheless eschew all forms of violence and are, instead, based on an appeal to common reason (dialogical rationality), were the "activist" campaigns of Mahatma Gandhi and Martin Luther King.

37 The Charter of Paris for a New Europe states: "Human rights and fundamental freedoms are the birthright of all human beings, are inalienable and are guaranteed by law" (see *Twenty-Four Human Rights Documents* 1992).

38 See also Havel's statement:

> I favour a political system based on the citizen and recognizing all fundamental and civil and human rights in their universal validity, equally applied; that is, no member of a single race, a single nation, a single sex, or a single religion may be endowed with basic rights that are any different from anyone else's. In other words, I favour what is called a civil society.
>
> (Havel 1992b, pp. 31–2)

39 See also in this regard Rhoda E. Howard 1995. Anticipating, as it were, the attack on "possessive individualism" on the part of communitarian critics of liberalism, Donnelly points out that "This individualism, however, is quite compatible with recognizing individual persons as members of a variety of social groups, and even with the idea of rights – not just *human* rights – held by these groups" (Donnelly 1989, p. 4).

40 Mises entitled his major work *Human Action: A Treatise on Economics* (1966).
41 Speaking of the view of the human person that informs the thought of John Paul II, Michael Novak writes:

> The underlying principle of the Polish Pope's anthropology is the "creative subjectivity" of the human person, together with the resulting "subjectivity of society." From his earliest work on, including his phenomenological inquiry *The Acting Person*, the Pope has been struck by the human being's most arresting characteristic: his or her capacity to originate action; that is, to imagine and to conceive of new things and then to do them. He found in creative acts the clue to human identity. Humans, he held, cannot take refuge from this responsibility by hiding behind "society" – there, too, they are responsible for their acts. Being in society does not absolve them of the burdens of subjectivity.
>
> (Novak 1993, p. 117)

42 Hayek provides a good characterization of what I mean by "order":

> a state of affairs in which a multiplicity of elements of various kinds are so related to each other that we may learn from our acquaintance with some spatial or temporal part of the whole to form correct expectations concerning the rest, or at least expectations which have a good chance of proving correct.
>
> (Hayek 1973, p. 36)

What makes an *order* a "spontaneous order" is that it possesses a *logic* peculiar to it, and which it is the task of interpretation (hermeneutics) to explicate. This is accomplished primarily by constructing "ideal types" (to be discussed in greater detail in Chapter 5).

2 A NEW THREAT TO AN OLD IDEA

1 For excellent studies of this often misunderstood (or misrepresented) period in Soviet history, see Boettke 1990a and Malia 1994.
2 For a structural analysis of why this is so, see Milanovic 1989.
3 Martin Malia offers the following thumbnail sketch of the history of Socialism in the USSR:

> Communist history . . . has been a series of oscillations between a hard and a soft variant of the basic model. The basic model of the Soviet total society was created in the first years of the regime, under Lenin. The two variants are his War Communism of 1918–1921 and his semimixed, but still essentially statist, New Economic Policy, or NEP, of 1921–1929. Stalin then put the system into its definitive and classic form in the 1930s with a regime of Five-Year Plans that was in fact an institutionalized version of War Communism. And after World War II he imposed this "command-administrative regime" throughout Eastern Europe. Ever since, the leaders of the various communist countries have periodically set sail for the reform of this system, to find the fabled route to "Socialism with a human face."
>
> (Malia 1992, p. 61)

4 A point clearly demonstrated in Malia 1994. This is something that those who conspired in the coup attempt against Gorbachev in August, 1990 obviously realized – like Brezhnev and Stalin before them. They were not nearly so naive as Gorbachev himself (assuming that he had no hand in the coup). As an illustration

of what I referred to above as the eternal to-and-fro of socialist regimes, consider the following historical observations of that foremost historian of the Soviet Union, Robert Conquest:

> In March 1930, Stalin's policies had collapsed. The Soviet cattle herds had been half-destroyed, and Stalin had no option but to allow the mass of the peasants to leave the collective farms into which they had been forced. In any other political system this would have been the occasion for those who had predicted ruin, and been proved right, to come forward with an alternative. A break with Stalin and his leadership in 1930 would have been dangerous; but above all, radical change would have had to appeal for support outside the Party, and would have meant an "opening to the Right" – that is to the nonpolitical, or non-Communist, majority. Bukharin's own attitude to any such "liberal" policy was summed up in his remark that two parties could exist in the USSR, provided one of them was in jail. In fact, the idea and possibility of "liberal" communism broke down on the issue of the one-party state.
>
> (Conquest 1993, p. 25)

Although he was no doubt more mild-mannered than Stalin, at least Bukharin, as Conquest's article clearly demonstrates, was under no illusions as to the possibility of "liberalizing" Communism (since this would have called for the Communist Party to relinquish its monopoly on political power, something which was incompatible with the logic of the system). It is therefore ironic that Gorbachev should have attempted to resurrect ("rehabilitate") Bukharin in his own attempt to create a "liberal Communism." And it is no less ironic that Stephen Cohen, author of an authoritative biography of Bukharin, should have continued to the end to have defended Gorbachev on the McNeil/Lehrer Newshour with a naiveté equal to that of Gorbachev himself.

Unlike Gorbachev, Alexander Yakovlev realized early on in *perestroika* the futility of attempts at reforming the Soviet system: "At some point in 1987, I personally realized that a society based on violence and fear could not be reformed and that we faced a momentous historical task of dismantling the entire social and political system with all its ideological, economic, and political roots" (Yakovlev 1993, p. 227).

5 Taking full advantage of Gorbachev's policy of *glasnost*, at the May Day celebrations in Moscow in 1990 one of the banners in the crowd proclaimed: "Seventy-Two Years on the Road to Nowhere."

6 In a subsequent article Nodia remarks on how the collapse of communist totalitarianism "was bound to leave behind a rubble of atomized, marginalized individuals. The building of a new system," he states, "can commence only after this last stage of collapse has unfolded; postcommunist society must touch bottom before it can bounce back up out of the abyss of social destruction" (Nodia 1995, pp. 105–6). In this article Nodia describes how the former Soviet republic of Georgia "played out most if not all of the nightmare scenarios that a pessimistic political scientist might devise for postcommunist states" (ibid.).

7 Compare the observations of the Czech philosopher Miroslav Bednář:

> The lesson of our present disillusion teaches us that the totalitarian menace is by no means an issue of the past. Contemporary chauvinist nationalism in post-communist regions are [*sic*] not comparable to the native nationalism in Western Europe. The essential difference consists in the obvious abuse and manipulation by powerful communist networks of basic national needs in these areas, including the secession of Slovakia from the Czech Lands. Such

"post-communist" nationalism is in reality the last stage of communism. It results in the preservation of communist power in changed circumstances; by the same token it paralyses any radical political and economic transformation of previously totalitarian regimes toward stable democracy and a free market. The phenomenon of "nation" is being manipulated against the citizens in order to suppress the civic dimension of human existence, for the manipulation consists in an identification of the nation with strong totalitarian authority on the part of the central power, eliminating the personal responsibility of the citizens. In this way, effective neo-communist abuse of the national principle fosters a totalitarian pseudo-citizenship.

(Bednář 1994, pp. 140–41)

8 Although he saw perfectly well why Socialism was unworkable, Mises, unlike Hayek, did not always have a clear understanding of the structural imperatives of a free society (he was, temperamentally, inclined in the direction of libertarianism or laissez-faire, and thus indisposed to appreciating some of the finer points of classical liberal theory); in particular, he did not see that the "right to self-determination" was nothing more than a recipe for anarchy. See in this regard Mises 1979, p. 109.
9 As the Soviet academician Igor Shafarevich demonstrated in his critical history of Socialism (1980; first published in Paris in 1975).
10 The same repressive function Zinoviev perceives to be the chief characteristic of Russian communes is perfectly well illustrated by China's "work units." In urban China, work units are an all-pervasive feature of social life, from factories to universities. The work unit to which one belongs literally determines all aspects of a person's life, from subsistence to housing to marriage...and beyond. The Chinese "work unit" is indeed the most fitting instrument of "total rule." As Chinese economic reformers have come to realize, however, this form of social organization is a definite impediment as regards the economic reforms advocated by the Chinese government itself. The Chinese dilemma is that, since the work unit is the basis for the entire communist edifice, it cannot be scrapped (inefficient though it may be from an economic point of view) without compromising fatally the leadership role of the Chinese Communist Party. For a revealing discussion of the role and function of the work unit in Chinese communist society, see Link 1992.
11 For an overview of the key concepts of philosophical hermeneutics, see Madison 1994a.
12 This is the old socialist idea of "social justice" (stealing from the rich to give to the poor). In Chapter 5 I shall attempt to spell out the meaning of "social justice" as it pertains to a genuine civil society.
13 One of the more eloquent criticisms of group-based, affirmative action programs is that of Shelby Steele, when he speaks of the need to repudiate "the pattern of social reform that America has offered its former victims for 25 years: entitlements offered to groups by race, sex, ethnicity and sexual orientation – entitlements like affirmation action and diversity Programs – rather than rights guaranteed to individuals and developmental help to those in need." He goes on to say:

This is a pattern of reform that brings out the Farrakans in every group so that they can be used as wedges in the group's negotiations with the larger society....
If you are seeking entitlements on the basis of oppression, you must have your Farrakhan or your Act-Up or your radical feminists: oppression must be seen to have driven these groups to hate, to have spoiled their reason and

made them dangerous. They are icons of oppression, and their role in America's group politics is to embody a degree of alienation and anger that could become manifest in the entire group if entitlements are not forthcoming.

... Whether justified by past oppression or notions of racial superiority, a group's entitlements always require thugs and goons to patrol its borders and ignorant mythologies to justify its advantages.

... To compensate for centuries of white entitlements, we do not enforce the democratic principles that those entitlements violated; instead, we grant precisely the same undemocratic entitlement to minorities and women in the name of redress. We use the old sin to correct its own damage. The only difference is that we now let the claim of oppression stand in for the claim of white superiority.

... Today, political correctness is a propriety that, among other things, makes objections to group entitlements indecent.

And these entitlements are a powerful incentive for groups to define their very identity around the claims that justify their advantage ...

Entitlements by race, sex, ethnicity and sexual orientation – categories that in no way reflect merit – are at the root of the great social evils in American life. Aside from the obvious unfairness of such entitlements, it is the distorted claims that groups must conjure to gain their benefit that absolutely require racism, sexism, anti-Semitism and all manner of collective animosities. Every such claim is backlit by the hatreds that try to make it singular and urgent.

The reformers of the last few decades have not admitted this. But the means to genuine reform have been here all along – a democracy of individuals that has the discipline never to entitle any group for any reason.

(Steele 1994, p. E 17)

14. In this connection, Rauch remarks:

In a liberal society, to upset people is not, *and must never be*, the same thing as to be wrong. ... [T]he establishment of a right not to be offended would lead not to a more civil culture but to a lot of shouting matches over who was being offensive to whom, and who could claim to be more offended.

(Rauch 1993, pp. 129, 130)

Moreover, as in the case of rent seeking, one can expect claims for redress to escalate dramatically when legal grievance procedures are established for those claiming to have had their "self-esteem" damaged or to have been "symbolically harmed." As Rauch points out: "Those who claim to be hurt by words must be led to expect nothing as compensation. Otherwise, once they learn they can get something by claiming to be hurt, they will go into the business of being offended" (Rauch 1993, p. 159).

The sad fact about left-wing communitarianism is that – as a form of fanaticized consciousness – it has a kind of built-in tendency to degenerate into a kind of practical fascism, its appeal to noble ideals notwithstanding, as one prominent advocate of human rights (and defender of what she refers to as social democracy) points out:

Left collectivist views on social justice ["communitarianism"] that deny the need for the separation of powers and protection of individual civil and political rights [such as, precisely the right to freedom of expression] can easily be transformed into ideological justification for fascism, which

216

can also be supported by traditionalist arguments about the nature of community and the need for the group to take precedence over the individual.

(Howard 1992b, p. 18)

15 See in this regard D'Souza 1991. For an account of one such case at the University of New Hampshire see Bernstein 1994a, and for a more extensive treatment of this and other cases see Bernstein 1994b. (The case in question involved a tenured professor of technical writing, J. Donald Silva, who was suspended without pay in April 1993 and ordered to undergo counselling at his own expense for classroom remarks to which some women took offense. In response to a ruling by a Federal judge in October 1994 that found that the University's sexual harassment policy violated Silva's constitutional right to free speech, the University agreed in December to reinstate his back pay, compensate him for damages and legal fees, and remove from his record any reference to his suspension and the charges brought against him.)

16 The expression is that of Bob Herbert, writing about the racist rantings of Leonard Jeffries, the black supremacist and director of the black studies program at City College, New York (see Herbert 1944, p. E 15).

17 For a detailed critical analysis of the panic-driven, adversarial politics of victimization as practiced by radical, biopolitical feminism (or "gender-feminism," as Sommers [1994] refers to it), see Fekete 1994. "Biopolitics," Fekete observes, "is intrinsically and aggressively adversarial, and there is no competition more fierce than the struggle over oppression credentials" (Fekete 1994, p. 175).

18 As Hughes oberves:

> The range of victims available ten years ago – blacks, chicanos, Indians, women, homosexuals – has now expanded to include every permutation of the halt, the blind, the lame and the short, or, to put it correctly, the differently abled, the other-visioned and the vertically challenged. Never before in human history were so many acronyms pursuing identity. It's as though all human encounter were one big sore spot, inflamed with opportunities to unwittingly give, and truculently receive, offence.

(Hughes 1993, p. 17)

19 For a critical analysis of this sociological phenomenon and a discussion of the "false memory syndrome," see Loftus and Ketchan 1994. One particularly virulent instance of the "need to stay as angry as possible" are the numerous "self-help" manuals directed at the putative victims of childhood sexual abuse that began to hit the market in the late 1980s and which, in the words of Frederick Crews, "are not about surmounting one's tragic girlhood but about keeping the psychic wounds open, refusing forgiveness or reconciliation, and joining the permanently embittered corps of 'survivors'" (Crews 1994b, p. 49).

20 I am quoting from a somewhat different version of this text, presented as a conference paper at McMaster University in April, 1993. Translations from the French are my own.

21 As Angenot points out, *ressentiment* is "fatally turned towards the past." In this regard it invents a "history" or "tradition" to justify the rancors of the victims and to bolster their "self-esteem" (cf. some of the more mythical histories invented by Afrocentrists).

22 The feminist in question is Sandra Harding, a philosophy professor at the University of Delaware (see Park 1995).

23 Speaking of proposals for a multicultural, "inclusive" curriculum at Hunter College, New York, a lecturer in political science at that institution, Cynthia

Roberts, stated in a letter to the editor of *The New York Times* October 10 (Roberts 1991):

> The third proposed requirement, for a course on non-Western culture, would be more defensible [than requirements for courses on women and American minorities] if Hunter first required students to study Western civilization. There are many good reasons to study foreign countries and cultures, especially at a time of revolutionary changes in international politics and growing global economic competition. But it makes no sense to explore other cultures and civilizations without standards of historical and comparative perspective.
>
> Increasingly, it seems only the best students are acquainted with the ideals of the European Enlightenment. An alarming number cannot even identify the differences between democracy and totalitarianism. More than 15 percent of the students in one of my classes recently equated the policies of Nazi Germany and the Bush administration, stating that both: "systematically oppressed lots of people, including the homeless"; "were imperialists who started wars," and sought a "new world order to take over the world."

24 This sort of active engagement in the affairs of the community on the part of Americans of an earlier age was not, however, of the sort longed for by communitarian critics of contemporary American society, who often appear to entertain a highly romanticized notion of what they believe we have now "lost." Even in Tocqueville's time, Americans did not live in "settled," life-long "communities." One of the things that in fact impressed Tocqueville the most was how the community spirit in America coexisted with a high degree of mobility – physical, social, and economic – on the part of its citizens.

25 Freedom of religion is an extremely important human right, since it is by belonging to a religious community that a great many people achieve meaning in their lives. And, as in the case of any "community" or corporate body, religious communities have the (group) right to make and enforce their own internal rules. These, however, can never be anything more than "by-laws" and may never be allowed to supersede the fundamental (constitutional) law of the land and the rights and freedoms of citizens guaranteed by this law. Unfortunately, there are still large portions of the world where people are brutally punished and even executed for no other reason than because they have been found guilty of religious heresy or apostasy, i.e., in violation of the rules of their community. A basic principle of civil society (which the West learned only by long and painful experience) is that religion must always be a voluntary matter, which entails the concomitant principle of the separation of Church and State. For a classic text in this regard, see James Madison, "Memorial and Remonstrance Against Religious Assessments" (1785); Madison's views on this matter are reflected in the "Bill of Rights" of the American Constitution that he sponsored. When in 1826 Thomas Jefferson wrote his own epitaph, he declared that he wanted written on his grave marker "the following inscription, & not a word more, 'Here was buried Thomas Jefferson, Author of the Declaration of American Independence, of the Statute of Virginia for religious freedom, & Father of the University of Virginia.'" As Jefferson had already noted, the Virginia Act for Religious Freedom (1785) passed the Virginia legislature owing to the efforts of Madison (see Jefferson 1984, pp. 702, 706).

26 The freedom of "opting-out" is related to two other fundamental human rights: the freedom to choose one's place of residence, i.e., to move from one "community" within a nation to another – referred to by some as "voting with one's

feet" – and the freedom to emigrate, moving from one nation-state or society to another, in pursuit of a better life.

27 See Cohen and Arato 1992, p. 97:

> As any reader of Hobbes knows, the road to statism is prepared by the identification of society outside the state with egotistic competition and conflict. Such is also the outcome of the well-known Marxian identification of civil and bourgeois society. The traditional German translation of *societas civilis* as *bürgerliche Gesellschaft* is not the only basis of this theoretical move. Hegel himself repeatedly identifies *bürgerlich* as *bourgeois*, and nowhere does he use the adjectival form in the classical sense of *Bürger* or *citoyen*. When he states that individuals as *Bürger* of civil society, the "external state," are private persons, he participates in a fundamental shift in the concept of civil society away from the original meaning of citizen society.

28 As we shall see in Chapter 5, the right to private property is a fundamental human right. It is listed as such in the *Déclaration des droits de l'homme et du citoyen* of 1789 and, more recently, in the *Charter of Paris for a New Europe* issued at the 1990 Conference on Security and Cooperation in Europe. As Havel has remarked: "ownership is not a vice, not something to be ashamed of, but rather a commitment, and an instrument by which the general good can be served" (Havel 1992c, p. 10). This is precisely the point I shall want to make in Chapter 5.

29 As Claude Lefort observes:

> The spread of Marxism throughout the whole of the French Left has long gone hand in hand with a devaluation of rights in general and with the vehement, ironic or "scientific" condemnation of the bourgeois notion of human rights. And we should note in passing, before coming back to this point, that, for once, Marxism was not unfaithful to the inspiration of its founder; Marx's famous critique of the "rights of man" in *On the Jewish Question*, though a product of his youth, was not contradicted by his later works, nor by the contributions of his heirs.
>
> (Lefort, 1986, p. 240)

In *On the Jewish Question* Marx wrote:

> None of the supposed rights of man . . . go beyond the egoistic man, man as he is, as a member of civil society in Hegel's sense; that is, an individual separated from the community, withdrawn into himself, wholly preoccupied with his private interest and acting in accordance with his private caprice.
>
> (Marx 1964, p. 26)

30 Although Diamond's definition of civil society is ambiguous and problematic, his article highlights many of the central features of civil society. What must *not*, however, be included under the rubric of civil society are "mafias, terrorism and warlords" (see Chilton 1994, p. 178, n. 9). The latter are, properly speaking, anti-social, extra-societal elements. The idea of civil society is, and always has been, a *normative* concept; it is not a mere empirical, social science concept which would include absolutely everything which is not a part of the government ("state"). Groups which engage in nonviolent civil disobedience in order to claim their rights are part of civil society, whereas terrorist groups are not.

31 Cicero defines a *res publica* or *res populi* as "an assemblage of people in large numbers associated in agreement with respect to justice and a partnership for the common good" (Cicero 1977, bk. I, ch. XXV).

32 I am borrowing this analytic distinction from Novak 1993. A similar distinction

(between the technical-economic, the social-political, and the moral-cultural) was made by sociologist Daniel Bell; see Bell 1976 and 1980.

33 An example of what I mean when I say that, for instance, the political and the economic orders have different logics whose integrity must be respected if civil society is not to be corrupted, is afforded by Jane Jacobs (1992). Jacobs refers to these two orders as "taking and trading," and she argues that when the integrity of either of these "self-organizing systems" or "syndromes" is violated by systemic imperatives appropriate to the other, what otherwise would be a virtue turns into a vice. She says, for instance:

> Any significant breach of a syndrome's integrity – usually by adopting an inappropriate function – causes some normal virtues to convert automatic-ally to vices. . . . [P]icking and choosing as we please from precepts in the two syndromes and mixing them up together breeds endless chains of injustice: great wickedness, great harm. (p. 132)

> Taking and trading are themselves fundamentally different from each oth-er. . . . It's bootless to try to harmonize commerce and guardianship [politics] into one joint system of morality [the socialist, totalitarian ideal]. Trying to do it can't produce harmony [social justice] – quite the opposite. The con-tradictions are innate. We have no way to escape them. To seek harmony in the sense of oneness is a profoundly false lead. But harmony can be sought by seeking to maintain each syndrome's own integrity. Then the two can support and complement each other. (p. 106)

> (Jacobs 1992)

What I am calling the "logic" of an order, Jacobs refers to as "syndrome integrity," and she argues that each order is (or should be) structured in accordance with an underlying moral principle appropriate to it (she refers to these as "moral syn-dromes"). In the following chapters I shall also be arguing that there is a *moral* principle proper to each order (this being one or another variant of the principle of communicative rationality). It may be noted in passing that "taking" is a most appropriate term with which to designate the political order, since it cannot exist except on the basis of *taxation*, which is a form of "taking" *par excellence*.

34 From one point of view, this work could be viewed as an elaborate reply to Seligman, who has expressed doubts as to the possibility of working out a viable theory of civil society in terms of discourse ethics or communicative rationality. Seligman's doubts in this regard are likely a result of his having taken Habermas as the prime example of such an approach. As we shall be seeing, there are serious difficulties in Habermas' position, and it is likely that these are what led Seligman to conclude that the attempt "to resurrect the idea of civil society by grounding it in the principles of discourse ethics ... will ultimately leave us empty-handed" (Seligman 1992, p. 195). It is my hope that the extended treatment of the problems inherent in the idea of civil society in the pages to follow will be such as to convince a writer such as Seligman that an elucidation of the idea of civil society in terms of communicative rationality can indeed be such as to give the idea "concrete meaning."

3 THE MORAL-CULTURAL ORDER

1 The idea in this case is the age-old one of chiliastic Socialism, as described by Shafarevich (1980). Although Shafarevich appears at first glance to be greatly exaggerating the matter, he does make an altogether convincing case for his central thesis, viz.: *"The death of mankind is not only a conceivable result of the triumph of socialism*

– it constitutes the goal of socialism" (Shafarevich 1980, p. 106; emphasis in original). Hayek develops a somewhat similar thesis in his last book, *The Fatal Conceit* (1988). For an attempt to show concretely and in detail how Socialism is essentially "destructionistic," see Mises 1981.

2 See Frank H. Knight:

> The vital fact is that any single scientific or positive theory of motivation is self-stultifying, especially in connection with any sort of propaganda. For any general theoretical explanation of behavior or motive must apply to the activities of the (explainer and) propagandist himself, and any intellectually satisfactory explanation reduces his propaganda to nonsense, to selling talk, if not to mere noise. The suggestion of an economic interpretation of the economic interpretation is all that should be needed as an answer to it. . . . What seems most philosophically significant about Marxism is its bearing upon the problem of ethics. For what it primarily means in practice is the complete futility and even the unreality of any intellectual-moral discussion, especially of group policy. It teaches that economic self-interest is the exclusive principle of human action (except that of the teacher?), that all human conduct is to be understood in terms of such interests, backed up by force. It is essentially the repudiation of real discussion and of reason.
>
> (Knight 1982, pp. 309–10)

What he calls "rational freedom" in particular, Knight says elsewhere "is a presupposition of all thinking and cannot be denied without asserting it" (p. 351).

3 This is one reason why "hate literature" laws passed in a number of countries (e.g., those prohibiting people from denying that the Holocaust ever occurred) are not only ineffective but also, very often, counter-productive ("If the goverment won't allow us to hear about it, there must be something to it"). Thus the liberal doctrine, as John Stuart Mill stated it, is that "there ought to exist the fullest liberty of professing and discussing, as a matter of ethical conviction, any doctrine, however immoral it may be considered" (Mill 1947, ch. 2, n. 1). The basic point here is that it is the function of the cultural sphere, not the political sphere, to determine what is and what is not "true." It is therefore not only ludicrous but also a fundamental violation of civil liberties when governments pass "hate laws." There can be no more justification for modern courts of law to arbitrate matters (such as the issue of the Holocaust) that properly belong to the realm of scholarship than there was for the Roman Inquisition to decide on the truth or falsity of the heliocentric theory.

4 For a succinct account of how the Soviets managed in the early 1930s to absorb the cultural realm into the political realm, thereby eliminating the last vestiges of civil society in Russia, see Malia 1994, pp. 227–43.

5 Animals (at least the more intelligent among them) are capable of dying for the sake of protecting their offspring (as any sociobiologist would readily point out), but this is a totally different phenomenon from that of humans *sacrificing* their lives for something of no material benefit or interest to them (such as preserving one's own genes). For one of the best treatments of the distinctively human phenomenon of risking one's life for something that carries no biological worth, see Hegel's discussion of the master-slave dialectic in his *Phenomenology of Spirit* (1963). See also the remarks of Karl Jaspers on the willingness to sacrifice one's life (Jaspers 1961, Chapter 4).

6 For a more detailed discussion of communicative rationality than that provided in what follows, see Madison 1986, Chapters 10 and 11. Schrag for his part writes:

The inmixing of truth and communication in expressive rhetoric as hermeneutic, we have attempted to show, forges a new and expanded notion of rationality as this rationality descends into discourse. The rationality of rationalism [what I have called intrumental rationality], with its Enlightenment concept of reason, is destroyed. But from the ashes of this destruction the phoenix of a new form of rationality arises within the discourse of mankind. However, this new form of rationality is displayed not only in discourse but also in action. Here we discern a further broadening of the logos of rhetoric. The descent of rationality into the texture of communicative praxis occasions a broadening of the notion of the reasonable to include not only the genre of discourse but also that of action. The rhetoric of discourse slides into an explicit rhetoric of action.

(Schrag 1986, p. 194)

7 Especially so, perhaps, if Knight is contrasted with Max Weber, as well as with some of the earlier representatives of the Frankfurt School (Horkheimer, Adorno, Marcuse).
8 For an argument that the liberal view of the self does not, contrary to what communitarian critics of liberalism such as Michael Sandel allege, presuppose an atomistic, "unencumbered concept of the self," see Macedo 1990.
9 Invoking Aristotle, Knight writes: "there really is no such thing as individual rationality. Rationality itself is social in nature and a product of stable group life. . . . Man is a social, or political, animal" (Knight 1982, p. 411).
10 See also Knight 1982, p. 372: "Human nature is a cultural phenomenon, and the individual exists as the bearer of a culture." Alluding to Aristotle's definition of man as the "social animal," Knight remarked: "The supreme paradox of man, in our civilization, is that he is an individual – unique, creative, and dynamic – yet is the creature of institutions which must be accounted for in terms of historical processes" (ibid., p. 363). "The human being does not achieve individuality or freedom, or the idea of freedom, except through a culture made and continued by the various groups ['communities'] in which he lives" (ibid., p. 373).
    F. A. Hayek was subsequently to argue (against *laissez-faire* individualism) in much the same manner. See, in this regard, Madison 1989b.
11 See p. 255:

The nearest approach to the pure ideal of free social action or democracy which is at all possible in reality is undoubtedly the discussion community, or intellectual association at the various levels – art, science, and philosophy, and also morals and politics, apart from mechanical organization and ritual. This community has no definite membership or boundaries and very little formal organization or formulated law [it is what I shall be referring to as a "spontaneous order"]. Practically any individual [apart from, as Protagoras would say, manifest abnormalities] is free to be a member, to participate in the activity, at will, subject to the momentary *de facto* consent of others. A similar degree of freedom is realized in small, spontaneous, and temporary groups, active in such fields as conversation, sociability, and play.

(Knight 1982, p. 255)

12 In these remarks I am drawing on my earlier essay "Being and Speaking," *Beyond the Symbol Model* (Stewart 1966), to which the reader is referred for a detailed discussion of the nature of (human) language. The word "human" should perhaps be stressed, since (as I argue) human language (usually referred to as "natural language") is *essentially* different from the "language" computers are said to "speak" (i.e., formal or logistic language).

13 This view of human rights as rational rights (based on communicative rationality) has only been fully articulated in the last several years, but it was clearly anticipated much earlier in this century by the famous historian of liberalism, Guido de Ruggiero (see 1981, p. 208). This major recasting or, as Ruggiero would say, *refonte* of liberal theory is unfortunately ignored by Shapiro in his study of the evolution of the liberal conception of rights, which remains much too narrowly focused on the Anglo-Saxon tradition.

14 Cf., for instance:

> What such [civilized and reflective] beings as we call men (normal adults) most conspicuously have in common, and in distinction from the other main recognized orders of existence – inert objects, plants, and animals – is the faculty of speech. . . . The "highest" form of mental activity, and use of speech, is in formulating and expressing reasons for judgments.
>
> (Knight 1982, 345)

15 In philosophy itself, the notion of truth as intersubjective agreement was fully articulated only many years later in Hans-Georg Gadamer's philosophical hermeneutics.

16 As William James was one of the first to argue earlier in this century.

17 The only time that a basic unanimity is both demanded by and necessary to a civil, free society is when that society finds itself in a state of war. In such circumstances, civil and human rights are normally, and quite legitimately, suspended (within limits), the overriding law then prevailing being the old Roman law: *salus populi, suprema lex*. (After the war situation has passed, governments will, given the nature of power, attempt to retain the emergency powers [such as income tax] that they had been granted for the period of the emergency; civil society then faces the difficult task of reasserting itself. How well a civil society manages to reconvert to peace time will depend, in large measure, on the soundness of its constitution, and the degree to which that constitution is generally respected.)

18 Seyla Benhabib, a student of the Frankfurt School, rightly corrects Habermas (in a decidedly liberal fashion) when she writes:

> Consent [unanimous consensus] alone can never be a criterion of anything, neither of truth nor of moral validity; rather, it is always the rationality of the procedure for attaining agreement which is of philosophical interest. We must interpret consent not as an end-goal but as a process for the cooperative generation of truth or validity. . . . "Consent" is a misleading term for capturing the core idea behind communicative ethics: namely, the processual generation of reasonable agreement about moral principles via an open-ended moral conversation. . . . [W]hen we shift the burden of the moral test in communicative ethics from consensus to the idea of an ongoing moral conversation, we begin to ask not what all would or could agree to as a result of practical discourses to be morally permissible or impermissible, but what would be allowed and perhaps even necessary from the standpoint of continuing and sustaining the practice of the moral conversation among us. The emphasis now is less on *rational agreement*, and more on sustaining those normative practices and moral relationships within which reasoned agreement *as a way of life* can flourish and continue.
>
> (Benhabib 1990, pp. 12–3)

19 As Mill further states:

> The fact . . . is, that not only the grounds of the opinion are forgotten in the absence of discussion, but too often the meaning of the opinion itself. The

words which convey it, cease to suggest ideas, or suggest only a small portion of those they were originally employed to communicate. Instead of a vivid conception and a living belief, there remain only a few phrases retained by rote; or, if any part, the shell and husk only of the meaning is retained, the finer essence being lost.

(Mill 1947, pp 38–39: lines 898–906)

20 Two pages further on Mouffe explicitly takes exception to Habermas' consensus theory of truth: "For a radical and plural democracy, the belief that a final resolution of conflicts is eventually possible, even if envisaged as an asymptotic approach to the regulative ideal of a free and unconstrained communication, as in Habermas, far from providing the necessary horizon for the democratic project, is something that puts it at risk" (Mouffe 1993, p.8).

21 This is the way Adam Przeworski defines democracy; see Przeworski 1991, p. 13.

22 This basic feature of civil society sets it in fundamental opposition to the practice of the former communist countries. As expressed in the crucial doctrine of *partiinost*, debate and discussion of issues was allowed (within strict limits) only so long as an official decision had not been arrived at, after which all discussion of the issues was prohibited (in these societies people were not free not to "toe the party-line"). (Naturally, human nature being what it is, people did, as they still do in China, express opinions deviating from the official party-line – but only in devious, "Byzantine" ways and with a great deal of "double-speak.")

23 In a civil society no politician may exert political pressures on an intellectual because of his or her views, nor may anyone who is not an elected representative interrupt legislative proceedings. In a civil society, the general public may not be allowed (through invariably political means) to exert pressure on the members of the academic community, who must always be allowed freely to pursue the truth as they see it (even if it conflicts with "the truth" as many other people, intellectuals or mere citizens alike, see it). Herein lies the rationale for academic tenure, whose purpose is to safeguard academic freedom, not, as the popular mind would have it, to provide "job security" in any ordinary sense of the term.

24 It is commonly asserted that no liberal democracies have ever waged war on one another. Peace (communicative rationality) is, in fact, the state of affairs that prevails between nations organized in the form of civil societies. Peace, however, does not mean "harmony" and the absence of conflict, sometimes of a serious nature. No two nations have peacefully coexisted for as long a period as have the United States and Canada, and yet they have regularly found themselves in serious dispute over various issues. In any event, from the fact that peace is the normal mode of relationship between civil societies, it follows, as a practical maxim of politics, that, if peace is sought beween any two nations, it can genuinely be achieved only to the degree that those nations democratize themselves (this is, *a contrario*, why the former socialist countries, despite their official ideology of universal brotherhood and "solidarity", were usually in a state of suppressed or open warfare [as, for instance, in the war that communist China waged against communist Vietnam]).

25 The phenomenon of globalization furnishes an example. No sooner had the nations of the world responded in a productive way to the demands of globalization by working out freer trade arrangements in 1994 (the World Trade Organization that was to replace GATT) than a new problem adversely affecting world trade arose, and due to the same forces at work in producing a global economy: wildly fluctuating exchange rates among national currencies on the world financial market posed a threat to the stability of world trade. As one observer remarked: "The more trade barriers come down, the more international cooperation . . . is

going to be required to modulate currency swings, because exporters, importers and investors simply cannot take advantage of free-trade zones if currency rates are bouncing around like golf balls on cement" (Friedman 1994c, p. E 5).

26 Stephen Toulmin explictly notes in this regard the intimate connection between a rational (democratic) society and a rational discipline such as science:

> The existence of regular procedures for criticizing the consequences of social or political institutions, and for advocating changes in social or polit-ical practice [what I am calling communicative rationality], is what makes the conduct of political affairs a "rational" matter, rather than a mere exercise of arbitrary authority or contest for power. In politics, as in science, the "rationality" of our present institutions requires the existence of accepted procedures ["rules"] for the self-transformation of social and political insti-tutions. . . . So, instead of social and political concepts being totally unlike the concepts of the natural sciences – as one might initially suppose – the relations between thought and practice in science and politics are very simi-lar. . . . [I]n both fields, the overall "rationality" of the existing procedures or institutions depends on the scope that exists for criticizing and changing them from within the enterprise itself.
>
> (Toulmin 1972, p. 168)

27 The use of force and intimidation for achieving social cohesion can be thoroughly rational, in a purely instrumentalist sense. Indeed, the effective use of force must be instrumentally rational in order to be effective. Thus the fundamental distinc-tion I am attempting to draw could equally well be between "spontaneous orders," on the one hand, and "instrumental organizations," on the other. The latter distinction is central to the excellent discussion of spontaneous orders by Gus diZerega (1989). One of the great merits of diZerega's article is the insightful way in which he compares and contrasts the spontaneous orders of the political and economic realms.

28 As I have argued on another occasion, from the point of view of liberal theory there are basically only two forms of governance: constitutional (*état de droit*) and nonconstitutional (arbitrary; see Madison 1986, p. 140). This is the same distinc-tion that Benjamin Constant made in 1815 when he declared: "[T]here are only two sorts of power in the world: one, illegitimate, is force; the other, legitimate, is the general will" (Constant 1988, p. 175). Rousseau had already stated in *Du contrat social:* "All legitimate governments are republican" (Rousseau 1977, II, 6); by "repub-lican" Rousseau meant "all governments guided by the general will, which is the law." In his "Perpetual Peace" (sec. II), Kant for his part stated that "government is either republican or despotic."

29 Hayek goes on to say:

> That there existed among the phenomena of society such spontaneous orders was often perceived [by the Greeks]. But as men were not aware of the ambiguity of the established natural/artificial terminology, they endeavoured to express what they perceived in terms of it, and inevitably produced confusion: one would describe a social institution as "natural" because it had never been deliberately designed, while another would describe the same institution as "artificial" because it resulted from human actions.
>
> (Hayek 1978, p. 254)

As I have argued elsewhere, thinking in terms of "either/or's" is the dominant characteristic of metaphysical thought.

30 See in this regard Charles Taylor's "Interpretation and the Sciences of Man," reprinted in Taylor 1985.
31 As Peirce states in "The Fixation of Belief": "This is the only one of the four methods which presents any distinction of a right and a wrong way" (Peirce 1955, p. 19).
32 As we shall see in the following chapter, this is also the chief characteristic of a liberal-democratic political order: In such an order, a civil society, truth ("justice") is solely a function of the (liberal-democratic) means of arriving at it.
33 For an extensive argument as to why it is so, see McCloskey 1994.
34 See also:

> [I]n both today's postmodern natural and human sciences and the critical disciplines of the humanities, we are concerned with a mix, or blend, of explanation and interpretation. All of our scientific explanations and critical readings start from, embody, and imply some interpretive standpoint, conceptual framework, or theoretical perspective. The relevance and adequacy of our explanations can never be demonstrated with Platonic rigor or geometrical necessity. . . . [T]he operative question is, Which of our positions are rationally warranted, reasonable, or defensible – that is, well-founded rather than groundless opinions. (p. 115)

> [W]e should ask scholars to pay more attention to the elements of interpretation – even of hermeneutics – that have nowadays become essential to both the natural and human sciences and to base their comparisons between the sciences and the humanities not on the assumed *absence* of hermeneutic interpretation from natural science but rather on the different *modes* of interpretation characteristic of the two general fields. (p. 101)
>
> (Toulmin 1982)

Another writer remarks in this regard:

> It is the contention of this article that a rightful concern to demonstrate the autonomy of the human sciences from the natural sciences had led to a lack of understanding of the parallels between the methodologies of the two, and a neglect of the fundamentally hermeneutical nature of the perceptual process underlying natural science. . . . [T]he thesis here is that the activity of a perceiving subject confronting a world is so radically identical with the activity of an interpreter confronting a text that the natural sciences can give no account of their starting point without using the tools of hermeneutics.
>
> (Franklin 1984, p. 511).

35 The "progress of knowledge" is to a very large extent due to the way in which various intellectual orders are made to interact in unanticipated and thus spontaneous ways; see in this regard Madison 1982, Chapters 6 and 7.
     Hayek defines "order" in the following manner: "a state of affairs in which a multiplicity of elements of various kinds are so related to each other than we may learn from our acquaintance with some spatial or temporal part of the whole to form correct expectations concerning the rest, or at least expectations which have a good chance of proving correct" (Hayek 1973, p. 36). The characteristic of orders that Hayek is describing is what I have referred to as their "logic." Hegel appropriately remarked in this connection:

> To discover the necessity at work here is the object of political economy, a science which does credit to thought because it finds the laws underlying a mass of contingent occurrences. It is an interesting spectacle to observe

here how all the interconnections have repercussions on others, and are helped or hindered by these. This interaction, which is at first sight incredible since everything seems to depend on the arbitrary will of the individual, is particularly worthy of note; it bears a resemblance to the planetary system, which presents only irregular movements to the eye, yet whose laws can nevertheless be recognized.

(Hegel 1991, §189)

36 Pragmatically speaking, "objectivity" is simply another name for what is intersubjectively agreed upon.
37 This is why the charge of *relativism* ("anything goes") cannot legitimately be levelled against the hermeneutical conception of truth. As Chantal Mouffe appropriately observes: "To assert that one cannot provide an ultimate foundation for any given system of values [or truths] does not imply that one considers all views to be equal" (Mouffe 1993, pp. 14–15). See also in this regard Madison 1991b.
38 See Hayek 1973:

[T]he rules that govern action will often be much more general and abstract than anything language can yet express. Such abstract rules are learnt by imitating particular actions, from which the individual acquires "by analogy" the capacity to act in other cases on the same principles which, however, he could never state as principles.

(Hayek 1973, p. 77)

39 This stress laid on the tacit element in all understanding is also a central feature of philosophical hermeneutics (which Gadamer discusses under the heading of "prejudice" [in a non-pejorative sense]); it is also the cornerstone of Hayek's theory of human understanding.

Philip Mirowski has similarly argued that "mathematics cannot be considered an independent mechanical decision procedure (as portrayed in the Cartesian tradition), because there are no self-enforcing rules concerning the sufficiency of mathematical analogy" (Mirowski 1988a, p. 126).
40 This is, in effect, the underlying thesis of the highly noteworthy study of Hubert Dreyfus (1979). For a critique of my critique (along with that of Dreyfus) of the Artificial Intelligence agenda, see Eric Dietrick, "AI and the Mechanistic Forces of Darkness," (Dietrick 1995, p. 155 and passim).
41 Hubert Dreyfus and Paul Rabinow address this issue when they remark:

Why is there a historical difference in the way the disciplinary matrix functions in the natural and the social sciences? To answer this question we must first look in more detail at the way background practices work in the natural sciences. Increasingly, sophisticated skills and techniques have enabled modern scientists to "work-over" objects so as to fit them into a formal framework. This allows modern scientists to isolate properties from their context of human relevance, and then to take the meaningless properties thus isolated and relate them by strict laws. Like any skills, the practices which make natural science possible involve a kind of know-how which cannot be captured by strict laws. Kuhn ... stresses that these skills are acquired by working through exemplary problems, and Polanyi adds that often these skills cannot be learned from textbooks but must be acquired by apprenticeship.

(Dreyfus and Rabinow 1982, pp. 162–63)

42 See in particular Feyerabend 1975. Another writer on science who has stressed the

essential affinities between the natural sciences and the human disciplines is Jacob Bronowski (see Bronowski 1971 and 1965).

43 As Paul Ricoeur has argued, in the human sciences "explanation" and "understanding" are simply "two different stages of a unique *hermeneutical arc*"; see in this regard his classic text, "The Model of the Text: Meaningful Action Considered as a Text" in Ricoeur 1981. See also in the same volume "What is a Text? Explanation and Understanding."

44 To be sure, this too, as regards the differences between the natural sciences and the human sciences, is a matter of degree and not of kind. The science of biology, for instance, is easily susceptible to ideological influences of a racist, sexist, or politically partisan nature. See for instance in this regard Lowontin 1994, as well as Zuckerman 1991.

45 Actually, Ricoeur is perhaps not altogether correct in asserting that this phenomenon is not at work in the natural sciences. An analogy (perhaps somewhat distant, but an analogy nonetheless) can be found in quantum mechanics, where the very act of "observing" a micro particle necessarily alters its "behavior" (a point that Toulmin stresses in his 1982 article cited above).

46 As a number of cultural anthropologists have noted, "natives" are often not only reticent in communicating information about their cultural practices and beliefs, but the information they do provide is often disinformation.

47 As Knight also stated: "[T]here is no such thing as individual rationality. Rationality itself is social in nature and a product of stable group life" (Knight 1982, p. 411).

48 This is a point greatly stressed by Gadamer, with his notion of "historically effective consciousness" (*Wirkungsgeschichtlichebewusstsein*): All understanding on the part of the individual is historical through and through; whenever any individual can say "I understand" (this or that), it is because, precisely as an individual, he or she is part of a *tradition* of inquiry and understanding.

49 In a later work, Hayek states:

In the marketplace (as in other institutions of our extended order), unintended consequences are paramount: a distribution of resources is effected by an impersoanl process in which individuals, acting for their own ends (themselves also often rather vague), literally do not and cannot know what will be the net result of their interactions.

(Hayek 1988, p. 71)

50 For an excellent account of what has come to be known as the "interpretive turn" in the philosophy of science, see Bernstein 1983, and see as well Polkinghorne 1983.

51 As Zygmunt Bauman has most insistently – and persuasively – argued (Bauman 1993, p. 245). If there is a point at which I diverge from Bauman's lefitst and generally "pessimistic" reading of our late-modern or postmodern times, it is with regard to his (in my opinion totally nostalgic) view that only a revival of "face-to-face" morality can save us now. I believe, on the contrary, that what we need today, in a veritable postmodern, postindustrial, and global society, is not a revival of old-fashioned morality but the cultivation of a "new morality," that required by the bringing-into-being of *civil society* (as defined by Václav Havel), on a global scale. The entire argument of this book is directed to this effect.

52 For a more thorough discussion of this issue, see Madison 1986, Chapter 7.

53 As Ricoeur remarks:

Violence and discourse are the two opposite poles of human existence. . . . Violence is always the interruption of discourse: discourse is always the interruption of violence. A violence that speaks is already a violence that is trying to be in the right, that is exposing itself to the gravitational pull of

Reason and already beginning to renegue on its own character as violence. The prime example of this is that the "tyrant" always tries to get discourse on his side.

(Ricoeur 1979, p. 226)

54 It is of course true, from a purely factual point of view, that there are many (powerful) people who are incapable of thinking this "principle of reason," and that is why the contest between reason and (sheer) power can be expected to continue for an indefinite future.

55 Another way of expressing the matter would be to say that freedom cannot *rationally* be rejected as a value inasmuch as it is, as Knight would say, the operative presupposition of communicative rationality, such that it is necessarily, albeit implicitly, affirmed by anyone engaging in communicative rationality, i.e., seeking genuine, uncoerced agreement with others (see Knight 1982, pp. 474, 476).

56 James Madison, in a report to the House of Delegates of Virginia, session of 1799–1800; cited in Meyers, 1981, p. 244.

57 For an analysis of the intersubjective nature of subjectivity, see my "The Hermeneutics of (Inter)Subjectivity, or: The Mind-Body Problem Deconstructed" (in Madison 1988).

58 Education would, however, be turned into indoctrination were the politically correct to have their way. To use the words of Giovanni Sartori (talking about totalitarian regimes):

> [T]he process of education becomes a process of indoctrination in which one doctrine only exists, and all other doctrines are banned. In all the areas that are not strictly technical, education is displaced and replaced by *propaganda fidei*, by the official, exclusive, faith of state. From womb to tomb the bombardment is both incessant and unopposed, for the artillery is all one one side and commanded by the same general.
>
> (Sartori 1987, I, p. 100)

It is significant that the PC agenda always relies on bureaucratic ("state") regulation.

59 "Sexual Harassment and Academic Freedom: A Statement of the National Association of Scholars," *The New York Review of Books* (February 17, 1994), p. 5.

60 As Doreen Kimura, Professor of Neuropsychology at the University of Western Ontario, stated in a Convocation address delivered on June 2, 1993 at Simon Fraser University in Vancouver.   ·

61 It was most disingenuous on the part of the Minister when, in an attempt to save face, he insisted that the Framework amounted only to a handful of helpful "suggestions" and did not at all have the force of imperial bureaucratic regulation; it most certainly and obviously did.

62 In another directive to Ontario universities, Minister of Education Dave Cooke had, in the subtle way of bureaucrats (in the words of Saul Ross, President of the Ontario Confederation of University Faculty Associations):

> Unilaterally, without public consultation or discussion with the institutions ... redefined the mission of Ontario's universities, narrowing our task to concerns for economic development, job creation and social justice. While these are obviously important social goals which we all want to see attained, they misrepresent and debase the centuries-old traditional central mission of the university: the generation and transmission of knowledge, the pursuit of truth. No government minister has the right to arbitrarily change the mission of the university.
>
> (OCUFA 1994a, p. 2)

63 From hints emanating from the Ministry, it was fairly clear that zero-tolerance was part of a wider campaign against academic freedom and university autonomy, namely, government control over university curricula and overt checks on what is taught in classrooms, the point not being simply to ban "offensive" speech but to insure in a "positive" way that what is taught is sufficiently "inclusive" and "equitable." After speech regulation, thought control. A natural progression. For a detailed critical analysis of the totalitarian (and racist) aspects of "zero tolerance" and "educational equity," see Fekete 1994.

64 Phyllis Granoff and Koici Shinohara, professors of religious studies at McMaster University, very appropriately observe:

> The very notion of a pluralistic society implies a diversity of opinion; diversity of opinion in turn entails that some individuals will reject what others believe or say. There is simply no way in which some individuals will not feel "uncomfortable" with what others believe and express in a society that allows more than one point of view. If we permit some individuals to bring charges against others because they feel that a "negative" atmosphere has been created for them, we will either create an atmosphere of terror for everyone, or a homogenized, bland environment in which people will simply not stand up for what they believe. The academic mission of the university will be fundamentally compromised under such circumstances. The recent abuses of "zero-tolerance" policies at the University of New Hampshire should be a warning that however well meant they may have been, efforts to define and legislate correct behaviour in this manner are dangerous and encourage the very abuses they were designed to avoid.
>
> (Granoff and Shinohara 1994, p. 13)

65 Cf. in this regard the very instructive remarks of John Fekete:

> Julie Mason, a feminist activist, and former director of communications for the federal NDP [the socialist party of Canada], worked for a year at the new Employment Equity Commission in Ontario. According to journalist Thomas Walcom, she called it the most racist workplace she had ever experienced. In his study of the follies of the NDP, Walcom quotes Mason: "I've never seen anything like it. It was absolutely vicious. . . . The blacks hated the Indians; the Indians were the most anti-Semitic; everyone hated the lesbians and gays. . . . There was a real pecking order. At the bottom were people with disabilities. Next to the bottom were white women. There were no white men, not until they had to bring in John DeMarco (a senior bureaucrat in Citizenship) to fix up the mess.
>
> (Fekete 1994, pp. 176–77)

66 The PC movement is a full-fledged embodiment of intolerance, in that the principle animating this movement is "If we are right, no one else with conflicting opinions can – by definition – be right." This is the most fundamental principle of dogmatic rationalism: there is, and can be, only one correct version of the Truth.

67 That this is in fact so is perhaps more obvious if the point is put "negatively": it is not so much that people everywhere explicitly view freedom as a *value* (in the philosophical sense of the term), as that they invariably, and by whatever means possible, seek to avoid the *harms* produced by a *lack of freedom*, e.g., slavery, torture, arbitrary arrest, imprisonment, or execution. See in this regard Sartori 1995, p. 103.

68 For an empirical survey of the democratic movement ("democratization"), see Huntington 1991.

69 A position very similar to the one I choose to call "hermeneutical universalism" (see my paper, "Hermeneutics, the Lifeworld, and the Universality of Reason"

[Madison 1995]) is argued for by Agnes Heller (see Heller 1990, Chapter 8). She writes for instance:

> Modernity is about the concretization of "freedom". Every form of life in modernity is by definition the concretization of the abstract possibility of having been born free. This is meant not as a predictive, rather as an analytical statement. There is no longer a "social pyramid". The modern world is flat because it is symmetrical. This is precisely why modern values can be universal. The universality of a value is a perfectly simple thing. It means that the opposite of the value cannot be chosen as a value. Freedom is certainly such a universal value, since no one is publicly committed to unfreedom as a value.
>
> (Heller 1990, p. 152)

70 For an account of how liberal concepts of Western origin, such as representative government, human rights, and the rule of law, can be creatively appropriated and applied in other cultural contexts (Burma, in this case), see A. S. Suu Kyi 1992.

4 THE POLITICAL ORDER

1 For a detailed analysis of the heuristic and cognitive function of metaphor, see Madison 1982.
2 In Seligman's estimation, when the various associations or groups which go to make up civil society (to be discussed below) "are built around the principle of interest [which they undeniably are], they cannot as such mediate or mitigate interest-motivated action in the name of some other or higher ethical unity" (Seligman 1992, pp. 197–98). This is a common and widely held view to which I shall nevertheless take exception in what follows.
3 The Virginia Constitution of 1776 (of whose drafting committee Madison was a member) stated (sec. 2): "That all power is vested in, and consequently derived from, the people."
4 Cf. in this regard Sunstein:

> In important respects, the departure from traditional republicanism could not have been greater. Madison willingly abandoned the classical republican understanding that citizens generally should participate directly in the processes of government. Far from being a threat to freedom, a large republic could help to guarantee it. At the same time, Madison's understanding was · sharply distinct from that of the modern pluralists [on the specialized meaning of this term as used by Sunstein see note 7 of this chapter, p. 232]. He hoped that national representatives, operating above the fray, would be able to disentangle themselves from local pressures and deliberate on and bring about something like an objective common good.
>
> (Sunstein 1993, p. 184)

5 On the essential difference between laws, in the proper sense of the term, and decrees or orders, see Hayek 1972, ch. 10.
   Sunstein very interestingly points out that in the United States judge-made public law has sought to uphold the Madisonian ideal of deliberative government by demanding that "measures taken by legislatures or administrators must be 'rational.'" He goes on to say:

> The rationality requirement may ... be understood precisely as a requirement that regulatory measures be something other than a response to political pressure. In the rationality cases, the Court requires some independent

"public interest" to justify regulation. A deference to political power is, by itself, insufficient. In no modern case has the Court recognized the legitimacy of pluralist compromise as the exclusive basis for legislation. In many cases, modern and not so modern, the Court has indicated that such compromise is impermissible if it is the sole reason for the legislative enactment at issue. Much of modern constitutional doctrine reflects a single perception of the underlying evil: the distribution of resources or opportunities to one group rather than another solely because those benefited have exercised the raw power to obtain governmental assistance.

(Sunstein 1993, pp. 190–91)

The situation Sunstein describes is a good illustration of how well crafted Madison's Constitution was (having, in this case, to do with judicial review), even though American government has never fully lived up to the Madisonian ideal of deliberative democracy.

6 Sunstein goes on to point out: "The requirement of deliberation does not exclude compromises among those with different conceptions of appropriate government ends. But it does demand that representatives engage in some form of discussion about those ends, rather than responding mechanically to political power or to existing private preferences" (Sunstein 1993, p. 201).

7 As Sunstein points out, such is the "pluralist" view of politics (favored by many a political scientist) as opposed to the "republican" or Madisonian view. He writes:

Distinct from the republican understanding of government is a competing conception that might be called pluralist [references provided]. Under the pluralist view, politics mediates the struggle among self-interested groups for scarce social resources. Only nominally deliberative, politics is a process of conflict and compromise among various social interests. Under the pluralist conception, people come to the political process with preselected interests that they seek to promote through political conflict and compromise. Preferences are not shaped through governance, but enter into the process as exogenous variables. . . . The pluralist conception treats the republican notion of a separate common good as incoherent, potentially totalitarian, or both.

(Sunstein 1993, p. 176)

8 As Sunstein (1993, p. 189) refers to it, Madisonian republicanism occupies "an intermediate position between interest group pluralism and traditional [civic virtue] republicanism."

9 It may be noted that this "deliberative or transformative function of politics" (as Sunstein refers to it [1993, p. 200]) is in perfect conformity to the hermeneutical view of understanding in general, viz., that all genuine understanding is of a transformative nature, rather than (as traditional epistemology always held) of a merely representational or reproductive sort.

10 In his short history of liberal theory, Pierre Manent credits the French politician François Guizot for "his resolute rejection of the founding political role of the human will, whether individual or collective." In this regard, Manent says, Guizot "breaks with the entire tradition of modern philosophy" (Manent 1994, p. 101). It was above all Madison, I maintain, who effected the decisive break. (In his study Manent does not even consider Madison's contributions to liberal theory, his history being in this respect entirely "eurocentric".)

11 The great advantage of this view of reason, as Manin himself points out with reference to the view of Habermas (see Manin 1994, p. 199, n. 23), is that it avoids the need to equate a *rational* agreement with a *unanimous* agreement (consensus or agreement in the Habermasian sense of the term): "As long as we accept the

predetermined will of individuals as the unique basis for legitimacy, we must inevitably conclude that only the object of unanimous agreement is legitimate" (ibid., p. 197). Thus as Manin observes, "deliberation makes it possible to avoid the exorbitant requirements of . . . unanimity" (ibid., p. 198).

12 The foremost twentieth-century exponent of this view of reason or rationality was Chaim Perelman (see in particular Perelman 1979 and 1982). Perelman referred to his revival of classical rhetoric as "The New Rhetoric" or "The Theory of Argumentation," and he explicitly linked up this view of reason with the practice of liberal democracy. (For a discussion of Perelman's New Rhetoric, see Madison 1989a.)

13 When one considers the populist passion that large numbers of Americans developed in the 1990s for imposing term limits on their elected representatives, one is inclined to think that it was perhaps no accident if the Founding Fathers included no such provision in the Constitution they drafted. Increasing the *responsiveness* of elected representatives to popular and transient demands in no way contributes to greater *responsibility* and *accountability* on their part, quite the opposite. The case of Mexico, where severe term limits have long been the norm, lends empirical confirmation to this theoretical precept (see DePalma 1994).

14 "As long as the reason of man continues fallible, and he is at liberty to exercise it, different opinions will be formed." As Madison also observed: human beings are "much more disposed to vex and oppress each other than to co-operate for their common good. So strong is this propensity of mankind to fall into mutual animosities, that where no substantial occasion presents itself, the most frivolous and fanciful distinctions have been sufficient to kindle their unfriendly passions and excite their most violent conflicts."

Madison's anti-utopianism, a basic trait of liberal thought, was rearticulated in a most superb and succinct fashion a number of years later by John Stuart Mill when he wrote: "Governments must be made for human beings as they are or as they are capable of speedily becoming" (Mill 1958, p. 98). Mill's remark points to the essential, irreconcilable difference between two fundamentally opposed conceptions of society: socialist society and civil society. The underlying premise of the latter is that, given the appropriate institutional framework, people can, in the here and now, behave in a communicatively rational way and can thereby bring into being a just (though by no means "perfect") society.

15 Cf. in this regard Hamilton (*The Federalist*, No. 27) where he speaks of "those occasional ill-humors, or temporary prejudices and propensities, which, in smaller societies ['communities,' as the communitarians would say], frequently contaminate the public councils, beget injustice and oppression of a part of the community, and engender schemes which, though they gratify a momentary inclination or desire, terminate in general distress, dissatisfaction, and disgust."

Although, like some of the "theoretic politicians" Madison refers to, Quintin Skinner lauds the "participatory" nature of medieval Italian city-republics and recommends it as a possible solution to the problems confronting modern democratic societies, he nevertheless (rather self-contradictingly) concedes that these small-scale, "participatory" republics were, throughout their often short-lived existence, beset with factional conflicts of the most destructive nature (see Skinner 1993 and, for an earlier discussion on his part of civic republicanism, Skinner 1984).

16 Madison observed:

When a majority is included in a faction, the form of popular government . . . enables it to sacrifice to its ruling passion or interest both the public good and the rights of other citizens. To secure the public good and private rights against the danger of such a faction, and at the same time to preserve the spirit and the form of popular government, is then the great object to which our inquiries are directed.

(The Federalist No. 76)

17 And indeed, the most important challenge facing the Western, industrially developed democracies is (from the point of view of human rights) not that of creating "more democracy"; it is rather that of both safeguarding and improving upon the basic structures of civil society in all its domains, cultural, political, and economic.

18 Contrary to the view of many classical thinkers, party politics is not a source of divisiveness in a polity but actually contributes to its overall cohesion. As Sartori observes:

> Only as parties and party systems developed in the nineteenth century did it come to be acknowledged and realized that a *pluralistic consensus*, or (depending on the emphasis) a *pluralistic dissensus*, was not only compatible with, but also beneficial to, the good polity. The crucial point is, therefore, that dissent, opposition, adversary politics, and contentation are all notions that acquire a positive value, and a positive role, within the context of *pluralism*, that is, within the pluralistic conception of society and history. Prior to whatever else it may be, pluralism is the belief in the *value* of diversity.
>
> (Sartori 1987, I, p. 92)

19 On the important role of *in camera* or closed session committee meetings in decision making (and the compromises needed to arrive at agreement), see Przeworski 1991.

20 Hamilton was echoing Madison when he said that the "supposition of universal venality in human nature is little less an error in political reasoning, than the supposition of universal rectitude.... [T]here is a portion of virtue and honor among mankind, which may be a reasonable foundation of confidence; and experience justifies the theory" *(The Federalist*, No. 76).

21 Schumpeter stated: "our chief troubles about the classical theory centered on the proposition that 'the people' hold a definite and rational opinion about every individual question and that they give effect to this opinion – in a democracy – by choosing 'representatives' who will see to it that that opinion is carried out" (Schumpeter 1976, p. 269).

22 In his review article, Brinkley observes how, after women did get the right of vote, their political power *actually declined.*

23 As diZerega rightly observes:

> As a spontaneous order, democracy refers to *the entire ensemble of citizens and their interactions when they observe the basic rules of democratic politics:* free elections, one-person-one vote, freedom of speech and of organization, and the like.... Democracy encompasses all of society *insofar as it is a political community.* It is not coterminous with society, but it is equally the case that no part of a democratic society is in principle removed from being subject to political discussion and, possibly, action.
>
> (diZerega 1989, pp. 215–16)

24 Thus in Japan, where the people were always highly subdued by a government-imposed and meticulously maintained ideology of group-consciousness *(nakamaishiki)* but where a freedom of information revolution is now underway, ordinary Japanese are today beginning to organize and speak their own minds (all the way from consumers' legitimate demands for lower prices for commercial and

food goods to neighborhood groups protesting government attempts to run new rail lines through their neighborhoods without consultation).

25 As Hayek says:

> [P]articular societies within the Great Society [i.e., a large-scale civil society] may arise as the result of spatial proximity, or of some other special circumstances which produce closer relations among their members. And different partial societies of this sort will often overlap and every individual may, in addition to being a member of the Great Society, be a member of numerous other spontaneous sub-orders or particular societies of this sort as well as of various organizations existing within the comprehensive Great Society.
>
> (Hayek 1973, p. 47)

This is far from being a trivial observation. Hayek's remark signals an important point, having far-reaching and highly significant implications for democratic political theory (which I can only allude to here). The point is that the more developed a society is in sociological/economic terms, the more likely it is that there will be both an increased diversification of sub-groups within civil society, on the one hand, and, on the other, an increased complexification of overlapping memberships in these groups. In other words, the more likely it is that there will be an increased tendency for the "identity" of individuals *not* to be a function of their belonging to any one group in particular (e.g., gender, race, ethnicity).

26 The Internet, by means of which many of these citizens communicate and which currently links together millions of individuals dispersed throughout the world, is itself, as a means of communication, a superb example of a "spontaneous order." The Internet as it now exists was never "centrally planned" and is not the creation of telecommunication organizations or large computer companies but is, rather, a "bottom-up information infrastructure" and the anarchic outgrowth, as it were, of numerous individuals acting on their own. Moreover, like other spontaneous orders, the Internet lacks a "center," being more like a huge and immensely complex web of interconnected nodal points – ordered anarchy (see Anderson 1995).

27 Mouffe errs, however, when she goes on to say: "Such a view of the political is profoundly at odds with liberal thought" (Mouffe 1993, p. 3). Mouffe's own profound error is a common and extremely widespread one, especially among leftist critics of liberalism, who continue to mouth standard clichés, such as the the idea that liberalism is synonymous with "possessive individualism" (see Macpherson 1962). Their error consists in taking too literally some of the, admittedly, "individualist" rhetoric of many of the classical liberals. The error could have been avoided if they had ever taken the time to read that most liberal of liberals, Frank H. Knight.

28 This of course is not to say that modern governments, socialist-type ones in particular, do not have a natural tendency to want to absorb as much as possible of civil society into the political sphere in the narrow sense of the term. They do indeed tend to operate under the "assumption that governments are the only vehicle whereby public concerns are addressed and public policy is articulated" (OCUFA 1994b, p. 3). (These are the words used by the Ontario Confederation of University Faculty Associations to describe the operative policy of the socialist [NDP] government of Ontario in the first half of the 1990s, which systematically sought to override university autonomy by making universities directly responsible to the social engineering dictates of the Ontario Ministry of Education.)

29 Madison wrote:

> In the compound republic of America, the power surrendered by the people is first divided between two distinct governments, and then the portion

allotted to each subdivided among distinct and separate departments. Hence a double security arises to the rights of the people. The different governments will control each other, at the same time that each will be controlled by itself.

(*The Federalist*, No. 51)

30 For a succinct statement of Madison's formula, see Alexander Hamilton, *The Federalist* No. 9.
31 See also *The Federalist*, No. 51: "[T]he larger the society, provided it lie within a practical sphere, the more duly capable it will be of self-government."

It is a properly Madisonian formula that a contemporary writer is recommending when, speaking of the prospects of democracy in the Arab world, he writes:

[T]he sheer presence of a multiplicity of organizations (whether "democratic" or not) in the political arena [by which he means what I have called the public realm] serves to create checks and balances. These groups limit one another's power, and all together they tend to limit the state, thus creating a situation favorable to democracy.

(Harik 1994, p. 56)

32 I do not, to be sure, mean "pluralism" in the specialized sense employed by Sunstein, see note 7 of this chapter.

In the case of countries in the process of democratization, one of the single most important factors in the development of pluralism, and thus of freedom, in the public realm is the abolition of state control over the economy. As one analyst observes: "[M]arket-oriented reforms are fundamental to the emergence of more autonomous interest groups, political parties, and media, and a much stronger legislative [as opposed to bureaucratic] role in public policy" (Nelson 1994, p. 60). This is one area in which the "synergetic" relation between the political order and the economic order is particularly in evidence: "A strong case can be made that largely market economics and open and competitive political systems, once both become established, are mutually reinforcing" (ibid., p. 61).

33 It is not without significance in this regard that the preamble to the US Constitution of 1778 lists as its aims: "to form a more perfect Union, establish Justice, insure domestic Tranquility, provide for the common defense, promote the general Welfare, and secure the Blessings of Liberty to ourselves and our Posterity."

34 Compare Madison, *The Federalist*, No. 10:

The diversity in the faculties of men, from which the rights of property originate, is not less an insuperable obstacle to a uniformity of interests. The protection of these faculties is the first object of government. From the protection of different and unequal faculties of acquiring property, the possession of different degrees and kinds of property immediately results; and from the influence of these on the sentiments and views of the respective proprietors, ensues a division of the society into different interests and parties. ... The latent causes of faction are thus sown in the nature of man; and we see them everywhere brought into different degrees of activity, according to the different circumstances of civil society.

35 It is my conviction that Kant was picking up on Madison (without referring to or acknowledging him) and Madison's notion that, people not being angels, the function of politics is to supply "by opposite and rival interests, the defect of better motives," when Kant subsequently rejected the idea that "a republic would have to be a nation of angels, because men with their selfish inclinations are not capable of

a constitution of such a sublime form" (Kant 1963, p.112). The truth of the matter, Kant said, is that "precisely with these inclinations nature comes to the aid of the general will established on reason" (ibid.). In a thoroughly and remarkably Madisonian fashion, he declared: "It is only a question of a good organization of the state (which does lie in man's power), whereby the powers of each selfish inclination are so arranged in opposition that one moderates or destroys the ruinous effects of the other. The consequence for reason is the same as if none of them existed, and man is forced to be a good citizen even if not a morally good person." Kant went on to say that, however hard a problem it may be to organize properly a State, it "can be solved even for a race of devils, if only they are intelligent." The problem is, he said: "Given a multitude of rational beings requiring universal laws for their preservation, but each of whom is secretly inclined to exempt himself from them, to establish a constitution in such a way that, although their private intentions conflict, they check each other, with the result that their public conduct is the same as if they had no such intentions" ("Perpetual Peace," in Kant 1963b, p. 112). Kant's essay was published in 1795, while Madison's observations in *The Federalist* date from 1788. Kant's reference to "a race of devils" also perhaps owed something to an earlier observation of John Adams who in his "A Defense of the Constitutions of the Government of the United States of America" had written:

> The best republics will be virtuous, and have been so; but we may hazard a conjecture that the virtues have been the effect of the well ordered constitution rather than the cause. And, perhaps, it would not be impossible to prove that a republic cannot exist even among highwaymen by setting one rogue to watch another, and the knaves themselves may in time be made honest men by the struggle.
>
> (Adams 1954, p. 162)

It would be tempting to compare and contrast the Madison–Adams–Kant point of view on constitutionalism (and its ability to create "virtuous" government) to contemporary, social-scientistic game theory ("the prisoner's dilemma") with its outright cynicism as to the possibilities of republican, constitutional government. I shall, however, resist that temptation at the present time.

36 A contrasting, more socialist view, so to speak, was expressed at the same time by Benjamin Rush (an advocate of civic republicanism) who declared:

> each citizen should be taught that he does not belong to himself, but that he is public property. Let him be taught to have his family, but let him be taught at the same time that he must forsake and even forget them when the welfare of his country requires it. . . . I consider it . . . possible to convert men into republican machines. This must be done if we expect them to perform their parts properly in the great machine of the government of the state.
>
> (*A Plan for the Establishment of Public Schools and the Diffusion of Knowledge in Pennsylvania* [1786], as cited by Sunstein 1993, p. 182, nt. 17)

(Note: At the time Rush produced this document, the State of Pennsylvania was governed by a radically democratic form of government, one which was subsequently abolished by its own citizens.)

For anyone who is familiar with the basic themes of classical Soviet ideology/propaganda, Rush's document is an absolutely incredible text. Just as Rush called for converting men into "republican machines," so likewise the whole Soviet socialist system was geared to expressly inculcating in people the idea that they were mere *machines* (or cogs) in the grandiose socialist system. So much for human freedom and dignity.

As Rush's demand so vividly demonstrates, socialist-type thinking is nothing new, and is not by any means foreign to the human make-up.

37 Compare with the remarks of Smith's fellow member of the Scottish Enlightenment, David Hume:

> Your corn is ripe today; mine will be so to-morrow. 'Tis profitable for us both, that I shou'd labour with you to-day, and that you shou'd aid me to-morrow. I have no kindness for you, and know you have as little for me. I will not, therefore, take any pains upon your account; and should I labour with you upon my own account, in expectation of a return, I know I shou'd be disappointed, and that I shou'd in vain depend upon your gratitude. Here then I leave you to labour alone: You treat me in the same manner. The seasons change; and both of us lose our harvests for want of mutual confidence and security.
>
> All this is the effect of the natural and inherent principles and passions of human nature; and as these passions and principles are inalterable, it may be thought, that our conduct, which depends on them, must be so too, and that 'twou'd be in vain, either for moralists or politicians, to tamper with us, or attempt to change the usual course of our actions, with a view to public interest. And indeed, did the success of their designs depend upon their success in correcting the selfishness and ingratitude of men, they wou'd never make any progress, unless aided by omnipotence, which is alone able to new-mould the human mind, and change its character in such fundamental articles. All they can pretend to, is to give a new direction to those natural passions, and teach us that we can better satisfy our appetites in an oblique and artificial manner, than by their headlong and impetuous motion. Hence I learn to do a service to another, without bearing him any real kindness; because I forsee, that he will return my service, in expectation of another of the same kind, and in order to maintain the same correspondence of good offices with me or with others. And accordingly, after I have serv'd him, and he is in possession of the advantage arising from my action, he is induc'd to perform his part, as forseeing the consequences of his refusal.
>
> (Hume 1978, bk. III, pt. II, sec. V, pp. 520–21)

38 Karen Vaughn points to the crucial difference between Smith and Mandeville when she writes: "The philosophers of the Scottish Enlightenment, of whom Smith was one, rejected Mandeville's sensational equating of self-interest with greed, but they developed as a major theme of their writing the underlying idea that private actions can have beneficial public effects that were not intended by the actors" (Vaughn 1989, p. 169).

39 Vaughn also notes the all-importance of correct institutional arrangements:

> [T]he overall beneficial nature of Smith's "simple system of natural liberty" depends not on the benevolence of individuals, but upon the operation of self-love *in a system* [emphasis added] of free exchange.... The desirability of the order that emerges as the unintended consequence of human action depends ultimately on the kind of rules and institutions within which human beings act.
>
> (Vaughn 1989, pp. 170–71)

There is a natural link between Madisonian constitutionalism (as well as Kant's reflections on "a perfectly just civic constitution") and the work of Adam Smith in that Smith's thought is an instance of what James Buchanan calls "constitutional economics" (Buchanan 1989). And as Buchanan points out, constitutional economics falls within the parameters of *moral philosophy*; it deals with the "central question of social philosophy," viz., "How can persons live together in liberty, peace, and prosperity?" (Buchanan 1989, p. 81)

40 As Paul Ricoeur observes, self-esteem is inseparable from solicitude for others, from "reciprocity" (see Ricoeur 1991, pp. 257–58). As a general rule, one's true interests are best served by cooperation with others, and the cooperation of others is most likely to be secured when one respects their right to pursue their own interests.

41 I call this the Enlightenment Thesis, since it was formulated in opposition to (or as a corrective to) the position defended by classical or civic humanists which typically stigmatized the pursuit of individual well-being ("commercialism," now referred to as the "consumer society") and which maintained that wealth is incompatible with "virtue." It is this Enlightenment Thesis which furnished the moral basis (the "institutional premise") for modern political economy or what Smith called freedom "in our present sense of the word" (see Robertson 1989, p. 241).

It follows as a converse to this thesis – one which has now been spelled out by Public Choice Theory – that there is every reason to *distrust* those – public officials, for example – who claim to be acting solely for the public good. Smith undoubtedly knew what he was talking about when he said: "I have never known much good done by those who affected to trade for the publick good" (Smith 1979, p. 456).

42 Arendt seems to admit to her excessive reading of Jeffersonian "happiness" when she writes:

> [T]he Declaration of Independence, though it blurs the distinction between private and public happiness, at least still intends us to hear the term "pursuit of happiness" in its twofold meaning: private welfare as well as the right to public happiness, the pursuit of well-being as well as being a "participator in public affairs." But the rapidity with which the second meaning was forgotten and the term used and understood without its original qualifying adjective may well be the standard by which to measure, in America no less than in France, the loss of the original meaning and the oblivion of the spirit that had been manifest in the Revolution.
>
> (Arendt 1965, p. 129)

Along with Benjamin Constant, whose views I shall consider in what follows, I would want to maintain for my part that the loss of "the original meaning" was not an instance of "oblivion" but of genuine progress in the notion of "happiness" and that of liberty in general.

43 Also more or less representative of this desire to rehabilitate the old idea of civic republicanism are Michael Walzer (1983) and Charles Taylor (1985). As Sartori has pointed out, however (1987, pp. 111–20), all appeals to the notion of participatory democracy are hopelessly underdefined and nebulous to the extreme; about the only really concrete meaning that can be given to the term is what he calls "referendum democracy," which is a formula for populist democracy of the most unreflective, knee-jerk, intolerant, and generally undesirable sort imaginable – the finest means ever thought of for realizing the "tyranny of the majority." For a careful assessment of both the virtues and the vices of "direct democracy" see Cronin 1989.

44 For a lucid exposition of Constant's political philosophy, see Holmes 1984.

45 A feminist writer, Anna Yeatman, makes the follow pertinent observations in this regard:

The alternative to representative models of democracy has been participatory democracy, which has been understood in terms of face-to-face community and a politics of equality. Everyone is put on the same level, difference is not able to be worked with, and, inevitably, those most adept at manipulating the communitarian ethos of the interaction prevail.

(Yeatman 1994, p. 52)

46 For an example of the customary opposition of civil society to the state, see Fish 1994. Contrasting with this view, an Arab affairs scholar, Iliya Harik, makes the following interesting remark: "The dichotomy between government and civil society that is posited in many of the standard scholarly accounts of democratization is more apt to be confusing than helpful when it comes to the Arab countries, where the role of government in the democratization process is so prominent" (Harik 1994, pp. 50–51). As we shall be seeing, government has, as a matter of principle, an important role in cultivating the structures of civil society.

47 In a totalitarian society such as the USSR, in contrast, the state indeed amounted in fact to nothing more than the Party that monopolized government and that spoke in its name.

48 As Rousseau remarked, the terms "republic," "state," and "city" (*cives*) are different ways of referring to the same thing, namely, the *people* as associated in a social contract (constitution) (see Rousseau 1977, bk. 1, ch. 6 [*"Du pacte social"*]). Although the word "state" has several different meanings, its ultimate meaning, Madison said, is "the people composing ... political societies [as organized into governments], in their highest sovereign capacity" ("Report on the Virginia Resolution," 1799–1800; cited in Meyers 1981, p. 233).

49 When using the term in the sense just defined I shall always spell it with a capital "S"; when spelled without a capital, the term will function in what has become its more common usage, i.e., meaning for all practical purposes the "government."

50 That "security" is the essential element in the "modern" conception of freedom is something that Montesquieu realized full well. Speaking of what we would call civil liberty, Montesquieu wrote: "Political liberty in a citizen is that tranquility of spirit which comes from the opinion each one has of his security, and in order for him to have this liberty the government must be such that one citizen cannot fear another citizen" (Montesquieeu 1989, bk. 11, ch. 6).

51 As Acton says a few pages further on:

[T]he possession of unlimited power, which corrodes the conscience, hardens the heart, and confounds the understanding of monarchs, exercised its demoralising influence on the illustrious democracy of Athens. It is bad to be oppressed by a minority, but it is worse to be oppressed by a majority. ... [F]rom the absolute will of an entire people there is no appeal, no redemption, no refuge but by treason. ... In this way the emancipated people of Athens became a tyrant; and their Government, the pioneer of European freedom, stands condemned with a terrible unanimity by all the wisest of the ancients. ... But the lesson of their experience endures for all times, for it teaches that government by the whole people, being the government of the most numerous and most powerful class, is an evil of the same nature as unmixed monarchy, and requires, for nearly the same reasons, institutions that shall protect it against itself, and shall uphold the permanent reign of law against arbitrary revolutions of opinion.

(Acton 1985, pp. 13–15)

52 Compare with the observations of Alain Touraine : "Today ... democracy is defined less by the sovereignty of the people than by the disappearance of any

240

sovereign. Democracy tends to be defined by respect for minorities and above all individual rights, and thus as an ensemble of rules which prevent the formation of absolute power" (Touraine 1992, p. 189).

53 For a further discussion of this issue see Madison 1986, pp. 74, 91.

54 While the Soviet (Brezhnev) Constitution adopted in 1977 (*Constitution* 1977) contained, like its previous Stalinist version, many references to human or civil rights (which never failed to impress a number of uncritical Western observers), these were, given the mode in which the Soviet regime invariably operated, no more than scratches on paper without any effective force in law, no enabling legislation having ever been passed in order to made them effective (the rule of law was never implemented in the USSR).

55 Section 1 of Article 14 reads: "All persons born or naturalized in the United States and subject to the jurisdiction thereof, are citizens of the United States and of the State wherein they reside. No State shall make or enforce any law which shall abridge the privileges or immunities of citizens of the United States; nor shall any State deprive any person of life, liberty, or property, without due process of law; nor deny to any person within its jurisdiction the equal protection of the laws."

Section 1 of Article 15 reads: "The right of citizens of the United States to vote shall not be denied or abridged by the United States or by any State on account of race, color, or previous condition of servitude."

56 This applies equally, if not especially, to the principle of taxation (a unique power granted only to government [but which, in their customarily uncivil fashion, mafias always attempt to usurp]). Taxation can be constitutionally justified only if it is uniform and universal, and if the revenues generated thereby are always dispensed only for the public good, never for the good of private individuals, purely as such (legitimate welfare programs excepted). All attempts on the part of governments to use taxation as a means for a (supposedly more egalitarian) "redistribution of wealth" have been a dismal failure, in all respects (see in this regard Drucker 1993). For a detailed study on the matter of taxation and its necessary relation to the common good, see Adams 1993.

Already in 1815, long before personal income tax and corporate taxes were introduced in Western countries, Benjamin Constant wrote in his "Principles of Politics":

> Any tax, of whatever kind, always has a more or less pernicious influence: it is a necessary evil, but like all necessary evils it must be made as negligible as possible. The more means are left for the use of private industry, the more a state prospers. Taxation, for the simple reason that it subtracts some portion of those means from that industry is inevitably damaging. . . . Excessive taxation leads to the subversion of justice, to the destruction of individual liberty.

> (Constant 1988, p. 271)

57 In all economically developed societies, the issuance of money – money being such an important factor in the "general Welfare" (and, as we shall see in the following chapter, in the communicative rationality of civil society) – has, as if by a Madisonian logic, now been removed from government control (at least in principle). Money is now issued no longer by government treasury departments but by autonomous central banks (in the US, the Federal Reserve), in accordance (in theory at least) solely with the judgment of the Governers of these banks and their readings of current financial/economic situations. A stop-gap measure, to be sure, as some would undoubtedly argue, but progress nonetheless.

58 It is interesting in this regard to note that in the constitutional debates in

Philadelphia in 1787 Madison proposed as an insert to the list of powers vested in Congress a power "to establish an University, in which no preferences or distinctions should be allowed on account of Religion." The motion was defeated (see Madison 1984, p. 639).

59 The reason being to combat the tendency towards corruption. An astute observer of human behavior, Smith wrote:

> When high roads, bridges, canals, etc. are in this manner made and supported by the commerce which is carried on by means of them, they can be made only when that commerce requires them, and consequently where it is proper to make them. Their expence too, their grandeur and magnificence, must be suited to what that commerce can afford to pay. They must be made consequently as it is proper to make them. A magnificent high road cannot be made through a desart [sic] country where there is little or no commerce, or merely because it happens to lead to the country villa of the intendant of the province, or to that of some great lord to whom the intendant finds it convenient to make his court. A great bridge cannot be thrown over a river at a place where nobody passes, or merely to embellish the view from the windows of a neighbouring palace: things which sometimes happen, in countries where works of this kind are carried on by any other revenue than that which they themselves are capable of affording.
>
> (Smith 1979, II, p. 725)

60 Peter F. Drucker, the well-known writer on economic affairs and business management and whose views on income redistribution policies will be cited in the following chapter, is often credited with coining the term "privatization."

61 The reason being that bureaucrats do not have and, by the nature of the beast, cannot have "the guts" required to be good entrepreneurs. The good entrepreneur is a risk-taker, whereas the good bureaucrat, by defintion, always "goes by the book." The logic under which the one operates is the "maximization of profits," while the logic under which the other operates is the "minimization of losses." These are incompatible systems, and they cannot be combined without producing a hybrid, and totally sterile, monster.

62 In addition to the economic inefficiency to which it invariably gives rise, direct government intervention in the economy is, in the twentieth century, one of the major factors contributing to the corruption of the political realm. Any number of instances could be cited in this regard (not the least of which being Italy), but for observations on the situation in France see Revel 1993.

63 The more, through "social self-organization," civil society can do for itself, the more bureaucrats are out of a job. A classic instance of "conflict of interests."

64 The policy in many American cities of creating self-taxing districts for the delivery of various public services and for neighborhood improvement known as business improvement districts (BIDs) is one way of going about implementing the principles of subsidiarity and self-responsibility.

65 It should perhaps be pointed out that, because a civil society is, by definition, self-organizing or self-regulating, the notion of the liberal State is altogether incompatible with that of the Welfare State, if by the latter one understands a state which assumes, as one of its major responsibilities, and on a permanent or on-going basis, direct responsibility for the economic well-being of the citizenry (this was, in theory at least, the principal legitimation for the Soviet regime [see Harding 1993]). In a genuine civil society, it is in the mutual interests of everyone that everyone should assume the maximum responsibility for their own welfare and should be as productive members of society as they possibly can be. For it is in this way, as Adam Smith pointed out, that the general welfare is best served. This is not to say

that a liberal State may not institute welfare measures of a temporary sort for those who, through no fault of their own, momentarily find themselves down and out. The rationale for liberal welfare measures is, however, that they should be such as, ideally, to cancel out the need for them, by enabling the recipients of public welfare to become productive members of society once again. Since, I said, this is in the interests of society as a whole, welfare measures of a liberal sort (what in former times was generally referred to as "relief") are a legitimate function of government, a legitimate "public good."

As the neo-leftists Arato and Cohen point out: "welfare state intervention in the name of serving the needs of civil society foster its disintegration" (Arato and Cohen 1992, P. 207).

66 Reported in *The Hamilton Spectator*, August 16, 1994.

67 A liberal democratic society must always be prepared to exercise "power" (force) in defense of the rule of law. It must, in particular, be prepared to utilize fully its police power to combat the extremely serious threat posed to civil society by organized crime.

68 Madison said: "[Justice] ever has been and ever will be pursued until it be obtained, or until liberty be lost in the process" (*The Federalist*, No. 51). One way of defining justice, a highly nebulous concept in most of the literature, would be to say that it is that state of affairs (always temporary) that results ("spontaneously") from the operation of a social-political order designed in accordance with the principle of the "equal liberty of all," in other words, an order designed to "maximize" the common good.

69 As Hayek says:

> [T]he "public sector" should not be conceived of as a range of purposes for the pursuit of which government has a monopoly, but rather as a range of needs that government is asked to meet so long and in so far as they cannot be met better in other ways. . . .To develop this independent sector and its capacities is in many fields the only way to ward off the danger of complete domination of social life by government.
>
> (Hayek 1979b, pp. 49, 51)

70 Compare with Rhoda Howard:

> Liberal democracy is, in a sense, the most difficult political system to honour. It requires tolerance of those who are different. It requires protecting the rights of those whom you hate. The price of having your own rights protected is protecting the rights of those whom you would rather see punished for their crimes, whether the crimes be economic exploitation, ethnic or religious difference, or refusal to defer to the authority of people considered superior.
>
> (Howard 1992b, p. 18)

71 Compare with the remarks of Yegor Yakovlev, editor of *Moscow News*:

> You see, when we say we are learning democracy, it doesn't just mean we are learning to vote. It means we are learning that democracy is a two-way street that requires a two-way psychology – the ability to tolerate opposing views. We even have to learn to coexist with the [ultra nationalistic] Pamyat Society, which I detest. A few years ago I would not have objected if those people had been sent to Siberia to hold their meetings. Now I understand that if the Pamyat Society is sent to Siberia, eventually I'll be on my way there, too. Not everybody thinks this way. There is a group that wants to impose order by punishing people who say something wrong. People on both sides of our

debates still want to prove that their opponent has dirty underwear. The problem is, we just aren't used to normal debate. God grant us the wisdom to learn to act democratically.

(Yakovlev 1988, p. 211)

As Mouffe says in this regard:

[W]ithin the context of the political community, the opponent should be considered not as an enemy to be destroyed, but as an adversary whose existence is legitimate and must be tolerated. We will fight against his ideas but we will not question his right to defend them. The category of the "enemy" does not disappear but is displaced; it remains pertinent with respect to those who do not accept the democratic "rules of the game" and who thereby exclude themselves from the political community.... This "agonistic pluralism" is constitutive of modern democracy and, rather than seeing it as a threat, we should realize that it represents the very condition of existence of such democracy.... The great strength of liberal democracy ... is precisely that it provides the institutions that, if properly undersood, can shape the element of hostility in a way that defuses its potential.

(Mouffe 1993, pp. 4–5)

Compare Mouffe's observations with those of Hayek:

We must face the fact that we here encounter a limit ot the universal application of ... liberal principles.... These limits do not constitute fatal flaws ... since they imply merely that, like tolerance in particular, liberal pinciples can be consistently applied only to those who themselves obey liberal principles, and cannot always be extended to those who do not.

(Hayek 1979b, p. 56)

72 Mouffe's only error – which she falls into on a regular basis – is in thinking that somehow this does not describe "the liberal idea of political association."

73 As Oakeshott observes:

The government of a collectivist society can tolerate only a very limited opposition to its plans; indeed, that hard-won distinction, which is one of the elements of our liberty, between opposition and treason is rejected: what is not obedience is sabotage. Having discouraged all other means of social and industrial integration, a collectivist government must enforce its imposed order or allow the society to relapse into chaos.

(Oakeshott 1962, p. 51)

74 See Samuel P. Huntington: "How were democracies made: They were made by the methods of democracy; there was no other way.... They were made by leaders in government and opposition who had the wisdom to recognize that in politics no one has a monopoly on truth or virtue" (Huntington 1991, pp. 164–65).

75 A point also stressed by Huntington:

In Eastern Europe, Solidarity from the start opposed revolutionary tactics and supported nonviolence. As one Solidarity leader put it during the organization's underground phase, when the temptation to use violence was presumably strongest, Solidarity was "against any acts of violence, street battles, hit squads, acts of terror, armed organization – and we do not accept any responsibility for violent acts." "We know lots of revolutions, great revolutions, and magnificent people, said Walesa, "who after taking over power, produced systems that were much worse than the ones they destroyed."

Those who start by storming bastilles, Adam Michnik similarly warned, end up building their own.

(Huntington 1991, p. 21)

Chile in the late 1980s and South Africa in the early 1990s are two other notable examples of self-limiting democratic revolutions.

76 For an account of the demise of revolutionism (the ideology of revolution) in what was formerly called the Third World, see Colburn 1994. Colburn defines revolution ("the accession of the extremists") as

the sudden, violent, and drastic substitution of one group governing a territorial political entity for another group formerly excluded from the government, *and* an ensuing assault on state and society for the purpose of radically transforming society. . . . An attempt at social transformation entails a massive, and inescapably violent, restructuring of social stratification.

(Colburn 1994, pp. 6–7)

77 Lefort observes how what is new in the various demands for human rights is that

they are not looking for an overall solution to conflicts through the conquest or destruction of established power. Their ultimate objective is not that famous inversion which would place the dominated in the position of the dominators and pave the way for the dissolution of the state. . . . Thus one sees the formation of a *social power* in which a multiplicity of elements, apparently distinct, and less and less formally independent, combine around political power.

(Lefort 1986, p. 262)

It may be noted in this regard how the Chinese Democracy Movement, even in its momentary failure, stood for this new kind of civil politics. As the writer Liu Xiabo stated in a manifesto issued at the time:

We must use a democratic spirit of tolerance and cooperation to begin the construction of democracy in China. For democratic politics [as opposed to the Leninist-Maoist politics of "class struggle" – "this traditional mentality of hatred, this enemy consciousness, and the practice of meeting violence with violence"] is a politics without enemies and without a mentality of hatred, a politics of consultation, discussion, and decision by vote, based on mutual respect, mutual tolerance, and mutual accommodation.

(in "Han Minzhu" 1990, p. 350)

78 One reason which may account for why the Tiananmen Square demonstrations in 1989 ended in disaster is the confrontational tactics pursued by extremists such as Chai Ling and Li Lu, whose deliberate purpose was, apparently, to provoke a bloody confrontation with government forces (see Tyler 1995a, p. 12).

79 As one Chinese citizen very dramatically points out, trust is a virtue which is noticeably absent from socialist society. In such a society: "Any person can choose to become an informer for a day if he has a grievance against you. You can never be sure whom to suspect and therefore never know whom to trust either. The result is that you suspect and fear almost everyone. . . . The whole environment seems hostile" (see Link 1992, p. 190).

80 In regard to economic matters, trust is a function of a citizen's assurance that government will be fiscally and monetarily responsible and "self-limiting."

81 In §199 of *Elements of the Philosophy of Right* Hegel, in speaking of "the interlinked dependence of each on all," remarked (in a somewhat German mode):

In this dependence and reciprocity of work and the satisfaction of needs, *subjective selfishness* turns into a *contribution towards the satisfaction of the needs of everyone else*. By a dialectical movement, the particular is mediated by the universal so that each individual, in earning, producing, and enjoying on his own account, thereby earns and produces for the enjoyment of others.

(Hegel 1991, §199)

82 In regard to this phenomenon, see for instance Wriston 1992. The loss of sovereignty on the part of nation-states due to postmodern economic developments (greater free trade and the macroeconomic adjustments on the part of nation-states required to facilitate this) should in no way be cause for lament ("lament for a nation," as a famous Canadian social theorist once put it). For as one political scientist has carefully demonstrated in the case of four countries (Taiwan and Mexico, Japan and Italy), these developments, in calling forth greater international solidarity, have at the same time been a major factor in world-wide democratization (Ferdinand 1994). In contrast, attempts in the opposite direction, at protectionism, autarky and national self-sufficiency, have always increased international tensions and have been a major factor making for war.

83 Lindblom writes: "By several criteria, the most elaborate mutual adjustment process in the world flourishes in the form of market systems" (Lindblom 1990, p. 241).

84 See also pp. 473–74:

What occurred in the spring of 1990 was a revolution of consciousness, and not just in the former Soviet bloc but throughout the world. There was suddenly a general consensus that the market, private property, and democracy formed an organic whole; that one could not have the rule of law, human rights, constitutional government, and political pluralism without a material "base" for civil society in personal property and freedom of economic choice. This package suddenly came to define the only possible form of a feasible society – or what people in Eastern Europe now called a "normal" society – as opposed to the abnormal ideological world of scarcity, servitude, and structural inefficiency.

(Malia 1994, pp. 473–74)

5 THE ECONOMIC ORDER

1 On p. 7 Przeworksi writes:

What was it that collapsed in Eastern Europe? "Communism" is a neutral answer to this question, since it is a label that has no more advocates. But was it not socialism? Many of those who believe that there can be no socialism without democracy contend that the system that failed in Eastern Europe was perhaps Stalinism, statism, bureaucracy, or communism, but not socialism. Yet I fear that the historical lesson is more radical, that what died in Eastern Europe is the very idea of rationally administering things to satisfy human needs – the feasibility of implementing public ownership of productive resources through centralized command; the very project of basing a society on disinterested cooperation – the possibility of dissociating social contributions from individual rewards. If the only ideas about a new social order originate today from the Right, it is because the socialist project – the project that was forged in Western Europe between 1848 and 1891 and that had animated social movements all over the world since then – failed, in the East and in the West. True, the values of political democracy and of social justice continue to guide social democrats such as myself, but social democracy is a program to mitigate the effects of private ownership and market allocation, not an alternative project of society.

(Przeworski 1991, p.7)

2 I do not mean to single Cohen and Arato out for special criticism. I am simply using them as examples of what I find to be an extremely widespread tendency among neoleftist thinkers, however skilled and refined they might otherwise be in political theory (and Cohen and Arato are nothing, if not that), a tendency, that is, to fall into the grossest of naïvetés when they issue pronouncements on economic matters (this, it would appear, is a general failing of members of the Frankfurt School who are not particularly renowned for their expertise in economic science). It is, for instance, utter nonsense to claim, as Cohen and Arato nevertheless do repeatedly and as a matter of common course and in a fashion which, I repeat, is typical and not a failing peculiar only to them: "Institutions which must be coordinated communicatively come under the heading of [']civil society', whereas those which must be *steered* by money and/or power come under the institutional level of system" (Cohen and Arato 1992, p. 214). What such a pronouncement fails to take account of is the fact that to the degree that an economic "system" *is* "steered" or controlled and *is not* "coordinated communicatively," to that precise degree it *is not* a free market economy.

3 Mouffe says, for instance: "One of my main theses ... is that in order to develop fully the potentialities of the liberal ideals of individual freedom and personal autonomy, we need to dissociate them from the other discourses in which they have been articulated and to rescue political liberalism from its association with economic liberalism" (Mouffe 1993, p. 7). On p. 18 Mouffe proclaims her allegiance to "anticapitalism" – along with "antiracism" and "antisexism."

4 A good example of this sort of conceptual confusion (amounting in point of fact to sheer nonsense) is reflected in the following remarks of one such neoleftist who, in reflecting on the "disturbingly novel" events of 1989, says in an article with the revealing title, "The World Reconsidered: A Brief Aggionamento for Leftist Intellectuals":

It has been quite clear for a long time that the Soviet-type economy does not function well. It has also become clear that the traditional Yugoslav model, based on decentralization and self-rule on the enterprise level, had severe difficulties. I thus assume that most leftist intellectuals tend to support some kind of market economy within political frames which allow for some version of the planned market. These are deep changes among Western leftist intellectuals: the pure market economy remains unattractive, but also the Yugoslav model of economic life has lost its attraction, and the Soviet model has lost its plausibility; what remains is some kind of mixed economy, of a social democratic nature.

(Skirbekk 1992, pp. 121–22)

Having both a planned economy and a free market would seem to be the socialist version of having your cake and eating it too! For a hermeneutical inquiry into the Yugoslav system of "workers' self-management," see Prychitko 1991.

5 Milton Friedman, for instance, would have us believe that when one buys a particular product one is in effect "casting a vote" and that there is, accordingly, no difference between this and voting in a democratic election (the implication being that "economic democracy" is no different from political democracy). This is, to be sure, utter nonsense, a gross *abuse* of metaphor. For an excellent treatment of how economic freedom – while indeed being freedom in a very real sense – nevertheless differs in important ways from political freedom, see diZirega 1989.

6 For a critical discussion of the largely *socialist* policies advocated by the American Catholic hierarchy, see Block 1986.

7 The best analysis (in many ways, the only study of its kind) of the logic of socialist systems is the monumental work of the Hungarian economist, Janos Kornai (1992). As an economist, Kornai analyses the total political economy of Socialism from a chiefly economic point of view. Malia (1994) does much the same sort of thing (in regard to the Soviet Union), but from a chiefly political point of view. These are, to be sure, arbitrary distinctions, since the chief characteristic of socialist regimes is that they allow for no distinction between the economic and the political (as well as the cutural). This is the reason why throughout this study I spell Socialism with a capital 'S': Socialism is a *total* (and totalizing) system. In contrast, "capitalism" designates not a total, homogeneous system (and is thus never capitalized); "capitalism" designates but one, autonomous realm of civil society. (In line with what is perhaps the most atavistically fundamental of all socialist fairy tales, most leftist "conspiracy" theories would have us believe that "capitalists" – Jewish bankers in particular – dominate all of civil society.)

   As an "ideal type" (a concept to be discussed later in this chapter), the market economy is the same everywhere and is universal, but the way in which an economy of this type is institutionalized in practice will vary from country to country, due to differing historical and cultural factors.

8 As Kornai writes (speaking about both the highly developed and the developing capitalist economies):

> There too one finds excessive centralization, a propensity for the bureaucracy to overspend, and bargaining between superiors and subordinates in hierarchical organizations. There too one encounters shortage phenomena, particularly in sectors subsidized by the state. There too one observes cases of paternalistic authorities intent on deciding on the citizen's behalf. There too experiments are made with central planning and price control. There too it occurs that large firms on the brink of insolvency are rescued from their financial predicament. I need not continue. The socialist system presented such phenomena in their ultimate form, which makes it a particularly instructive environment for studying them.
>
> (Kornai 1992, p. xxii)

9 Both Michael Polanyi (1962) and Don Lavoie have drawn instructive comparisons between the functioning of the scientific (knowledge) enterprise and the economic market place. Lavoie says for instance:

> The role controversy plays in ferreting out less defensible belief in science has its counterpart in the role rivalrous competition and the calculation of profit and loss play in eliminating less economically viable methods of production. . . . It is only through the intricate pressure being exerted by this rivalrous struggle of competition (or criticism) that new workable productive (or acceptable scientific) discoveries are made and that unworkable (or unacceptable) ones are discarded.
>
> (Lavoie 1995, p. 132)

10 For a discussion of the contribution of the Greek Sophists and rhetoricians to the ideal of communicative rationality, see Madison 1982 and Madison 1989a.

11 For a detailed description of this new phenonemon, see Wriston 1992.

12 "Yet I am persuaded that the central Marxist argument for the irrationality of capitalism is both fundamental and valid" (Przeworski 1991, p. 105).

13 For readers not overly familiar with economic theory, the following remarks of Przeworski may help to clarify what economists mean by "equilibrium":

The model [developed by Walras (1874), Edgeworth (1881), Pareto (1927), Pigou (1932), and others] is simple: Individuals know that [*sic*; no doubt "what"] they need, they have endowments, and they exchange and engage in production whenever they want. In equilibrium no one wants to do anything else given what others have done or will do; or, equivalently, the expectations under which individual agents act are all fulfilled. Moreover, in equilibrium all markets clear. Hence, the prices at which individuals exchange reflect their preferences and relative scarcities; these prices inform individuals about the opportunities they forsake. As a result, resources are allocated in such a way that all gains from trade are exhausted, no one can be better off without someone else being worse off, and the resulting distribution of welfare would not be altered under a unanimity rule. These are three equivalent definitions of collective rationality (optimality in Pareto's sense).

(Przeworski 1991, p. 105)

For observations on the history of the concept of equilibrium, see Pribram 1983, pp. 612–23.

14 For a clarification of the meaning of "objectivism," see Madison 1991a.

15 These writers also make the following interesting point:

If one argues that the equilibrating tendencies of markets are an empirical regularity, then human society must be tending toward a state of affairs without money, without firms, without any market institutions....[T]he very existence of coordinating processes in markets depends upon non-equilibrium situations. Moreover, the closer one gets to an equilibrium state the less effective the coordinating role of institutions becomes. What, then, does this say about the theory of spontaneous order? It seems that the very ordering processes that arise spontaneously in a market are undermined by the mechanical metaphor of equilibration.

(Boettke, Horwitz, and Prychitko 1994, p. 64)

For a listing of the "appallingly unrealistic assumptions" underlying the notion of general economic equilibrium, see Prychitko 1993a, p. 569.

16 Odd it is too that main line neoclassical economics should have nothing to say about the real world, human agents, apart from whom the object of economic science, viz., human transactions, would not exist. It is indeed a methodological absurdity when a central doctrine such as equilibrium, in order to have any scientific meaning, must in effect postulate that individuals do not exist. As Boettke points out, quoting Frank Hahn (*On the Notion of Equilibrium* [1973]: "Traditional equilibrium theory does best when the individual is of no importance – he is a measure zero" (see Boettke 1990c, p. 36).

17 Przeworski can maintain that the "anarchy critique" of the market economy is vindicated only in as much as "recent developments of economic theory" have proven incapable of sustaining equilibrium theory (see Przeworski 1991, p. 108). If the Austrian critique of neoclassical economics is right however, all that this proves is that the concept of equilibrium is not the right one for understanding the market economy.

In a passing reference to Austrian economics, Przeworski remarks on how "Austrian models, which assume that trades are consummated out of equilibrium, cannot substantiate the Pareto conclusions" (ibid., p. 108). As if these "models" were meant to do that! In the light of the rejection of equilibrium on the part of the neo-Austrians, this is truly an ironic remark. See for instance the remarks of Sanford Ikeda:

From the point of view of market process theory, the usefulness of an equilibrium-based, normative construct such as Pareto optimality, long the centerpiece of neoclassical welfare economics, is severely limited as a normative criterion. Its chief weakness has little to do with the traditional criticisms that have been levelled against it (for example, those of Kaldor, Hicks, Scitovsky, and Arrow). Indeed, most of its alternatives share the same limitation as the Pareto criterion, namely an exclusive focus on situations in which radical ignorance [a basic principle in Austrian economics] is absent and agents possess all relevant information. They fail to recognize what modern market process theorists refer to as the "knowledge problem", wherein decision makers find themselves radically ignorant of relevant information dispersed among different individuals across the market. The impossibility of complete knowledge on the part of an actor about the current and future states of the world renders moot the question of whether an actual change produces a Pareto improvement.

(Ikeda 1994, pp. 24–25)

18 The antipathy of Marxists and other leftists towards *money*, which they consider to be an "alienating" force in human affairs (cf. the all-important Marxist conceptual distinction between "use value" and "exchange value"), is on a par with the antipathy of metaphysicians ever since the time of Plato and his war against the rhetoricians towards *words*. Just as Plato believed that words alienate thought from itself, so likewise Marxists believe that money alienates the products of human labor from human workers. Whether it be in Lenin's Soviet Union under "war Communism" or Pol Pot's revolutionary Kampuchea, one measure Marxists invariably seek to take at one point or another is that of abolishing money altogether, just as they seek to abolish the free exchange of words. (In Pol Pot's socialist regime, any use of words after the day's work, if even only for humor, was punishable by immediate, on-the-spot execution.)

19 It may be noted that in the purely ideal world of general equilibrium there is no real place for money (see Horwitz 1992b, pp. 17–18).

20 Cf. Fernand Braudel

.a forest that is not made use of by man, or the money hoarded by a miser are outside [social] production and cannot be considered capital goods. But money that passes from hand to hand, stimulating commerce, or is used to pay rents, incomes, profits and wages – money that is in circuits, forcing open doors and dictating the speed of flow, is a capital good.

(Braudell 1982, vol. 2, p. 241)

21 In socialist systems, the free exchange of goods and services always continued to occur, even though they were prohibited by socialist law. These exchanges involved, however, hefty "transaction costs" of an illegal nature, to wit, bribes, pay-offs, or kick-backs.

22 Addressing the "paradox of value" that had long bedevilled economic reasoning (why is it that things with an "intrinsically" higher value nevertheless fetch a lower price in the market?), Molina wrote:

In the first place, it should be observed that a price is considered just or unjust not because of the nature of the things themselves – this would lead us to value them according to their nobility or perfection – but due to their ability to serve human utility. Because this is the way in which they are appreciated by men, they therefore command a price in the market and in exchanges. . . . What we have just described explains why rats, which, accord-

250

ing to their nature, are nobler than wheat, are not esteemed or appreciated by men. The reason is that they are of no utility whatsoever. This also explains why a house can be justly sold at a higher price than a horse and even a slave, even though the horse and the slave are, by nature, more noble than the house.

(Chafuen 1986, pp. 100–1)

Molina went on to point out how *utility* should not be interpreted in a narrow "utilitarian" sense:

In the second place, we should observe that the just price of goods is not fixed according to the utility given to them by man, as if, *caeteris paribus*, the nature and the need of the use given them determined the quantity of price … it *depends on the relative appreciation which each man has for the use of the good.* This explains why the just price of a pearl, which can be used only to decorate, is higher than the just price of a great quantity of grain, wine, meat, bread or horses, even if the utility of these things (which are also nobler in nature) is more convenient and superior to the use of a pearl. That's why *we can conclude that the just price for a pearl depends on the fact that some men wanted to grant it value* as an object of decoration.

(Chafuen 1986, p. 101)

23 The increasing practice for employers to screen just about every aspect of their employees' private lives (Do they smoke? Do they consume alcohol? Do they eat too much? Do they exercise? Do they engage in hazardous recreational activities? etc., etc.) is a case in point.

Even Humbolt, who argued for an extremely limited role for the state, this being restricted almost exclusively to providing for the *security* of individual citizens, would have to agree that government intervention is fully justified in this case – precisely in order to defend the security of individuals (see Humbolt 1993).

24 For an explicit attempt to conceive of economic science itself in terms of rhetoric, see McCloskey 1985, as well as Klamer, McCloskey, and Solow 1988.

25 See also in this regard Lavoie 1992. Arguing against the sort of position defended by Habermas, Lavoie maintains that free market processes are not "steered"; they are "driven by no one." Lavoie explicitly likens the "creative discovery procedure" of the market to the kind of *conversations* that characterize the cultural realm of a civil society: "Just as verbal discourse is a communicative process that must be set free to do its work of discovery, so are markets. . . . The free market's discovery process is open-ended in the same sense that a conversation [in the Gadamerian sense] is" (Lavoie 1992, p. 445). On the open-endedness of the market process see the seminal work of Hayek, "Competition as a Discovery Procedure," in Hayek 1978.

26 For a treatment of money as a "linguistic" phenomenon, bringing Gadamerian insights to bear on the matter, see Horwitz 1992a and 1992b. Many of the insights that Simmel expressed in *The Philosophy of Money* have been incorporated into Austrian economic theory. For a discussion of Simmel's views on money, see Frankel 1977.

27 Thus, as Lavoie further says,

Without the benefit of a price system, decision-makers who are faced with the bewildering variety of technologically possible methods of production would hit upon a set of economically feasible methods only by the most bizarre accident. . . . [B]y reducing to a manageable size the mind-boggling variety of conceivable methods of production, the price system performs an indispensable service.

(Lavoie 1995, p. 128)

28 To maintain that monetary prices in a free market economy are a form of communicative rationality is, of course, to maintain that the understanding of the economic world requires interpretation and that economics is, so to speak, a "regional hermeneutics." Peter Boettke underscores this point when he remarks:

> [T]he ideas of money as a language and the market as a text necessitate a recognition of the role of interpretation. What happens in the market is a constant process of interpretation and reinterpretation that acquires inter-subjective validity through the social institutions of the market – money, prices, profits, and the like. As well, what happens during the economist's attempts to make sense of the market is a process of interpretation. The theorist is interpreting the texts of the market within the common framework of economic theory. Finally, what happens between economists as they engage in conflict over these interpretations of the market is itself an interpretive process. . . .Approaches to economics that ignore or discount these interpretive dimensions (as does neoclassical economics) are unlikely to provide much help in rendering the institutions of the market process, and the scientific process, intelligible to any great degree.
> (Boettke 1990b, p. 104)

Like numerous other social scientists, Boettke is following up on Paul Ricoeur's suggestion that human action can appropriately be understood on the model of text-interpretation, as a text-analogue (see Ricoeur's seminal article, "The Model of the Text: Meaningful Action Considered as a Text," reprinted in Ricoeur 1981).

29 Don Lavoie remarks on how Gadamer's notion of *play* (*Spiel*) is ideally suited to conceptualize the market process as a communicative or dialogical process (see Lavoie 1989).

30 As Palmer observes:

> There was no "given" demand for portable computers, video games, genetic engineering, or CD players, to take four recent examples, before they were developed by inventor/entrepreneurs who "created" (i.e., persuaded) the demand for them. In such cases, the end result could not have been implicit in the "initial" conditions, which did not include *any* demand for these items.
> (Palmer 1987, p. 103)

Another example of a product for which there was no demand before it was dreamed up by a clever entrepreneur is gourmet dog water, marketed under the label "The Thirsty Dog" by the Original Pet Drink Co. based in Fort Lauderdale, Florida. and which, within two months of its introduction in 1994, sold over 10,000 cases.

31 Lavoie remarks in this regard:

> Hayek's knowledge-dispersal argument is really an entirely different kind of justification for "private enterprise" than the welfare economists' notion that perfect competition represents an ideal state of efficiency. In a sense one might say that the argument is not that competition gives us the optimal combination of resources but rather that competition represents a procedure for the discovery and dissemination of information that would otherwise not be available in any usable form.
> (Lavoie 1995, p. 116)

32 Things do not work this way in the real world. The fact of the matter is that expansionary policy tends never to remain constant but always to increase at an accelerating rate (see Hayek 1960, ch. 21). In this regard Simmel remarked:

It may appear ... that the inconveniences of an unlimited increase in the volume of money are attributable not so much to the increase itself, but rather to the way in which it is distributed. Shocks, hypertrophy and stagnation occur only because the newly created money is initially in one hand and spreads from there in an uneven and inappropriate manner. This might be avoidable if a way could be found of distributing the money equally or according to some principle of equity. Thus, it has been said that if every Englishman were suddenly to find that he had twice as much money in his pocket, all prices would increase correspondingly but no one would gain any advantage; the only difference would be that the pounds, shillings and pence would have to be calculated in larger amounts. ... There is little to be gained from a discussion of such hypotheses, based upon quite unrealizable presuppositions.

(Simmel 1990, pp. 161–62)

Attempts to cope with inflation by means of "indexation," such as practiced by Brazil in the 1970s, proved not to be the panacea they were touted as but dismal failures (Brazil has long since abandoned its "indexation" policy and is now attempting to deal with its endemic problem of inflation by strictly monetary means [i.e., by limiting the supply of money]).

33 As Simmel states:

The excessive increase in money creates pessimism and mistrust among the people, so that they attempt to dispense with money and to fall back upon barter and promissory notes. This reduction of the demand for money leads to a further decline in the value of the money in circulation. The authority responsible for issuing money attempts to counteract the decline in value by further increasing the supply of money; thus supply and demand drift apart, and the reciprocal effects that we have noted produce a cumulative decline in the value of money.

(Simmel 1990, p. 161)

34 According to Przeworski, there is nothing inherently wrong with the socialist blueprint for society – if, that is to say, the following assumptions were to obtain: "If individuals truthfully revealed their needs and their productive potential, if they exerted effort independently of reward, if planners behaved as perfect agents and could solve problems of optimal allocation, then socialism would generate all the wonderful effects its proponents advertise" (Przeworski 1991, pp. 112–13). Socialism and capitalism as conceptualized by neoclassical equilibrium theory have at least one thing in common: the unreality of their assumptions! See Lebowitz (1991, pp. 366–67) for a frank admission that the building of Socialism would require the building of the "new man," a fundamental transformation of human nature.

35 It is almost as if Yakovlev were responding to Novak when he says that

in the real life of a totalitarian society. ... for decades antimoral phenomena increased almost daily. This was encouraged not only by the replacement of family ties with class affiliation, by the contempt for the principles of a civil society, and by bans on religion, but by the even greater need to cheat and act evasively in every respect. I do not refer here to the amorality of politics as a whole in which the individual was regarded only as a means and not as the end of social initiatives.

(Yakovlev 1993, p. 199)

Not only does a free market economy "favor in its citizens forms of generosity, trust, extroversion, and reliance on the good faith of others," as Novak says, it also promotes *civility*.

> Decades under Communist rule have shaped people's thinking about trade, and the differences in attitudes and behavior between East and West can, [James] Buchanan suggests, be explained in terms of economic theory. In the West, the buyer is typically at an advantage: he offers money to the seller in exchange for goods or services, and money is more generally desired than other goods. The result is that sellers of goods adopt a deferential attitude toward buyers; they tend to treat potential buyers with courtesy and to advertise in order to attract their business. In the East, this deferential attitude is wholly absent.
>
> (Paul et al., 1993, p. ix)

36 See in this regard Mittermaier. Of this particular "category mistake" that economists are ever so prone to make, Mittermaier says:

> [A]n economist engages in mechanomorphism when he ascribes mechanical properties to what is otherwise recognized as an aspect of human affairs or when he treats an economic system as though it were a mechanical system. In its most general sense we may understand mechanics to be concerned with matter in motion. In the Newtonian formulation, a mechanical system involves concepts of space, time, force, point mass, and derivations from these. Equilibrium clearly comes from this domain of thought and talk of equilibrating or market forces must be regarded as mechanomorphic. Consumption and saving, which normally are regarded as activities, acquire a mechanical aspect as macroeconomic aggregates. They are treated as though they were quantities of a substance, perhaps a liquid flowing through some kind of system – the conception Coddington called hydraulicism.
>
> (Mittermaier 1986, p. 237)

Like the Austrians, I prefer to refer to the central problem of economic theory as that of *coordination*, deliberately avoiding the term often used by neoclassical economists, viz., "allocation mechanisms." The latter term has undesirable instrumentalist and "mechanistic" implications, whereas "coordination" underlines the fact that it is the lifeworld activity of real human beings that constitutes the true object of economics. As Kornai very aptly observes:

> Neoclassical economists frequently use the expression "allocation mechanism"; they consider analysis of the allocation of scarce resources as the purpose of economics. In the usage of this book coordination embraces allocation, but the emphasis is on the fact that it is living people who transfer inanimate objects, resources, and information from one place of availability to another and utilize them. It is living people who need coordination if the inanimate resources are to be allocated by their agency and direction.
>
> (Kornai 1992, p. 95)

37 For a detailed historical study of how neoclassical economics has, in the most uncritical of ways, sought to model itself after classical physics, see Mirowski 1989 (as well as Mirowski 1988a). For an early critique of the physicalistic approach to economics, see Hayek 1979a and, for a discussion of Hayek's position, Madison 1989c.

38 The tight monetary policy I have implicitly advocated in my preceding remarks on inflation is in no way the kind of steering mechanism that writers speak about

when they view the economy in a purely instrumentalist way. Monetary policy of this sort is not intended to produce any "quick fixes" or to exert direct control over specific outcomes. Its purpose is merely of the "cultivating" sort (mentioned in the preceding chapter). Its *raison d'être* is simply that of creating a stable monetary climate in which individual economic agents can go about their own business in security and trust. As I shall be arguing in the following section, government can and should do what it can to promote a favorable economic *climate*, but it should under no circumstances attempt to control the day-to-day economic *weather* (a distinction I borrow from Drucker 1993).

39 The important thing in the economic realm, as in the political realm, is not just that citizens have rights but that they should feel *secure* in their rights. As William Riker and David Weiner observe:

> The efficient use of economic resources requires not only that rights to property be currently effective (clearly allocated to individuals, alienable at low cost, and secure from trespass), but that those now exercising the rights believe that they will continue to enjoy their effectiveness in the future. In other words, they must believe that they have a credible commitment from government to preserve the rights. The less credible the commitment, the less willing individuals will be to forgo current consumption to accumulate capital and preserve the economic value of natural resources, activities that contribute to future private and social wealth. A fear that one will not be able to enjoy the potential future gains from risky efforts to invent, adapt, and adopt new technologies, both in production and organization, slows the innovation that drives long-term economic growth.
>
> (Riker and Weiner 1993, p. 87)

These remarks point out the reason why the "right to property" should be clearly listed in the *constitution* of a civil society (see in this regard Siegan 1994).

40 On the role played by law and the political sphere in the rise of capitalism, see North and Thomas 1973.

41 And, in any event, the right to property is now fully "entrenched" in most human rights documents.

42 For phenomenological observers of the human condition, there is a great irony in the proclamation on the part of seventeenth- and eighteenth-century thinkers of the "natural rights of man." No one much before that time ever really suspected that there were any such things. This is obviously a case where the rhetoric of human rights far exceeded at the time the philosophical justification that was needed for them (Jefferson admitted as much; see Madison 1986, pp. 263–64); and thus we witness one of those curious "historical inversions" that are so common in human affairs. Norberto Bobbio describes this particular hermeneutical curiosity in the following fashion:

> The course of history led from an initial state of servitude, by way of a gradual process of liberalization, to the conquest by the subject of growing areas of liberty, but the doctrine proceeds in the opposite direction: only by taking as its starting-point a hypothetical initial state of liberty, and conceiving of man as naturally free, does it arrive at the construction of a political society [civil society] in which sovereignty is limited. Thus it is that the doctrine – here the doctrine of natural rights – inverts the course of historical events, treating as origin or foundation, as *prius*, that which is historically the result, which occurs *posterius*.
>
> (Bobbio 1990, p. 8)

43 Although, like all liberals of his time, Constant paid lip-service to the notion of "natural" rights (no better theoretical notion being yet available), he did (in contrast with Locke) recognize that the right to private property is a *social* right through and through. Society guarantees the right to private property because this is what is in the best interests of society as a whole. As Constant said:

> Property is by no means prior to society, as without the security which gives it a guarantee, property would simply be the right of the first occupant, in other words, the right of force, that is to say a right which is not a right at all. Property is not independent from society, because a social condition, albeit a very miserable one, can be conceived without property, while it is impossible to imagine property without a social condition. Property exists only through society.... Property is merely a social convention. But if we recognize it as such, it does not follow from this that we consider it as less sacred, less inviolable, less necessary, than those writers who subscribe to a different system.
>
> (Constant 1988, p. 262)

44 While there is a quasi-universal recognition that this is indeed the way things should appropriately work in the cultural realm ("excelling" in your chosen field is here considered to be the most natural of things [who would ever propose stamping out all the budding Einsteins and Mozarts?]), the idea that people should be allowed to excel in the economic realm often runs into a great deal of opposition. As the on-going attempt to privatize the state property of the former Soviet Union demonstrates, however, "privatization" can work for the overall betterment of society. As one writer observed in early 1994:

> In addition to influencing interest formation, privatization promises to recast the relationship between the citizen and the state. In the old Soviet system, the workplace served as the main locus of social control. The state's monopoly on employment and control over enterprises, combined with management's ability to grant or deny access to scarce goods and services supplied through the workplace [such as housing], guaranteed the state's hegemony over the citizen. The system also killed off the professions and professional organizations as autonomous entities and as possible sources of intermediation between the individual and the state [exactly, as we saw in Chapter 4, as the policy of the Ontario Government is designed to do]. Privatization, along with the fragmentation of the old *nomenklatura* system, has already released some Russians from direct dependence on the beneficience of the state. Political control over employment and occupations has fallen off, opening the way for genuine professions and professional associations to emerge. The spread of property ownership has also created pools of autonomous resources in society – sources that political parties, interest groups, independent trade unions, and church organizations might draw on for material support.
>
> (Fish 1994, p. 37)

45 Cf. Malia (1994, pp. 498–99): "[T]he suppression of 'capitalism' – in the form of private property, profit, and the market – means the extermination of civil society and the statization of all aspects of life."

46 On the economic virtues of owner-based autonomy, see Arnold 1992.

47 Speaking of the post-revolutionary situation in Eastern Europe, Riker and Weiner observe:

> When the legal system – especially criminal law, tort law, and the judicial

resources to implement them with certainty, fairness and swiftness – fails to guarantee freedom from trespass, those who control property may find that certain of its uses are not feasible because they expose property to easy trespass, and that other uses demand high investments in self-protection. The opportunity for profitable trespass may induce predatory behavior that hinders efficient use of property and diverts labor and entrepreneurial effort from socially productive activities. An extreme example is the formation of "mafia," organizations that threaten the use of force to extort or steal from businesses. As in the case of contracts, the formerly socialist countries face difficulty in creating freedom from trespass because an appropriate legal tradition and adequate judicial resources are lacking.

(Riker and Weimer 1993, p. 87)

On the lack of a proper legal framework and the upsurge of crime in the former USSR, see A. Cohen 1995.

48 As one commentator observes: "The creation of the market cannot be left to the market itself. An external agency is required if anything more than a freebooting, carpet-bagging market is to be created, and this is the strong state" (Sakwa 1994, pp. 65–6). For a description of the *un*civil market economy see also Milanovic 1989, p. 68.

49 For information on the background role played by Hayek and the Austrian school of economics in the construction of the German social market economy, see the numerous references to these subjects in Peacock and Willgerodt 1989a. Erhard, along with Walter Eucken and Wilhelm Roepke, was a member of the Mont Pèlerin Society founded by Hayek in 1947.

50 Ever the socialist J.K. Galbraith, then Chief of the Division of Occupied Areas in the U.S. State Department, wrote in March of 1948:

During the past two years it has been asserted with increasing frequency and vehemence that if, somehow, the German economy could be freed from materials and manpower regulations, price controls and other bureaucratic paraphernalia then recovery would be expedited. . . . Yet there never has been the slightest possibility of getting German recovery by this wholesale repeal, and it is quite possible that its reiteration has delayed German recovery. The question is not whether there must be planning – the assignment of priorities to industries for reconstruction and rehabilitation, the allocation of materials and manpower, the supplying of incentive goods and all the rest – but whether that planning has been forthright and effective.

(cited in Willgerodt 1976, p. 64)

51 As one commentator observes: "Private property, another of [Walter] Eucken's formative principles, is not only intended to ensure the workability of the system, but also to have regard to human dignity" (Lenel 1989, p. 30).

52 The underlying idea here was that social solidarity and the promotion of the common good is best served by creating a legal order which maximizes the opportunies for individuals to pursue their own well-being. As one writer remarks:

In a workable market economy, free initiative and individual self-interest are guided by competition in the direction of the general interest. Competition is therefore an indispensable complement of freedom. It should not only favourably influence innovative activity and the process of price formation, which is important for coordination; it should also contribute to the safeguarding of freedom by the provision of alternatives. Then private initiative should produce an overall economic and also socially beneficial increase in performance. The obstruction of privite initiative . . . is likely to harm the general interest.

(Lenel 1989, p. 29)

53 Hayek formulated this principle in the following way:

> [O]ne of the guiding considerations in resorting to the technique of deliberate organization where this is indispensable for the achievement of particular goals, must always be that we do not do so in a manner which impairs the functioning of the spontaneous market order on which we remain dependent for many other and often more important needs.
>
> (Hayek 1979b, p. 46)

54 Another notable way in which the German neoliberal *Wirtschaftsverfassung* parallels Madisonian constitutionalism is the way in which it was premised on the same fundamental philosophical principle, viz., that "governments" should be designed for people as they actually are (creatures of limited virtue) and not as they might be capable of becoming in an ideal world (see Chapter 4, note 14, p. 233). Wilhelm Roepke summed up this principle in the following way:

> When studying so many projects of economic and social reform one has the uneasy feeling that their authors never asked themselves the simple question: Who is to carry through all those fine-spun schemes? . . . In all those projects, and particularly those of a collectivist kind, there is above all the "human bottleneck" to consider, but it is exactly this which is all too often entirely overlooked. . . . There is indeed little use in making blueprints of theoretically perfect machines for the economic process with the one but capital fault that they do not work because men, governments and societies are as they are. . . . We need economic systems and monetary standards which correspond both to the average intelligence and the average morality of men. They have to be [institutionally] fool-proof, and they must suppose neither heroes nor saints nor intellectual giants but men with their average ethics and brains.
>
> (Roepke 1987, p. 12)

55 The predictive value of ideal type analysis is noted by Hayek in his discussion of Mengerian economics; see Hayek 1992, p. 103.
56 According to Menger, the three-fold function of ideal-type (hermeneutical) analysis is that of "understanding, predicting, and controlling" (Menger 1985, p. 64). As I have argued elsewhere (Madison 1991c), the ultimate justification of hermeneutical *theory* (as a theory *of* practice) is its significance *for* practice.
57 This is the basic reason why (as I argued in Chapter 1) attempts to institute a free market economy in formerly socialist countries should eschew a "gradualist" approach and should opt instead for global and radical reform. "Shock therapy" is required precisely because of *the mutual exclusivity of the logics of the two systems.* Speaking on the basis of his own experience as finance minister in the first Solidarity-led government of Poland which launched the radical liberalization program that became known as "the big bang" on January 1, 1990, Leszek Balcerowicz writes:

> From our analysis, a clear conclusion emerges. Given the typical initial conditions of a socialist economy, a country will be better off politically and economically in the medium-to-long run if it adopts a radical and comprehensive economic reform program as quickly as possible after the political transition, implements as much of this program as possible during

the brief period of extraordinary politics, and then stays the course of reform by implementing far-reaching institutional changes.

(Balcerowicz 1994, p. 88)

For a detailed analysis by Harvard economist Jeffrey Sachs of Poland's successful transition to a market economy, see Sachs 1994. Sachs helped to design Poland's transition strategy, and he gives a good description of how all the key elements in the radical reform package were – as one would expect that they would have to be given that every system has its own logic – systematically interrelated and mutually reinforcing (see in particular Sachs 1994 pp. 48–57).

58 Sullivan goes on to say:

On the contrary, markets are well-developed institutions based on highly complex sets of politically formulated, government-enforced rules – in other words, laws. The formation of modern limited-liability corporations, for example, presupposes sound and enforceable commercial law – something that postcommunist societies need to develop if they hope to become state market democracies.

(Sullivan 1994, p. 149)

59 There is, for instance, a lesson in this for reformers in China, as the Chinese scholar Nien Cheng points out:

[I]n my view, the limits placed on ownership and the insistence on adhering to "half and half" – that is, to a socialist economy and a market economy existing side by side – are the two most serious stumbling blocks to a thorough and speedy transformation of China's economy and any real improvement in the standard of living. . . . China is faced with the choice between socialism and a market system; a mixed system is doomed to failure. The obstacles to China's development can be removed only if China goes all the way toward a private market system with constitutional protections for both economic and civil liberties. . . . Reality . . . requires that China embark on thoroughgoing reform or face the prospect of being left behind in the wake of the liberal revolution that is now sweeping the globe.

(Cheng 1990, pp. 333–34)

60 Even in the most "capitalist" of countries, the state will likely have some direct involvement in the economy. Publicly owned companies will, however, operate in accordance with the principle of market coordination – posing in this way no threat to the system as such – when they are relatively few in number and importance. As Kornai says: "The behavioral norms of the narrow public sector then resemble the behavior of the dominant private sector of the economy" (Kornai 1992, p. 495, n. 35).

61 I am here using the word "revolution" in the way in which Kornai does (see Kornai 1992, sec. 16.3).

62 The words "in theory" should perhaps be emphasized. While a *laissez-faire* economy is arguably a "pure" type, the idea of such an economy operates with thoroughly unrealistic assumptions and is thus, for this very reason, not an *ideal* type, i.e., a construct which can usefully describe real world economics.

Sociologist Peter Berger also views capitalism and Socialism as two ideal types (see Berger 1986, pp. 21–2). He does not, however, emphasize the "distinctiveness" of these two different types as much as I wish to. Indeed, he locates different types of economies on a continuum, one pole of which being "a pure market economy" (by which he means "an imagined paradise of laissez-faire economics") and the other pole being "an economy in which all decisions are determined by political allocation," i.e., Socialism – everything else in between being, presumably, some form or other of "mixed economy." In my opinion, this is a misleading way of viewing things. While "capitalism" – the civil market economy as I have described it – and Socialism are indeed polar opposites, the idea of a pure *laissez-faire* economy should be situated on a wholly different conceptual register. The reason for this is that *laissez-faire* is a purely economic concept (as its advocates portray it, such an economy is totally independent of the political order), whereas both Socialism and the civil market economy are not pure economic concepts but rather *political-economic* concepts (both of these types are dependent on state "intervention" – albeit of two altogether different sorts).

63 To express the point in question in a slightly different way, it is not a requirement for an order to be "spontaneous" that it have arisen "spontaneously," i.e., by gradual "evolution" (as in the case of the British Constitution). A spontaneous order can equally well be the result of deliberate design – the Madison Republic and the German Social Market Economy being prime instances in this regard. Market economist Karen Vaughn recognizes this when she writes:

> Spontaneous orders can be thought of in two, related ways. They can describe a set of regularities in a social system that is self-organizing in some way within the context of a set of social rules. In this interpretation, the constraints in the system could well be set by human design and can work for good or ill. Alternatively, spontaneous orders can be thought of as evolved orders where the rules themselves are the unintended products of human actions.
>
> (Vaughn 1989, p. 171)

It may be noted in this regard that Hayek often tends to fall into the error of equating spontaneous orders solely with the latter alternative.

64 Peter Drucker, the well-known writer on economic and business issues, observes in this regard:

> The Megastate has been least successful as fiscal state. Nowhere has it succeeded in bringing about a meaningful redistribution of income. In fact, the past forty years have amply confirmed Pareto's Law, according to which income distribution between major classes in society is determined by two factors, and two factors only: the culture of the society, and the level of productivity within the economy. The more productive an economy, the greater the equality of income; the less productive, the greater the inequality of income. Taxes, so Pareto's Law asserts, cannot change this. But the advocates of the fiscal state based their case in large measure on the assertion that taxation could effectively and permanently change income distribution. All our experience of the last forty years disproves this claim. . . . Despite all its corruptions and scandals, the most egalitarian country is now Japan – the country of the fastest productivity increases and the fewest attempts to redistribute income through taxation.
>
> (Drucker 1993, pp. 131–32)

Evidence of a different sort – of a reverse kind, so to speak – of the futility of government-imposed redistribution measures is furnished by the case of the "Four Little Dragons" (South Korea, Taiwan, Hong Kong, and Singapore) where in the 1960s and 1970s a clean break with what could be called the Third World Syndrome and a resolute reliance on capitalist value-added production geared to the world market resulted in a dramatic reduction in income inequalities and in an income distribution comparing very favorably with Western advanced industrial societies – *and this in the absence of the kind of redistributionist and welfarist policies advocated by Western social democrats*. By contrast, Latin America, which only began to shed its traditional anticapitalist, mercantilist mentality in the late 1980s and early 1990s, has the world's most uneven distribution of wealth (according to World Bank statistics, in 1994 the richest 20 per cent of Brazilians earned 26 times as much as the poorest 20 per cent; in the U.S. that ratio was 9 to 1).

65 See Cohen and Arato 1992, pp. 464, 466. As they also remark:

> Directly or indirectly, the forms of economic dysfunction of the welfare state not only interfere with the mechanisms of the capitalist economy but are harmful to many of the strata that redistributive politics are designed to support. This is true because the expansion of the unproductive public sector becomes a drag on capital accumulation, which in turn restricts the fiscal resources available for public spending.
>
> (Cohen and Arato 1992, p. 465)

66 For an attempt to articulate systematically a theory of participatory democracy in the tradition of C. B. Macpherson and focusing in particular on "economic democracy" and workers' self-management, see Gould 1988.

67 In the past, advocates of "workplace democracy" regularly appealed to the "Yugoslav Model." What this form of economic organization most clearly demonstrates, however, is the economic inefficiency of "workers' self-management." See in this regard Prychitko 1991.

68 For an account of the baleful effects of the "corporatist mentality," see Barry 1987, Chapter 5. As Barry observes:

> Corporatism rests on foundations diametrically opposed to liberal individualism. It rejects the idea of a society as a "civil association" of individuals held together by general rules. . . . Instead the corportist presupposes that such an association will mutate into a system of power blocks which will confront each other in a socially destructive manner unless their behaviour is not co-ordinated *artificially*.
>
> (Barry 1987, p. 132)

69 Communication in the market place, Lavoie reminds us, extends well beyond mere verbal communication. As he says:

> Democracy must subsume not only the situations of literal dialogues, but also the many ways in modern society in which we are able to communicate at a distance with one another. When applied to our discourse, democracy lets us make verbal transactions with whomever we want to talk to. But if we truly extend democracy to cover the economy, we must be able to make any other kinds of voluntary transactions with whomever we want to. Economic democracy should borrow the core values of democracy but should apply them to both those situations where people exchange words and those where they exchange deeds.
>
> (Lavoie 1992, p. 446)

Economic democracy so conceived is precisely what permits the creative discovery process to operate in economic matters, contributing thereby, as all democratic practices should, to the general welfare. As Lavoie goes on to say:

> For the same reasons that science and the arts should not be under the control of any single institution but should be left to freely evolve, so should markets. . . . Removing obstacles to free-market interaction unleashes the same kind of social power as opening up discourse. The driving engine of

261

intellectual development is freedom of discourse; the driving engine of economic development is freedom of economic action.

(Lavoie 1992, p. 446)

70 "If we return to the model of conversation," he says,

we see that what makes a discourse democratic is precisely the fact that it is *not* under any participant's control. Just as a good discussion takes on a life of its own and participants are carried along by its flow [Lavoie is alluding here to Gadamer's notion of "play"], so markets constitute an open-ended process with its own systematic dynamic.

(Lavoie 1992, p. 451)

71 Madison, "Property," *National Gazette*, March 29, 1792; cited in Meyers 1981, p. 187.

72 Although it would seem that the "right to work" in this sense is guaranteed by the *Universal Declaration of Human Rights*, art. 20, sec. 2, which states: "No one may be compelled to belong to an association."

73 Cf. Madison:

That is not a just government, nor is property secure under it, where arbitrary restrictions, exemptions, and monopolies deny to part of its citizens that free use of their faculties and free choice of their occupations which not only constitute their property in the general sense of the word [i.e., their "indubitable, unalienable, and indefeasible rights"], but are the means of acquiring property strictly so called.

(cited in Meyers 1981, p. 187)

74 Thus, for example, in order to protect the "right to work" on the part of all of its citizens, the state has an obligation to combat attempts on the part of special interest groups to "corner" the market for themselves.

75 The reason why rights should be constitutionally specified is to remove them from the vicissitudes of political whim. As Peter C. Ordeshook states: "Constitutional specifications of rights should be viewed as an attempt to remove issues from the domain of politics so as to reduce the opportunities to create unstable outcomes" (Ordeshook 1993, p. 216). It is especially important that rights issues should be removed from the domain of politics in the case of multi-ethnic, -racial, etc. societies. Multiculturalism of the undesirable sort I described in Chapter 2 (granting quasi-constitutional status – rights – to diverse groups) is one of the worst policies imaginable in a civil society. By its very nature it weakens the structural cohesion of society and undermines the constitution order – which is to say that it works directly against the promotion of human rights and against the equal justice and liberty for all that these rights are meant to ensure.

76 Siegan cites the following remarks of the US Supreme Court:

[T]he intractable economic, social and even philosophical problems presented by public welfare assistance programs are not the business of this Court. . . . [T]he Constitution does not empower this Court to second-guess state officials charged with the difficult responsibility of allocating limited public welfare funds among the myriad of poential recipients.

(Siegan 1994, p. 67; Dandridge v. Williams, 397 U.S. 471, 487 [1970])

77 When economic rights are viewed not as "negative" but as "positive" rights, i.e., as entitlements, as something that people have come to regard as their due regardless of what they may or may not have done to merit these benefits, or when, as in the case of affirmative action and so-called equity programs, social benefits are allo-

cated without regard to what the *Declaration* of 1789 referred to as people's talents and abilities, the result is that there develops in the general population a number of uncivil dispositions – such as envy and ill will – which are destructive of social trust and solidarity and thus of civil society itself. This is something that Mill noted when he wrote:

> Where there exists a desire for advantages not possessed, the mind which does not potentially possess them by means of its own energies is apt to look with hatred and malice on those who do. The person bestirring himself with hopeful prospects to improve his circumstances is the one who feels good will toward others engaged in, or who have succeeded in, the same pursuit. And where the majority are so engaged, those who do not attain the object have had the tone given their feelings by the general habit of the country, and ascribe their failure to want of effort or opportunity or to their personal ill luck. But those who, while desiring what others possess, put no energy into striving for it, are either incessantly grumbling that fortune does not do for them what they do not attempt to do for themselves or overflowing with envy and ill will toward those who possess what they would like to have.
>
> In proportion as success in life is seen or believed to be the fruit of fatality or accident, and not of exertion, in the same relation does envy develop itself as a point of national character.
>
> (Mill 1958, p. 49)

78 Consider for instance the matter of paid holidays (listed as a "right" in the *Universal Declaration of Human Rights* [art. 24] and in the *International Covenant on Economic, Social and Cultural Rights* [art. 7(d)]). This is properly speaking not a right but an entitlement. There is, moreover, no need even to list it as a "right," since the matter can be quite adequately dealt within the context of what *is* a human right in the proper sense of the term, viz., the right to association. Paid holidays and other such material benefits are matters to be *negotiated* between employees and employers. In contrast, rights, being absolute, are never negotiable (although they may, in states of emergency, be suspended or severly restricted).
   It is as if the authors of the documents mentioned assumed that all workers worked for either the state or large firms. What about the self-employed? Does it make any sense to say that a family of Korean immigrants, for instance, who work seven days a week in their corner store in order to amass capital so as to improve their living standards in the future have a "right" to paid holidays? Who owes them this right? To what tribual can they address themselves in order to claim it as a right? A fundamental maxim of effective human rights legislation is, as Jack Donnelly formulates it: "If human rights are to continue to be conceived of as paramount moral rights, we need to keep their number as small as possible" (Donnelly 1989, p. 159).

79 On the following page, Elshtain states: "I am not so naive or foolish as to believe we can do without the state. The state, properly chastened, plays a vital role in a democratic society. Rather, I am worried about the *logic* of statism, which looks to the state as the only entity capable of 'solving a problem' or responding to a concern" (Elshtain 1995, p. 18).

80 It is not justly acquired property that, as Proudhon wildly proclaimed, is theft; it is, rather, government mandated redistribution of wealth that is theft. It is a form of social *in*justice when some are made to lose so that others may win and when government intervention in the economy does not promote the common good. As Abraham Lincoln pointed out, "You cannot help the poor by ruining the rich."

NOTES: CHAPTER 5

It may also be noted that in many instances the principal beneficiaries of state welfarism are not the poor but the middle class administrators of state welfare programs. As Moises Naim points out with regard to Latin America:

> Those familiar with the inner workings of Latin-American public bureau-cracies know that discharging an agency's formal functions weighs much less in determining its daily operations than does the need to serve as a welfare agency for its employees and their families. Even the social security system is as much a means to transfer resources to its employees as it is a mechanism to serve the outside clients that justify its existence.
>
> (Naim 1994, p. 38)

81 Referring to what he calls the "conventional statist conception of social justice," Michael Novak writes:

> Most leftists who use the term social justice wish (unwisely) to employ the power of the state to allocate goods and positions to selected groups. They should have learned long since that history knows no surer way to heighten inter-group antagonisms. By contrast, true social justice begins by removing systems of political allocation and group favoritism, so that the rule of law may be applicable to every individual equally: "the rule of law, not of men." Individuals differ so in personality, ability, character, talent, effort, family background, and even luck that no just system can predetermine or enforce equal outcomes. Therefore, true social justice inspires the just to design general rules and procedures, rooted in experience that (1) apply to all impersonally; and (2) produce economic growth, from whose benefits none are excluded. The first condition defeats envy, summoning personal accountability to center stage. The second furthers the common good of all and raises the hope of all.
>
> (Novak 1993, pp. 176–77)

For a detailed analysis which attempts to show how attempts to achieve through multiculturalism, affirmative action, and other such statist means – and which ignore those cultural differences between individuals and groups which are mainly decisive for their economic performance and well-being – are only likely to make things worse off, see Sowell 1994.

82 As Marx pointed out, no other "mode of production" has done more to raise human productive capacities and to transform the material condition of human life. As he and Engles stated in *The Communist Manifesto*:

> The bourgeoisie, during its rule of scarce one hundred years, has created more massive and more colossal productive forces than have all preceding generations together. Subjection of nature's forces to man, machinery, application of chemistry to industry and agriculture, steam-navigation, rail-ways, electric telegraphs, clearing of whole continents for cultivation, canalization of rivers, whole populations conjured out of the ground – what earlier century had ever a presentiment that such productive forces slumbered in the lap of social labor?

Were this assessment to be up-dated to take account of all the productive forces that the "bourgeoisie" *has continued to unleash* over the course of the subsequent century and a half, it would be no less true today than it was in 1848. It would, in fact, be even more true now that Socialism, the "alternative society" that Marx and Engels claimed would supersede capitalism and would be even more efficient than it, has been tried out on a grand scale and has been found wanting, has in fact proven to be a decidedly less efficient means for promoting the general welfare.

264

83 This means that to the degree that in a market economy exchanges are voluntary, they are also, to that degree *just* (which means in turn that *social justice* is best served by an economic system that promotes free market transactions). As the Spanish scholastics maintained, truly voluntary exchanges are always just (*Volenti non fit injuria*) (Chafuen 1994, p. 491). However, like Hayek who underscored the need in a free market system for legislation designed to prevent "fraud and deception (including exploitation of ignorance)" (see p. 152 above), the Salamanca school of economic thinkers maintained that "ignorance on the part of the buyer or seller could, in certain cases, render the transactions involuntary" – and thus unjust (Chafuen 1994, p. 491). As Chafuen goes on to say: "Although the late scholastics tolerated the pursuit of profit due to better knowledge of the market, they morally condemned those who took advantage of an ignorant customer." The sixteenth-century scholastic Francisco Garcia maintained that transactions are coercive and "implicitly violent," and thus unjust, when market forces are distorted either by monopoly (the privileging of some sellers over others by the state) or cornering the market (preventing others from buying) (Chafuen 1986, pp. 111–12). And Adam Smith himself clearly observed how the "private interest" of "merchants and manufactures" easily leads them to indulge in fraudulent and deceptive practices and to enter into conflict with the "general interest" that a genuinely free market promotes.

84 Cf. Braudel:

> Mercantilism was ... quite simply a policy of each for himself, as both Montaigne and Voltaire wrote, the first in general terms: "One man's advantage can only mean another man's loss"; the second more specifically: "It is clear that one country can only gain if another country loses." (1764)
>
> And the best way to gain advantage, according to the mercantilist states, was to attract to one's shores the greatest quantity of the world's stock of precious metals, and thereafter to prevent it from leaving the kingdom.
>
> (Braudel 1982, p. 544)

85 The crucial words here are "in the short run." What principally serves to distinguish the liberal version of welfare from that of the Welfare State is that the latter would grant "welfare rights" to the citizenry on a permanent and on-going basis, fundamentally transforming thereby the relation between the individual and the state in such a way as to undermine individual autonomy and responsibility.

86 Cf. the following remarks of Adam Smith in defense of a policy of high wages over against the mercantilist policy of low wages:

> Servants, labourers and workmen of different kinds, make up the far greater part of every great political society. But what improves the circumstances of the greater part can never be regarded as an inconveniency to the whole. No society can surely be flourishing and happy, of which the far greater part of the members are poor and miserable. It is but equity, besides, that they who feed, cloath and lodge the whole body of the people, should have such a share of the produce of their own labour as to be themselves tolerably well fed, cloathed and lodged. . . .
>
> The liberal reward of labour, as it encourages the propagation, so it increases the industry of the common people. The wages of labour are the encouragement of industry, which, like every other human quality, improves in proportion to the encouragement it receives. A plentiful subsistence increases the bodily strength of the labourer, and the comfortable hope of bettering his condition, and of ending his days perhaps in ease and plenty,

animates him to exert that strength to the utmost. Where wages are high, accordingly, we shall alway find the workment more active, diligent, and expeditious, than where they are low.

(Smith 1979, pp. 96, 99)

APPENDIX: ON CIVIL SOCIETY AND INTERNATIONAL JUSTICE

1 The potential "downside" to global developments currently underway is that the new world order may in fact turn out to be a new world *dis*order (see in this regard Hoffmann 1992). The demise of national sovereignty and the weakening of the power of central governments concomitant upon the rise of ethnonationalistic tribalism could well mean an increase, everywhere, in local hostilities and, indeed, in a transformation of the very nature of warfare itself. The former Yugoslavia furnishes a vivid example of the kind of "postmodern" warfare we have to fear (see R. Cohen 1995). Unlike the Gulf War which was of a traditional sort with nation-states confronting nation-states, the actors in postmodern warfare would be numerous mutually antagonistic groupings and ethnically-based militias (cf. Rwanda) relying on relatively unsophisticated (and readily available) weaponry and engaging in what has come to be called "low-intensity warfare" without set battles. Precisely because these conflicts would not be between states, there would be no ready means for resolving them through negotiation and binding arbitration. In addition, they would likely be extremely bloody conflicts, since no readily discernible distinction would exist between armies and populations. Even where peace-keeping forces are introduced, they would, as in Bosnia, tend to become simply one warring faction among others. In such a situation, everyone would become the enemy of everyone else in a kind of Hobbesian global civil war.

2 As Latin American and African countries have begun to realize, the formation of regional blocks of free trade (such as Mercosur, grouping together Brazil, Argentina, Uruguay, and Paraguay) is a most important factor in development. It could in fact be stated as a general principle that the more free trade is facilitated, the greater will be the pay-off in terms of development. For a discussion of the forces of a patrimonial sort that continue however to militate against the creation of regional free trade in west Africa, see Howard W. French (1995). One factor in particular is the way in which hitherto the World Bank has operated in areas such as west Africa; as French observes: "[T]he World Bank and other lenders duplicate Africa's balkanization and ultimately help perpetuate it by organizing their projects on a country-by-country basis" (French 1995, p. E14).

It can be expected that the more countries in, for example, west Africa or southern Africa engage in free trade and the more they are able in this way to develop competitive and profitable industries, the more attractive they will be to foreign capital investment – a crucial element, along with technology transfers (largely through transnational corporations), in making for sustainable development. (On the issue of foreign capital investment, see for instance Rohatyn 1994.)

3 In 1981 Reagan stated that "unless a nation puts its own financial and economic house in order by providing economic incentives and commercial opportunities, no amount of aid will produce progress" ("Reagan Cautions Developing Lands on Economic Help," *New York Times* [September 30, 1981]; cited in Krauss 1983, p. 15).

4 As a study of twenty-nine sub-Saharan African economies (*Adjustment in Africa: Reforms, Results, and the Road Ahead*) released by the World Bank in March of 1994 reveals, those countries – six altogether (Ghana, Tanzania, Gambia, Burkina Faso,

Nigeria, and Zimbabwe) – which instituted radical economic reform also managed, from 1987 to 1991, to achieve net growth in per capita terms while others which resisted liberalization "saw their median GDP growth fall to a level of minus 2 percent a year" (1994a):

> The countries that made the biggest economic changes, like Ghana, saw their growth rates and consumption rise and more goods to buy in the marketplace, the study found. Those that made the fewest changes, like the Ivory Coast and Cameroon, became further mired in recession and saw increases of as much as 50 percent in the number of their people living in poverty.
>
> (Friedman 1994a)

5 It is interesting to compare the views of Michael Manley, a real-world politician attuned to reality and capable of learning from it, with those, published at roughly the same time, of Kai Nielson, a Canadian-American philosopher and long-time Marxist who apparently remains unaffected by global developments and firmly attached to the old shibboleths. Writes Nielson:

> What I think is plainly true is this: our capitalist masters, in principal control of the consciousness industry, have a plain interest in maintaining something not very different from the present North-South state of affairs. Capitalism requires . . . at most a somewhat improved and efficient version of the present that, in turn, requires a great injustice and inhumanity. A necessary but not sufficient condition for attaining the end of such global injustice and inhumanity is the shedding of capitalism.
>
> (Nielson 1992, p. 32)

6 When in 1982 the Canadian Broadcasting Corporation (CBC) produced a program ("Up the Down Elevator") detailing widespread abuses of the foreign aid allotted to Tanzania by Canada (then totaling the not insignificant sum of 25 million dollars), the Nyerere government responded by banning visits on the part of all Canadian journalists. Money, it's true, does not buy respect. For an exposition of the ideology of *Ujaama*, see Nyerere 1962.

7 Cf. Pei:

> Despite their recent impressive economic performance records, East Asian neoautocracies such as China, Vietnam, Indonesia, and Burma face many of the well-known political problems associated with autocracies undergoing rapid socioeconomic changes. The most serious peril confronted by all these regimes is the pervasive official corruption in the economy, weak legal institutions, and low-quality civil service.
>
> (Pei 1994a, p. 100)

8 Despite its spectacular economic progress, South Korea still suffers from the disruptive effects of state interventionism under its former dictator, General Park Chung Hee, and has a great deal yet to accomplish by way of institutional reforms: "South Korea presents a cautionary tale. Its policy-makers resolved to switch to liberal policies 15 years ago. They are still struggling" (*The Economist*, June 3, 1195, survey 17).

9 Economist Shyam J. Kamath says of India:

> Today, after forty-five years of planned economic development, India's per capita income remains around $300. Almost 40 percent of Indians live below the official poverty line, and the absolute number of Indians in that category increased sharply between the late 1950s and the mid-1980s. India

lags behind the majority of nations on most indicators of the quality of life such as literacy, life expectancy, nourishment, access to safe drinking water and sanitation, and so forth. Considering that almost one-sixth of humanity resides in India, the failure of centrally directed development planning has produced an economic and social debacle of much larger proportions than was witnessed by the collapse of socialism in Eastern Europe and the Soviet Union.

(Kamath 1994, p. 91)

10 As of 1994, India's bloated public sector employed more than 18 million people, of which about 2.1 million were workers in India's vast job-for-life, state-run enterprises (see Burns 1994, p. F5).

11 A personal note: when I visited Buenos Aires in 1972, I made a point of changing money twice a day, once in the morning and later in the afternoon. By late afternoon, I would receive additional pesos for my dollars, inflation having proceeded apace in the meantime. When I attempted to phone La Plata, some twenty miles distant, it took close to an hour for the state-owned telephone company to get the call through. I was told that business people will often pay a visit in person to those with whom they wish to talk, the frustrations involved in trying to make a telephone call being just too great. Apprehensive of the civil unrest I feared might follow, I advanced my departure time and left Argentina for Paraguay only hours before Peron was due to return from exile in Spain – recalled to power in what was predictably to turn out to be yet another failed attempt at "national salvation."

12 Though it is not the same in the two. Since gaining independence in 1947, India has adhered to the basic principles of (liberal) political democracy and is indeed, as is often said, the world's largest democracy. Under Nehru's guidance, however, it also adhered to a version of the Soviet system of a planned economy and thus did not permit – indeed, effectively outlawed – *economic democracy*. Because of this, the forces of civil society in India have been severely constrained (the basic human right to private ownership of property, even residential housing, has been grotesquely handicapped [see Kamath 1994]). Postcolonial, sub-Saharan Africa has not only not allowed civil societies to develop but has, until recently, rejected political liberalism as well. Since, as the historical record shows, nationalist and statist policies serve only to exacerbate social tensions in ethnically diverse countries, the only way of overcoming the kinds of ethnic (or religious) hostilities endemic to India or Africa is through the development of civil society, i.e., a society in which individual liberties take precedence over communal "values," and the market economy necessary for the existence of the former.

13 The Ghanaian economist and journalist George B. N. Ayittey provides the following illustration of the institutionalized thievery long practiced by Africa's socialist regimes:

Unbelievable brutalities were heaped upon peasant farmers and traders under Ghana's inane price controls (1982–83). Furthermore, Ghanaian cocoa farmers in 1983 were paid less than 10 percent of the world market price for their produce.

In Gambia, peanut producers received about 20 percent for their produce the same year. According to *West Africa* (Feb. 15, 1989, 250):

"On the average, between 1964/65 and 1984/85, the peasants of Gambia were robbed of 60 percent of the international price of their groundnuts! For 20 years, the Jawara Government 'officially' took, free of charge, 3 out of every 5 bags, leaving the peasant with a gross of 2. With deductions for subsistence credit fertiliser, seeds, etc., the peasant would end up with a net one bag out of five. . . . With these facts, it is simply wrong to say that the poverty of the peasant derives from the defects of nature – drought, over-population, laziness, and so on."

(Ayittey 1994, p. 163)

14 A good example of how universal standards must be adjusted to the exigencies of time and place is furnished by the attempt to formulate electoral laws guaranteeing "free and fair elections." Possible variants of electoral laws that can legitimately lay claim to being democratic are quasi-infinite, and no one model can prevail over all others. For a more detailed discussion of the theoretical bases of this issue, which could properly be labelled that of "hermeneutical application," see Madison 1995.

15 In a news release dated July 21, 1994, a contrite World Bank, on the occasion of its fiftieth anniversary, confessed to its past sins, having formerly, as it says, put more emphasis on "huge dams and power plants" rather than on "human development projects." As journalist Thomas L. Friedman writes: "Human resource develop-ment now accounts for 17 percent of all World Bank loans, as opposed to 5 percent a decade ago" (Friedman 1994b). A significant, if not overwhelming, improvement in the Bank's record.

One example of how the Bank can do better (and at negligible cost) by helping people more directly is its Road Maintenance Initiative (RMI) undertaken in the mid 1990s. After discovering that every dollar "saved" by cash-starved African governments in road repairs increased the operating costs of vehicles by at least $2 or $3, the Bank organized seminars in various African countries to receive input not only from bureaucrats but, most importantly, from the actual users of the road system. It was discovered that users were willing to pay more for road use through fuel tax, licences fees, and tolls, on the condition that the revenue thereby gener-ated be specifically earmarked for road maintenance. Besides discouraging governments from squandering the funds they receive by way of general revenue (governments find it much more glamorous to spend their money on building things rather than merely keeping them in good repair), a scheme such as this has the great merit of generating two very important by-products, so to speak, of a permanent or "institutional" sort. As *The Economist* states:

> Getting road users involved in the system for managing roads is akin to establishing a market: civil servants and construction companies are sud-denly made aware of their ultimate customers. Users can influence the choice of new roads to build, and the split between new construction and maintaining the existing network.

(*The Economist* June 10, 1995, p. 72)

In the second instance, this kind of scheme based on popular involvement helps to resolve the perennial free-rider problem. As *The Economist* also states:

> Any public good such as roads gives people scope to benefit without paying. The opportunity is greatest in Africa, where tax collectors are ineffectual and easily bribed. In Zambia, for example, the Bank reported that half of all vehicles were not licensed. But once road funds receive licence fees, each user has an incentive to ensure that everyone pays his share.

(ibid.)

16 Ayittey refers to this state of affairs as "economic barbarism," of which he says:

> Elsewhere in Africa [outside of Tanzania], the experience with development planning proved to be an unmitigated disaster. From 1965 to 1986, Africa's annual rate of growth of gross national product (GNP) averaged a

deplorable 0.9 percent. With a population growth rate of 3 percent, that meant declining levels of economic welfare for the average African. Real income per capita dropped by 14.6 percent for all of Black Africa from its level in 1965. Unadjusted for inflation, GNP per capita grew by a mere 1.4 percent in the 1960s and 0.5 percent in the 1970s. The 1980s began with declines in income per capita.

(Ayittey 1994, p. 155)

17 As I mentioned in Chapter 4, patriotism, as I there defined it, is a laudable virtue. Nationalism, especially in its "ethno" versions, is, however, a debilitating vice which serves only to reinforce a people's political and economic backwardness.
On the growing wave of "internationalization," Scalapino says:

> Although various forms of economic nationalism are still resilient and may be expected to mount new challenges in response to the trauma of rapid internationalization, virtually every nation now recognizes that the autarkic economy is outmoded; and all of them are seeking, in one way or another, to participate in the international division of labor. Thus, a growing transfer of skills and technology to the developing societies is underway, and economic regionalism of various types is coming into being, cutting across ideological-political lines.

(Scalapino 1989, pp. 127–28)

18 Callaghty also points to the inner contradiction in "alternatives" such as Adedeji's when he says: "These imagined republics and imagined economies are rarely fleshed out in any detail, and when an effort is made to elaborate on them, it often concludes with a demand that the outside world pay for their implementation – again showing a fundamental lack of insight into the hard realities of 'self-reliant development'" (Callaghty 1994, p. 141).

19 For a sobering account of the economic havoc wrought on Burma under the decades-long tyranny of General Ne Win in his dogged pursuit of the "Burmese Road to Socialism," see Chirot 1994.

20 It amounts to a refusal to grant people the fundamental human rights they are entitled to when third world critics of "eurocentrism" allege that they are not needed in their countries, since they have other, more "traditional" means of respecting the dignity of the person. For an argument against this version of exceptionalism, see Donnelly 1989.

21 Moreover, in the modern world, appeals to tradition can all too easily lead to populist authoritarianism and even fascism, which can, as Howard notes, look for support to "traditionalist arguments about the nature of community and the need for the group to take precedence over the individual" (Howard 1992b, p. 18). Umberto Eco has pointed out how one of the abiding traits of the fascist mind-set is its "cult of tradition" (see Eco 1995, p. 14). In his study of modern tyrannies, Daniel Chirot observes how "it is not the increasing individualism and destruction of old communal values that has produced modern tyranny, but the attempt to reverse these trends by reimposing mythologized and exaggerated old solidarities" (Chirot 1994, p. 259). In his book Chirot shows how anti-individualistic communalism, vindictive nationalism, and obsessive autarky invariably work to promote tyranny, of either a "rightist" or "leftist" sort.

22 For a general discussion of development issues from the point of view of Austrian economics, see Boettke (1994b), *The Collapse of Development Planning*.

23 An extremely important element in the development role that NGOs – such as the Grameen Bank in Bangladesh – have to play is the promotion of human rights for women.

270

24 It is not merely because of their own extreme fiscal difficulties that most Western nations have been reducing the amounts of their budgets earmarked for foreign aid. It is above all due to the increasing realization that years of foreign aid has not only for the most part been unproductive; in many instances it has even been counterproductive and, ironically, one of the factors accounting for the *lack* of development in "third world" countries. This is not just because foreign aid was often used to finance grandiose, "white elephant" projects – the "edifice complex" – but also, more generally, because it helped to neutralize the costs on the part of third world governments of their failures to act in an economically and financially responsible way; in economic terms, the incentive-effect of foreign aid was and is largely negative. (If a major colonial power such as France continues to disburse generous sums of monies to its former African colonies, it is principally not for facilitating their own social and economic development but rather for political reasons of a self-serving nature.)

It is interesting to note that, in anticipation of the cut-off of US aid in 1965, Taiwan radically altered its economic thinking, abandoned its old import-substitution policies, and adopted the export-driven policies that account for its subsequent "economic miracle" (see Krauss 1983, p. 160).

25 For a general discussion of the legitimate – and necessary – role of government (the "state") in society, see Chapter 4. Just as there is, as I argued in Chapter 5, a legitimate form of "welfare," so likewise there is a legitimate form of foreign aid. Its purpose is not income redistribution or on-going budgetary support but assistance in (1) the creation of institutions conducive to democratic governance and the rule of law and (2) economic reforms aiming at (a) macroeconomic stabilization and (b) long-term economic liberalization.

26 Cf. Ayittey:

> Total African foreign debt has risen nineteen-fold since 1970 to a staggering $270 billion in 1990 which was equal to its gross national product (GNP), making the region the most heavily indebted of all (Latin America's debt amounted to around 60 percent of GNP). Debt service obligations absorbed 47 percent of export revenue in 1988, but only half were actually paid. The arrears were constantly being rescheduled.
>
> (Ayittey 1994, p. 157)

27 Income redistribution had in fact become the main business of the World Bank under McNamara. David Osterfeld observes:

> Under Robert McNamara, president of the Bank from 1968 to 1981, the Bank shifted its focus from creating wealth by stimulating development to transferring wealth by initiating social welfare programs (see Clark 1981). As Ann Hughey commented (1980, 123), McNamara seemed almost possessed with redistribution of income. He seems to have turned away from the concept of helping the poor by raising overall national economic standards.
>
> (Osterfeld 1994, p. 191)

Despite enormous transfers of funds by the World Bank to LDCs (mostly in sub-Saharan Africa), no noteworthy development or rise in living standards has been produced as a result. As Osterfeld points out, World Bank aid has actually served as a *dis*incentive for development in numerous instances. It is no exaggeration to say that for all the preferential treatment and billions of dollars in aid it has received over the decades, sub-Saharan Africa has little, if anything, to show for it.

28 For a systematic treatment of Chinese economic reforms since 1978 and the way in which these reforms have served to create a gap between the Marxist ideology of the Chinese communist Party and the new (liberal) economic realities, undermining in the process the legitimacy of the former, see Chen 1995.

REFERENCES

[...] signifies that the date indicated was not that of the original publication of the text in question (contemporary foreign literature translations excepted, as well as current English-language re-editions).

Acton, (Lord). [1985]. *Essays in the History of Liberty.* Indianapolis: Liberty Classics.

Adams, Charles. 1993. *For Good and Evil: The Impact of Taxes on the Course of Civilization.* Lanham, Md.: Madison Books.

Adams, John. [1954]. "A Defense of the Constitutions of the Government of the United States of America." In G. A. Peek, Jr., ed., *The Political Writings of John Adams.* Indianapolis: Bobbs-Merrill.

Adams, Roy. 1993. "The North American Model of Employee Representative Participation: A Hollow Mockery." *Comparative Labor Law Journal* 15, no. 1 (Fall).

Adedeji, Adebayo. 1994. "An Alternative for Africa." *Journal of Democracy* 5, no. 4 (October).

Aganbegyan, Abel. 1988. "Economic Reform." In Abel Aganbegyan, ed., *Perestroika 1989.* New York: Charles Scribner's Sons.

———. 1989. *Inside Perestroika: The Future of the Soviet Economy.* Trans. Helen Szamuely. New York: Harper and Row.

Aganbegyan, Abel, ed. 1988. *Perestroika 1989.* New York: Charles Scribner's Sons.

Allison, Lincoln. 1994. "On the Gap between Theories of Democracy and Theories of Democratization?" *Democratization* 1, no. 1 (Spring).

Anderson, Christopher. 1995. "The Internet." *The Economist* (July 1).

Angenot, Marc. 1992. "Les idéologies du ressentiment." *Discours social/Social Discourse* 4, nos. 3 and 4.

Anonymous. 1994. "Documents on Democracy: Africa." *Journal of Democracy* 5, no. 4 (October).

Anyang' Nyong'o, Peter. 1992. "Africa: The Failure of One-Party Rule." *Journal of Democracy* 3, no. 1 (January).

Apel, Karl-Otto. 1990. "Is the Ethics of the Ideal Communication Community a Utopia? On the Relationship between Ethics, Utopia, and the Critique of Utopia." In Seyla Benhabib and Fred Dallmayer, eds., *The Communicative Ethics Controversy.* Cambridge, Mass.: Massachusetts Institute of Technology.

Aquinas, Thomas. [1945]. *Basic Writings of Saint Thomas Aquinas.* 2 vols. Ed. Anton C. Pegis. New York: Random House.

Arato, Andrew and Cohen, Jean. 1992. "Civil Society and Social Theory." In Peter Beilharz; Gillian Robinson; and John Rundell, eds., *Between Totalitarianism and Democracy: A Thesis Eleven Reader.* Cambridge, Mass.: Massachusetts Institute of Technology.

273

Arendt, Hannah. 1951. 1973 (new edition). *The Origins of Totalitarianism.* New York: Harcourt, Brace, Jovanovich.

———. 1965. *On Revolution.* New York: Viking Press.

———. 1968. *Between Past and Future: Eight Exercises in Political Thought.* New York: Viking Press.

———. 1973 (reedition of 1951). *The Origins of Totalitarianism.* New York: Harcourt Brace, Jovanovich.

Aristotle. [1941] *Politica.* Trans. B. Jowett. In R. McKeon, ed., *The Basic Writings of Aristotle.* New York: Random House.

Armijo, Leslie Elliott; Biersteker, Thomas J.; and Lowenthal, Abraham F. 1994. "The Problems of Simultaneous Transitions." *Journal of Democracy* 5, no. 4 (October).

Ash, Timothy Garton. 1989. *The Uses of Adversity: Essays on the Fate of Central Europe.* New York: Random House.

———. 1990. *The Magic Lantern: The Revolution of '89 Witnessed in Warsaw, Budapest, Berlin and Prague.* New York: Random House.

———. 1993. *In Europes's Name: Germany and the Divided Continent.* New York: Random House.

———. 1994. "Journey to the Post-communist East." *The New York Review of Books* 61, no. 12 (June 23).

Aslund, Anders. 1989. *Gorbachev's Struggle for Economic Reform: The Soviet Reform Process, 1985–88.* Ithaca, N.Y.: Cornell University Press.

———. 1992. "Russia's Road from Communism." *Daedalus* (Spring).

———. 1994. "The Case for Radical Reform." *Journal of Democracy* 5, no. 4 (October).

———. 1995. *How Russia Became a Market Economy.* Washington, D.C.: Brookings Institute.

Auerbach, Dennis. 1987. "Liberalism in Search of Its Self," *Critical Review* 1, no. 3 (Summer).

Ayittey, George B. N. 1994. "The Failure of Development Planning in Africa." In Peter J. Boettke, ed., *The Collapse of Development Planning.* New York: New York University Press.

Baechler, Jean. 1975. *The Origins of Capitalism.* Trans. Barry Cooper. Oxford: Basil Blackwell.

Bakhtin, Mikhail. 1986. *Speech Genres and Other Late Essays.* Austin: University of Texas Press.

Balcerowicz, Leszek. 1994. "Understanding Postcommunist Transitions." *Journal of Democracy* 5, no. 4 (October).

Barkey, Henri. 1995. "Can the Middle East Compete?" *Journal of Democracy* 6, no. 2 (April).

Barry, Norman P. 1987. *The New Right.* London: Croom Helm.

Batemareo, Robert J. (1994) "Austrian Business Cycle Theory." In Peter J. Boettke, ed., *The Elgar Companion to Austrian Economics.* Aldershot: Edward Elgar.

Bauer, P.T. 1972. *Dissent on Development: Studies and Debates on Development Economics.* Cambridge, Mass.: Harvard University Press.

———. 1981. *Equality, the Third World and Economic Delusion.* Cambridge, Mass.: Harvard University Press.

———. 1984. *Reality and Rhetoric: Studies in the Economics of Development.* Cambridge, Mass.: Harvard University Press.

———. 1991. *The Development Frontier: Essays in Applied Economics.* Cambridge, Mass.: Harvard University Press.

Bauman, Zygmunt. 1993. *Postmodern Ethics.* Oxford: Blackwell.

Bednář, Miroslav. 1994. "The Character of the 1989 Revolution in East-Central Europe and Czech Political Traditions." In Miroslav Bednář and M. Vejražba, eds.,

Traditions and Present Problems of Czech Political Culture. Washington, D.C.: The Council for Research in Values and Philosophy.

Beilharz, Peter; Robinson, Gillian; and Rundell, John, eds. 1992. *Betweeen Totalitarianism and Democracy: A Thesis Eleven Reader.* Cambridge, Mass.: Massachusetts Institute of Technology.

Bell, Daniel. 1976. *The Cultural Contradictions of Capitalism.* New York: Basic Books.

———. 1980. *The Winding Passage.* Cambridge, Mass.: ABT Books.

Bellarmy, Richard. 1994. "Moralizing Markets." *Critical Review* 8, no. 3. (Summer).

Benhabib, Seyla. 1990. "In the Shadow of Aristotle and Hegel: Communicative Ethics and Current Controversies in Practical Philosophy." In Michael Kelly, ed., *Hermeneutics and Critical Theory in Ethics and Politics.* Cambridge, Mass.: Massachusetts Institute of Technology.

Benhabib, Seyla and Dallmayr, Fred, eds. 1990. *The Communicative Ethics Controversy.* Cambridge, Mass.: Massachusetts Institute of Technology.

Berger, Peter C. 1986. *The Capitalist Revolution: 50 Propositions about Prosperity, Equality, and Liberty.* New York: Basic Books.

Berlin, Isaiah. 1969. *Four Essays on Liberty.* Oxford: Oxford University Press.

Bernholz, Peter. 1989. "Ordo-liberals and the Control of the Money Supply." In Alan Peacock and Hans Willgerodt, eds., *German Neo-Liberals and the Social Market Economy.* New York: St. Martin's Press.

Bernstein, Richard. 1994a. "Guilty If Charged." *The New York Review of Books* (January 13).

———. 1994b. *Dictatorship of Virtue: Multiculturalism and the Battle for America's Future.* New York: Alfred A. Knopf.

Bernstein, Richard J. 1983. *Beyond Objectivism and Relativism: Science, Hermeneutics, and Praxis.* Philadelphia: University of Pennsylvania Press.

Blausten, Albert P. and Sigler, Jay A. 1988. *Constitutions That Made History.* New York: Paragon House.

Block, Walter. 1986. *The U.S. Bishops and Their Critics: An Economic and Ethical Perspective.* Vancouver: The Fraser Institute.

Bobbio, Norberto. 1990. *Liberalism and Democracy.* Trans. Maring Ryle and Kate Soper. London: Verso.

Boettke, Peter J. 1990a. *The Political Economy of Soviet Socialism: The Formatiave Years, 1918–1928.* Boston: Kluwer Academic.

———. 1990b. "The Theory of Spontaneous Orders and Cultural Evolution in the Social Theory of F. A. Hayek." *Cultural Dynamics* 3, no. 1.

———. 1990c. "Interpretive Reasoning and the Study of Social Life," *Methodus* 2, no. 2 (December). Reprinted in David L. Prychitko, ed., *Individuals, Institutions, Interpretations: Hermeneutics Applied to Economics.* Aldershot: Avebury.

———. 1993. *Why Perestroika Failed: The Politics and Economics of Socialist Transformation.* London: Routledge.

Boettke, Peter J., ed. 1994a. *The Elgar Companion to Austrian Economics.* Aldershot: Edward Elgar.

———. ed. 1994b. *The Collapse of Development Planning.* New York: New York University Press.

Boettke, Peter J.; Horwitz, Steven; and Prychitko, David L. 1994. "Beyond Equilibrium Economics: Reflections on the Uniqueness of the Austrian Tradition." In Peter J. Boettke and David L. Prychitko, eds., *The Market Process*: *Essays in Contemporary Austrian Economics.* Aldershot: Edward Elgar.

Boettke, Peter J. and Prychitko, David L., eds. 1994. *The Market Process: Essays in Contemporary Austrian Economics.* Aldershot: Edward Elgar.

Booth, Wayne C. 1974. *Modern Dogma and the Rhetoric of Assent.* Notre Dame, Ind.: University of Notre Dame Press.

275

Braudel, Fernand. 1982. *The Wheels of Commerce*. Vol. 2: *Civilization and Capitalism, 15th-18th Century*. New York: Harper and Row.

Brezinski, Zbigniew. 1989. *The Grand Failure: The Birth and Death of Communism in the Twentieth Century*. New York: Charles Scribner's Sons.

Brinkley, Alan. 1994. "For Their Own Good." *The New York Review of Books* (May 26).

Bronowski, Jacob. 1965. *Science and Human Values*. New York: Harper Torchbooks.

———. 1971. *The Identity of Man*. Garden City, N.Y.: Natural History Press.

Brooke, James. 1995. "Columbia's Rebels Grow Rich from Banditry." *New York Times* (July 2).

Buchanan, James. 1975. *The Limits of Liberty: Between Anarchy and Leviathan*. Chicago: University of Chicago Press.

———. 1977. *Freedom in Constitutional Contract*. College Station: Texas A & M University Press.

———. 1979. *What Should Economists Do?* Indianapolis: Liberty Press.

———. 1982. "Order Defined in the Process of Its Emergence," *Literature of Liberty* 5, no. 4 (Winter).

———. 1989. "Constitutional Economics." In John Eatwell, Murray Milgate, and Peter Newmwn, eds, *The Invisible Hand (The New Palgrave)*. New York: W. W. Norton.

Buchanan, James and Tullock, Gordon. 1965. *The Calculus of Consent*. Ann Arbor: University of Michigan Press.

Burns, John F. 1994. "Unlikely Reformer Coaxes India Toward a Market Economy." *New York Times* (May 8).

Callaghty, Thomas. 1994. "Africa: Back to the Future?" *Journal of Democracy* 5, no. 4 (October).

Camus, Albert. 1955. *The Myth of Sisyphus and Other Essays*. Trans. Justin O'Brien. New York: Vintage Books.

———. 1951. *L'homme revolté*. Paris: Gallimard.

Canon, Lou. 1991. *President Reagan: The Role of a Lifetime*. New York: Simon and Schuster.

CAUT (Canadian Association of University Teachers). 1994. *Reply to the Ontario Government: Academic Staff and the Ontario Government's Framework Document*. Ottawa.

Chafuen, Alejandro A. 1986. *Christians for Freedom: Late Scholastic Economics.* San Francisco: Ignatius Press.

———. 1994. "The Late Scholastics." In Peter J. Boettke, ed., *The Elgar Companion to Austrian Economics*. Aldershot: Edward Elgar.

Chen, Feng. 1995. *Economic Transition and Political Legitimacy in Post-Mao China*. Albany: State University of New York Press.

Cheng, Nien. 1990. "The Roots of China's Crisis." In James A. Dorn and Wang Xi, eds., *Economic Reform in China: Problems and Prospects*. Chicago: University of Chicago Press.

Chilton, Patricia. 1994. "Mechanisms of Change: Social Movements, Transnational Coalitions, and the Transformation Processes in Eastern Europe." *Democratization* 1, no. 1 (Spring).

Chirot, Daniel. 1994. *Modern Tyrants: The Power and Prevalence of Evil in Our Age*. New York: The Free Press.

Chirot, Daniel, ed. 1991. *The Crisis of Leninism and the Decline of the Left: The Revolutions of 1989*. Seattle: Univeristy of Washington Press.

Christian, Shirley. 1990. "Chilean Communists in Turmoil About the Future." *The New York Times* (September 23).

Cicero. [1977]. *De Re Publica*. Trans. C. W. Keyes. London: William Heinemann.

Coarse, Ronald H. 1988. *The Firm, the Market and the Law*. Chicago: University of Chicago Press.

Cohen, Ariel. 1995. "Crime Without Punishment." *Journal of Democracy* 6, no. 2 (April).

REFERENCES

Cohen, Jean. 1990. "Discourse Ethics and Civil Society." In David Rasmussen, ed. *Universalism vs. Communitarianism: Contemporary Debates in Ethics.* Cambridge, Mass.: Massachusetts Institute of Technology.

Cohen, Jean L. and Arato, Andrew. 1992. *Civil Society and Political Theory.* Cambridge, Mass.: Massachusetts Institute of Technology.

Cohen, Robert. 1995. "In Sarajevo, Victims of a 'Postmodern' War." *New York Times* (May 21).

Cohen, Stephen E. and Heuvel, Katrian vanden. 1989. *Voices of Glasnost: Interviews with Gorbachev's Reformers.* New York: W. W. Norton & Co.

Colburn, Forrest D. 1994. *The Vogue of Revolution in Poor Countries.* Princeton, N.J.: Princeton University Press.

Conquest, Robert. 1993. "The Evil of This time." *The New York Review of Books* (September 23).

Constant, Benjamin. [1988]. In *Political Writings.* Trans. and ed. Biancamaria Fontana. Cambridge: Cambridge University Press.

Constitution (Fundamental Law) of the Union of Soviet Socialist Republics. 1977. Moscow: Novosti Press Agency Publishing House.

Crews, Frederick. 1994a. "The Revenge of the Repressed." *The New York Review of Books* 41, no. 19 (November 17).

———. 1994b. "The Revenge of the Repressed: Part II." *The New York Review of Books* 41, no. 20 (December 1).

Cronin, Thomas E. 1989. *Direct Democracy: The Politics of Initiative, Referendum, and Recall.* Cambridge, Mass.: Harvard University Press.

Crossette, Barbara. 1994. "The 'Third World' Is Dead, but Spirits Linger." *New York Times* (November 13).

———. 1995a. "New Watchdog Group Ranks Nations in 'Corruption Index.'" *New York Times* (August 13).

———. 1995b. "A Global Gauge of Greased Palms." *New York Times* (August 20).

———. 1995c. "The Second Sex in the Third World." *New York Times* (Sept. 10).

Daedalus. 1992. "The Exit from Communism," vol. 121. no. 2, Spring.

Dahl, Robert. 1956. *A Preface to Democratic Theory.* Chicago: University of Chicago Press.

———. 1971. *Polyarchy.* New Haven, Conn.: Yale University Press.

———. 1989. *Democracy and Its Critics.* New Haven, Conn.: Yale University Press.

Dahrendorf, Ralf. 1988. *The Modern Social Conflict: An Essay on the Politics of Liberty.* Cambridge, Mass.: Ballinger.

———. 1990. *Reflections on the Revolution in Europe.* New York: Random House.

DePalma, Anthony. 1994. "Do Term Limits Work? Ask Mexico." *The New York Times,* February 4.

de Soto, Hernando. 1989. *The Other Path: The Invisible Revolution in the Third World.* New York: Harper and Row.

Diamond, Larry. 1994. "Toward Democratic Consolidation." *Journal of Democracy* 5, no. 3 (July).

Dietrick, Eric. 1995. "AI and the Mechanistic Forces of Darkness." *Journal of Experimental and Theoretical Artificial Intelligence* 7.

diZerega, Gus. 1989. "Democracy as a Spontaneous Order," *Critical Review* 3, no. 2 (Spring).

———. 1992. "Social Ecology, Deep Ecology, and Liberalism." *Critical Review* 6, nos. 2–3 (Spring–Summer).

Dijilas, Milovan. 1966 *The New Class: An Analysis of the Communist System.* London: George Allen and Unwin.

Donnelly, Jack. 1989. *Universal Human Rights in Theory and Practice.* Ithaca, N.Y.: Cornell University Press.

277

REFERENCES

Dorn, James A. 1994. "The Collapse of Communist and Post-communist Reform." In Peter J. Boettke, ed., *The Elgar Companion to Austrian Economics*. Aldershot: Edward Elgar.

Dorn, James A. and Xi, Wang, eds. 1990. *Economic Reform in China: Problems and Prospects*. Chicago: University of Chicago Press.

Dreyfus, Hubert L. 1979. *What Computers Can't Do: The Limits of Artificial Intelligence*. Revised edition. New York: Harper and Row.

Dreyfus, Hubert and Rabinow, Paul. 1982. *Michel Foucault: Beyond Structuralism and Hermeneutics*. Chicago: University of Chicago Press.

Drucker, Peter F. 1993. *Post-Capitalist Society*. New York: Harper Business.

D'Souza, Dinesh. 1991. *Illiberal Education: The Politics of Race and Sex on Campus*. New York: The Free Press.

Dunn, John, ed. 1993. *Democracy: The Unfinished Journey, 508 BC to AD 1993*. Oxford: Oxford University Press.

Dworkin, Ronald. 1991. "Liberty and Pornography." *The New York Review of Books* (August 15).

———. 1992. "The Coming Battles over Free Speech." *The New York Review of Books* (June 11).

Eatwell, John; Milgate, Murray; and Newman, Paul, eds. 1989. *The Invisible Hand (The New Palgrave)*. New York: W. W. Norton.

Ebeling, Richard M. 1986. "Toward a Hermeneutical Economics: Expectations, Prices, and the Role of Interpretation in a Theory of the Market Process." In Israel Kirzner, ed., *Subjectivism, Intelligibility, and Economic Understanding*. New York: New York University Press. Reprinted in David L. Prychitko, ed., *Individuals, Institutions, Interpretations: Hermeneutics Applied to Economics*. Aldershot: Avebury.

———. 1987. "Cooperation in Anonymity." *Critical Review* 1, no. 4 (Fall). Reprinted in David L. Prychitko, ed., *Individuals, Institutions, Interpretations: Hermeneutics Applied to Economics*. Aldershot: Avebury.

———. 1994. "Expectations and Expectations Formation in Mises' Theory of the Market Process." In Peter J. Boettke and David L. Prychitko, *The Market Process: Essays in Contemporary Austrian Economics*. Aldershot: Edward Elgar.

Eco, Umberto. 1995. "Ur-Fascism." *The New York Review of Books* 42, no. 11 (June 22).

Elkin, Stephen L. and Soltan, Karol Edward, eds. 1993. *A New Constitutionalism: Designing Political Institutions for a Good Society*. Chicago: University of Chicago Press.

Ellul, Jacques. 1978. *The Betrayal of the West*. New York: Seabury Press.

Elon, Amos. 1995. "One Foot on the Moon." *The New York Review of Books* (April 6).

Elshtain, Jean Bethke. 1995. *Democracy on Trial*. New York: Basic Books.

Fehér, Ferenc. 1992. "The Left After Communism." In Peter Beilharz; Gillian Robinson; and John Rundell, eds., *Between Totalitarianism and Democracy: A Thesis Eleven Reader*. Cambridge Mass.: Massachusetts Institute of Technology.

Fehl, Ulrich, 1994. "Spontaneous Order." In Peter J. Boettke, ed., *The Elgar Companion to Austrian Economics*. Aldershot: Edward Elgar.

Fekete, John. 1994. *Moral Panic: Biopolitics Rising*. Montreal-Toronto: Robert Davies Publishing.

Ferdinand, Peter. 1994. "The Party's Over – Market Liberalization and the Challenges for One-Party and One-Party Dominant Regimes: The Cases of Taiwan and Mexico, Italy and Japan." *Democratization* 1, no. 1 (Spring).

Ferguson, Adam. [1980]. *An Essay on the History of Civil Society*. New Brunswick, N.J.: Transaction Publishers.

Ferry, Luc, and Renaut, Alain. 1990. *French Philosophy of the Sixties: An Essay on Anti-humanism*. Trans. Mary H.S. Cattani. Amherst: University of Massachusetts Press.

Feyerabend, Paul. 1975. *Against Method*. London: Verso.

278

Finkielkraut, Alain. 1995. *The Defeat of the Mind*. Trans. Judith Friedlander. New York: Columbia University Press.

Fish, M. Steven. 1994. "Russia's Fourth Transition." *Journal of Democracy* 5, no. 3 (July).

Foucault, Michel. 1980. *Power/Knowledge: Selected Interviews and Other Writings 1972 – 1977*. Ed. Colin Gordon. New York: Pantheon Books.

"Framework Regarding Prevention of Harassment and Discrimination in Ontario Universities." 1993. Toronto: Ontario Ministry of Education and Training.

Frankel, S. Herbert. 1977. *Money. Two Philosophies: The Conflict of Trust and Authority*. Oxford: Basil Blackwell.

Franklin, James. 1989. "Natural Sciences as Textual Interpretation: The Hermeneutics of the Natural Sign." *Philosophy and Phenomenological Research* 45, no. 4 (June).

French, Howard W. 1994. "An Ignorance of Africa as Vast as the Continent." *New York Times* (November 20).

———. 1995. "West Africans Find Prosperity Is Elusive." *New York Times* (April 9).

Friedman, Thomas L. 1994a. "Africa's Economies: Reforms Pay Off." *New York Times* (March 13).

———. 1994b. "It's a Mad, Mad, Mad, Mad World Money Market·Economy." *New York Times* (May 8).

———. 1994c. "World Bank at 50, Vows to do Better." *New York Times* (July 24).

Fukuyama, Francis. 1989. "The End of History?" *The National Interest* (Summer).

———. 1992. *The End of History and the Last Man*. New York: The Free Press.

———. 1995. "The Primacy of Culture." *Journal of Democracy* 6, no. 1 (January).

Gadamer, Hans-Georg. 1975. *Truth and Method*. New York: Seabury.

———. 1976. *Philosophical Hermeneutics*. Berkeley: University of California Press.

———. 1981. *Reason in the Age of Science*. Trans. F. Lawrence. Cambridge, Mass.: Massachusetts Institute of Technology.

———. 1990a. "Afterword" to *Truth and Method*. New York: Crossroad.

———. 1990b. "Reply to My Critics" in Gayle L. Ormiston and Alan D. Schrift, *The Hermeneutical Tradition: From Ast to Ricoeur*. Albany: State University of New York Press.

Garrison, Roger W. and Kirzner, Israel M. (1989) "Friedrich August von Hayek." In John Eatwell; Murray Milgater; and Paul Newman, eds., *The Invisible Hand (The New Palgrave)*. New York: W. W. Norton.

Geertz, Clifford. 1973. *The Interpretation of Cultures*. New York: Basic Books.

Gould, Carol C. 1988. *Rethinking Democracy: Freedom and Social Cooperation in Politics, Economy, and Society*. Cambridge: Cambridge University Press.

Grahman, Carol. 1995. "The Politics of Safety Nets." *Journal of Democracy* 6, no. 2 (April).

Granoff, Phyliss and Shinohara, Koici. 1994. *Newsletter* (The McMaster University Faculty Association). Vol 20, special no. ("The Meaning of Academic Freedom") (April).

Gray, John. 1993. "From Post communist to Civil Society: The reemergence of History and the Decline of the Western Model." In Ellen Frankel Paul; Fred D. Miller, Jr.; and Jeffrey Paul, eds., *Liberalism and the Economic Order*. Cambridge: Cambridge University Press.

Grossman, Lawrence K. 1995. *The Electronic Republic: Reshaping Democracy in the Information Age*. New York: Viking.

Guie, Honoré Koffi. 1993. "Organizing Africa's Democrats." *Journal of Democracy* 4, no. 2 (April).

Gutmann, Amy, ed. 1994. *Multiculturalism: Examining the Politics of Recognition*. Princeton, N.J.: Princeton University Press.

Habermas, Jürgen. 1971. *Knowledge and Human Interests*. Boston: Beacon Press.

———. 1987. *The Philosophical Discourse of Modernity*. Trans. Frederick Lawrence. Cambridge, Mass.: Massachusetts Institute of Technology.

279

——. 1990. *Moral Consciousness and Communicative Action.* Trans. Christian Lenhardt and Shierry Weber Nicholsen. Cambridge, Mass.: Massachusetts Institute of Technology.

——. 1994. "Struggles for Recognition in the Democratic Constitutional State." In Amy Gutmann, ed., *Multiculturalism: Examining the Politics of Recognition.* Princeton, N.J.: Princeton University Press.

Hacker, Andrew. 1993. "'Diversity' and Its Dangers." *New York Review of Books* (October 7).

Haggard, Stephan and Kaufman, Robert R. 1992. *The Politics of Economic Adjustment.* Princeton, N.J.: Princeton University Press.

Hamm, Walter. 1989. "The Welfare State at Its Limits." In Alan Peacock and Hans Willgerodt, *German Neo-Liberalism and the Social Market Economy.* New York: St. Martin's Press.

"Han Minzhu," ed. 1990. *Cries for Democracy: Writings and Speeches from the 1989 Chinese Democracy Movement.* Princeton: Princeton University Press.

Handelman, Stephen. 1995. *Comrade Criminal: Russia's New Mafiya.* New Haven, Conn.: Yale University Press.

Harding, Neil. 1993. "The Marxist-Leninist Detour." In John Dunn, ed., *Democracy: The Unfinished Journey, 508 BC to AD 1993.* Oxford: Oxford University Press.

Harik, Iliya. 1994. "Pluralism in the Arab World." *Journal of Democracy* 5, no. 3 (July).

Havel, Václav. 1985. *The Power of the Powerless: Citizens Against the State in Central-Eastern Europe.* London: Hutchinson.

——. 1990. "The Future of Central Europe." *The New York Review of Books* (March 29).

——. 1992a. "The End of the Modern Era" (an address to the World Economic Forum, Davos, Switzerland, February 4, 1992). *The New York Times.* (March 1, op-ed section).

——. 1992b. *Summer Meditations.* New York: Alfred A. Knopf.

——. 1992c. "A Dream for Czechoslovakia." *The New York Review of Books* (June 15).

——. 1992d. "How Europe Could Fall (address given on October 3, 1992 to the General Assemboy of the Council of Europe in Vienna)." *New York Times,* op-ed section (November 18).

——. 1993. "The Post-communist Nightmare." *The New York Review of Books* (May 27).

——. 1995. "The Responsibility of Intellectuals." *The New York Review of Books* (June 22).

Hayek, Friedrich A. 1944. *The Road to Serfdom.* Chicago: University of Chicago Press.

——. 1960. *The Constitution of Liberty.* South Bend, Ind.: Gateway Editions.

——. 1973. *Law, Legislation, and Liberty,* Vol. I: *Rules and Order.* Chicago: Univeristy of Chicago Press.

——. 1976. *Law, Legislation, and Liberty.* Vol. II: *The Mirage of Social Justice.* Chicago: University of Chicago Press.

——. 1978. *New Studies in Philosophy, Politics, Economics, and the History of Ideas.* Chicago: University of Chicago Press.

——. 1979a. *The Counter-Revolution of Science: Studies on the Abuse of Reason.* 2nd edition. Indianapolis: Liberty Press.

——. 1979b. *Law, Legislation, and Liberty.* Vol. III: *The Political Order of a Free People.* Chicago: University of Chicago Press.

——. 1988. *The Fatal Conceit.* Chicago: Univeristy of Chicago Press.

——. 1992. *The Fortunes of Liberalism: Essays on Austrian Economics and the Ideal of Freedom.* Ed. Peter G. Klein. Chicago: University of Chicago Press.

Hedges, Charles. 1994. "Battle of Algiers, the Sequel." *New York Times* (February 6).

Hegel, G. W. F. [1956]. *The Philosophy of History.* New York: Dover Publications.

REFERENCES

——. [1991]. *Elements of the Philosophy of Right.* Ed. Allen W. Wood. Cambridge: Cambridge University Press.

——. [1963]. *Phenomenology of Spirit.* Trans. A. V. Miller. Oxford: Oxford University Press.

Heller, Agnes. 1990. *Can Modernity Survive?* Berkeley: University of California Press.

Heller, Agnes and Fehér, Ferenc. 1988. *The Postmodern Political Condition.* New York: Columbia University Press.

Herbert, Bob. 1994. "Racism 101." *New York Times* (December 1).

Himmelfarb, Gertrude. 1985. *The Idea of Poverty: England in the Early Industrial Age.* New York: Vintage Books.

Hobhouse, L. T. [1974]. *Liberalism.* New York: Oxford University Press.

Hodgson, Geoffrey M. 1988. *Economics and Institutions: A Manifesto for a Modern Institutional Economics.* Philadelphia: University of Pennsylvania Press.

Hoffmann, Stanley. 1992. "Delusions of World Order." *The New York Review of Books* (April 9).

Holmes, Stephen. 1984. *Benjamin Constant and the Making of Modern Liberalism.* New Haven, Conn.: Yale University Press.

Horne, Thomas A. 1994. "Liberalism and the Problem of Poverty: A Reply to Ashcroft." *Critical Review* 8, no. 3 (Summer).

Horowitz, Donald L. 1993. "Democracy in Divided Societies." *Journal of Democracy* 4, no. 4 (October).

Horwitz, Stephen. 1992a. "Monetary Exchange as an Extra-Linguistic Social Communication Process." *Review of Social Economy* 50, no. 2 (Summer). Reprinted in David L. Prychitko, ed., *Individuals, Institutions, Interpretations: Hermeneutics Applied to Economics.* Aldershot: Avebury

——. 1992b. *Monetary Evolution, Free Banking, and Economic Order.* Boulder, Colo.: Westview Press.

——. 1994a. "Inflation." In Peter J. Boettke, ed., *The Elgar Companion to Austrian Economics.* Aldershot: Edward Elgar.

——. 1994b. "Subjectivism." In Peter J. Boettke, ed., *The Elgar Companion to Austrian Economics* Aldershot: Edward Elgar.

——. 1994c. "Does Eastern Europe Need a New (Marshall) Plan?" In Peter J. Boettke, ed., *The Collapse of Development Planning.* New York: New York University Press.

Hoskin, Geoffrey. 1990. *The Awakening of the Soviet Union.* Cambridge, Mass.: Harvard University Press.

Howard, Rhoda E. 1990. "Group Versus Individual Identity in the African Debate on Human Rights." In Abdullahi Ahmed An-Na'im and Francis M. Deng, eds., *Human Rights in Africa: Cross-Cultural Perspectives.* Washington, D.C.: Brookings Institution.

——. 1992a. "Human Rights and the Necessity for Cultural Change." *Focus on Law Studies* 8, no. 1 (Fall).

——. 1992b. "Communitarianism and Liberalism in Debate on Human Rights in Africa." *Journal of Contemporary African Studies* 1, no. 4.

——. 1993. "Women's Rights and the Right to Development." In Ronald Cohen, Goran Hyden, and Winston P. Magan, eds., *Human Rights and Governance in Africa.* Gainsville: University Press of Florida.

——. 1995. *Human Rights and the Search for Community.* Boulder, Colo.: Westview Press.

Howard, Rhoda (with Jack Donnelly). 1989. "Human Dignity, Human Rights, and Political Regimes." In Jack Donnelly, *Universal Human Rights in Theory and Practice.* Ithaca, N.Y.: Cornell University Press.

Hughes, Robert. 1993. *Culture of Complaint: The Fraying of America.* New York: Oxford University Press.

Humbolt, Wilhelm von. [1993]. *The Limits of Government.* Indianapolis: Liberty Fund.

Hume, David. [1978]. *A Treatise of Human Nature.* Oxford: Clarendon Press.

Huntington, Samuel P. 1991. *The Third Wave: Democratization in the Late Twentieth Century.* Norman: University of Oklahoma Press.

Ignatieff, Michael. 1993. *Blood and Belonging: Journeys into the New Nationalism.* New York: Farrar, Strauss and Giroux.

Ikeda, Sanford. 1994. "Market Process." In Peter J. Boettke, ed., *The Elgar Companion to Austrian Economics.* Aldershot: Edward Elgar.

Jacobs, Jane. 1992. *Systems of Survival: A Dialogue on the Moral Foundations of Commerce and Politics.* New York: Random House.

James, William. [1956]. *The Will to Believe/Human Immortality.* New York: Dover Books.

Jaspers, Karl. 1961. *The Future of Mankind.* Trans. R. B. Aston. Chicago: University of Chicago Press.

Jefferson, Thomas. [1984]. *Thomas Jefferson: Writings.* New York: The Library of America.

John Paul II. 1991. *Centesimus Annus.* Montréal: Editions Paulines.

Judt, Tony. 1994. "The New Old Nationalism," *The New York Review of Books* 41, no. 10 (May 20).

Kamath, Shyam J. 1994. "The Failure of Development Planning in India." In Peter J. Boettke, ed., *The Collapse of Development Planning.* New York: New York University Press.

Kant, Immanuel. [1963a]. "Ideas for a Universal History from a Cosmopolitan Point of View." In Lewis White Beck, ed., *Kant, On History.* Indianapolis: Bobbs-Merril.

———. [1963b]. "Perpetual Peace." In Lewis White Beck, ed., *Kant, On History.* Indianapolis: Bobbs-Merril.

Karol, Marcin. 1994. "Poland's Longing for Paternalism." *Journal of Democracy* 5, no. 1 (January).

Kelly, Michael, ed. 1990. *Hermeneutics and Critical Theory in Ethics and Politics.* Cambridge, Mass.: Massachusetts Institute of Technology.

Keynes, John M. [1964]. *The General Theory of Employment, Interest and Money.* New York: Harcourt Brace.

Khalifa, Aymen M. 1995. "Reviving Civil Society in Egypt." *Journal of Democracy* 6, no. 3 (July).

Kimura, Doreen. 1993. "Fear of Offending Stifles Intellectual Debate." *Newsletter* (The Society for Academic Freedom and Scholarship). No. 4 (October).

Kirzner, Israel, ed. 1986. *Subjectivism, Intelligibility, and Economic Understanding.* New York: New York University Press.

Klamer, Arjo; McCloskey, Donald N.; and Solow, Robert M., eds. 1988. *The Consequences of Economic Rhetoric.* Cambridge: Cambridge University Press.

Kloten, Norbert. 1989. "The Role of the Public Sector in the Social Market Economy." In Alan Peacock and Hans Willgerodt, eds. *German Neo-Liberalism and the Social Market Economy.* New York: St. Martin's Press.

Knight, Frank H. 1921. *Risk, Uncertainty, and Profit.* Boston: Houghton Mifflin.

———. 1956. *On the History and Method of Economics.* Chigago: University of Chicago Press.

———. [1982]. *Freedom and Reform: Essays in Economics and Social Philosophy.* Indianapolis: Liberty Press.

Kornai, Janos. 1990. *The Road to a Free Economy. Shifting from a Socialist System: The Example of Hungary.* New York: W.W. Norton.

———. 1992. *The Socialist System: The Political Economy of Communism.* Princeton, N.J.: Princeton University Press.

Krauss, Melvyn B. 1983. *Development Without Aid: Growth, Poverty and Government.* New York: McGraw-Hill.

Kristeva, Julia. 1993. *Nations Without Nationalism.* Trans. Leon S. Roudiez. New York: Columbia University Press.

282

REFERENCES

Laqueur, Walter. 1994. *The Dream That Failed: Reflections on the Soviet Union*. New York: Oxford University Press.

Lal, Deepak. 1985. *The Poverty of "Development Economics"*. Cambridge, Mass.: Harvard University Press.

Lavoie, Don. 1985a. *National Economic Planning: What is Left?* Cambridge, Mass.: Ballinger.

———. 1985b. *Rivalry and Central Planning: The Social Calculation Debate Reconsidered*. Cambridge: Cambridge University Press.

———. 1987. "The Accounting of Interpretations and the Interpretation of Accounts: The Communicative Function of 'The Language of Business.'" *Accounting Organizations and Society* 12, no. 6.

———. 1988. "Editor's Notes." *Market Process* 6, no. 2 (Fall).

———. 1989. "Understanding Differently: Hermeneutics and the Social Order of Communicative Processes." Paper presented at the conference on "Carl Menger and His Legacy," Duke University, April 14–16. Photocopy.

———. 1992. "Glasnost and the Knowledge Problem: Rethinking Economic Democracy." *Cato Journal* 11, no. 3 (Winter).

———. 1993. "Democracy, Markets, and the Legal Order: Notes on the Nature of Politics in a Radically Liberal Society." In Ellen Frankel Paul, Fred D. Miller, Jr. and Jeffrey Paul, et al., eds, *Liberalism and the Economic Order*. Cambridge: Cambridge University Press.

———. 1994. "A Political Philosophy for the Market Process." In Peter J. Boettke and David L. Prychitko, eds., *The Market Process: Essays in Contemporary Austrian Economics*. Aldershot: Edward Elgar.

———. 1995. "The Market as a Procedure for the Discovery and Conveyance of Inarticulate Knowledge." In David L. Prychitko, ed., *Individuals, Institutions, Interpretations: Hermeneutics applied to Economics*. Aldershot: Avebury.

Lavoie, Don, ed. 1990. *Economics and Hermeneutics*. London: Routledge.

Lebowitz, Michael A. 1991. "The Socialist Fetter: A Cautionary Tale." In Ralph Miliband and Leo Panitch, eds., *Communist Regimes: The Aftermath*. London: Merlin Press.

Lefort, Claude. 1986. *The Political Forms of Modern Society: Bureaucracy, Democracy, Totalitarianism*. Ed. John B. Thompson. Cambridge, Mass.: Massachusetts Institute of Technology.

Lenel, Hans Otto. 1989. "Evolution of the Social Market Economy." In Alan Peacock and Hans Willgerodt, eds., *German Neo-Liberalism and the Social Market Economy*. New York: St Martin's Press.

Lepenies, Wolf. 1993. "Three Years After the Revolution: The View from Germany." *Ideas from the National Humanities Center* 2, no. 1 (Summer).

Lewis, Flora. 1984. "A Third-World Spring?" *New York Times* (April 8).

Lewis, Peter M. 1995. "'Civil' and Other Societies." *Journal of Democracy* 6, no. 2 (April).

Lewontin, R. C. 1994. "Women Versus the Biologists." *The New York Review of Books* (April 4).

———. 1995. "Reply." *The New York Review of Books* (May 25).

Lindblom, Charles E. 1977. *Politics and Markets*. New York: Basic Books.

———. 1990. *Inquiry and Change: The Troubled Attempt to Understand and Shape Society*. New Haven, Conn.: Yale University Press.

Lincoln, Abraham. [1989]. *Speeches and Writings*. 2 vols. New York: The Library of America.

Link, Perry. 1992. *Evening Chats in Beijing: Probing China's Predicament*. New York: W. W. Norton.

Lipset, Seymour Martin. 1991. "No Third Way: A Comparative Perspective on the Left." In Daniel Chirot, ed., *The Crisis of Leninism and the Decline of the Left: The Revolutions of 1989*. Seattle: University of Washington Press.

———. 1993. "Reflections on Capitalism, Socialism and Democracy." *Journal of Democracy* 4, no. 2 (April).

Locke, John. [1952]. *The Second Treatise of Government.* Ed. Thomas P. Peardon. Indianapolis: Bobbs-Merrill.

Loftus, Elizabeth and Ketchan, Katherine. 1994. *The Myth of Repressed Memory: False Memories and Allegations of Sexual Abuse.* New York: St. Martin's Press.

Lowi, Theodore J. 1993. "Two Roads to Serfdom: Liberalism, Conservatism, and Administrative Power." In Stephen L. Elkin and Karol Edward Soltan, eds., *A New Constitutionalism: Designing Political Institutions for a Good Society.* Chicago: University of Chicago Press.

Macedo, Stephen. 1990. *Liberal Virtues: Citizenship, Virtue, and Community in Liberal Constitutionalism.* Oxford: Clarendon Press.

Macpherson, C. B. (1962) *The Political Theory of Possessive Individualism.* Oxford: Clarendon Press.

Madison, G. B. 1981. *The Phenomenology of Merleau-Ponty: A Search for the Limits of Consciousness.* Athens: Ohio University Press.

———. 1982. *Understanding: A Phenomenological-Pragmatic Analysis.* Westport, Conn.: Greenwood Press.

———. 1986. *The Logic of Liberty.* New York: Greenwood Press.

———. 1988. *The Hermeneutics of Postmodernity: Figures and Themes.* Bloomington: Indiana University Press.

———. 1989a. "The New Philosophy of Rhetoric." *Texte: Revue de critique et de théorie littéraire* 8/9.

———. 1989b. "How Individualistic is Methodological Individualism?," *Critical Review* 4, nos 1/2 (Winter/Spring). Reprinted in David L. Prychitko, ed., *Individuals, Institutions, Interpretations: Hermeneutics Applied to Economics.* Aldershot: Avebury.

———. 1989c. "Hayek and the Interpretive Turn," *Critical Review* 3, no. 2 (Spring).

———. 1990. "Between Theory and Practice: Hayek on the Logic of Cultural Dynamics." *Cultural Dynamics* 3, no. 1.

———. 1991a. "Getting Beyond Objectivism: The Philosophical Hermeneutics of Gadamer and Ricoeur." In Don Lavoie, ed., *Economics and Hermeneutics.* London: Routledge.

———. 1991b. "Philosophy Without Foundations." *Reason Papers* 16 (Fall).

———. 1991c. "The Practice of Theory, the Theory of Practice," *Critical Review* 5, no. 2 (Spring).

———. 1993. "Merleau-Ponty Alive." *Man and World* 26: 19–44.

———. 1994a. "Hermeneutics: Gadamer and Ricoeur." In Richard Kearney, ed., *Twentieth-Century Continental Philosophy. Routledge History of Philosophy,* vol. viii. London: Routledge.

———. 1994b. "Visages de la postmodernité." *Etudes littéraires* 27, no. 1 (été).

———. 1994c. "The Primacy of Action and Its Scientific Consequences for the Hermeneutics of the Human Sciences." In Vincent Shen, Richard Knowles, and Tran Van Doan, eds. *Psychology, Phenomenology, and Chinese Philosophy (Chinese Philosophical Studies, VI).* Washington, D.C.: The Council for Research in Values and Philosophy.

———. 1995a. "Hermeneutics, the Lifeworld, and the Universality of Reason." *Dialogue and Universalism* (Polish Academy of Sciences) 7.

Madison, James (with Alexander Hamilton and John Jay). N. D. *The Federalist: A Commentary on The Constitution of the United States (Being a Collection of Essays written in Support of the Constitution agreed upon September 17, 1787, by the Federal Convention).* New York: The Modern Library.

Madison, James. 1785. "Memorial and Remonstrance Against Religious Assessments." In Gaillard Hunt, ed. (1900–1910) *The Writings of James Madison.* 9 vols. Vol II. New York: G.P. Putnam's & Sons.

———. 1984. *Notes on Debates in the Federal Convention of 1787 Reported by James Madison.* Athens: Ohio University Press.

Maier, Charles S. 1993. "Democracy Since the French Revolution." In John Dunn, ed., *Democracy: The Unfinished Journey, 508 BC to AD 1993.* Oxford: Oxford University Press.

Malia, Martin. 1992. "Leninist Endgame." *Daedalus* (Spring).

———. 1994. *The Soviet Tragedy: A History of Socialism in Russia, 1917–1991.* New York: The Free Press.

Mandeville, Bernard. [1970]. *The Fable of the Bees.* Harmondsworth: Penguin Books.

Manent, Pierre. 1994. *An Intellectual History of Liberalism.* Trans. Rebecca Balinski. Princeton, N.J.: Princeton University Press.

Manin, Bernard. 1994. "On Legitimacy and Political Deliberation." In Mark Lilla, ed., *New French Thought: Political Philosophy.* Princeton, N.J.: Princeton University Press.

Manley, Michael. 1992a. "Adam Smith's New Fan." *Washington Times* (April 27).

———. 1992b. "Illusory New Economic Order." *Washington Times* (April 28).

Maravall, José María 1994. "The Myth of the Authoritarian Advantage." *Journal of Democracy* 5, no. 4 (October).

Marx, Karl. [1964]. *Karl Marx: Early Writings,* ed. Tom Bottomore. New York: McGraw Hill.

Marx, Karl and Engels, Friedrich. [1946]. *Essentials of Marx.* New York: Rand School Press.

McCarthy, Thomas. 1981. *The Critical Theory of Jürgen Habermas.* Cambridge, Mass.: Massachusetts Institute of Technology.

McCloskey, Donald N. 1985. *The Rhetoric of Economics.* Madison: University of Wisconsin Press.

———. 1994. *Knowledge and Persuasion in Economics.* Cambridge: Cambridge University Press.

Menger, Carl. [1976]. *Principles of Economics.* Trans. James Dingwall and Bert F. Hoselitz. New York: New York University Press.

———. [1985]. *Investigations into the Method of the Social Sciences with Special Reference to Economics.* Trans. Francis J. Noch. New York: New York University Press.

Merleau-Ponty, Maurice. 1962. *Phenomenology of Perception.* Trans. Colin Smith. London: Routledge and Kegan Paul.

Meyers, Marvin, ed. 1981. *The Mind of the Founder: Sources of the Political Thought of James Madison.* Hanover: University Press of New England.

Milanovic, Branko. 1989. *Liberalization and Entrepreneurship: Dynamics of Reform in Socialism and Capitalism.* Armonk, N.Y.: M. E. Sharp.

Miliband, Ralph and Panitch, Leo, eds. 1991. *Communist Regimes: The Aftermath.* London: Merlin Press.

Mill, John Stuart. [1947]. *On Liberty.* Northbrook, Ill.: AHM Publishing.

———. [1958]. *Considerations on Representative Government.* Indianapolis: Bobbs-Merrill.

Mirowski, Philip. 1988a. "Shall I Compare Thee to a Minkowki-Ricardo-Leontief-Metzler Matrix of the Mosak-Hicks Type?" In Arjo Klamer, Donald N. McCloskey, and Robert M. Solow, eds., *The Consequences of Economic Rhetoric.* Cambridge: Cambridge University Press.

———. 1988b. *Against Mechanism: Protecting Economics from Science.* Totowa, N.J.: Rowman and Littlefield.

———. 1989. *More Heat than Light: Economics as Social Physics, Physics as Nature's Economics.* Cambridge: Cambridge University Press.

Mirsky, Jonathan. 1994. "Unmasking the Monster." *The New York Review of Books* 41, no. 19 (November 17).

Mises, Ludwig von. [1963]. *Human Action: A Treatise on Economics.* 3rd revised ed. Chicago: Contemporary Books.

———. [1966]. *Human Action: A Treatise on Economics.* Chicago: Contemporary Books.

REFERENCES

——. [1978]. *The Ultimate Foundation of Economic Science: An Essay on Method.* Kansas City: Sheed, Andrews, and McMeel.

——. [1979]. *Liberalism: A Socio-Economic Exposition.* Kansas City: Sheed, Andrews, and McMeel.

——. [1981]. *Socialism: An Economic and Sociological Analysis.* Indianapolis: Liberty Classics.

Mittermaier, Karl. 1986. "Mechanomorphism." In Israel Kirzner, ed., *Subjectivism, Intelligibility and Economic Understanding.* New York: New York University Press.

Montesquieu. [1989]. *The Spirit of the Laws.* Trans. Anne M. Cohler, et al. Cambridge: Cambridge University Press.

Morgan, Edmund S. 1988. *Inventing the People: The Rise of Popular Sovereignty in England and America.* New York: W. W. Norton.

——. 1993. "Power to the People?" *The New York Review of Books* (December 2).

Möschel, Wernhard. 1989. "Competition Policy from an Ordo Point of View." In Alan Peacock and Hans Willgerodt, eds., *German Neo-Liberalism and the Social Market Economy.* New York: St. Martin's Press.

Mouffe, Chantal. 1993. *The Return of the Political.* London: Verso.

Naim, Moses. 1994. "Latin America: The Second Stage of Reform." *Journal of Democracy* 5, no. 4 (October).

Ndue, Paul Ntungwe. 1994. "Africa's Turn Toward Pluralism." *Journal of Democracy* 5, no. 1 (January).

Nelson, Joan M. 1990. *Economic Crisis and Policy Choice: The Politics of Adjustment in the Third World.* Princeton, N.J.: Princeton University Press.

——. 1994. "Linkages Between Politics and Economics." *Journal of Democracy* 5, no. 4 (October).

Nelson, John; Megill, Allan; and McCloskey, Donald N., eds. 1987. *The Rhetoric of the Human Sciences: Language and Argument in Scholarship and Public Affairs.* Madison: University of Wisconsin Press.

Nielson, Kai. 1992. "Global Justice, Capitalism and the Third World." In Robin Attfield and Barry Wilkins, eds., *International Justice and the Third World.* London: Routledge.

Nietzsche, Friedrich. [1964]. *The Complete Works of Friedrich Nietzsche.* Vol 7: *Mixed Opinions and Aphorisms.* Trans. P. Cohen. New York: Russell and Russell.

Nodia, Ghia. 1992. "Nationalism and Democracy." *Journal of Democracy* 3, no. 4 (October).

——. 1995. "Georgia's Identity Crisis." *Journal of Democracy* 6, no. 1 (January).

North, Douglas and Thomas, Robert. 1973. *The Rise of the Western World: A New Economic History.* Cambridge: Cambridge University Press.

Novak, Michael. 1982. *The Spirit of Democratic Capitalism.* New York: Simon and Schuster.

——. 1984. "The Case Against Liberation Theology." *New York Times Magazine* (October 21).

——. 1986. *Will It Liberate? Questions about Liberation Theology.* New York: Paulist Press.

——. 1989. *Free Persons and the Common Good.* Landham, Md.: Madison Books.

——. 1993. *The Catholic Ethic and the Spirit of Capitalism.* New York: The Free Press.

Nozick, Robert. 1974. *Anarchy, State, and Utopia.* New York: Basic Books.

Nyerere, Julius K. 1962. *Ujamma: The Basis of African Socialism.* Dar es Salaam: Government Printer.

Nyong'o, Peter Anyang'. 1992. "Africa: The Failure of One-Party Rule." *Journal of Democracy* 3, no. 1 (January).

Oakeshott, Michael. 1962. *Rationalism in Politics and Other Essays.* London: Methuen.

O'Brien, Conor Cruise. 1991. "Nationalists and Democrats." *The New York Review of Books* (August 15).

REFERENCES

OCUFA (Ontario Confederation of University Faculty Associations). 1994a. *OCUFA Forum* 9, no. 5 (June).
———. 1994b. *OCUFA Forum* 10, no. 2 (November).
Ontario Ministry of Education and Training. 1993. *Framework Regarding Prevention of Harassment and Discrimination in Ontario Universities.* Toronto.
Ordeshook, Peter C. 1993. "Some Rules of Constitutional Design." In Ellen Frankel Paul et al., eds., *Liberalism and the Economic Order.* Cambridge: Cambridge University Press.
Osterfeld, David. 1994. "The World Bank and the IMF: Misbegotten Sisters." In Peter J. Boettke, ed., *The Collapse of Development Planning.* New York: New York University Press.
Paine, Thomas. [1995]. *Rights of Man.* In *Collected Writings.* New York: Library of America.
Palmer, Tom G. 1984. "Industrial Policy, Business Failures, and Economic Evolution." *Policy Report.* Washington: The Cato Institute 6, no. 3. (March).
———. 1987. "Gadamer's Hermeneutics and Social Theory," *Critical Review* 1, no. 3 (Summer).
Park, Robert L. 1995. "The Danger of Voodoo Science." *New York Times* (July 9).
Parnas, David Lorge. 1994. "Academic Freedom: An 'Egregious' Case." *McMaster University Faculty Association Newsletter* 21, no. 4 (December).
Paul, Ellen Frankel, Miller, Fred D., Jr. and Paul, Jeffrey. eds. 1993. *Liberalism and the Economic Order.* Cambridge: Cambridge University Press.
Peacock, Alan and Willgerodt, Hans, eds. 1989a. *German Neo-Liberals and the Social Market Economy.* New York: St. Martin's Press.
———. 1989b. *Germany's Social Market Economy: Origins and Evolution.* New York: St. Martin's Press.
Peck, Merton J. and Richardson, Thomas J., eds. 1991. *What Is To Be Done?: A Proposal for the Soviet Transition to the Market.* New Haven, Conn.: Yale University Press.
Pei, Minxin. 1992. "Societal Takeover in China and the USSR." *Journal of Democracy* 3, no. 1 (January).
———. 1994a. "The Puzzle of East Asian Exceptionalism." *Journal of Democracy* 5, no. 4 (October).
———. 1994b. *From Reform to Revolution: The Demise of Communism in China and the Soviet Union.* Cambridge, Mass.: Harvard University Press.
Peirce, Charles S. [1955]. *Philosophical Writings of Peirce.* New York: Dover Publications.
Perelman, Chaim. 1979. *The New Rhetoric and the Humanities: Essays on Rhetoric and Its Applications.* Dordrecht: D. Reidel.
———. 1982. *The Realm of Rhetoric.* Trans. William Klubach. Notre Dame, Ind.: University of Notre Dame Press.
Pesic, Vesna. 1993. "The Cruel Face of Nationalism." *Journal of Democracy* 4, no. 4 (October).
Polanyi, Michael. 1958. *Personal Knowledge: Towards a Post-Critical Philosophy.* Chicago: University of Chicago Press.
———. 1962. "The Republic of Science: Its Political and Economic Theory." In Polanyi, *Knowing and Being.* Ed. Majorie Green. Chicago: University of Chicago Press.
———. 1964 (1946). *Science, Faith, and Society.* Chicago: Uuniversity of Chicago Press.
Polkinghorne, Donald. 1983. *Methodology for the Human Sciences.* Albany: State University of New York Press.
Prendergast, Christopher. 1986. "Alfred Schutz and the Austrian School of Economics." *American Journal of Sociology* 92, no. 1 (July).
Pribram, Karl. 1983. *A History of Economic Reasoning.* Baltimore: The Johns Hopkins University Press.
Prybyla, Jan S. 1994, "The Political Economy of Development in Communist China:

China and the Market." In Peter J. Boettke, ed., *The Collapse of Development Planning*. New York: New York University Press.

Prychitko, David L. 1988. "Marxism and Decentralized Socialism," *Critical Review* 2, no. 4 (Fall).

———. 1991. *Marxism and Workers' Self-Management*. Wesport, Conn.: Greenwood Press.

———. 1993a. "After Davidson Who Needs the Austrians? Reply to Davidson." *Critical Review* 7, nos. 2–3 (Spring-Summer).

———. 1993b. "Formalism in the Austrian-School Welfare Economics: Another Pretense of Knowledge?" *Critical Review* 7, no. 4 (Fall).

Prychitko, David L., ed. 1995. *Individuals, Institutions, Interpretations: Hermeneutics Applied to Economics*. Aldershot: Avebury.

Przeworski, Adam. 1991. *Democracy and the Market: Political and Economic Reform in Eastern Europe and Latin America*. Cambridge: Cambridge University Press.

Quezada, Sergio Aguayo. 1995. "A Mexican Milestone." *Journal of Democracy* 6, no. 2 (April).

Raico, Ralph. 1994. "The Theory of Economic Development and the 'European Miracle'." In Peter J. Boettke, ed., *The Collapse of Development Planning*. New York: New York University Press.

Rauch, Jonathan. 1993. *Kindly Inquisitors: The New Attacks on Free Thought*. Chicago: University of Chicago Press.

Rector, Ralph A. 1990. "The Economics of Rationality and the Rationality of Economics." In Don Lavoie, ed., *Economics and Hermeneutics*. London: Routledge.

Reddaway, Peter. 1994. "Instability and Fragmentation." *Journal of Democracy* 5, no. 2 (April).

Reinhold, Robert. 1991. "Class Struggle." *New York Times Magazine* (September 29).

Remnick, David. 1993. *Lenin's Tomb: The Last Days of the Soviet Empire*. New York: Random House.

Revel, Jean-François. 1993. *Democracy Against Itself: The Future of the Democratic Impulse*. New York: The Free Press.

Ricoeur, Paul. 1969. "La philosophie et la politique devant la question de la liberté." In *La Liberté et l'ordre social*. Neuchâtel: La Baconnière.

———. 1979. *Main Trends in Philosophy*. New York: Holmes and Meier.

———. 1981. *Hermeneutics and the Human Sciences*. Cambridge: Cambridge University Press.

———. 1991. *Lectures 1: Autour du politique*. Paris: Editions du Seuil.

Riker, William H. and Weiner, David L. 1993. "The Economic and Political Liberalization of Socialism: The Fundamental Problem of Property Rights." In Ellen Frankel Paul et al., eds., *Liberalism and the Economic Order*. Cambridge: Cambridge University Press.

Roberts, Cynthia. 1991. Letter to *New York Times* (October 10).

Robertson, John. 1989. "Scottish Enlightenment." In John Eatwell, Murray Milgate and Paul Newman, eds., *The Invisible Hand*. (*The New Palgrave*). New York: W. W. Norton.

Roepke, Wilhelm. [1987]. *Two Essays by Wilhelm Roepke: The Problem of Economic Order; Welfare, Freedom and Inflation*. Ed. Johannes Overbeek. Lanham, Md.: University Press of America.

Rohatyn, Felix. 1994. "World Capital: The Need and the Risks." *The New York Review of Books* (July 14).

Rohter, Larry. 1987. "A Radical Diagnosis of Latin America's Economic Malaise." *New York Times* (December 27).

Rorty, Richard. 1985. "Postmodern Bourgeois Liberalism." In R. Hollinger, ed., *Hermeneutics and Praxis*. Notre Dame, Ind.: University of Notre Dame Press.

——— 1987. "Science as Solidarity." In John Nelson, Allan Magill, and Donald N.

McCloskey, eds., *The Rhetoric of the Human Sciences: Language and Argument in Scholarship and Public Affairs*. Madison: University of Wisconsin Press.

——. 1994. "The Unpatriotic Academy." *New York Times* (February 13).

Rose, Richard. 1992. "Toward a Civil Economy," *Journal of Democracy* 3, no. 2 (April).

——. 1994. "Postcommunism and the Problem of Trust." *Democratization* 1, no. 1 (July).

Rousseau, Jean-Jacques. [1977]. *Du contrat social.* Paris: Editions du Seuil.

Ruggiero, Guido de. [1981]. *The History of European Liberalism.* Trans. R. G. Collingwood. Gloucester, Mass.: Peter Smith.

Rupnik, Jacques. 1995. "The Post-Totalitarian Blues." *Journal of Democracy* 6, no. 2 (April).

Sachs, Jeffrey. 1994. *Poland's Jump to the Market Economy.* Cambridge, Mass.: Massachusetts Institute of Technology.

Sakwa, Richard. 1994. "Democratic Challenge in Russia and Ukraine." *Democratization* 1, no. 1. (Spring).

Sandel, Michael J. 1982. *Liberalism and the Limits of Justice.* Cambridge: Cambridge University Press.

Sartori, Giovanni. 1979. "Liberty and Law." In K. S. Templeton, Jr. ed., *The Politicization of Society.* Indianapolis: Liberty Press.

——. 1987. *The Theory of Democracy Revisited.* 2 vols. Chatham, N.J.: Chatham House.

——. 1995. "How Far Can Free Government Travel?" *Journal of Democracy* 6, no. 3 (July).

Sartre, Jean-Paul. [1973]. *Existentialism and Humanism.* Trans. Philip Mairet. London: Methuen.

Scalapino, Robert A. 1989. *The Politics of Development: Perspectives on Twentieth-Century Asia.* Cambridge, Mass.: Harvard University Press.

Schrag, Calvin O. 1986. *Communicative Praxis and the Space of Subjectivity.* Bloomington: Indiana University Press.

Schumpeter, Joseph A. 1976. *Capitalism, Socialism and Democracy.* New York: Harper Torchbooks.

Schutz, Alfred. 1962. *Collected Papers I: The Problem of Social Reality.* The Hague: Martinus Nijhoff.

Scott, Arnold N. 1992. "Market Socialism." *Critical Review* 6, no. 4 (Fall).

Seligman, Adam. 1992. *The Idea of Civil Society.* New York: The Free Press.

"Sexual Harassment and Academic Freedom: A Statement of the National Association of Scholars." 1994. *The New York Review of Books.* (February 17).

Shafarevich, Igor. 1980. *The Socialist Phenomenon.* Trans. William Tjalsma. New York: Harper and Row (first published in Paris in 1975).

Shapiro, Ian. 1986. *The Evolution of Rights in Liberal Theory.* Cambridge: Cambridge University Press.

Shenon, Philip. 1995. "Either Filthy and Free or Clean and Mean." *New York Times* (May 2).

Siegan, Bernard H. 1994. *Drafting a Constitution for a Nation or Republic Emerging into Freedom.* Fairfax, Va.: George Mason University Press.

Simmel, Georg. [1990]. *The Philosophy of Money.* Trans. Tom Bottomore and David Frisby. London: Routledge.

Simpson, Evan. 1994. "Humanities: Frill or Major Force?" *Bulletin: The Canadian Federation for the Humanities* 16, no. 3 (Winter).

Skinner, Andrew S. 1989. "Adam Smith." In John Eatwell, Murray Milgate, and Paul Newman, eds., *The Invisible Hand (The New Palgrave).* New York: W. W. Norton.

Skinner, Quentin. 1984. "The Idea of Negative Liberty: Philosophical and Historical

Perspectives." In Richard Rorty, J. B. Schneewind and Quentin Skinner, *Philosophy In History*, Cambridge: Cambridge University Press.

———. 1993. "The Italian City-Republics." In Dunn, ed., *Democracy: The Unfinished Journey, 508 BC to AD 1993*. Oxford: Oxford University Press.

Skirbekk. 1992. "The World Reconsidered: A Brief Aggionamento for Leftist Intellectuals." In Peter Beilharz, Gillian Robinson and John Rundell, eds, *Between Totalitarianism and Democracy: A Thesis Eleven Reader*. Cambridge, Mass.: Massachusetts Institute of Technology.

Smith, Adam. [1978]. *Lectures on Jurisprudence*. Oxford: Oxford University Press.

———. [1979]. *An Inquiry into the Nature and the Causes of the Wealth of Nations*. 2 vols. Oxford: Oxford University Press.

———. [1982]. *The Theory of Moral Sentiments*. Indianapolis: Liberty Classics.

Smolar, Aleksander. 1994. "The Dissolution of Solidarity," *Journal of Democracy* 5, no. 1 (January).

Sołtan, Karol Edward. 1993. "Genuine Constitutionalism." In Stephen L. Elkin and Karol Edward Sołtan, eds., *A New Constitutionalism: Designing Political Insitutions for a Good Society*. Chicago: University of Chicago Press.

Solzhenitsyn, Alexander I. 1974a. *Letter to the Soviet Leaders*. New York: Harper and Row.

———. 1974b. *The Gulag Archipelago*. Trans. Thomas P. Whitney. Glasgow: William Collins Sons & Co.

———. 1980. *The Mortal Danger: How Misconceptions about Russia Imperil America*. New York: Harper Colophon Books.

Sommers, Christina Hoff. 1994. *Who Stole Feminism? How Women Have Betrayed Women*. New York: Simon and Schuster.

Sopinka, John. 1994. "Freedom of Speech Under Attack." *University Affairs* (Canada). (April).

Sowell, Thomas. 1994. *Race and Culture: A World View*. New York: Basic Books.

Stewart, John, ed. 1966. *Beyond the Symbol Model*. Albany: State University of New York Press.

Steele, Shelby. 1994. "How to Grow Extremists." *New York Times* (March 13).

Strauss, Leo. 1953. *Natural Rights and History*. Chicago: University of Chicago Press.

Streit, M. E. 1994. "The Freiburg School of Law and Economics." In Peter J. Boettke, ed., *The Elgar Companion to Austrian Economics*. Aldershot: Edward Elgar.

Strossen, Nadine. 1995. *Defending Pornography: Free Speech, Sex, and the Fight for Women's Rights*. New York: Scribner.

Sullivan, John D. 1994. "Democratization and Business Interests." *Journal of Democracy* 5, no. 4 (October).

Sunstein, Cass R. 1993. "The Enduring Legacy of Republicanism." In Stephen J. Elkin and Karol Edward Sołtan, eds., *A New Constitutionalism: Designing Political Institutions for a Good Society*. Chicago: University of Chicago Press.

Suu Kyi, Aung San. 1992. "Burma's Quest for Democracy." *Journal of Democracy* 3, no. 1 (January).

———. 1995. "Freedom, Development, and Human Worth." *Journal of Democracy* 6, no. 2 (April).

Taylor, Charles. 1985. *Philosophy and the Human Sciences*. Cambridge: Cambridge University Press.

———. 1994. "The Politics of Recognition." In Amy Gutmann, ed., *Multiculturalism: Examining the Politics of Recognition*. Princeton, N.J.: Princeton University Press.

Templeton, K. S., Jr., ed. 1979. *The Politicization of Society*. Indianapolis: Liberty Press.

Tocqueville, Alexis de. [1955]. *The Old Regime and the French Revolution*. Trans. Stuart Gilbert. New York: Doubleday.

———. [1961]. *De la Démocratie en Amérique*. 2 vols. Paris: Gallimard.

Toro, Fernando de. 1994. "Ontario's Zero-Tolerance Policy or the End of Academic

Freedom: Between the Reign of Intellectual Terrorism and University Cleansing."
CAUT (Canadian Association of University Teachers) Bulletin (June).

Toulmin, Stephen. 1972. *Human Understanding.* Princeton, N.J.: Princeton University Press.

———. 1982. "The Construal of Reality: Criticism in Modern and Postmodern Science". In W. J. T. Mitchell, ed., *The Politics of Interpretation.* Chicago: University of Chicago Press.

Touraine, Alain. 1992. "Is Sociology Still the Study of Society?" In Peter Beilharz; Gillain Robinson; and John Rundell, eds., *Between Totalitarianism and Democracy: A Thesis Eleven Reader.* Cambridge, Mass.: Massachusetts Institute of Technology.

———. 1995. *Critique of Modernity.* Trans. David Macey. Oxford: Basil Blackwell.

Twenty-Four Human Rights Documents. 1992. New York: Columbia University (Center for the Study of Human Rights).

Tyler, Patrick E. 1995a. "Six Years After the Tiananmen Massacre, Survivors Clash Anew on Tactics." *New York Times* (April 30).

———. 1995b. "Beijing Arrests Rights Defender." *New York Times* (July 9).

van de Walle, Nicolas. 1995. "Crisis and Opportunity in Africa." *Journal of Democracy* 6, no. 2 (April).

Varga, György. 1992. "Economics and Human Values." In W. Robert Connor, ed. *The Idea of a Civil Society.* Research Triangle Park, N.C.: The National Humanities Center.

Vargas Llosa, Mario. 1987. "In Defense of the Black Market." *New York Times Magazine* (February 22).

———. 1989. "Foreword" to Hernando de Soto, *The Other Path: The Invisible Revolution in the Third World.* New York: Harper and Row.

Varian, Hal R. 1993. "Markets for Public Goods?" *Critical Review* 7, no. 4 (Fall).

Vaughn, Karen I. 1989. "Invisible Hand." In John Eatwell, Murray Milgate and Paul Newman, eds., *The Invisible Hand (The New Palgrave).* New York: W. W. Norton.

———. 1994. "The Socialist Calculation Debate." In Peter J. Boettke, ed., *The Elgar Companion to Austrian Economics.* Aldershot: Edward Elgar.

Walicki, Andrzej. 1988. "Karl Marx as Philosopher of Freedom," *Critical Review* 2, no. 4 (Fall).

———. 1989. "Totalitarianism and Liberalism: Rejoinder to Mizgala," *Critical Review* 3, no. 2 (Spring).

Walzer, Michael. 1983. *Spheres of Justice: Exodus and Revolution.* New York: Basic Books.

Weil, Eric. 1971. *Philosophie politique.* Paris: J. Vrin.

White, Gordon. 1994. "Civil Society, Democratization and Development (I): Clearing the Analytic Ground." *Democratization* 1, no. 3 (Autumn).

"Why *Balance* is Needed." 1994. *Balance* 1, no. 1 (Fall).

Willgerodt, Hans. 1976. "Planning in West Germany: The Social Market Economy." In A. L. Chichering, ed. *The Politics of Planning: A Review and Critique of Centralized Economic Planning.* San Francisco: Institute for Contemporary Studies.

Wiseman, Jack. 1989. "Social Policy and the Social Market Economy." In Alan Peacock and Hans Willgerodt, eds., *German Neo-Liberalism and the Social Market Economy.* New York: St. Martin's Press.

Wojtiła, Karol. 1979. *The Acting Person.* Trans. Andrzei Potocki. Dordrecht: D. Reidel.

Wriston, Walter B. 1992. *The Twilight of Sovereignty: How the Information Revolution Is Transforming Our World.* New York: Charles Scribner's Sons.

Wu, Hongda Harry. 1995. *Logai: The Chinese Gulag.* Foreword by Fang Lizhi. Boulder, Colo.: Westview Press.

Yakovlev, Alexander N. 1988. "The Political Philosophy of Perestroika." In Abel Aganbegyan, ed., *Perestroika 1989.* New York: Charles Scribner's Sons.

——. 1993. *The Fate of Marxism in Russia*. Trans. Catharine A. Fitzpatrick. New Haven, Conn.: Yale University Press.

Yan, Jiaqi. 1992. *Toward a Democratic China*. Honolulu: University of Hawaii Press.

Yeatman, Anna. 1994. *Postmodern Revisionings of the Political*. London: Routledge.

Zuckerman (Lord). 1991. "Apes 'Я' Not Us," *The New York Review of Books* (May 30).

NAME INDEX

SUBJECT INDEX

public realm 89–91, 102

rationality 135, 221n6, 231n5;
   communicative or dialogical xii, 37,
   41–51, 63, 87, 89, 121–2, 126, 138,
   142, 148, 149, 170, 220n34; economic
   42, 133; ethics of 62–6; instrumental
   42–3, 126, 142; rules of 57–62
reason 42–4, 82, 138–9
reasonableness 41, 44, 122
reciprocity 11, 77, 122, 148, 149, 201
rent seeking 29, 105, 176, 216n14
revolution: revolutions of 1989 ix ff, 1,
   117–18, 127; self-limiting 117–18
revolutionism x, 104, 117–20, 210n22
rhetoric 44, 138, 221n6
rights 262n75; collective (group) 16;
   economic 172, 173–7, 262n77; and
   entitlements 174–7, 262n77; to free
   association 170; human 8, 10, 11–18,
   32, 40, 44, 84, 93, 100, 103, 111, 128,
   193–7, 201, 204, 263n78, 270n20;
   individual 15–17, 32, 34, 116; natural
   45, 153, 255n42; to privacy 40; to
   private property 125, 153–6, 167, 179,
   255n39, 256n43; rational 45, 153,
   223n13; social 40, 153; to work
   173–4, 180, 262n74

School of Salamanca 137
Socialism 6, 9, 19–21, 38, 73, 77, 98, 114,
   116, 124–7, 130, 143, 164, 169, 171,

192, 205n1, 246n1, 248n7, 253n34;
   market 129, 162, 165–6, 170, 206n4,
   208n16; really existing ix, 3, 73;
society 98, 99, 169
solidarity 74, 93–4, 123, 129, 146–7, 183,
   204, 257n52
sovereignty: national 183, 246n82;
   popular 78, 103–4
State: and civil society 35–6; liberal
   102–5; role of in the economy
   151–81; see also government
subsidiarity 86, 108–9, 169
Swedish model 3

taxation 179–81, 241n56
third way 3, 5–6, 124, 125, 157, 161, 167,
   187, 205n1, 206n5
third-worldism 184–5, 187
totalitarianism 9, 12–14, 20–2, 36–7, 116,
   211n30
trust 120–1, 146–9
truth 40, 45–51, 57, 66, 116

unsocial sociability 94–8, 148

victim, cult of the 30–3, 186, 199
violence 228n53

welfare state 109, 165, 167–70, 184, 198,
   206n6, 210n25, 242n65, 265n85
will of the people 79–82, 88, 103, 115

For Product Safety Concerns and Information please contact our EU
representative GPSR@taylorandfrancis.com
Taylor & Francis Verlag GmbH, Kaufingerstraße 24, 80331 München, Germany

www.ingramcontent.com/pod-product-compliance
Lightning Source LLC
Chambersburg PA
CBHW070559270326
41926CB00013B/2368